THE DUCHESS OF MALFI

AND OTHER PLAYS

BY JOHN WEBSTER

The Duchess of Malfi and Other Plays
By John Webster

Print ISBN 13: 978-1-4209-6565-0
eBook ISBN 13: 978-1-4209-6566-7

Cover Image: a detail of "View of the Gulf of Naples", by Gaspare Vanvitelli (1653-1736) / Photo © Luisa Ricciarini / Bridgeman Images.

Please visit *www.digireads.com*

CONTENTS

THE WHITE DEVIL

OR, VITTORIA COROMBONA.

TO THE READER

In publishing this tragedy, I do but challenge myself that liberty, which other men have taken before me; not that I affect praise by it, for, *nos hæc novimus esse nihil,* only since it was acted in so dull a time of winter, presented in so open and black a theatre, that it wanted (that which is the only grace and setting-out of a tragedy) a full and understanding auditory; and that since that time I have noted, most of the people that come to that playhouse resemble those ignorant asses (who, visiting stationers' shops, their use is not to inquire for good books, but new books), I present it to the general view with this confidence:

> Nec rhoncos metues maligniorum,
> Nec scombris tunicas dabis molestas.

If it be objected this is no true dramatic poem, I shall easily confess it, *non potes in nugas dicere plura meas, ipse ego quam dixi*; willingly, and not ignorantly, in this kind have I faulted: For should a man present to such an auditory, the most sententious tragedy that ever was written, observing all the critical laws as height of style, and gravity of person, enrich it with the sententious Chorus, and, as it were Life and Death, in the passionate and weighty Nuntius: yet after all this divine rapture, *O dura messorum ilia,* the breath that comes from the incapable multitude is able to poison it; and, ere it be acted, let the author resolve to fix to every scene this of Horace:

> —Hæc hodie porcis comedenda relinques.

To those who report I was a long time in finishing this tragedy, I confess I do not write with a goose-quill winged with two feathers; and if they will need make it my fault, I must answer them with that of Euripides to Alcestides, a tragic writer: Alcestides objecting that Euripides had only, in three days composed three verses, whereas himself had written three hundred: Thou tallest truth (quoth he), but here's the difference, thine shall only be read for three days, whereas mine shall continue for three ages.

Detraction is the sworn friend to ignorance: for mine own part, I have ever truly cherished my good opinion of other men's worthy labours, especially of that full and heightened style of Mr. Chapman, the laboured and understanding works of Mr. Johnson, the no less worthy composures of the both worthily excellent Mr. Beaumont and Mr. Fletcher; and lastly (without wrong last to be named), the right happy and copious industry of Mr. Shakespeare, Mr. Dekker, and Mr. Heywood, wishing what I write may be read by their light: protesting that, in the strength of mine own judgment, I know them so worthy, that though I rest silent in my own work, yet to most of theirs I dare (without flattery) fix that of Martial;

—non norunt hæc monumenta mori.

DRAMATIS PERSONAE

MONTICELSO, *a cardinal, afterwards Pope.*
FRANCISCO DE MEDICIS, *Duke of Florence.*
BRACHIANO, *otherwise Paulo Giordano Ursini, Duke of Brachiano, husband to Isabella.*
GIOVANNI, *his son.*
COUNT LODOVICO.
CAMILLO, *husband to Vittoria.*
FLAMINEO, *his brother; Secretary to Brachiano.*
MARCELLO, *brother to Vittoria, attendant on Francisco de Medicis.*
HORTENSIO.
ANTONELLI.
GASPARO.
FARNESE.
CARLO.
PEDRO.
DOCTOR.
CONJURER.
JAQUES.
JULIO.
CRISTOPHERO.
ISABELLA, *sister to Francisco De Medicis, and wife to Brachiano.*
VITTORIA COROMBONA, *married to Camillo, afterwards to Brachiano.*
CORNELIA, *mother to Vittoria.*
ZANCHE, *a Moor.*

Ambassadors, Courtiers, Lawyers, Officers, Physicians, Conjurer, Armourer, Attendants.

In mentem auctoris
Scire velis quid sit mulier? Quo percitet œstro?
En tibi, si sapias, cum sale, mille sales.

J. WILSON

THE WHITE DEVIL

OR, VITTORIA COROMBONA.

ACT I.

SCENE I.

[*Enter* COUNT LODOVICO, ANTONELLI, *and* GASPARO.]

LODOVICO. Banish'd!
ANTONELLI. It griev'd me much to hear the sentence.
LODOVICO. Ha, ha, O Democritus, thy gods
    That govern the whole world! courtly reward
    And punishment. Fortune 's a right whore:
    If she give aught, she deals it in small parcels,
    That she may take away all at one swoop.
    This 'tis to have great enemies! God 'quite them.
    Your wolf no longer seems to be a wolf
    Than when she's hungry.
GASPARO. You term those enemies,
    Are men of princely rank.
LODOVICO. Oh, I pray for them:
    The violent thunder is adored by those
    Are pash'd in pieces by it.
ANTONELLI. Come, my lord,
    You are justly doom'd; look but a little back
    Into your former life: you have in three years
    Ruin'd the noblest earldom.
GASPARO. Your followers
    Have swallowed you, like mummia, and being sick
    With such unnatural and horrid physic,
    Vomit you up i' th' kennel.
ANTONELLI. All the damnable degrees
    Of drinking have you stagger'd through. One citizen,
    Is lord of two fair manors, call'd you master,
    Only for caviare.
GASPARO. Those noblemen

Which were invited to your prodigal feasts,
(Wherein the phœnix scarce could 'scape your throats)
Laugh at your misery, as fore-deeming you
An idle meteor, which drawn forth, the earth
Would be soon lost i' the air.

ANTONELLI. Jest upon you,
And say you were begotten in an earthquake,
You have ruin'd such fair lordships.

LODOVICO. Very good.
This well goes with two buckets: I must tend
The pouring out of either.

GASPARO. Worse than these.
You have acted certain murders here in Rome,
Bloody and full of horror.

LODOVICO. 'Las, they were flea-bitings:
Why took they not my head then?

GASPARO. O, my lord!
The law doth sometimes mediate, thinks it good
Not ever to steep violent sins in blood:
This gentle penance may both end your crimes,
And in the example better these bad times.

LODOVICO. So; but I wonder then some great men 'scape
This banishment: there's Paulo Giordano Ursini,
The Duke of Brachiano, now lives in Rome,
And by close panderism seeks to prostitute
The honour of Vittoria Corombona:
Vittoria, she that might have got my pardon
For one kiss to the duke.

ANTONELLI. Have a full man within you:
We see that trees bear no such pleasant fruit
There where they grew first, as where they are new set.
Perfumes, the more they are chaf'd, the more they render
Their pleasing scents, and so affliction
Expresseth virtue fully, whether true,
Or else adulterate.

LODOVICO. Leave your painted comforts;
I'll make Italian cut-works in their guts
If ever I return.

GASPARO. Oh, sir.

LODOVICO. I am patient.
I have seen some ready to be executed,
Give pleasant looks, and money, and grown familiar
With the knave hangman; so do I; I thank them,
And would account them nobly merciful,
Would they dispatch me quickly.

ANTONELLI. Fare you well;
  We shall find time, I doubt not, to repeal
  Your banishment.
LODOVICO. I am ever bound to you.
  This is the world's alms; pray make use of it.
  Great men sell sheep, thus to be cut in pieces,
  When first they have shorn them bare, and sold their fleeces.

[*Exeunt.*]

SCENE II.

[*Enter* BRACHIANO, CAMILLO, FLAMINEO, VITTORIA COROMBONA,
  and attendants.]

BRACHIANO. Your best of rest.
VITTORIA. Unto my lord the duke,
  The best of welcome. More lights: attend the duke.

[*Exeunt* CAMILLO *and* VITTORIA COROMBONA.]

BRACHIANO. Flamineo.
FLAMINEO. My lord.
BRACHIANO. Quite lost, Flamineo.
FLAMINEO. Pursue your noble wishes, I am prompt
  As lightning to your service. O my lord!
  The fair Vittoria, my happy sister, [*Whisper.*]
  Shall give you present audience—Gentlemen,
  Let the caroch go on—and 'tis his pleasure
  You put out all your torches and depart.

[*Exeunt attendants.*]

BRACHIANO. Are we so happy?
FLAMINEO. Can it be otherwise?
  Observ'd you not to-night, my honour'd lord,
  Which way soe'er you went, she threw her eyes?
  I have dealt already with her chambermaid,
  Zanche the Moor, and she is wondrous proud
  To be the agent for so high a spirit.
BRACHIANO. We are happy above thought, because 'bove merit.
FLAMINEO. 'Bove merit!—we may now talk freely—'bove merit! what
  is 't you doubt? her coyness! that's but the superficies of lust most
  women have; yet why should ladies blush to hear that named,
  which they do not fear to handle? Oh, they are politic; they know

our desire is increased by the difficulty of enjoying; whereas
satiety is a blunt, weary, and drowsy passion. If the buttery-hatch
at court stood continually open, there would be nothing so
passionate crowding, nor hot suit after the beverage.

BRACHIANO. Oh, but her jealous husband!

FLAMINEO. Hang him! a gilder that hath his brains perished with
quicksilver is not more cold in the liver. The great barriers moulted
not more feathers, than he hath shed hairs, by the confession of his
doctor. An Irish gamester that will play himself naked, and then
wage all downward, at hazard, is not more venturous. So unable to
please a woman, that, like a Dutch doublet, all his back is shrunk
into his breaches.

    Shroud you within this closet, good my lord;
Some trick now must be thought on to divide
My brother-in-law from his fair bed-fellow.

BRACHIANO. Oh, should she fail to come!

FLAMINEO. I must not have your lordship thus unwisely amorous. I
myself have not loved a lady, and pursued her with a great deal of
under-age protestation, whom some three or four gallants that have
enjoyed would with all their hearts have been glad to have been rid
of. 'Tis just like a summer bird-cage in a garden: the birds that are
without despair to get in, and the birds that are within despair and
are in a consumption for fear they shall never get out. Away, away,
my lord.

[*Exit* BRACHIANO.]

[*Enter* CAMILLO.]

    See here he comes. This fellow by his apparel
Some men would judge a politician;
But call his wit in question, you shall find it
Merely an ass in 's foot-cloth. How now, brother?
What, travelling to bed with your kind wife?

CAMILLO. I assure you, brother, no. My voyage lies
More northerly, in a far colder clime.
I do not well remember, I protest,
When I last lay with her.

FLAMINEO. Strange you should lose your count.

CAMILLO. We never lay together, but ere morning
There grew a flaw between us.

FLAMINEO. 'T had been your part
To have made up that flaw.

CAMILLO. True, but she loathes I should be seen in 't.

FLAMINEO. Why, sir, what 's the matter?

CAMILLO. The duke your master visits me, I thank him;
 And I perceive how, like an earnest bowler,
 He very passionately leans that way
 He should have his bowl run.
FLAMINEO. I hope you do not think—
CAMILLO. That nobleman bowl booty? faith, his cheek
 Hath a most excellent bias: it would fain
 Jump with my mistress.
FLAMINEO. Will you be an ass,
 Despite your Aristotle? or a cuckold,
 Contrary to your Ephemerides,
 Which shows you under what a smiling planet
 You were first swaddled?
CAMILLO. Pew wew, sir; tell me not
 Of planets nor of Ephemerides.
 A man may be made cuckold in the day-time,
 When the stars' eyes are out.
FLAMINEO. Sir, good-bye you;
 I do commit you to your pitiful pillow
 Stuffed with horn-shavings.
CAMILLO. Brother!
FLAMINEO. God refuse me.
 Might I advise you now, your only course
 Were to lock up your wife.
CAMILLO. 'Twere very good.
FLAMINEO. Bar her the sight of revels.
CAMILLO. Excellent.
FLAMINEO. Let her not go to church, but, like a hound
 In Leon, at your heels.
CAMILLO. 'Twere for her honour.
FLAMINEO. And so you should be certain in one fortnight,
 Despite her chastity or innocence,
 To be cuckolded, which yet is in suspense:
 This is my counsel, and I ask no fee for 't.
CAMILLO. Come, you know not where my nightcap wrings me.
FLAMINEO. Wear it a' th' old fashion; let your large ears come through, it will be more easy—nay, I will be bitter—bar your wife of her entertainment: women are more willingly and more gloriously chaste, when they are least restrained of their liberty. It seems you would be a fine capricious, mathematically jealous coxcomb; take the height of your own horns with a Jacob's staff, afore they are up. These politic enclosures for paltry mutton, makes more rebellion in the flesh, than all the provocative electuaries doctors have uttered since last jubilee.
CAMILLO. This doth not physic me——

FLAMINEO. It seems you are jealous: I'll show you the error of it by a familiar example: I have seen a pair of spectacles fashioned with such perspective art, that lay down but one twelve pence a' th' board, 'twill appear as if there were twenty; now should you wear a pair of these spectacles, and see your wife tying her shoe, you would imagine twenty hands were taking up of your wife's clothes, and this would put you into a horrible causeless fury.

CAMILLO. The fault there, sir, is not in the eyesight.

FLAMINEO. True, but they that have the yellow jaundice think all objects they look on to be yellow. Jealousy is worse; her fits present to a man, like so many bubbles in a basin of water, twenty several crabbed faces, many times makes his own shadow his cuckold-maker.

[*Enter* VITTORIA COROMBONA.]

See, she comes; what reason have you to be jealous of this creature? what an ignorant ass or flattering knave might be counted, that should write sonnets to her eyes, or call her brow the snow of Ida, or ivory of Corinth; or compare her hair to the blackbird's bill, when 'tis liker the blackbird's feather? This is all. Be wise; I will make you friends, and you shall go to bed together. Marry, look you, it shall not be your seeking. Do you stand upon that, by any means: walk you aloof; I would not have you seen in 't.—Sister, my lord attends you in the banqueting-house: your husband is wondrous discontented.

VITTORIA. I did nothing to displease him; I carved to him at supper-time.

FLAMINEO. You need not have carved him, in faith; they say he is a capon already. I must now seemingly fall out with you. Shall a gentleman so well descended as Camillo—a lousy slave, that within this twenty years rode with the black guard in the duke's carriage, 'mongst spits and dripping-pans—

CAMILLO. Now he begins to tickle her.

FLAMINEO. An excellent scholar [one that hath a head fill'd with calves' brains without any sage in them,] come crouching in the hams to you for a night's lodging? [that hath an itch in 's hams, which like the fire at the glass-house hath not gone out this seven years] Is he not a courtly gentleman?—when he wears white satin, one would take him by his black muzzle to be no other creature than a maggot.—You are a goodly foil, I confess, well set out—but cover'd with a false stone, yon counterfeit diamond.

CAMILLO. He will make her know what is in me.

FLAMINEO. Come, my lord attends you; thou shalt go to bed to my lord—

CAMILLO. Now he comes to 't.

FLAMINEO. With a relish as curious as a vintner going to taste new wine.—I am opening your case hard. [*to* CAMILLO.]

CAMILLO. A virtuous brother, o' my credit!

FLAMINEO. He will give thee a ring with a philosopher's stone in it.

CAMILLO. Indeed, I am studying alchemy.

FLAMINEO. Thou shalt lie in a bed stuffed with turtle's feathers; swoon in perfumed linen, like the fellow was smothered in roses. So perfect shall be thy happiness, that as men at sea think land, and trees, and ships, go that way they go; so both heaven and earth shall seem to go your voyage. Shalt meet him; 'tis fix'd, with nails of diamonds to inevitable necessity.

VITTORIA. How shalt rid him hence?

FLAMINEO. I will put [the] brize in's tail [shall] set him gadding presently.—I have almost wrought her to it; I find her coming: but, might I advise you now, for this night I would not lie with her, I would cross her humour to make her more humble.

CAMILLO. Shall I, shall I?

FLAMINEO. It will show in you a supremacy of judgment.

CAMILLO. True, and a mind differing from the tumultuary opinion; for, *quæ negata, grata.*

FLAMINEO. Right: you are the adamant shall draw her to you, though you keep distance off.

CAMILLO. A philosophical reason.

FLAMINEO. Walk by her a' th' nobleman's fashion, and tell her you will lie with her at the end of the progress.

CAMILLO. Vittoria, I cannot be induc'd, or as a man would say, incited—

VITTORIA. To do what, sir?

CAMILLO. To lie with you to-night. Your silkworm used to fast every third day, and the next following spins the better. To-morrow at night, I am for you.

VITTORIA. You 'll spin a fair thread, trust to 't.

FLAMINEO. But do you hear, I shall have you steal to her chamber about midnight.

CAMILLO. Do you think so? why look you, brother, because you shall not say I'll gull you, take the key, lock me into the chamber, and say you shall be sure of me.

FLAMINEO. In troth I will; I'll be your jailor once.

CAMILLO. A pox on 't, as I am a Christian! tell me to-morrow how scurvily she takes my unkind parting.

FLAMINEO. I will.

CAMILLO. Didst thou not mark the jest of the silkworm?
    Good-night; in faith, I will use this trick often.

FLAMINEO. Do, do, do.

[*Exit* CAMILLO.]

So, now you are safe. Ha, ha, ha, thou entanglest thyself in thine own work like a silkworm. Come, sister, darkness hides your blush. Women are like cursed dogs: civility keeps them tied all daytime, but they are let loose at midnight; then they do most good, or most mischief. My lord, my lord.

[*Enter* BRACHIANO. ZANCHE *brings out a carpet, spreads it, and lays on it two fair cushions.*]

BRACHIANO. Give credit: I could wish time would stand still,
    And never end this interview, this hour;
    But all delight doth itself soon'st devour.

[*Enter* CORNELIA *behind, listening.*]

Let me into your bosom, happy lady,
    Pour out, instead of eloquence, my vows.
    Loose me not, madam, for if you forgo me,
    I am lost eternally.
VITTORIA. Sir, in the way of pity,
    I wish you heart-whole.
BRACHIANO. You are a sweet physician.
VITTORIA. Sure, sir, a loathed cruelty in ladies
    Is as to doctors many funerals:
    It takes away their credit.
BRACHIANO. Excellent creature!
    We call the cruel fair; what name for you
    That are so merciful?
ZANCHE. See now they close.
FLAMINEO. Most happy union.
CORNELIA. My fears are fall'n upon me: oh, my heart!
    My son the pander! now I find our house
    Sinking to ruin. Earthquakes leave behind,
    Where they have tyranniz'd, iron, or lead, or stone;
    But woe to ruin, violent lust leaves none.
BRACHIANO. What value is this jewel?
VITTORIA. 'Tis the ornament of a weak fortune.
BRACHIANO. In sooth, I'll have it; nay, I will but change
    My jewel for your jewel.
FLAMINEO. Excellent;
    His jewel for her jewel: well put in, duke.
BRACHIANO. Nay, let me see you wear it.

VITTORIA. Here, sir?
BRACHIANO. Nay, lower, you shall wear my jewel lower.
FLAMINEO. That 's better: she must wear his jewel lower.
VITTORIA. To pass away the time, I'll tell your grace
    A dream I had last night.
BRACHIANO. Most wishedly.
VITTORIA. A foolish idle dream:
    Methought I walked about the mid of night
    Into a churchyard, where a goodly yew-tree
    Spread her large root in ground: under that yew,
    As I sat sadly leaning on a grave,
    Chequer'd with cross-sticks, there came stealing in
    Your duchess and my husband; one of them
    A pickaxe bore, th' other a rusty spade,
    And in rough terms they 'gan to challenge me
    About this yew.
BRACHIANO. That tree?
VITTORIA. This harmless yew;
    They told me my intent was to root up
    That well-grown yew, and plant i' the stead of it
    A wither'd blackthorn; and for that they vow'd
    To bury me alive. My husband straight
    With pickaxe 'gan to dig, and your fell duchess
    With shovel, like a fury, voided out
    The earth and scatter'd bones: Lord, how methought
    I trembled, and yet for all this terror
    I could not pray.
FLAMINEO. No; the devil was in your dream.
VITTORIA. When to my rescue there arose, methought,
    A whirlwind, which let fall a massy arm
    From that strong plant;
    And both were struck dead by that sacred yew,
    In that base shallow grave that was their due.
FLAMINEO. Excellent devil!
    She hath taught him in a dream
    To make away his duchess and her husband.
BRACHIANO. Sweetly shall I interpret this your dream.
    You are lodg'd within his arms who shall protect you
    From all the fevers of a jealous husband,
    From the poor envy of our phlegmatic duchess.
    I'll seat you above law, and above scandal;
    Give to your thoughts the invention of delight,
    And the fruition; nor shall government
    Divide me from you longer, than a care
    To keep you great: you shall to me at once

Be dukedom, health, wife, children, friends, and all.
CORNELIA. Woe to light hearts, they still forerun our fall!

[*Coming forward.*]

FLAMINEO. What fury raised thee up? away, away.

[*Exit* ZANCHE.]

CORNELIA. What make you here, my lord, this dead of night?
    Never dropp'd mildew on a flower here till now.
FLAMINEO. I pray, will you go to bed then,
    Lest you be blasted?
CORNELIA. O that this fair garden
    Had with all poison'd herbs of Thessaly
    At first been planted; made a nursery
    For witchcraft, rather than a burial plot
    For both your honours!
VITTORIA. Dearest mother, hear me.
CORNELIA. O, thou dost make my brow bend to the earth.
    Sooner than nature! See the curse of children!
    In life they keep us frequently in tears;
    And in the cold grave leave us in pale fears.
BRACHIANO. Come, come, I will not hear you.
VITTORIA. Dear my lord.
CORNELIA. Where is thy duchess now, adulterous duke?
    Thou little dream'st this night she is come to Rome.
FLAMINEO. How! come to Rome!
VITTORIA. The duchess!
BRACHIANO. She had been better—
CORNELIA. The lives of princes should like dials move,
    Whose regular example is so strong,
    They make the times by them go right, or wrong.
FLAMINEO. So, have you done?
CORNELIA. Unfortunate Camillo!
VITTORIA. I do protest, if any chaste denial,
    If anything but blood could have allay'd
    His long suit to me—
CORNELIA. I will join with thee,
    To the most woeful end e'er mother kneel'd:
    If thou dishonour thus thy husband's bed,
    Be thy life short as are the funeral tears
    In great men's—
BRACHIANO. Fie, fie, the woman's mad.
CORNELIA. Be thy act Judas-like; betray in kissing:

May'st thou be envied during his short breath,
And pitied like a wretch after his death!

VITTORIA. O me accurs'd! [Exit.

FLAMINEO. Are you out of your wits? my lord,
I'll fetch her back again.

BRACHIANO. No, I'll to bed:
Send Doctor Julio to me presently.
Uncharitable woman! thy rash tongue
Hath rais'd a fearful and prodigious storm:
Be thou the cause of all ensuing harm. [*Exit.*]

FLAMINEO. Now, you that stand so much upon your honour,
Is this a fitting time a' night, think you,
To send a duke home without e'er a man?
I would fain know where lies the mass of wealth
Which you have hoarded for my maintenance,
That I may bear my beard out of the level
Of my lord's stirrup.

CORNELIA. What! because we are poor
Shall we be vicious?

FLAMINEO. Pray, what means have you
To keep me from the galleys, or the gallows?
My father prov'd himself a gentleman,
Sold all 's land, and, like a fortunate fellow,
Died ere the money was spent. You brought me up
At Padua, I confess, where I protest,
For want of means—the University judge me—
I have been fain to heel my tutor's stockings,
At least seven years; conspiring with a beard,
Made me a graduate; then to this duke's service,
I visited the court, whence I return'd
More courteous, more lecherous by far,
But not a suit the richer. And shall I,
Having a path so open, and so free
To my preferment, still retain your milk
In my pale forehead? No, this face of mine
I'll arm, and fortify with lusty wine,
'Gainst shame and blushing.

CORNELIA. O that I ne'er had borne thee!

FLAMINEO. So would I;
I would the common'st courtesan in Rome
Had been my mother, rather than thyself.
Nature is very pitiful to whores,
To give them but few children, yet those children
Plurality of fathers; they are sure
They shall not want. Go, go,

Complain unto my great lord cardinal;
It may be he will justify the act.
Lycurgus wonder'd much, men would provide
Good stallions for their mares, and yet would suffer
Their fair wives to be barren.
CORNELIA. Misery of miseries! [*Exit.*]
FLAMINEO. The duchess come to court! I like not that.
We are engag'd to mischief, and must on;
As rivers to find out the ocean
Flow with crook bendings beneath forced banks,
Or as we see, to aspire some mountain's top,
The way ascends not straight, but imitates
The subtle foldings of a winter's snake,
So who knows policy and her true aspect,
Shall find her ways winding and indirect. [*Exit.*]

[*Enter* FRANCISCO DE MEDICIS, CARDINAL MONTICELSO,
MARCELLO, ISABELLA, *young* GIOVANNI, *with little* JAQUES
the Moor.]

FRANCISCO. Have you not seen your husband since you arrived?
ISABELLA. Not yet, sir.
FRANCISCO. Surely he is wondrous kind;
If I had such a dove-house as Camillo's,
I would set fire on 't were 't but to destroy
The polecats that haunt to it—My sweet cousin!
GIOVANNI. Lord uncle, you did promise me a horse,
And armour.
FRANCISCO. That I did, my pretty cousin.
Marcello, see it fitted.
MARCELLO. My lord, the duke is here.
FRANCISCO. Sister, away; you must not yet be seen.
ISABELLA. I do beseech you,
Entreat him mildly, let not your rough tongue
Set us at louder variance; all my wrongs
Are freely pardon'd; and I do not doubt,
As men to try the precious unicorn's horn
Make of the powder a preservative circle,
And in it put a spider, so these arms
Shall charm his poison, force it to obeying,
And keep him chaste from an infected straying.
FRANCISCO. I wish it may. Begone, 'void the chamber.

[*Exeunt* ISABELLA, GIOVANNI, *and* JAQUES.]

[*Enter* BRACHIANO *and* FLAMINEO.]

You are welcome; will you sit?—I pray, my lord,
Be you my orator, my heart 's too full;
I'll second you anon.
MONTICELSO. Ere I begin,
Let me entreat your grace forgo all passion,
Which may be raised by my free discourse.
BRACHIANO. As silent as i' th' church: you may proceed.
MONTICELSO. It is a wonder to your noble friends,
That you, having as 'twere enter'd the world
With a free scepter in your able hand,
And having to th' use of nature well applied
High gifts of learning, should in your prime age
Neglect your awful throne for the soft down
Of an insatiate bed. O my lord,
The drunkard after all his lavish cups
Is dry, and then is sober; so at length,
When you awake from this lascivious dream,
Repentance then will follow, like the sting
Plac'd in the adder's tail. Wretched are princes
When fortune blasteth but a petty flower
Of their unwieldy crowns, or ravisheth
But one pearl from their scepter; but alas!
When they to wilful shipwreck lose good fame,
All princely titles perish with their name.
BRACHIANO. You have said, my lord——
MONTICELSO. Enough to give you taste
How far I am from flattering your greatness.
BRACHIANO. Now you that are his second, what say you?
Do not like young hawks fetch a course about;
Your game flies fair, and for you.
FRANCISCO. Do not fear it:
I'll answer you in your own hawking phrase.
Some eagles that should gaze upon the sun
Seldom soar high, but take their lustful ease,
Since they from dunghill birds their prey can seize.
You know Vittoria?
BRACHIANO. Yes.
FRANCISCO. You shift your shirt there,
When you retire from tennis?
BRACHIANO. Happily.
FRANCISCO. Her husband is lord of a poor fortune,
Yet she wears cloth of tissue.

BRACHIANO. What of this?
  Will you urge that, my good lord cardinal,
  As part of her confession at next shrift,
  And know from whence it sails?
FRANCISCO. She is your strumpet——
BRACHIANO. Uncivil sir, there 's hemlock in thy breath,
  And that black slander. Were she a whore of mine,
  All thy loud cannons, and thy borrow'd Switzers,
  Thy galleys, nor thy sworn confederates,
  Durst not supplant her.
FRANCISCO. Let 's not talk on thunder.
  Thou hast a wife, our sister; would I had given
  Both her white hands to death, bound and lock'd fast
  In her last winding sheet, when I gave thee
  But one.
BRACHIANO. Thou hadst given a soul to God then.
FRANCISCO. True:
  Thy ghostly father, with all his absolution,
  Shall ne'er do so by thee.
BRACHIANO. Spit thy poison.
FRANCISCO. I shall not need; lust carries her sharp whip
  At her own girdle. Look to 't, for our anger
  Is making thunderbolts.
BRACHIANO. Thunder! in faith,
  They are but crackers.
FRANCISCO. We 'll end this with the cannon.
BRACHIANO. Thou 'lt get naught by it, but iron in thy wounds,
  And gunpowder in thy nostrils.
FRANCISCO. Better that,
  Than change perfumes for plasters.
BRACHIANO. Pity on thee!
  'Twere good you 'd show your slaves or men condemn'd,
  Your new-plough'd forehead. Defiance! and I'll meet thee,
  Even in a thicket of thy ablest men.
MONTICELSO. My lords, you shall not word it any further
  Without a milder limit.
FRANCISCO. Willingly.
BRACHIANO. Have you proclaim'd a triumph, that you bait
  A lion thus?
MONTICELSO. My lord!
BRACHIANO. I am tame, I am tame, sir.
FRANCISCO. We send unto the duke for conference
  'Bout levies 'gainst the pirates; my lord duke
  Is not at home: we come ourself in person;
  Still my lord duke is busied. But we fear

When Tiber to each prowling passenger
Discovers flocks of wild ducks, then, my lord—
'Bout moulting time I mean—we shall be certain
To find you sure enough, and speak with you.
BRACHIANO. Ha!
FRANCISCO. A mere tale of a tub: my words are idle.
But to express the sonnet by natural reason,
When stags grow melancholic you 'll find the season.

[*Enter* GIOVANNI.]

MONTICELSO. No more, my lord; here comes a champion
Shall end the difference between you both;
Your son, the Prince Giovanni. See, my lords,
What hopes you store in him; this is a casket
For both your crowns, and should be held like dear.
Now is he apt for knowledge; therefore know
It is a more direct and even way,
To train to virtue those of princely blood,
By examples than by precepts: if by examples,
Whom should he rather strive to imitate
Than his own father? be his pattern then,
Leave him a stock of virtue that may last,
Should fortune rend his sails, and split his mast.
BRACHIANO. Your hand, boy: growing to a soldier?
GIOVANNI. Give me a pike.
FRANCISCO. What, practising your pike so young, fair cousin?
GIOVANNI. Suppose me one of Homer's frogs, my lord,
Tossing my bulrush thus. Pray, sir, tell me,
Might not a child of good discretion
Be leader to an army?
FRANCISCO. Yes, cousin, a young prince
Of good discretion might.
GIOVANNI. Say you so?
Indeed I have heard, 'tis fit a general
Should not endanger his own person oft;
So that he make a noise when he's a-horseback,
Like a Danske drummer,—Oh, 'tis excellent!—
He need not fight! methinks his horse as well
Might lead an army for him. If I live,
I 'll charge the French foe in the very front
Of all my troops, the foremost man.
FRANCISCO. What! what!
GIOVANNI. And will not bid my soldiers up, and follow,
But bid them follow me.

BRACHIANO. Forward lapwing!
    He flies with the shell on 's head.
FRANCISCO. Pretty cousin!
GIOVANNI. The first year, uncle, that I go to war,
    All prisoners that I take, I will set free,
    Without their ransom.
FRANCISCO. Ha! without their ransom!
    How then will you reward your soldiers,
    That took those prisoners for you?
GIOVANNI. Thus, my lord:
    I'll marry them to all the wealthy widows
    That falls that year.
FRANCISCO. Why then, the next year following,
    You'll have no men to go with you to war.
GIOVANNI. Why then I'll press the women to the war,
    And then the men will follow.
MONTICELSO. Witty prince!
FRANCISCO. See, a good habit makes a child a man,
    Whereas a bad one makes a man a beast.
    Come, you and I are friends.
BRACHIANO. Most wishedly:
    Like bones which, broke in sunder, and well set,
    Knit the more strongly.
FRANCISCO. Call Camillo hither.—

[*Exit* MARCELLO.]

You have receiv'd the rumour, how Count Lodowick
    Is turn'd a pirate?
BRACHIANO. Yes.
FRANCISCO. We are now preparing to fetch him in. Behold your
duchess.
    We now will leave you, and expect from you
    Nothing but kind entreaty.
BRACHIANO. You have charm'd me.

[*Exeunt* FRANCISCO DE MEDICIS, MONTICELSO, *and* GIOVANNI.
    FLAMINEO *retires.*]

[*Enter* ISABELLA.]

You are in health, we see.
ISABELLA. And above health,
    To see my lord well.
BRACHIANO. So: I wonder much

What amorous whirlwind hurried you to Rome.
ISABELLA. Devotion, my lord.
BRACHIANO. Devotion!
  Is your soul charg'd with any grievous sin?
ISABELLA. 'Tis burden'd with too many; and I think
  The oftener that we cast our reckonings up,
  Our sleep will be the sounder.
BRACHIANO. Take your chamber.
ISABELLA. Nay, my dear lord, I will not have you angry!
  Doth not my absence from you, now two months,
  Merit one kiss?
BRACHIANO. I do not use to kiss:
  If that will dispossess your jealousy,
  I'll swear it to you.
ISABELLA. O, my loved lord,
  I do not come to chide: my jealousy!
  I am to learn what that Italian means.
  You are as welcome to these longing arms,
  As I to you a virgin.
BRACHIANO. Oh, your breath!
  Out upon sweetmeats and continued physic,
  The plague is in them!
ISABELLA. You have oft, for these two lips,
  Neglected cassia, or the natural sweets
  Of the spring-violet: they are not yet much wither'd.
  My lord, I should be merry: these your frowns
  Show in a helmet lovely; but on me,
  In such a peaceful interview, methinks
  They are too roughly knit.
BRACHIANO. O dissemblance!
  Do you bandy factions 'gainst me? have you learnt
  The trick of impudent baseness to complain
  Unto your kindred?
ISABELLA. Never, my dear lord.
BRACHIANO. Must I be hunted out? or was 't your trick
  To meet some amorous gallant here in Rome,
  That must supply our discontinuance?
ISABELLA. Pray, sir, burst my heart; and in my death
  Turn to your ancient pity, though not love.
BRACHIANO. Because your brother is the corpulent duke,
  That is, the great duke, 'sdeath, I shall not shortly
  Racket away five hundred crowns at tennis,
  But it shall rest 'pon record! I scorn him
  Like a shav'd Polack: all his reverend wit
  Lies in his wardrobe; he's a discreet fellow,

When he's made up in his robes of state.
Your brother, the great duke, because h' 'as galleys,
And now and then ransacks a Turkish fly-boat,
(Now all the hellish furies take his soul!)
First made this match: accursed be the priest
That sang the wedding-mass, and even my issue!

ISABELLA. Oh, too, too far you have curs'd!

BRACHIANO. Your hand I'll kiss;
This is the latest ceremony of my love.
Henceforth I'll never lie with thee; by this,
This wedding-ring, I'll ne'er more lie with thee!
And this divorce shall be as truly kept,
As if the judge had doomed it. Fare you well:
Our sleeps are sever'd.

ISABELLA. Forbid it the sweet union
Of all things blessed! why, the saints in heaven
Will knit their brows at that.

BRACHIANO. Let not thy love
Make thee an unbeliever; this my vow
Shall never, on my soul, be satisfied
With my repentance: let thy brother rage
Beyond a horrid tempest, or sea-fight,
My vow is fixed.

ISABELLA. O, my winding-sheet!
Now shall I need thee shortly. Dear my lord,
Let me hear once more, what I would not hear:
Never?

BRACHIANO. Never.

ISABELLA. Oh, my unkind lord! may your sins find mercy,
As I upon a woeful widow'd bed
Shall pray for you, if not to turn your eyes
Upon your wretched wife and hopeful son,
Yet that in time you 'll fix them upon heaven!

BRACHIANO. No more; go, go, complain to the great duke.

ISABELLA. No, my dear lord; you shall have present witness
How I'll work peace between you. I will make
Myself the author of your cursed vow;
I have some cause to do it, you have none.
Conceal it, I beseech you, for the weal
Of both your dukedoms, that you wrought the means
Of such a separation: let the fault
Remain with my supposed jealousy,
And think with what a piteous and rent heart
I shall perform this sad ensuing part.

[*Enter* FRANCISCO DE MEDICIS, *and* MONTICELSO.]

BRACHIANO. Well, take your course.—My honourable brother!
FRANCISCO. Sister!—This is not well, my lord.—Why, sister!—She
   merits not this welcome.
BRACHIANO. Welcome, say!
   She hath given a sharp welcome.
FRANCISCO. Are you foolish?
   Come, dry your tears: is this a modest course
   To better what is naught, to rail and weep?
   Grow to a reconcilement, or, by heaven,
   I'll ne'er more deal between you.
ISABELLA. Sir, you shall not;
   No, though Vittoria, upon that condition,
   Would become honest.
FRANCISCO. Was your husband loud
   Since we departed?
ISABELLA. By my life, sir, no,
   I swear by that I do not care to lose.
   Are all these ruins of my former beauty
   Laid out for a whore's triumph?
FRANCISCO. Do you hear?
   Look upon other women, with what patience
   They suffer these slight wrongs, and with what justice
   They study to requite them: take that course.
ISABELLA. O that I were a man, or that I had power
   To execute my apprehended wishes!
   I would whip some with scorpions.
FRANCISCO. What! turn'd fury!
ISABELLA. To dig that strumpet's eyes out; let her lie
   Some twenty months a-dying; to cut off
   Her nose and lips, pull out her rotten teeth;
   Preserve her flesh like mummia, for trophies
   Of my just anger! Hell, to my affliction,
   Is mere snow-water. By your favour, sir;—
   Brother, draw near, and my lord cardinal;—
   Sir, let me borrow of you but one kiss;
   Henceforth I'll never lie with you, by this,
   This wedding-ring.
FRANCISCO. How, ne'er more lie with him!
ISABELLA. And this divorce shall be as truly kept
   As if in thronged court a thousand ears
   Had heard it, and a thousand lawyers' hands
   Sealed to the separation.

BRACHIANO. Ne'er lie with me!
ISABELLA. Let not my former dotage
  Make thee an unbeliever; this my vow
  Shall never on my soul be satisfied
  With my repentance: *manet alta mente repostum.*
FRANCISCO. Now, by my birth, you are a foolish, mad,
  And jealous woman.
BRACHIANO. You see 'tis not my seeking.
FRANCISCO. Was this your circle of pure unicorn's horn,
  You said should charm your lord! now horns upon thee,
  For jealousy deserves them! Keep your vow
  And take your chamber.
ISABELLA. No, sir, I'll presently to Padua;
  I will not stay a minute.
MONTICELSO. Oh, good madam!
BRACHIANO. 'Twere best to let her have her humour;
  Some half-day's journey will bring down her stomach,
  And then she 'll turn in post.
FRANCISCO. To see her come
  To my lord for a dispensation
  Of her rash vow, will beget excellent laughter.
ISABELLA. 'Unkindness, do thy office; poor heart, break:
  Those are the killing griefs, which dare not speak. [*Exit.*]

[*Enter* MARCELLO *and* CAMILLO.]

MARCELLO. Camillo's come, my lord.
FRANCISCO. Where 's the commission?
MARCELLO. 'Tis here.
FRANCISCO. Give me the signet.

[FRANCISCO DE MEDICIS, MONTICELSO, CAMILLO, *and*
MARCELLO, *retire to the back of the stage.*]

FLAMINEO. My lord, do you mark their whispering? I will compound a
  medicine, out of their two heads, stronger than garlic, deadlier than
  stibium: the cantharides, which are scarce seen to stick upon the
  flesh, when they work to the heart, shall not do it with more silence
  or invisible cunning.

[*Enter* DOCTOR.]

BRACHIANO. About the murder?
FLAMINEO. They are sending him to Naples, but I'll send him to Candy.
  Here 's another property too.

BRACHIANO. Oh, the doctor!

FLAMINEO. A poor quack-salving knave, my lord; one that should have been lashed for 's lechery, but that he confessed a judgment, had an execution laid upon him, and so put the whip to a non plus.

DOCTOR. And was cozened, my lord, by an arranter knave than myself, and made pay all the colorable execution.

FLAMINEO. He will shoot pills into a man's guts shall make them have more ventages than a cornet or a lamprey; he will poison a kiss; and was once minded for his masterpiece, because Ireland breeds no poison, to have prepared a deadly vapour in a Spaniard's fart, that should have poisoned all Dublin.

BRACHIANO. Oh, Saint Anthony's fire!

DOCTOR. Your secretary is merry, my lord.

FLAMINEO. O thou cursed antipathy to nature! Look, his eye 's bloodshot, like a needle a surgeon stitcheth a wound with. Let me embrace thee, toad, and love thee, O thou abominable, loathsome gargarism, that will fetch up lungs, lights, heart, and liver, by scruples!

BRACHIANO. No more.—I must employ thee, honest doctor:
    You must to Padua, and by the way,
    Use some of your skill for us.

DOCTOR. Sir, I shall.

BRACHIANO. But for Camillo?

FLAMINEO. He dies this night, by such a politic strain,
    Men shall suppose him by 's own engine slain.
    But for your duchess' death——

DOCTOR. I'll make her sure.

BRACHIANO. Small mischiefs are by greater made secure.

FLAMINEO. Remember this, you slave; when knaves come to preferment, they rise as gallows in the Low Countries, one upon another's shoulders.

    [*Exeunt* BRACHIANO, FLAMINEO, *and* DOCTOR.]

MONTICELSO. Here is an emblem, nephew, pray peruse it:
    'Twas thrown in at your window.

CAMILLO. At my window!
    Here is a stag, my lord, hath shed his horns,
    And, for the loss of them, the poor beast weeps:
    The word, *Inopem me copia fecit.*

MONTICELSO. That is,
    Plenty of horns hath made him poor of horns.

CAMILLO. What should this mean?

MONTICELSO. I'll tell you; 'tis given out
    You are a cuckold.

CAMILLO. Is it given out so?
    I had rather such reports as that, my lord,
    Should keep within doors.
FRANCISCO. Have you any children?
CAMILLO. None, my lord.
FRANCISCO. You are the happier:
    I'll tell you a tale.
CAMILLO. Pray, my lord.
FRANCISCO. An old tale.
    Upon a time Phbus, the god of light,
    Or him we call the sun, would need to be married:
    The gods gave their consent, and Mercury
    Was sent to voice it to the general world.
    But what a piteous cry there straight arose
    Amongst smiths and felt-makers, brewers and cooks,
    Reapers and butter-women, amongst fishmongers,
    And thousand other trades, which are annoyed
    By his excessive heat! 'twas lamentable.
    They came to Jupiter all in a sweat,
    And do forbid the banns. A great fat cook
    Was made their speaker, who entreats of Jove
    That Phœbus might be gelded; for if now,
    When there was but one sun, so many men
    Were like to perish by his violent heat,
    What should they do if he were married,
    And should beget more, and those children
    Make fireworks like their father? So say I;
    Only I apply it to your wife;
    Her issue, should not providence prevent it,
    Would make both nature, time, and man repent it.
MONTICELSO. Look you, cousin,
    Go, change the air for shame; see if your absence
    Will blast your cornucopia. Marcello
    Is chosen with you joint commissioner,
    For the relieving our Italian coast
    From pirates.
MARCELLO. I am much honour'd in 't.
CAMILLO. But, sir,
    Ere I return, the stag's horns may be sprouted
    Greater than those are shed.
MONTICELSO. Do not fear it;
    I'll be your ranger.
CAMILLO. You must watch i' th' nights;
    Then 's the most danger.
FRANCISCO. Farewell, good Marcello:

All the best fortunes of a soldier's wish
Bring you a-shipboard.

CAMILLO. Were I not best, now I am turn'd soldier,
Ere that I leave my wife, sell all she hath,
And then take leave of her?

MONTICELSO. I expect good from you,
Your parting is so merry.

CAMILLO. Merry, my lord! a' th' captain's humour right,
I am resolved to be drunk this night.

[*Exeunt* CAMILLO *and* MARCELLO.]

FRANCISCO. So, 'twas well fitted; now shall we discern
How his wish'd absence will give violent way
To Duke Brachiano's lust.

MONTICELSO. Why, that was it;
To what scorn'd purpose else should we make choice
Of him for a sea-captain? and, besides,
Count Lodowick, which was rumour'd for a pirate,
Is now in Padua.

FRANCISCO. Is 't true?

MONTICELSO. Most certain.
I have letters from him, which are suppliant
To work his quick repeal from banishment:
He means to address himself for pension
Unto our sister duchess.

FRANCISCO. Oh, 'twas well!
We shall not want his absence past six days:
I fain would have the Duke Brachiano run
Into notorious scandal; for there 's naught
In such cursed dotage, to repair his name,
Only the deep sense of some deathless shame.

MONTICELSO. It may be objected, I am dishonourable
To play thus with my kinsman; but I answer,
For my revenge I 'd stake a brother's life,
That being wrong'd, durst not avenge himself.

FRANCISCO. Come, to observe this strumpet.

MONTICELSO. Curse of greatness!
Sure he'll not leave her?

FRANCISCO. There's small pity in 't:
Like mistletoe on sere elms spent by weather,
Let him cleave to her, and both rot together.

[*Exeunt.*]

[*Enter* BRACHIANO, *with one in the habit of a conjurer.*]

BRACHIANO. Now, sir, I claim your promise: 'tis dead midnight,
    The time prefix'd to show me by your art,
    How the intended murder of Camillo,
    And our loath'd duchess, grow to action.
CONJURER. You have won me by your bounty to a deed
    I do not often practise. Some there are,
    Which by sophistic tricks, aspire that name
    Which I would gladly lose, of necromancer;
    As some that use to juggle upon cards,
    Seeming to conjure, when indeed they cheat;
    Others that raise up their confederate spirits
    'Bout windmills, and endanger their own necks
    For making of a squib; and some there are
    Will keep a curtal to show juggling tricks,
    And give out 'tis a spirit; besides these,
    Such a whole ream of almanac-makers, figure-flingers,
    Fellows, indeed that only live by stealth,
    Since they do merely lie about stol'n goods,
    They 'd make men think the devil were fast and loose,
    With speaking fustian Latin. Pray, sit down;
    Put on this nightcap, sir, 'tis charmed; and now
    I'll show you, by my strong commanding art,
    The circumstance that breaks your duchess' heart.

A dumb Show.

[*Enter suspiciously* JULIO *and* CHRISTOPHERO: *they draw a curtain
    where* BRACHIANO'*s picture is*; *they put on spectacles of
    glass, which cover their eyes and noses, and then burn
    perfumes before the picture, and wash the lips of the picture*;
    *that done, quenching the fire, and putting off their spectacles,
    they depart laughing.*]

[*Enter* ISABELLA *in her night-gown, as to bedward, with lights,
    after her, count* LODOVICO, GIOVANNI, GUID-ANTONIO, *and
    others waiting on her: she kneels down as to prayers, then
    draws the curtain of the picture, does three reverences to it,
    and kisses it thrice; she faints, and will not suffer them to come
    near it*; *dies*; *sorrow expressed in* GIOVANNI, *and in* COUNT
    LODOVICO. *She is conveyed out solemnly.*]

BRACHIANO. Excellent! then she 's dead.
CONJURER. She's poisoned
　　By the fumed picture. 'Twas her custom nightly,
　　Before she went to bed, to go and visit
　　Your picture, and to feed her eyes and lips
　　On the dead shadow: Doctor Julio,
　　Observing this, infects it with an oil,
　　And other poison'd stuff, which presently
　　Did suffocate her spirits.
BRACHIANO. Methought I saw
　　Count Lodowick there.
CONJURER. He was; and by my art
　　I find he did most passionately dote
　　Upon your duchess. Now turn another way,
　　And view Camillo's far more politic fate.
　　Strike louder, music, from this charmed ground,
　　To yield, as fits the act, a tragic sound!

The second dumb Show.

[*Enter* FLAMINEO, MARCELLO, CAMILLO, *with four more as captains: they drink healths, and dance; a vaulting horse is brought into the room; Marcello and two more whispered out of the room, while* FLAMINEO *and* CAMILLO *strip themselves into their shirts, as to vault; compliment who shall begin; as* CAMILLO *is about to vault,* FLAMINEO *pitcheth him upon his neck, and, with the help of the rest, writhes his neck about; seems to see if it be broke, and lays him folded double, as 'twere under the horse; makes show to call for help;* MARCELLO *comes in, laments; sends for the cardinal and duke, who comes forth with armed men; wonders at the act; commands the body to be carried home; apprehends* FLAMINEO, MARCELLO, *and the rest, and go, as 'twere, to apprehend* VITTORIA.]

BRACHIANO. 'Twas quaintly done; but yet each circumstance
　　I taste not fully.
CONJURER. Oh, 'twas most apparent!
　　You saw them enter, charg'd with their deep healths
　　To their boon voyage; and, to second that,
　　Flamineo calls to have a vaulting horse
　　Maintain their sport; the virtuous Marcello
　　Is innocently plotted forth the room;
　　Whilst your eye saw the rest, and can inform you
　　The engine of all.

BRACHIANO. It seems Marcello and Flamineo
    Are both committed.
CONJURER. Yes, you saw them guarded;
    And now they are come with purpose to apprehend
    Your mistress, fair Vittoria. We are now
    Beneath her roof: 'twere fit we instantly
    Make out by some back postern.
BRACHIANO. Noble friend,
    You bind me ever to you: this shall stand
    As the firm seal annexed to my hand;
    It shall enforce a payment.

[*Exit* BRACHIANO.]

CONJURER. Sir, I thank you.
    Both flowers and weeds spring, when the sun is warm,
    And great men do great good, or else great harm. [*Exit.*]

[*Enter* FRANCISCO DE MEDICIS, *and* MONTICELSO, *their
    Chancellor and Register.*]

FRANCISCO. You have dealt discreetly, to obtain the presence
    Of all the great lieger ambassadors
    To hear Vittoria's trial.
MONTICELSO. 'Twas not ill;
    For, sir, you know we have naught but circumstances
    To charge her with, about her husband's death:
    Their approbation, therefore, to the proofs
    Of her black lust shall make her infamous
    To all our neighbouring kingdoms. I wonder
    If Brachiano will be here?
FRANCISCO. Oh, fie! 'Twere impudence too palpable.

[*Exeunt.*]

[*Enter* FLAMINEO *and* MARCELLO *guarded, and a* LAWYER.]

LAWYER. What, are you in by the week? So, I will try now whether
    they wit be close prisoner. Methinks none should sit upon thy
    sister, but old whore-masters.
FLAMINEO. Or cuckolds; for your cuckold is your most terrible tickler
    of lechery. Whore-masters would serve; for none are judges at
    tilting, but those that have been old tilters.
LAWYER. My lord duke and she have been very private.
FLAMINEO. You are a dull ass; 'tis threatened they have been very

public.

LAWYER. If it can be proved they have but kissed one another—

FLAMINEO. What then?

LAWYER. My lord cardinal will ferret them.

FLAMINEO. A cardinal, I hope, will not catch conies.

LAWYER. For to sow kisses (mark what I say), to sow kisses is to reap
    lechery; and, I am sure, a woman that will endure kissing is half
    won.

FLAMINEO. True, her upper part, by that rule; if you will win her neither
    part too, you know what follows.

LAWYER. Hark! the ambassadors are 'lighted—

FLAMINEO. I do put on this feigned garb of mirth,
    To gull suspicion.

MARCELLO. Oh, my unfortunate sister!
    I would my dagger-point had cleft her heart
    When she first saw Brachiano: you, 'tis said,
    Were made his engine, and his stalking horse,
    To undo my sister.

FLAMINEO. I am a kind of path
    To her and mine own preferment.

MARCELLO. Your ruin.

FLAMINEO. Hum! thou art a soldier,
    Followest the great duke, feed'st his victories,
    As witches do their serviceable spirits,
    Even with thy prodigal blood: what hast got?
    But, like the wealth of captains, a poor handful,
    Which in thy palm thou bear'st, as men hold water;
    Seeking to grip it fast, the frail reward
    Steals through thy fingers.

MARCELLO. Sir!

FLAMINEO. Thou hast scarce maintenance
    To keep thee in fresh chamois.

MARCELLO. Brother!

FLAMINEO. Hear me:
    And thus, when we have even pour'd ourselves
    Into great fights, for their ambition,
    Or idle spleen, how shall we find reward?
    But as we seldom find the mistletoe,
    Sacred to physic, on the builder oak,
    Without a mandrake by it; so in our quest of gain,
    Alas, the poorest of their forc'd dislikes
    At a limb proffers, but at heart it strikes!
    This is lamented doctrine.

MARCELLO. Come, come.

FLAMINEO. When age shall turn thee

White as a blooming hawthorn—
MARCELLO. I'll interrupt you:
    For love of virtue bear an honest heart,
    And stride o'er every politic respect,
    Which, where they most advance, they most infect.
    Were I your father, as I am your brother,
    I should not be ambitious to leave you
    A better patrimony.
FLAMINEO. I'll think on 't.
    The lord ambassadors.

[*Here there is a passage of the lieger Ambassadors over the stage severally.*]

LAWYER. Oh, my sprightly Frenchman! Do you know him? he's an admirable tilter.
FLAMINEO. I saw him at last tilting: he showed like a pewter candlestick fashioned like a man in armour, holding a tilting staff in his hand, little bigger than a candle of twelve i'th' pound.
LAWYER. Oh, but he's an excellent horseman!
FLAMINEO. A lame one in his lofty tricks; he sleeps a-horseback, like a poulter.
LAWYER. Lo you, my Spaniard!
FLAMINEO. He carried his face in 's ruff, as I have seen a serving-man carry glasses in a cypress hatband, monstrous steady, for fear of breaking; he looks like the claw of a blackbird, first salted, and then broiled in a candle.

[*Exeunt.*]

The Arraignment of VITTORIA

[*Enter* FRANCISCO DE MEDICIS, MONTICELSO, *the six lieger Ambassadors*, BRACHIANO, VITTORIA, ZANCHE, FLAMINEO, MARCELLO, LAWYER, *and a Guard.*]

MONTICELSO. Forbear, my lord, here is no place assign'd you.
    This business, by his Holiness, is left
    To our examination.
BRACHIANO. May it thrive with you.

[*Lays a rich gown under him.*]

FRANCISCO. A chair there for his Lordship.
BRACHIANO. Forbear your kindness: an unbidden guest

Should travel as Dutch women go to church,
Bear their stools with them.
MONTICELSO. At your pleasure, sir.
Stand to the table, gentlewoman. Now, signior,
Fall to your plea.
LAWYER. *Domine judex, converte oculos in hanc pestem, mulierum corruptissiman.*
VITTORIA. What 's he?
FRANCISCO. A lawyer that pleads against you.
VITTORIA. Pray, my lord, let him speak his usual tongue,
I'll make no answer else.
FRANCISCO. Why, you understand Latin.
VITTORIA. I do, sir, but amongst this auditory
Which come to hear my cause, the half or more
May be ignorant in 't.
MONTICELSO. Go on, sir.
VITTORIA. By your favour,
I will not have my accusation clouded
In a strange tongue: all this assembly
Shall hear what you can charge me with.
FRANCISCO. Signior,
You need not stand on 't much; pray, change your language.
MONTICELSO. Oh, for God's sake—Gentlewoman, your credit
Shall be more famous by it.
LAWYER. Well then, have at you.
VITTORIA. I am at the mark, sir; I'll give aim to you,
And tell you how near you shoot.
LAWYER. Most literated judges, please your lordships
So to connive your judgments to the view
Of this debauch'd and diversivolent woman;
Who such a black concatenation
Of mischief hath effected, that to extirp
The memory of 't, must be the consummation
Of her, and her projections—
VITTORIA. What 's all this?
LAWYER. Hold your peace!
Exorbitant sins must have exulceration.
VITTORIA. Surely, my lords, this lawyer here hath swallow'd
Some 'pothecaries' bills, or proclamations;
And now the hard and undigestible words
Come up, like stones we use give hawks for physic.
Why, this is Welsh to Latin.
LAWYER. My lords, the woman
Knows not her tropes, nor figures, nor is perfect
In the academic derivation

Of grammatical elocution.
FRANCISCO. Sir, your pains
    Shall be well spar'd, and your deep eloquence
    Be worthily applauded amongst thouse
    Which understand you.
LAWYER. My good lord.
FRANCISCO. Sir,
    Put up your papers in your fustian bag—

[Francisco speaks this as in scorn.]

    Cry mercy, sir, 'tis buckram and accept
    My notion of your learn'd verbosity.
LAWYER. I most graduatically thank your lordship:
    I shall have use for them elsewhere.
MONTICELSO. I shall be plainer with you, and paint out
    Your follies in more natural red and white
    Than that upon your cheek.
VITTORIA. Oh, you mistake!
    You raise a blood as noble in this cheek
    As ever was your mother's.
MONTICELSO. I must spare you, till proof cry whore to that.
    Observe this creature here, my honour'd lords,
    A woman of most prodigious spirit,
    In her effected.
VITTORIA. My honourable lord,
    It doth not suit a reverend cardinal
    To play the lawyer thus.
MONTICELSO. Oh, your trade instructs your language!
    You see, my lords, what goodly fruit she seems;
    Yet like those apples travellers report
    To grow where Sodom and Gomorrah stood,
    I will but touch her, and you straight shall see
    She'll fall to soot and ashes.
VITTORIA. Your envenom'd 'pothecary should do 't.
MONTICELSO. I am resolv'd,
    Were there a second paradise to lose,
    This devil would betray it.
VITTORIA. O poor Charity!
    Thou art seldom found in scarlet.
MONTICELSO. Who knows not how, when several night by night
    Her gates were chok'd with coaches, and her rooms
    Outbrav'd the stars with several kind of lights;
    When she did counterfeit a prince's court
    In music, banquets, and most riotous surfeits;

This whore forsooth was holy.

VITTORIA. Ha! whore! what 's that?

MONTICELSO. Shall I expound whore to you? sure I shall;
    I'll give their perfect character. They are first,
    Sweetmeats which rot the eater; in man's nostrils
    Poison'd perfumes. They are cozening alchemy;
    Shipwrecks in calmest weather. What are whores!
    Cold Russian winters, that appear so barren,
    As if that nature had forgot the spring.
    They are the true material fire of hell:
    Worse than those tributes i' th' Low Countries paid,
    Exactions upon meat, drink, garments, sleep,
    Ay, even on man's perdition, his sin.
    They are those brittle evidences of law,
    Which forfeit all a wretched man's estate
    For leaving out one syllable. What are whores!
    They are those flattering bells have all one tune,
    At weddings, and at funerals. Your rich whores
    Are only treasuries by extortion fill'd,
    And emptied by curs'd riot. They are worse,
    Worse than dead bodies which are begg'd at gallows,
    And wrought upon by surgeons, to teach man
    Wherein he is imperfect. What's a whore!
    She's like the guilty counterfeited coin,
    Which, whosoe'er first stamps it, brings in trouble
    All that receive it.

VITTORIA. This character 'scapes me.

MONTICELSO. You, gentlewoman!
    Take from all beasts and from all minerals
    Their deadly poison—

VITTORIA. Well, what then?

MONTICELSO. I'll tell thee;
    I'll find in thee a 'pothecary's shop,
    To sample them all.

FRENCH AMBASSADOR. She hath liv'd ill.

ENGLISH AMBASSADOR. True, but the cardinal 's too bitter.

MONTICELSO. You know what whore is. Next the devil adultery,
    Enters the devil murder.

FRANCISCO. Your unhappy husband
    Is dead.

VITTORIA. Oh, he's a happy husband!
    Now he owes nature nothing.

FRANCISCO. And by a vaulting engine.

MONTICELSO. An active plot; he jump'd into his grave.

FRANCISCO. What a prodigy was 't,

That from some two yards' height, a slender man
Should break his neck!

MONTICELSO. I' th' rushes!

FRANCISCO. And what's more,
Upon the instant lose all use of speech,
All vital motion, like a man had lain
Wound up three days. Now mark each circumstance.

MONTICELSO. And look upon this creature was his wife!
She comes not like a widow; she comes arm'd
With scorn and impudence: is this a mourning-habit?

VITTORIA. Had I foreknown his death, as you suggest,
I would have bespoke my mourning.

MONTICELSO. Oh, you are cunning!

VITTORIA. You shame your wit and judgment,
To call it so. What! is my just defence
By him that is my judge call'd impudence?
Let me appeal then from this Christian court,
To the uncivil Tartar.

MONTICELSO. See, my lords,
She scandals our proceedings.

VITTORIA. Humbly thus,
Thus low to the most worthy and respected
Lieger ambassadors, my modesty
And womanhood I tender; but withal,
So entangled in a curs'd accusation,
That my defence, of force, like Perseus,
Must personate masculine virtue. To the point.
Find me but guilty, sever head from body,
We'll part good friends: I scorn to hold my life
At yours, or any man's entreaty, sir.

ENGLISH AMBASSADOR. She hath a brave spirit.

MONTICELSO. Well, well, such counterfeit jewels
Make true ones oft suspected.

VITTORIA. You are deceiv'd:
For know, that all your strict-combined heads,
Which strike against this mine of diamonds,
Shall prove but glassen hammers: they shall break.
These are but feigned shadows of my evils.
Terrify babes, my lord, with painted devils,
I am past such needless palsy. For your names
Of 'whore' and 'murderess', they proceed from you,
As if a man should spit against the wind,
The filth returns in 's face.

MONTICELSO. Pray you, mistress, satisfy me one question:
Who lodg'd beneath your roof that fatal night

Your husband broke his neck?
BRACHIANO. That question
Enforceth me break silence: I was there.
MONTICELSO. Your business?
BRACHIANO. Why, I came to comfort her,
And take some course for settling her estate,
Because I heard her husband was in debt
To you, my lord.
MONTICELSO. He was.
BRACHIANO. And 'twas strangely fear'd,
That you would cozen her.
MONTICELSO. Who made you overseer?
BRACHIANO. Why, my charity, my charity, which should flow
From every generous and noble spirit,
To orphans and to widows.
MONTICELSO. Your lust!
BRACHIANO. Cowardly dogs bark loudest: sirrah priest,
I'll talk with you hereafter. Do you hear?
The sword you frame of such an excellent temper,
I'll sheath in your own bowels.
There are a number of thy coat resemble
Your common post-boys.
MONTICELSO. Ha!
BRACHIANO. Your mercenary post-boys;
Your letters carry truth, but 'tis your guise
To fill your mouths with gross and impudent lies.
SERVANT. My lord, your gown.
BRACHIANO. Thou liest, 'twas my stool:
Bestow 't upon thy master, that will challenge
The rest o' th' household-stuff; for Brachiano
Was ne'er so beggarly to take a stool
Out of another's lodging: let him make
Vallance for his bed on 't, or a demy foot-cloth
For his most reverend moil. Monticelso,
Nemo me impune lacessit. [*Exit.*]
MONTICELSO. Your champion's gone.
VITTORIA. The wolf may prey the better.
FRANCISCO. My lord, there's great suspicion of the murder,
But no sound proof who did it. For my part,
I do not think she hath a soul so black
To act a deed so bloody; if she have,
As in cold countries husbandmen plant vines,
And with warm blood manure them; even so
One summer she will bear unsavoury fruit,
And ere next spring wither both branch and root.

       The act of blood let pass; only descend
       To matters of incontinence.
VITTORIA. I discern poison
       Under your gilded pills.
MONTICELSO. Now the duke's gone, I will produce a letter
       Wherein 'twas plotted, he and you should meet
       At an apothecary's summer-house,
       Down by the River Tiber,—view 't, my lords,
       Where after wanton bathing and the heat
       Of a lascivious banquet—I pray read it,
       I shame to speak the rest.
VITTORIA. Grant I was tempted;
       Temptation to lust proves not the act:
       Casta est quam nemo rogavit.
       You read his hot love to me, but you want
       My frosty answer.
MONTICELSO. Frost i' th' dog-days! strange!
VITTORIA. Condemn you me for that the duke did love me?
       So may you blame some fair and crystal river,
       For that some melancholic distracted man
       Hath drown'd himself in 't.
MONTICELSO. Truly drown'd, indeed.
VITTORIA. Sum up my faults, I pray, and you shall find,
       That beauty and gay clothes, a merry heart,
       And a good stomach to [a] feast, are all,
       All the poor crimes that you can charge me with.
       In faith, my lord, you might go pistol flies,
       The sport would be more noble.
MONTICELSO. Very good.
VITTORIA. But take your course: it seems you've beggar'd me first,
       And now would fain undo me. I have houses,
       Jewels, and a poor remnant of crusadoes;
       Would those would make you charitable!
MONTICELSO. If the devil
       Did ever take good shape, behold his picture.
VITTORIA. You have one virtue left,
       You will not flatter me.
FRANCISCO. Who brought this letter?
VITTORIA. I am not compell'd to tell you.
MONTICELSO. My lord duke sent to you a thousand ducats
       The twelfth of August.
VITTORIA. 'Twas to keep your cousin
       From prison; I paid use for 't.
MONTICELSO. I rather think,
       'Twas interest for his lust.

VITTORIA. Who says so but yourself?
If you be my accuser,
Pray cease to be my judge: come from the bench;
Give in your evidence 'gainst me, and let these
Be moderators. My lord cardinal,
Were your intelligencing ears as loving
As to my thoughts, had you an honest tongue,
I would not care though you proclaim'd them all.
MONTICELSO. Go to, go to.
After your goodly and vainglorious banquet,
I'll give you a choke-pear.
VITTORIA. O' your own grafting?
MONTICELSO. You were born in Venice, honourably descended
From the Vittelli: 'twas my cousin's fate,
Ill may I name the hour, to marry you;
He bought you of your father.
VITTORIA. Ha!
MONTICELSO. He spent there in six months
Twelve thousand ducats, and (to my acquaintance)
Receiv'd in dowry with you not one Julio:
'Twas a hard pennyworth, the ware being so light.
I yet but draw the curtain; now to your picture:
You came from thence a most notorious strumpet,
And so you have continued.
VITTORIA. My lord!
MONTICELSO. Nay, hear me,
You shall have time to prate. My Lord Brachiano—
Alas! I make but repetition
Of what is ordinary and Rialto talk,
And ballated, and would be play'd a' th' stage,
But that vice many times finds such loud friends,
That preachers are charm'd silent.
You, gentlemen, Flamineo and Marcello,
The Court hath nothing now to charge you with,
Only you must remain upon your sureties
For your appearance.
FRANCISCO. I stand for Marcello.
FLAMINEO. And my lord duke for me.
MONTICELSO. For you, Vittoria, your public fault,
Join'd to th' condition of the present time,
Takes from you all the fruits of noble pity,
Such a corrupted trial have you made
Both of your life and beauty, and been styl'd
No less an ominous fate than blazing stars
To princes. Hear your sentence: you are confin'd

Unto a house of convertites, and your bawd——
FLAMINEO. Who, I?
MONTICELSO. The Moor.
FLAMINEO. Oh, I am a sound man again.
VITTORIA. A house of convertites! what 's that?
MONTICELSO. A house of penitent whores.
VITTORIA. Do the noblemen in Rome
    Erect it for their wives, that I am sent
    To lodge there?
FRANCISCO. You must have patience.
VITTORIA. I must first have vengeance!
    I fain would know if you have your salvation
    By patent, that you proceed thus.
MONTICELSO. Away with her,
    Take her hence.
VITTORIA. A rape! a rape!
MONTICELSO. How?
VITTORIA. Yes, you have ravish'd justice;
    Forc'd her to do your pleasure.
MONTICELSO. Fie, she's mad——
VITTORIA. Die with those pills in your most cursed maw,
    Should bring you health! or while you sit o' th' bench,
    Let your own spittle choke you!
MONTICELSO. She's turned fury.
VITTORIA. That the last day of judgment may so find you,
    And leave you the same devil you were before!
    Instruct me, some good horse-leech, to speak treason;
    For since you cannot take my life for deeds,
    Take it for words. O woman's poor revenge,
    Which dwells but in the tongue! I will not weep;
    No, I do scorn to call up one poor tear
    To fawn on your injustice: bear me hence
    Unto this house of—what's your mitigating title?
MONTICELSO. Of convertites.
VITTORIA. It shall not be a house of convertites;
    My mind shall make it honester to me
    Than the Pope's palace, and more peaceable
    Than thy soul, though thou art a cardinal.
    Know this, and let it somewhat raise your spite,
    Through darkness diamonds spread their richest light.

[*Exeunt* VITTORIA COROMBONA, LAWYER, *and Guards.*]

[*Enter* BRACHIANO.]

BRACHIANO. Now you and I are friends, sir, we'll shake hands
    In a friend's grave together; a fit place,
    Being th' emblem of soft peace, t' atone our hatred.
FRANCISCO. Sir, what's the matter?
BRACHIANO. I will not chase more blood from that lov'd cheek;
    You have lost too much already; fare you well. [*Exit.*]
FRANCISCO. How strange these words sound! what 's the
    interpretation?
FLAMINEO. Good; this is a preface to the discovery of the duchess'
    death: he carries it well. Because now I cannot counterfeit a
    whining passion for the death of my lady, I will feign a mad
    humour for the disgrace of my sister; and that will keep off idle
    questions. Treason's tongue hath a villainous palsy in 't; I will talk
    to any man, hear no man, and for a time appear a politic madman.

[*Enter* GIOVANNI, *and Count* LODOVICO, *and* ATTENDANT.]

FRANCISCO. How now, my noble cousin? what, in black!
GIOVANNI. Yes, uncle, I was taught to imitate you
    In virtue, and you must imitate me
    In colours of your garments. My sweet mother
    Is—
FRANCISCO. How? where?
GIOVANNI. Is there; no, yonder: indeed, sir, I'll not tell you,
    For I shall make you weep.
FRANCISCO. Is dead?
GIOVANNI. Do not blame me now,
    I did not tell you so.
LODOVICO. She's dead, my lord.
FRANCISCO. Dead!
MONTICELSO. Bless'd lady, thou art now above thy woes!
    Will 't please your lordships to withdraw a little?

[*Exeunt* AMBASSADORS.]

GIOVANNI. What do the dead do, uncle? do they eat,
    Hear music, go a hunting, and be merry,
    As we that live?
FRANCISCO. No, coz; they sleep.
GIOVANNI. Lord, Lord, that I were dead!
    I have not slept these six nights. When do they wake?
FRANCISCO. When God shall please.
GIOVANNI. Good God, let her sleep ever!
    For I have known her wake an hundred nights,
    When all the pillow where she laid her head

Was brine-wet with her tears. I am to complain to you, sir;
I'll tell you how they have us'd her now she's dead:
They wrapp'd her in a cruel fold of lead,
And would not let me kiss her.
FRANCISCO. Thou didst love her?
GIOVANNI. I have often heard her say she gave me suck,
And it should seem by that she dearly lov'd me,
Since princes seldom do it.
FRANCISCO. Oh, all of my poor sister that remains!
Take him away for God's sake!

[*Exeunt* GIOVANNI, *and* ATTENDANT.]

MONTICELSO. How now, my lord?
FRANCISCO. Believe me, I am nothing but her grave;
And I shall keep her blessed memory
Longer than thousand epitaphs.

[*Exeunt* FRANCISCO DE MEDICIS *and* MONTICELSO.]

[*Enter* FLAMINEO *as distracted.*]

FLAMINEO. We endure the strokes like anvils or hard steel, Till pain
itself make us no pain to feel. Who shall do me right now? is this
the end of service? I'd rather go weed garlic; travail through
France, and be mine own ostler; wear sheep-skin linings, or shoes
that stink of blacking; be entered into the list of the forty thousand
pedlars in Poland.

[*Enter* AMBASSADORS.]

Would I had rotted in some surgeon's house at Venice, built upon
the pox as well as on piles, ere I had served Brachiano!
SAVOY AMBASSADOR. You must have comfort.
FLAMINEO. Your comfortable words are like honey: they relish well in
your mouth that's whole, but in mine that's wounded, they go
down as if the sting of the bee were in them. Oh, they have
wrought their purpose cunningly, as if they would not seem to do it
of malice! In this a politician imitates the devil, as the devil
imitates a canon; wheresoever he comes to do mischief, he comes
with his backside towards you.
FRENCH AMBASSADOR. The proofs are evident.
FLAMINEO. Proof! 'twas corruption. O gold, what a god art thou! and O
man, what a devil art thou to be tempted by that cursed mineral!
Your diversivolent lawyer, mark him! knaves turn informers, as

maggots turn to flies, you may catch gudgeons with either. A cardinal! I would he would hear me: there's nothing so holy but money will corrupt and putrify it, like victual under the line. You are happy in England, my lord; here they sell justice with those weights they press men to death with. O horrible salary!

ENGLISH AMBASSADOR. Fie, fie, Flamineo.

[*Exeunt* AMBASSADORS.]

FLAMINEO. Bells ne'er ring well, till they are at their full pitch; and I hope yon cardinal shall never have the grace to pray well, till he come to the scaffold. If they were racked now to know the confederacy: but your noblemen are privileged from the rack; and well may, for a little thing would pull some of them a-pieces afore they came to their arraignment. Religion, oh, how it is commeddled with policy! The first blood shed in the world happened about religion. Would I were a Jew!

MARCELLO. Oh, there are too many!

FLAMINEO. You are deceived; there are not Jews enough, priests enough, nor gentlemen enough.

MARCELLO. How?

FLAMINEO. I'll prove it; for if there were Jews enough, so many Christians would not turn usurers; if priests enough, one should not have six benefices; and if gentlemen enough, so many early mushrooms, whose best growth sprang from a live by begging: be thou one of them practise the art of Wolner in England, to swallow all 's given thee: and yet let one purgation make thee as hungry again as fellows that work in a saw-pit. I'll go hear the screech-owl. [*Exit.*]

LODOVICO. This was Brachiano's pander; and 'tis strange
That in such open, and apparent guilt
Of his adulterous sister, he dare utter
So scandalous a passion. I must wind him.

[*Enter* FLAMINEO.]

FLAMINEO. How dares this banish'd count return to Rome,
His pardon not yet purchas'd! I have heard
The deceased duchess gave him pension,
And that he came along from Padua
I' th' train of the young prince. There's somewhat in 't:
Physicians, that cure poisons, still do work
With counter-poisons.

MARCELLO. Mark this strange encounter.

FLAMINEO. The god of melancholy turn thy gall to poison,

And let the stigmatic wrinkles in thy face,
Like to the boisterous waves in a rough tide,
One still overtake another.
LODOVICO. I do thank thee,
And I do wish ingeniously for thy sake,
The dog-days all year long.
FLAMINEO. How croaks the raven?
Is our good duchess dead?
LODOVICO. Dead.
FLAMINEO. O fate!
Misfortune comes like the coroner's business
Huddle upon huddle.
LODOVICO. Shalt thou and I join housekeeping?
FLAMINEO. Yes, content:
Let 's be unsociably sociable.
LODOVICO. Sit some three days together, and discourse?
FLAMINEO. Only with making faces;
Lie in our clothes.
LODOVICO. With faggots for our pillows.
FLAMINEO. And be lousy.
LODOVICO. In taffeta linings, that's genteel melancholy;
Sleep all day.
FLAMINEO. Yes; and, like your melancholic hare,
Feed after midnight.
We are observed: see how yon couple grieve.
LODOVICO. What a strange creature is a laughing fool!
As if man were created to no use
But only to show his teeth.
FLAMINEO. I'll tell thee what,
It would do well instead of looking-glasses,
To set one's face each morning by a saucer
Of a witch's congeal'd blood.
LODOVICO. Precious rogue!
We'll never part.
FLAMINEO. Never, till the beggary of courtiers,
The discontent of churchmen, want of soldiers,
And all the creatures that hang manacled,
Worse than strappadoed, on the lowest felly
Of fortune's wheel, be taught, in our two lives,
To scorn that world which life of means deprives.

[*Enter* ANTONELLI *and* GASPARO.]

ANTONELLI. My lord, I bring good news. The Pope, on 's death bed,
    At th' earnest suit of the great Duke of Florence,
    Hath sign'd your pardon, and restor'd unto you——
LODOVICO. I thank you for your news. Look up again,
    Flamineo, see my pardon.
FLAMINEO. Why do you laugh?
    There was no such condition in our covenant.
LODOVICO. Why?
FLAMINEO. You shall not seem a happier man than I:
    You know our vow, sir; if you will be merry,
    Do it i' th' like posture, as if some great man
    Sat while his enemy were executed:
    Though it be very lechery unto thee,
    Do 't with a crabbed politician's face.
LODOVICO. Your sister is a damnable whore.
FLAMINEO. Ha!
LODOVICO. Look you, I spake that laughing.
FLAMINEO. Dost ever think to speak again?
LODOVICO. Do you hear?
    Wilt sell me forty ounces of her blood
    To water a mandrake?
FLAMINEO. Poor lord, you did vow
    To live a lousy creature.
LODOVICO. Yes.
FLAMINEO. Like one
    That had for ever forfeited the daylight,
    By being in debt.
LODOVICO. Ha, ha!
FLAMINEO. I do not greatly wonder you do break,
    Your lordship learn'd 't long since. But I'll tell you.
LODOVICO. What?
FLAMINEO. And 't shall stick by you.
LODOVICO. I long for it.
FLAMINEO. This laughter scurvily becomes your face:
    If you will not be melancholy, be angry.

    [*Strikes him.*]

    See, now I laugh too.
MARCELLO. You are to blame: I'll force you hence.
LODOVICO. Unhand me.

    [*Exeunt* MARCELLO *and* FLAMINEO.]

    That e'er I should be forc'd to right myself,

Upon a pander!

ANTONELLI. My lord.

LODOVICO. H' had been as good met with his fist a thunderbolt.

GASPARO. How this shows!

LODOVICO. Ud's death! how did my sword miss him?
These rogues that are most weary of their lives
Still 'scape the greatest dangers.
A pox upon him; all his reputation,
Nay, all the goodness of his family,
Is not worth half this earthquake:
I learn'd it of no fencer to shake thus:
Come, I'll forget him, and go drink some wine.

[*Exeunt.*]

[*Enter* FRANCISCO DE MEDICIS *and* MONTICELSO.]

MONTICELSO. Come, come, my lord, untie your folded thoughts,
And let them dangle loose, as a bride's hair.
Your sister's poisoned.

FRANCISCO. Far be it from my thoughts
To seek revenge.

MONTICELSO. What, are you turn'd all marble?

FRANCISCO. Shall I defy him, and impose a war,
Most burthensome on my poor subjects' necks,
Which at my will I have not power to end?
You know, for all the murders, rapes, and thefts,
Committed in the horrid lust of war,
He that unjustly caus'd it first proceed,
Shall find it in his grave, and in his seed.

MONTICELSO. That 's not the course I 'd wish you; pray observe me.
We see that undermining more prevails
Than doth the cannon. Bear your wrongs conceal'd,
And, patient as the tortoise, let this camel
Stalk o'er your back unbruis'd: sleep with the lion,
And let this brood of secure foolish mice
Play with your nostrils, till the time be ripe
For th' bloody audit, and the fatal gripe:
Aim like a cunning fowler, close one eye,
That you the better may your game espy.

FRANCISCO. Free me, my innocence, from treacherous acts!
I know there's thunder yonder; and I'll stand,
Like a safe valley, which low bends the knee
To some aspiring mountain: since I know
Treason, like spiders weaving nets for flies,

By her foul work is found, and in it dies.
To pass away these thoughts, my honour'd lord,
It is reported you possess a book,
Wherein you have quoted, by intelligence,
The names of all notorious offenders
Lurking about the city.

MONTICELSO. Sir, I do;
And some there are which call it my black-book.
Well may the title hold; for though it teach not
The art of conjuring, yet in it lurk
The names of many devils.

FRANCISCO. Pray let 's see it.

MONTICELSO. I'll fetch it to your lordship. [*Exit.*]

FRANCISCO. Monticelso,
I will not trust thee, but in all my plots
I'll rest as jealous as a town besieg'd.
Thou canst not reach what I intend to act:
Your flax soon kindles, soon is out again,
But gold slow heats, and long will hot remain.

[*Enter* MONTICELSO, *presents* FRANCISCO DE MEDICIS *with the book.*]

MONTICELSO. 'Tis here, my lord.

FRANCISCO. First, your intelligencers, pray let 's see.

MONTICELSO. Their number rises strangely;
And some of them
You 'd take for honest men.
Next are panders.
These are your pirates; and these following leaves
For base rogues, that undo young gentlemen,
By taking up commodities; for politic bankrupts;
For fellows that are bawds to their own wives,
Only to put off horses, and slight jewels,
Clocks, defac'd plate, and such commodities,
At birth of their first children.

FRANCISCO. Are there such?

MONTICELSO. These are for impudent bawds,
That go in men's apparel; for usurers
That share with scriveners for their good reportage:
For lawyers that will antedate their writs:
And some divines you might find folded there,
But that I slip them o'er for conscience' sake.
Here is a general catalogue of knaves:
A man might study all the prisons o'er,

Yet never attain this knowledge.
FRANCISCO. Murderers?
    Fold down the leaf, I pray;
    Good my lord, let me borrow this strange doctrine.
MONTICELSO. Pray, use 't, my lord.
FRANCISCO. I do assure your lordship,
    You are a worthy member of the State,
    And have done infinite good in your discovery
    Of these offenders.
MONTICELSO. Somewhat, sir.
FRANCISCO. O God!
    Better than tribute of wolves paid in England;
    'Twill hang their skins o' th' hedge.
MONTICELSO. I must make bold
    To leave your lordship.
FRANCISCO. Dearly, sir, I thank you:
    If any ask for me at court, report
    You have left me in the company of knaves.

[*Exit* MONTICELSO.]

I gather now by this, some cunning fellow
That's my lord's officer, and that lately skipp'd
From a clerk's desk up to a justice' chair,
Hath made this knavish summons, and intends,
As th' Irish rebels wont were to sell heads,
So to make prize of these. And thus it happens:
Your poor rogues pay for 't, which have not the means
To present bribe in fist; the rest o' th' band
Are razed out of the knaves' record; or else
My lord he winks at them with easy will;
His man grows rich, the knaves are the knaves still.
But to the use I'll make of it; it shall serve
To point me out a list of murderers,
Agents for my villany. Did I want
Ten leash of courtesans, it would furnish me;
Nay, laundress three armies. That in so little paper
Should lie th' undoing of so many men!
'Tis not so big as twenty declarations.
See the corrupted use some make of books:
Divinity, wrested by some factious blood,
Draws swords, swells battles, and o'erthrows all good.
To fashion my revenge more seriously,
Let me remember my dear sister's face:
Call for her picture? no, I'll close mine eyes,

And in a melancholic thought I'll frame

[*Enter* ISABELLA's *ghost.*]

Her figure 'fore me. Now I ha' 't—how strong
Imagination works! how she can frame
Things which are not! methinks she stands afore me,
And by the quick idea of my mind,
Were my skill pregnant, I could draw her picture.
Thought, as a subtle juggler, makes us deem
Things supernatural, which have cause
Common as sickness. 'Tis my melancholy.
How cam'st thou by thy death?—how idle am I
To question mine own idleness!—did ever
Man dream awake till now?—remove this object;
Out of my brain with 't: what have I to do
With tombs, or death-beds, funerals, or tears,
That have to meditate upon revenge?

[*Exit Ghost.*]

So, now 'tis ended, like an old wife's story.
Statesmen think often they see stranger sights
Than madmen. Come, to this weighty business.
My tragedy must have some idle mirth in 't,
Else it will never pass. I am in love,
In love with Corombona; and my suit
Thus halts to her in verse.—

[*He writes.*]

I have done it rarely: Oh, the fate of princes!
I am so us'd to frequent flattery,
That, being alone, I now flatter myself:
But it will serve; 'tis seal'd. Bear this

[*Enter* SERVANT.]

To the House of Convertites, and watch your leisure
To give it to the hands of Corombona,
Or to the Matron, when some followers
Of Brachiano may be by. Away!

[*Exit* SERVANT.]

He that deals all by strength, his wit is shallow;
When a man's head goes through, each limb will follow.
The engine for my business, bold Count Lodowick;
'Tis gold must such an instrument procure,
With empty fist no man doth falcons lure.
Brachiano, I am now fit for thy encounter:
Like the wild Irish, I'll ne'er think thee dead
Till I can play at football with thy head,
Flectere si nequeo superos, Acheronta movebo. [*Exit.*]

[*Enter the* MATRON, *and* FLAMINEO.]

MATRON. Should it be known the duke hath such recourse
To your imprison'd sister, I were like
T' incur much damage by it.
FLAMINEO. Not a scruple.
The Pope lies on his death-bed, and their heads
Are troubled now with other business
Than guarding of a lady.

[*Enter* SERVANT.]

SERVANT. Yonder 's Flamineo in conference
With the Matrona.—Let me speak with you:
I would entreat you to deliver for me
This letter to the fair Vittoria.
MATRON. I shall, sir.

[*Enter* BRACHIANO.]

SERVANT. With all care and secrecy;
Hereafter you shall know me, and receive
Thanks for this courtesy. [*Exit.*]
FLAMINEO. How now? what 's that?
Matron. A letter.
FLAMINEO. To my sister? I'll see 't deliver'd.
BRACHIANO. What 's that you read, Flamineo?
FLAMINEO. Look.
BRACHIANO. Ha! 'To the most unfortunate, his best respected Vittoria'.
Who was the messenger?
FLAMINEO. I know not.
BRACHIANO. No! who sent it?
FLAMINEO. Ud's foot! you speak as if a man
Should know what fowl is coffin'd in a bak'd meat
Afore you cut it up.

BRACHIANO. I'll open 't, were 't her heart. What 's here subscrib'd!
  Florence! this juggling is gross and palpable.
  I have found out the conveyance. Read it, read it.
FLAMINEO. *Your tears I'll turn to triumphs, be but mine*:
  Your prop is fallen: I pity, that a vine
  Which princes heretofore have long'd to gather,
  Wanting supporters, now should fade and wither.
  (Wine, i'faith, my lord, with lees would serve his turn.)
  Your sad imprisonment I'll soon uncharm,
  And with a princely uncontrolled arm
  Lead you to Florence, where my love and care
  Shall hang your wishes in my silver hair.
  (A halter on his strange equivocation!)
  Nor for my years return me the sad willow,—
  Who prefer blossoms before fruit that's mellow?
  (Rotten, on my knowledge, with lying too long i' th' bed-straw.)
  And all the lines of age this line convinces;
  The gods never wax old, no more do princes.
  A pox on 't, tear it; let 's have no more atheists, for God's sake.
BRACHIANO. Ud's death! I'll cut her into atomies,
  And let th' irregular north wind sweep her up,
  And blow her int' his nostrils: where's this whore?
FLAMINEO. What? what do you call her?
BRACHIANO. Oh, I could be mad!
  Prevent the curs'd disease she 'll bring me to,
  And tear my hair off. Where 's this changeable stuff?
FLAMINEO. O'er head and ears in water, I assure you;
  She is not for your wearing.
BRACHIANO. In, you pander!
FLAMINEO. What, me, my lord? am I your dog?
BRACHIANO. A bloodhound: do you brave, do you stand me?
FLAMINEO. Stand you! let those that have diseases run;
  I need no plasters.
BRACHIANO. Would you be kick'd?
FLAMINEO. Would you have your neck broke?
  I tell you, duke, I am not in Russia;
  My shins must be kept whole.
BRACHIANO. Do you know me?
FLAMINEO. Oh, my lord, methodically!
  As in this world there are degrees of evils,
  So in this world there are degrees of devils.
  You're a great duke, I your poor secretary.
  I do look now for a Spanish fig, or an Italian sallet, daily.
BRACHIANO. Pander, ply your convoy, and leave your prating.
FLAMINEO. All your kindness to me, is like that miserable courtesy of

Polyphemus to Ulysses; you reserve me to be devoured last: you
would dig turfs out of my grave to feed your larks; that would be
music to you. Come, I'll lead you to her.

BRACHIANO. Do you face me?

FLAMINEO. Oh, sir, I would not go before a politic enemy with my back
towards him, though there were behind me a whirlpool.

[*Enter* VITTORIA COROMBONA.]

BRACHIANO. Can you read, mistress? look upon that letter:
  There are no characters, nor hieroglyphics.
  You need no comment; I am grown your receiver.
  God's precious! you shall be a brave great lady,
  A stately and advanced whore.

VITTORIA. Say, sir?

BRACHIANO. Come, come, let 's see your cabinet, discover
  Your treasury of love-letters. Death and furies!
  I'll see them all.

VITTORIA. Sir, upon my soul,
  I have not any. Whence was this directed?

BRACHIANO. Confusion on your politic ignorance!
  You are reclaim'd, are you? I'll give you the bells,
  And let you fly to the devil.

FLAMINEO. Ware hawk, my lord.

VITTORIA. Florence! this is some treacherous plot, my lord;
  To me he ne'er was lovely, I protest,
  So much as in my sleep.

BRACHIANO. Right! there are plots.
  Your beauty! Oh, ten thousand curses on 't!
  How long have I beheld the devil in crystal!
  Thou hast led me, like an heathen sacrifice,
  With music, and with fatal yokes of flowers,
  To my eternal ruin. Woman to man
  Is either a god, or a wolf.

VITTORIA. My lord.

BRACHIANO. Away!
  We 'll be as differing as two adamants,
  The one shall shun the other. What! dost weep?
  Procure but ten of thy dissembling trade,
  Ye 'd furnish all the Irish funerals
  With howling past wild Irish.

FLAMINEO. Fie, my lord!

BRACHIANO. That hand, that cursed hand, which I have wearied
  With doting kisses!—Oh, my sweetest duchess,
  How lovely art thou now!—My loose thoughts

Scatter like quicksilver: I was bewitch'd;
For all the world speaks ill of thee.

VITTORIA. No matter;
I'll live so now, I'll make that world recant,
And change her speeches. You did name your duchess.

BRACHIANO. Whose death God pardon!

VITTORIA. Whose death God revenge
On thee, most godless duke!

FLAMINEO. Now for two whirlwinds.

VITTORIA. What have I gain'd by thee, but infamy?
Thou hast stain'd the spotless honour of my house,
And frighted thence noble society:
Like those, which sick o' th' palsy, and retain
Ill-scenting foxes 'bout them, are still shunn'd
By those of choicer nostrils. What do you call this house?
Is this your palace? did not the judge style it
A house of penitent whores? who sent me to it?
To this incontinent college? is 't not you?
Is 't not your high preferment? go, go, brag
How many ladies you have undone, like me.
Fare you well, sir; let me hear no more of you!
I had a limb corrupted to an ulcer,
But I have cut it off; and now I'll go
Weeping to heaven on crutches. For your gifts,
I will return them all, and I do wish
That I could make you full executor
To all my sins. O that I could toss myself
Into a grave as quickly! for all thou art worth
I'll not shed one tear more—I'll burst first.

[*She throws herself upon a bed.*]

BRACHIANO. I have drunk Lethe: Vittoria!
My dearest happiness! Vittoria!
What do you ail, my love? why do you weep?

VITTORIA. Yes, I now weep poniards, do you see?

BRACHIANO. Are not those matchless eyes mine?

VITTORIA. I had rather
They were not matches.

BRACHIANO. Is not this lip mine?

VITTORIA. Yes; thus to bite it off, rather than give it thee.

FLAMINEO. Turn to my lord, good sister.

VITTORIA. Hence, you pander!

FLAMINEO. Pander! am I the author of your sin?

VITTORIA. Yes; he's a base thief that a thief lets in.

FLAMINEO. We 're blown up, my lord.
BRACHIANO. Wilt thou hear me?
    Once to be jealous of thee, is t' express
    That I will love thee everlastingly,
    And never more be jealous.
VITTORIA. O thou fool,
    Whose greatness hath by much o'ergrown thy wit!
    What dar'st thou do, that I not dare to suffer,
    Excepting to be still thy whore? for that,
    In the sea's bottom sooner thou shalt make
    A bonfire.
FLAMINEO. Oh, no oaths, for God's sake!
BRACHIANO. Will you hear me?
VITTORIA. Never.
FLAMINEO. What a damn'd imposthume is a woman's will!
    Can nothing break it? Fie, fie, my lord,
    Women are caught as you take tortoises,
    She must be turn'd on her back.—Sister, by this hand
    I am on your side.—Come, come, you have wrong'd her;
    What a strange credulous man were you, my lord,
    To think the Duke of Florenc would love her!
    Will any mercer take another's ware
    When once 'tis tows'd and sullied? And yet, sister,
    How scurvily this forwardness becomes you!
    Young leverets stand not long, and women's anger
    Should, like their flight, procure a little sport;
    A full cry for a quarter of an hour,
    And then be put to th' dead quat.
BRACHIANO. Shall these eyes,
    Which have so long time dwelt upon your face,
    Be now put out?
FLAMINEO. No cruel landlady i' th' world,
    Which lends forth groats to broom-men, and takes use
    For them, would do 't.
    Hand her, my lord, and kiss her: be not like
    A ferret, to let go your hold with blowing.
BRACHIANO. Let us renew right hands.
VITTORIA. Hence!
BRACHIANO. Never shall rage, or the forgetful wine,
    Make me commit like fault.
FLAMINEO. Now you are i' th' way on 't, follow 't hard.
BRACHIANO. Be thou at peace with me, let all the world
    Threaten the cannon.
FLAMINEO. Mark his penitence;
    Best natures do commit the grossest faults,

When they 're given o'er to jealousy, as best wine,
Dying, makes strongest vinegar. I'll tell you:
The sea 's more rough and raging than calm rivers,
But not so sweet, nor wholesome. A quiet woman
Is a still water under a great bridge;
A man may shoot her safely.
VITTORIA. O ye dissembling men!
FLAMINEO. We suck'd that, sister,
    From women's breasts, in our first infancy.
VITTORIA. To add misery to misery!
BRACHIANO. Sweetest!
VITTORIA. Am I not low enough?
    Ay, ay, your good heart gathers like a snowball,
    Now your affection 's cold.
FLAMINEO. Ud's foot, it shall melt
    To a heart again, or all the wine in Rome
    Shall run o' th' lees for 't.
VITTORIA. Your dog or hawk should be rewarded better
    Than I have been. I'll speak not one word more.
FLAMINEO. Stop her mouth
    With a sweet kiss, my lord. So,
    Now the tide 's turn'd, the vessel 's come about.
    He's a sweet armful. Oh, we curl-hair'd men
    Are still most kind to women! This is well.
BRACHIANO. That you should chide thus!
FLAMINEO. Oh, sir, your little chimneys
    Do ever cast most smoke! I sweat for you.
    Couple together with as deep a silence,
    As did the Grecians in their wooden horse.
    My lord, supply your promises with deeds;
    You know that painted meat no hunger feeds.
BRACHIANO. Stay, ungrateful Rome——
FLAMINEO. Rome! it deserve to be call'd Barbary,
    For our villainous usage.
BRACHIANO. Soft; the same project which the Duke of Florence,
    (Whether in love or gallery I know not)
    Laid down for her escape, will I pursue.
FLAMINEO. And no time fitter than this night, my lord.
    The Pope being dead, and all the cardinals enter'd
    The conclave, for th' electing a new Pope;
    The city in a great confusion;
    We may attire her in a page's suit,
    Lay her post-horse, take shipping, and amain
    For Padua.
BRACHIANO. I'll instantly steal forth the Prince Giovanni,

And make for Padua. You two with your old mother,
And young Marcello that attends on Florence,
If you can work him to it, follow me:
I will advance you all; for you, Vittoria,
Think of a duchess' title.

FLAMINEO. Lo you, sister!

Stay, my lord; I'll tell you a tale. The crocodile, which lives in the River Nilus, hath a worm breeds i' th' teeth of 't, which puts it to extreme anguish: a little bird, no bigger than a wren, is barber-surgeon to this crocodile; flies into the jaws of 't, picks out the worm, and brings present remedy. The fish, glad of ease, but ungrateful to her that did it, that the bird may not talk largely of her abroad for non-payment, closeth her chaps, intending to swallow her, and so put her to perpetual silence. But nature, loathing such ingratitude, hath armed this bird with a quill or prick on the head, top o' th' which wounds the crocodile i' th' mouth, forceth her open her bloody prison, and away flies the pretty tooth-picker from her cruel patient.

BRACHIANO. Your application is, I have not rewarded
The service you have done me.

FLAMINEO. No, my lord.

You, sister, are the crocodile: you are blemish'd in your fame, my lord cures it; and though the comparison hold not in every particle, yet observe, remember, what good the bird with the prick i' th' head hath done you, and scorn ingratitude.

It may appear to some ridiculous
Thus to talk knave and madman, and sometimes
Come in with a dried sentence, stuffed with sage:
But this allows my varying of shapes;
Knaves do grow great by being great men's apes.

[*Exeunt.*]

[*Enter* FRANCISCO DE MEDICIS, LODOVICO, GASPARO, *and six Ambassadors.*]

FRANCISCO. So, my lord, I commend your diligence.
Guard well the conclave; and, as the order is,
Let none have conference with the cardinals.

LODOVICO. I shall, my lord. Room for the ambassadors.

GASPARO. They 're wondrous brave to-day: why do they wear
These several habits?

LODOVICO. Oh, sir, they 're knights
Of several orders:

That lord i' th' black cloak, with the silver cross,
Is Knight of Rhodes; the next, Knight of St. Michael;
That, of the Golden Fleece; the Frenchman, there,
Knight of the Holy Ghost; my Lord of Savoy,
Knight of th' Annunciation; the Englishman
Is Knight of th' honour'd Garter, dedicated
Unto their saint, St. George. I could describe to you
Their several institutions, with the laws
Annexed to their orders; but that time
Permits not such discovery.
FRANCISCO. Where 's Count Lodowick?
LODOVICO. Here, my lord.
FRANCISCO. 'Tis o' th' point of dinner time;
    Marshal the cardinals' service.
LODOVICO. Sir, I shall.

[*Enter* SERVANTS, *with several dishes covered.*]

Stand, let me search your dish. Who 's this for?
SERVANT. For my Lord Cardinal Monticelso.
LODOVICO. Whose this?
SERVANT. For my Lord Cardinal of Bourbon.
FRENCH AMBASSADOR. Why doth he search the dishes? to observe
    What meat is dressed?
ENGLISH AMBASSADOR. No, sir, but to prevent
    Lest any letters should be convey'd in,
    To bribe or to solicit the advancement
    Of any cardinal. When first they enter,
    'Tis lawful for the ambassadors of princes
    To enter with them, and to make their suit
    For any man their prince affecteth best;
    But after, till a general election,
    No man may speak with them.
LODOVICO. You that attend on the lord cardinals,
    Open the window, and receive their viands.

[*A* CARDINAL *on the terrace.*]

A CARDINAL. You must return the service: the lord cardinals
    Are busied 'bout electing of the Pope;
    They have given o'er scrutiny, and are fallen
    To admiration.
LODOVICO. Away, away.
FRANCISCO. I'll lay a thousand ducats you hear news
    Of a Pope presently. Hark; sure he's elected:

Behold, my Lord of Arragon appears
On the church battlements.

[*A* CARDINAL *on the terrace.*]

ARRAGON. *Denuntio vobis gaudium magnum*: *Reverendissimus Cardinalis Lorenzo de Monticelso electus est in sedem apostolicam, et elegit sibi nomen Paulum Quartum.*
OMNES. *Vivat Sanctus Pater Paulus Quartus!*

[*Enter* SERVANT.]

SERVANT. Vittoria, my lord—
FRANCISCO. Well, what of her?
SERVANT. Is fled the city.
FRANCISCO. Ha!
SERVANT. With Duke Brachiano.
FRANCISCO. Fled! where 's the Prince Giovanni?
SERVANT. Gone with his father.
FRANCISCO. Let the Matrona of the Convertites
Be apprehended. Fled? O damnable!

[*Exit* SERVANT.]

How fortunate are my wishes! why, 'twas this
I only labour'd: I did send the letter
T' instruct him what to do. Thy fame, fond duke,
I first have poison'd; directed thee the way
To marry a whore; what can be worse? This follows:
The hand must act to drown the passionate tongue,
I scorn to wear a sword and prate of wrong.

[*Enter* MONTICELSO *in state.*]

MONTICELSO. *Concedimus vobis Apostolicam benedictionem, et remissionem peccatorum.*
       My lord reports Vittoria Corombona
Is stol'n from forth the House of Convertites
By Brachiano, and they 're fled the city.
Now, though this be the first day of our seat,
We cannot better please the Divine Power,
Than to sequester from the Holy Church
These cursed persons. Make it therefore known,
We do denounce excommunication
Against them both: all that are theirs in Rome

We likewise banish. Set on.

[*Exeunt* MONTICELSO, *his* TRAIN, AMBASSADORS, &c.]

FRANCISCO. Come, dear Lodovico;
　　You have ta'en the sacrament to prosecute
　　Th' intended murder?
LODOVICO. With all constancy.
　　But, sir, I wonder you 'll engage yourself
　　In person, being a great prince.
FRANCISCO. Divert me not.
　　Most of his court are of my faction,
　　And some are of my council. Noble friend,
　　Our danger shall be like in this design:
　　Give leave part of the glory may be mine.

[*Exit* FRANCISCO DE MEDICIS *and* GASPARO.]

[*Enter* MONTICELSO.]

MONTICELSO. Why did the Duke of Florence with such care
　　Labour your pardon? say.
LODOVICO. Italian beggars will resolve you that,
　　Who, begging of alms, bid those they beg of,
　　Do good for their own sakes; or 't may be,
　　He spreads his bounty with a sowing hand,
　　Like kings, who many times give out of measure,
　　Not for desert so much, as for their pleasure.
MONTICELSO. I know you 're cunning. Come, what devil was that
　　That you were raising?
LODOVICO. Devil, my lord?
MONTICELSO. I ask you,
　　How doth the duke employ you, that his bonnet
　　Fell with such compliment unto his knee,
　　When he departed from you?
LODOVICO. Why, my lord,
　　He told me of a resty Barbary horse
　　Which he would fain have brought to the career,
　　The sault, and the ring galliard: now, my lord,
　　I have a rare French rider.
MONTICELSO. Take your heed,
　　Lest the jade break your neck. Do you put me off
　　With your wild horse-tricks? Sirrah, you do lie.
　　Oh, thou 'rt a foul black cloud, and thou dost threat
　　A violent storm!

LODOVICO. Storms are i' th' air, my lord;
    I am too low to storm.
MONTICELSO. Wretched creature!
    I know that thou art fashion'd for all ill,
    Like dogs, that once get blood, they 'll ever kill.
    About some murder, was 't not?
LODOVICO. I'll not tell you:
    And yet I care not greatly if I do;
    Marry, with this preparation. Holy father,
    I come not to you as an intelligencer,
    But as a penitent sinner: what I utter
    Is in confession merely; which, you know,
    Must never be reveal'd.
MONTICELSO. You have o'erta'en me.
LODOVICO. Sir, I did love Brachiano's duchess dearly,
    Or rather I pursued her with hot lust,
    Though she ne'er knew on 't. She was poison'd;
    Upon my soul she was: for which I have sworn
    T' avenge her murder.
MONTICELSO. To the Duke of Florence?
LODOVICO. To him I have.
MONTICELSO. Miserable creature!
    If thou persist in this, 'tis damnable.
    Dost thou imagine, thou canst slide on blood,
    And not be tainted with a shameful fall?
    Or, like the black and melancholic yew-tree,
    Dost think to root thyself in dead men's graves,
    And yet to prosper? Instruction to thee
    Comes like sweet showers to o'er-harden'd ground;
    They wet, but pierce not deep. And so I leave thee,
    With all the furies hanging 'bout thy neck,
    Till by thy penitence thou remove this evil,
    In conjuring from thy breast that cruel devil. [*Exit.*]
LODOVICO. I'll give it o'er; he says 'tis damnable:
    Besides I did expect his suffrage,
    By reason of Camillo's death.

[*Enter* SERVANT *and* FRANCISCO DE MEDICIS.]

FRANCISCO. Do you know that count?
SERVANT. Yes, my lord.
FRANCISCO. Bear him these thousand ducats to his lodging.
    Tell him the Pope hath sent them. Happily
    That will confirm more than all the rest. [*Exit.*]
SERVANT. Sir.

LODOVICO. To me, sir?
SERVANT. His Holiness hath sent you a thousand crowns,
And wills you, if you travel, to make him
Your patron for intelligence.
LODOVICO. His creature ever to be commanded.

[*Exit* SERVANT.]

Why now 'tis come about. He rail'd upon me;
And yet these crowns were told out, and laid ready,
Before he knew my voyage. Oh, the art,
The modest form of greatness! that do sit,
Like brides at wedding-dinners, with their looks turn'd
From the least wanton jests, their puling stomach
Sick from the modesty, when their thoughts are loose,
Even acting of those hot and lustful sports
Are to ensue about midnight: such his cunning!
He sounds my depth thus with a golden plummet.
I am doubly arm'd now. Now to th' act of blood,
There's but three furies found in spacious hell,
But in a great man's breast three thousand dwell. [*Exit.*

[*A passage over the stage of* BRACHIANO, FLAMINEO, MARCELLO,
HORTENSIO, VITTORIA COROMBONA, CORNELIA, ZANCHE,
and others: *exeunt omnes* FLAMINEO *and* HORTENSIO.]

FLAMINEO. In all the weary minutes of my life,
Day ne'er broke up till now. This marriage
Confirms me happy.
HORTENSIO. 'Tis a good assurance.
Saw you not yet the Moor that's come to court?
FLAMINEO. Yes, and conferr'd with him i' th' duke's closet.
I have not seen a goodlier personage,
Nor ever talk'd with man better experience'd
In State affairs, or rudiments of war.
He hath, by report, serv'd the Venetian
In Candy these twice seven years, and been chief
In many a bold design.
HORTENSIO. What are those two
That bear him company?
FLAMINEO. Two noblemen of Hungary, that, living in the emperor's
service as commanders, eight years since, contrary to the
expectation of the court entered into religion, in the strict Order of
Capuchins; but, being not well settled in their undertaking, they
left their Order, and returned to court; for which, being after

troubled in conscience, they vowed their service against the enemies of Christ, went to Malta, were there knighted, and in their return back, at this great solemnity, they are resolved for ever to forsake the world, and settle themselves here in a house of Capuchins in Padua.

HORTENSIO. 'Tis strange.

FLAMINEO. One thing makes it so: they have vowed for ever to wear, next their bare bodies, those coats of mail they served in.

HORTENSIO. Hard penance!
Is the Moor a Christian?

FLAMINEO. He is.

HORTENSIO. Why proffers he his service to our duke?

FLAMINEO. Because he understands there's like to grow
Some wars between us and the Duke of Florence,
In which he hopes employment.
I never saw one in a stern bold look
Wear more command, nor in a lofty phrase
Express more knowing, or more deep contempt
Of our slight airy courtiers
As if he travell'd all the princes' courts
Of Christendom: in all things strives t' express,
That all, that should dispute with him, may know,
Glories, like glow-worms, afar off shine bright,
But look'd to near, have neither heat nor light.
The duke.

[*Enter* BRACHIANO, FRANCISCO DE MEDICIS *disguised like* MULINASSAR, MARCELLO, LODOVICO, ANTONELLI, GASPARO, FARNESE, CARLO, *and* PEDRO, *bearing their swords, their helmets.*]

BRACHIANO. You are nobly welcome. We have heard at full
Your honourable service 'gainst the Turk.
To you, brave Mulinassar, we assign
A competent pension: and are inly sorry,
The vows of those two worthy gentlemen
Make them incapable of our proffer'd bounty.
Your wish is, you may leave your warlike swords
For monuments in our chapel: I accept it,
As a great honour done me, and must crave
Your leave to furnish out our duchess' revels.
Only one thing, as the last vanity
You e'er shall view, deny me not to stay
To see a barriers prepar'd to-night:
You shall have private standings. It hath pleas'd

The great ambassadors of several princes,
In their return from Rome to their own countries,
To grace our marriage, and to honour me
With such a kind of sport.
FRANCISCO. I shall persuade them to stay, my lord.
BRACHIANO. Set on there to the presence.

[*Exeunt* BRACHIANO, FLAMINEO, MARCELLO, *and* HORTENSIO.]

LODOVICO. Noble my lord, most fortunately welcome;

[*The conspirators here embrace.*]

You have our vows, seal'd with the sacrament,
To second your attempts.
GASPARO. And all things ready;
He could not have invented his own ruin
(Had he despair'd) with more propriety.
LODOVICO. You would not take my way.
FRANCISCO. 'Tis better order'd.
LODOVICO. T' have poison'd his prayer-book, or a pair of beads,
The pummel of his saddle, his looking-glass,
Or th' handle of his racket,—O, that, that!
That while he had been bandying at tennis,
He might have sworn himself to hell, and strook
His soul into the hazard! Oh, my lord,
I would have our plot be ingenious,
And have it hereafter recorded for example,
Rather than borrow example.
FRANCISCO. There's no way
More speeding that this thought on.
LODOVICO. On, then.
FRANCISCO. And yet methinks that this revenge is poor,
Because it steals upon him like a thief:
To have ta'en him by the casque in a pitch'd field,
Led him to Florence——
LODOVICO. It had been rare: and there
Have crown'd him with a wreath of stinking garlic,
T' have shown the sharpness of his government,
And rankness of his lust. Flamineo comes.

[*Exeunt* LODOVICO, ANTONELLI, GASPARO, FARNESE, CARLO, *and*
PEDRO.]

[*Enter* FLAMINEO, MARCELLO, *and* ZANCHE.]

MARCELLO. Why doth this devil haunt you, say?

FLAMINEO. I know not:
    For by this light, I do not conjure for her.
    'Tis not so great a cunning as men think,
    To raise the devil; for here's one up already;
    The greatest cunning were to lay him down.

MARCELLO. She is your shame.

FLAMINEO. I pray thee pardon her.
    In faith, you see, women are like to burs,
    Where their affection throws them, there they 'll stick.

ZANCHE. That is my countryman, a goodly person;
    When he's at leisure, I'll discourse with him
    In our own language.

FLAMINEO. I beseech you do.

[*Exit* ZANCHE.]

    How is 't, brave soldier? Oh, that I had seen
    Some of your iron days! I pray relate
    Some of your service to us.

FRANCISCO. 'Tis a ridiculous thing for a man to be his own chronicle: I did never wash my mouth with mine own praise, for fear of getting a stinking breath.

MARCELLO. You're too stoical. The duke will expect other discourse from you.

FRANCISCO. I shall never flatter him: I have studied man too much to do that. What difference is between the duke and I? no more than between two bricks, all made of one clay: only 't may be one is placed in top of a turret, the other in the bottom of a well, by mere chance. If I were placed as high as the duke, I should stick as fast, make as fair a show, and bear out weather equally.

FLAMINEO. If this soldier had a patent to beg in churches, then he would tell them stories.

MARCELLO. I have been a soldier too.

FRANCISCO. How have you thrived?

MARCELLO. Faith, poorly.

FRANCISCO. That's the misery of peace: only outsides are then respected. As ships seem very great upon the river, which show very little upon the seas, so some men i' th' court seem Colossuses in a chamber, who, if they came into the field, would appear pitiful pigmies.

FLAMINEO. Give me a fair room yet hung with arras, and some great cardinal to lug me by th' ears, as his endeared minion.

FRANCISCO. And thou mayest do the devil knows what villainy.

FLAMINEO. And safely.

FRANCISCO. Right: you shall see in the country, in harvest-time, pigeons, though they destroy never so much corn, the farmer dare not present the fowling-piece to them: why? because they belong to the lord of the manor; whilst your poor sparrows, that belong to the Lord of Heaven, they go to the pot for 't.

FLAMINEO. I will now give you some politic instruction. The duke says he will give you pension; that's but bare promise; get it under his hand. For I have known men that have come from serving against the Turk, for three or four months they have had pension to buy them new wooden legs, and fresh plasters; but after, 'twas not to be had. And this miserable courtesy shows as if a tormentor should give hot cordial drinks to one three-quarters dead o' th' rack, only to fetch the miserable soul again to endure more dogdays.

[*Exit* FRANCISCO DE MEDICIS.]

[*Enter* HORTENSIO, *a* YOUNG LORD, ZANCHE, *and two more.*]

How now, gallants? what, are they ready for the barriers?

Young Lord. Yes: the lords are putting on their armour.

HORTENSIO. What 's he?

FLAMINEO. A new upstart; one that swears like a falconer, and will lie in the duke's ear day by day, like a maker of almanacs: and yet I knew him, since he came to th' court, smell worse of sweat than an under tennis-court keeper.

HORTENSIO. Look you, yonder 's your sweet mistress.

FLAMINEO. Thou art my sworn brother: I'll tell thee, I do love that Moor, that witch, very constrainedly. She knows some of my villainy. I do love her just as a man holds a wolf by the ears; but for fear of her turning upon me, and pulling out my throat, I would let her go to the devil.

HORTENSIO. I hear she claims marriage of thee.

FLAMINEO. 'Faith, I made to her some such dark promise; and, in seeking to fly from 't, I run on, like a frighted dog with a bottle at 's tail, that fain would bite it off, and yet dares not look behind him. Now, my precious gipsy.

ZANCHE. Ay, your love to me rather cools than heats.

FLAMINEO. Marry, I am the sounder lover; we have many wenches about the town heat too fast.

HORTENSIO. What do you think of these perfumed gallants, then?

FLAMINEO. Their satin cannot save them: I am confident
They have a certain spice of the disease;
For they that sleep with dogs shall rise with fleas.

ZANCHE. Believe it, a little painting and gay clothes make you loathe me.

FLAMINEO. How, love a lady for painting or gay apparel? I'll unkennel
one example more for thee. Æsop had a foolish dog that let go the
flesh to catch the shadow; I would have courtiers be better diners.

ZANCHE. You remember your oaths?

FLAMINEO. Lovers' oaths are like mariners' prayers, uttered in
extremity; but when the tempest is o'er, and that the vessel leaves
tumbling, they fall from protesting to drinking. And yet, amongst
gentlemen, protesting and drinking go together, and agree as well
as shoemakers and Westphalia bacon: they are both drawers on; for
drink draws on protestation, and protestation draws on more drink.
Is not this discourse better now than the morality of your sunburnt
gentleman?

[*Enter* CORNELIA.]

CORNELIA. Is this your perch, you haggard? fly to th' stews.

FLAMINEO. You should be clapped by th' heels now: strike i' th' court!

[*Exit* CORNELIA.]

ZANCHE. She's good for nothing, but to make her maids
Catch cold a-nights: they dare not use a bedstaff,
For fear of her light fingers.

MARCELLO. You 're a strumpet,
An impudent one. [*Kicks* ZANCHE.]

FLAMINEO. Why do you kick her, say?
Do you think that she's like a walnut tree?
Must she be cudgell'd ere she bear good fruit?

MARCELLO. She brags that you shall marry her.

FLAMINEO. What then?

MARCELLO. I had rather she were pitch'd upon a stake,
In some new-seeded garden, to affright
Her fellow crows thence.

FLAMINEO. You 're a boy, a fool,
Be guardian to your hound; I am of age.

MARCELLO. If I take her near you, I'll cut her throat.

FLAMINEO. With a fan of feather?

MARCELLO. And, for you, I'll whip
This folly from you.

FLAMINEO. Are you choleric?
I'll purge it with rhubarb.

HORTENSIO. Oh, your brother!

FLAMINEO. Hang him,
He wrongs me most, that ought t' offend me least:

I do suspect my mother play'd foul play,
When she conceiv'd thee.
MARCELLO. Now, by all my hopes,
Like the two slaughter'd sons of Œdipus,
The very flames of our affection
Shall turn two ways. Those words I'll make thee answer
With thy heart-blood.
FLAMINEO. Do, like the geese in the progress;
You know where you shall find me.
MARCELLO. Very good.

[*Exit* FLAMINEO.]

And thou be'st a noble friend, bear him my sword,
And bid him fit the length on 't.
YOUNG LORD. Sir, I shall.

[*Exeunt* YOUNG LORD, MARCELLO, HORTENSIO, *and two more.*]

ZANCHE. He comes. Hence petty thought of my disgrace!

[*Enter* FRANCISCO DE MEDICIS.]

I ne'er lov'd my complexion till now,
'Cause I may boldly say, without a blush,
I love you.
FRANCISCO. Your love is untimely sown; there's a spring at
Michaelmas, but 'tis but a faint one: I am sunk in years, and I have
vowed never to marry.
ZANCHE. Alas! poor maids get more lovers than husbands: yet you may
mistake my wealth. For, as when ambassadors are sent to
congratulate princes, there's commonly sent along with them a rich
present, so that, though the prince like not the ambassador's
person, nor words, yet he likes well of the presentment; so I may
come to you in the same manner, and be better loved for my dowry
than my virtue.
FRANCISCO. I'll think on the motion.
ZANCHE. Do; I'll now detain you no longer. At your better leisure, I'll
tell you things shall startle your blood:
        Nor blame me that this passion I reveal;
Lovers die inward that their flames conceal.
FRANCISCO. Of all intelligence this may prove the best:
Sure I shall draw strange fowl from this foul nest.

[*Exeunt.*]

[*Enter* MARCELLO *and* CORNELIA.]

CORNELIA. I hear a whispering all about the court,
    You are to fight: who is your opposite?
    What is the quarrel?
MARCELLO. 'Tis an idle rumour.
CORNELIA. Will you dissemble? sure you do not well
    To fright me thus: you never look thus pale,
    But when you are most angry. I do charge you,
    Upon my blessing—nay, I'll call the duke,
    And he shall school you.
MARCELLO. Publish not a fear,
    Which would convert to laughter: 'tis not so.
    Was not this crucifix my father's?
CORNELIA. Yes.
MARCELLO. I have heard you say, giving my brother suck
    He took the crucifix between his hands,

[*Enter* FLAMINEO.]

    And broke a limb off.
CORNELIA. Yes, but 'tis mended.
FLAMINEO. I have brought your weapon back.

[FLAMINEO *runs* MARCELLO *through.*]

CORNELIA. Ha! Oh, my horror!
MARCELLO. You have brought it home, indeed.
CORNELIA. Help! Oh, he's murder'd!
FLAMINEO. Do you turn your gall up? I'll to sanctuary,
    And send a surgeon to you. [*Exit.*]

[*Enter* CARLO, HORTENSIO, *and* PEDRO.]

HORTENSIO. How! o' th' ground!
MARCELLO. Oh, mother, now remember what I told
    Of breaking of the crucifix! Farewell.
    There are some sins, which heaven doth duly punish
    In a whole family. This it is to rise
    By all dishonest means! Let all men know,
    That tree shall long time keep a steady foot,
    Whose branches spread no wider than the root. [*Dies.*]
CORNELIA. Oh, my perpetual sorrow!
HORTENSIO. Virtuous Marcello!

He's dead. Pray leave him, lady: come, you shall.

CORNELIA. Alas! he is not dead; he's in a trance. Why, here's nobody shall get anything by his death. Let me call him again, for God's sake!

LODOVICO. I would you were deceived.

CORNELIA. Oh, you abuse me, you abuse me, you abuse me! how many have gone away thus, for lack of 'tendance! rear up 's head, rear up 's head! his bleeding inward will kill him.

HORTENSIO. You see he is departed.

CORNELIA. Let me come to him; give me him as he is, if he be turn'd to earth; let me but give him one hearty kiss, and you shall put us both in one coffin. Fetch a looking-glass: see if his breath will not stain it; or pull out some feathers from my pillow, and lay them to his lips. Will you lose him for a little painstaking?

HORTENSIO. Your kindest office is to pray for him.

CORNELIA. Alas! I would not pray for him yet. He may live to lay me i' th' ground, and pray for me, if you'll let me come to him.

[*Enter* BRACHIANO, *all armed, save the beaver, with* FLAMINEO, FRANCISCO DE MEDICIS, LODOVICO, *and* PAGE.]

BRACHIANO. Was this your handiwork?

FLAMINEO. It was my misfortune.

CORNELIA. He lies, he lies! he did not kill him: these have killed him, that would not let him be better looked to.

BRACHIANO. Have comfort, my griev'd mother.

CORNELIA. Oh, you screech-owl!

HORTENSIO. Forbear, good madam.

CORNELIA. Let me go, let me go.

[*She runs to* FLAMINEO *with her knife drawn, and coming to him lets it fall.*]

The God of heaven forgive thee! Dost not wonder
I pray for thee? I'll tell thee what 's the reason,
I have scarce breath to number twenty minutes;
I'd not spend that in cursing. Fare thee well:
Half of thyself lies there; and mayst thou live
To fill an hour-glass with his moulder'd ashes,
To tell how thou shouldst spend the time to come
In blessed repentance!

BRACHIANO. Mother, pray tell me
How came he by his death? what was the quarrel?

CORNELIA. Indeed, my younger boy presum'd too much
Upon his manhood, gave him bitter words,

Drew his sword first; and so, I know not how,
For I was out of my wits, he fell with 's head
Just in my bosom.
PAGE. That is not true, madam.
CORNELIA. I pray thee, peace.
One arrow 's graze'd already; it were vain
T' lose this, for that will ne'er be found again.
BRACHIANO. Go, bear the body to Cornelia's lodging:
And we command that none acquaint our duchess
With this sad accident. For you, Flamineo,
Hark you, I will not grant your pardon.
FLAMINEO. No?
BRACHIANO. Only a lease of your life; and that shall last
But for one day: thou shalt be forc'd each evening
To renew it, or be hang'd.
FLAMINEO. At your pleasure.

[LODOVICO *sprinkles* BRACHIANO'S *beaver with a poison.*]

Your will is law now, I'll not meddle with it.
BRACHIANO. You once did brave me in your sister's lodging:
I'll now keep you in awe for 't. Where 's our beaver?
FRANCISCO. [*aside.*] He calls for his destruction. Noble youth,
I pity thy sad fate! Now to the barriers.
This shall his passage to the black lake further;
The last good deed he did, he pardon'd murder.

[*Exeunt.*]

[*Charges and shouts. They fight at barriers; first single pairs,
    then three to three.*]

[*Enter* BRACHIANO, VITTORIA COROMBONA, GIOVANNI,
    FRANCISCO DE MEDICIS, FLAMINEO, *with others.*]

BRACHIANO. An armourer! ud's death, an armourer!
FLAMINEO. Armourer! where 's the armourer?
BRACHIANO. Tear off my beaver.
FLAMINEO. Are you hurt, my lord?
BRACHIANO. Oh, my brain 's on fire!

[*Enter* ARMOURER.]

The helmet is poison'd.
ARMOURER. My lord, upon my soul—

BRACHIANO. Away with him to torture.
    There are some great ones that have hand in this,
    And near about me.
VITTORIA. Oh, my lov'd lord! poison'd!
FLAMINEO. Remove the bar. Here 's unfortunate revels!
    Call the physicians.

    [*Enter two* PHYSICIANS.]

    A plague upon you!
    We have too much of your cunning here already:
    I fear the ambassadors are likewise poison'd.
BRACHIANO. Oh, I am gone already! the infection
    Flies to the brain and heart. O thou strong heart!
    There's such a covenant 'tween the world and it,
    They're loath to break.
GIOVANNI. Oh, my most loved father!
BRACHIANO. Remove the boy away.
    Where 's this good woman? Had I infinite worlds,
    They were too little for thee: must I leave thee?
    What say you, screech-owls, is the venom mortal?
PHYSICIANS. Most deadly.
BRACHIANO. Most corrupted politic hangman,
    You kill without book; but your art to save
    Fails you as oft as great men's needy friends.
    I that have given life to offending slaves,
    And wretched murderers, have I not power
    To lengthen mine own a twelvemonth?
    Do not kiss me, for I shall poison thee.
    This unctions 's sent from the great Duke of Florence.
FRANCISCO. Sir, be of comfort.
BRACHIANO. O thou soft natural death, that art joint-twin
    To sweetest slumber! no rough-bearded comet
    Stares on thy mild departure; the dull owl
    Bears not against thy casement; the hoarse wolf
    Scents not thy carrion: pity winds thy corse,
    Whilst horror waits on princes'.
VITTORIA. I am lost for ever.
BRACHIANO. How miserable a thing it is to die

    [*Enter* LODOVICO *and* GASPARO, *in the habit of Capuchins.*]

    'Mongst women howling!
    What are those?
FLAMINEO. Franciscans:

They have brought the extreme unction.

BRACHIANO. On pain of death, let no man name death to me:
It is a word infinitely terrible.
Withdraw into our cabinet.

[*Exeunt all but* FRANCISCO DE MEDICIS, *and* FLAMINEO.]

FLAMINEO. To see what solitariness is about dying princes! as
heretofore they have unpeopled towns, divorced friends, and made
great houses unhospitable, so now, O justice! where are their
flatterers now? flatterers are but the shadows of princes' bodies;
the least thick cloud makes them invisible.

FRANCISCO. There 's great moan made for him.

FLAMINEO. 'Faith, for some few hours salt-water will run most
plentifully in every office o' th' court; but, believe it, most of them
do weep over their stepmothers' graves.

FRANCISCO. How mean you?

FLAMINEO. Why, they dissemble; as some men do that live without
compass o' th' verge.

FRANCISCO. Come, you have thrived well under him.

FLAMINEO. 'Faith, like a wolf in a woman's breast; I have been fed
with poultry: but for money, understand me, I had as good a will to
cozen him as e'er an officer of them all; but I had not cunning
enough to do it.

FRANCISCO. What didst thou think of him? 'faith, speak freely.

FLAMINEO. He was a kind of statesman, that would sooner have
reckoned how many cannon-bullets he had discharged against a
town, to count his expense that way, than think how many of his
valiant and deserving subjects he lost before it.

FRANCISCO. Oh, speak well of the duke!

FLAMINEO. I have done.

[*Enter* LODOVICO.]

Wilt hear some of my court-wisdom? To reprehend princes is
dangerous; and to over-commend some of them is palpable lying.

FRANCISCO. How is it with the duke?

LODOVICO. Most deadly ill.
He's fallen into a strange distraction:
He talks of battles and monopolies,
Levying of taxes; and from that descends
To the most brain-sick language. His mind fastens
On twenty several objects, which confound
Deep sense with folly. Such a fearful end
May teach some men that bear too lofty crest,

Though they live happiest yet they die not best.
He hath conferr'd the whole state of the dukedom
Upon your sister, till the prince arrive
At mature age.
FLAMINEO. There's some good luck in that yet.
FRANCISCO. See, here he comes.

[*Enter* BRACHIANO, *presented in a bed,* VITTORIA COROMBONA,
    GASPARO, *and Attendants.*]

There's death in 's face already.
VITTORIA. Oh, my good lord!
BRACHIANO. Away, you have abus'd me:

[*These speeches are several kinds of distractions, and in the
    action should appear so.*]

You have convey'd coin forth our territories,
Bought and sold offices, oppress'd the poor,
And I ne'er dreamt on 't. Make up your accounts,
I'll now be mine own steward.
FLAMINEO. Sir, have patience.
BRACHIANO. Indeed, I am to blame:
For did you ever hear the dusky raven
Chide blackness? or was 't ever known the devil
Rail'd against cloven creatures?
VITTORIA. Oh, my lord!
BRACHIANO. Let me have some quails to supper.
FLAMINEO. Sir, you shall.
BRACHIANO. No, some fried dog-fish; your quails feed on poison.
That old dog-fox, that politician, Florence!
I'll forswear hunting, and turn dog-killer.
Rare! I'll be friends with him; for, mark you, sir, one dog
Still sets another a-barking. Peace, peace!
Yonder 's a fine slave come in now.
FLAMINEO. Where?
BRACHIANO. Why, there,
In a blue bonnet, and a pair of breeches
With a great cod-piece: ha, ha, ha!
Look you, his cod-piece is stuck full of pins,
With pearls o' th' head of them. Do you not know him?
FLAMINEO. No, my lord.
BRACHIANO. Why, 'tis the devil.
I know him by a great rose he wears on 's shoe,
To hide his cloven foot. I'll dispute with him;

He's a rare linguist.

VITTORIA. My lord, here 's nothing.

BRACHIANO. Nothing! rare! nothing! when I want money,
Our treasury is empty, there is nothing:
I'll not be use'd thus.

VITTORIA. Oh, lie still, my lord!

BRACHIANO. See, see Flamineo, that kill'd his brother,
Is dancing on the ropes there, and he carries
A money-bag in each hand, to keep him even,
For fear of breaking 's neck: and there's a lawyer,
In a gown whipped with velvet, stares and gapes
When the money will fall. How the rogue cuts capers!
It should have been in a halter. 'Tis there; what 's she?

FLAMINEO. Vittoria, my lord.

BRACHIANO. Ha, ha, ha! her hair is sprinkl'd with orris powder,
That makes her look as if she had sinn'd in the pastry.
What 's he?

FLAMINEO. A divine, my lord.

[BRACHIANO *seems here near his end*; LODOVICO *and* GASPARO,
in the habit of CAPUCHINS, *present him in his bed with a
crucifix and hallowed candle.*]

BRACHIANO. He will be drunk; avoid him: th' argument
Is fearful, when churchmen stagger in 't.
Look you, six grey rats that have lost their tails
Crawl upon the pillow; send for a rat-catcher:
I'll do a miracle, I'll free the court
From all foul vermin. Where 's Flamineo?

FLAMINEO. I do not like that he names me so often,
Especially on 's death-bed; 'tis a sign
I shall not live long. See, he's near his end.

LODOVICO. Pray, give us leave. *Attende, domine Brachiane.*

FLAMINEO. See how firmly he doth fix his eye
Upon the crucifix.

VITTORIA. Oh, hold it constant!
It settles his wild spirits; and so his eyes
Melt into tears.

LODOVICO. *Domine Brachiane, solebas in bello tutus esse tuo clypeo*;
nunc hunc clypeum hosti tuo opponas infernali.

[*By the crucifix.*]

GASPARO. *Olim hastâ valuisti in bello*; *nunc hanc sacram hastam
vibrabis contra hostem animarum.*

[*By the hallowed taper.*]

LODOVICO. *Attende, Domine Brachiane, si nunc quoque probes ea, quæ acta sunt inter nos, flecte caput in dextrum.*

GASPARO. *Esto securus, Domine Brachiane; cogita, quantum habeas meritorum; denique memineris mean animam pro tuâ oppignoratum si quid esset periculi.*

LODOVICO. *Si nunc quoque probas ea, quæ acta sunt inter nos, flecte caput in lvum.*
He is departing: pray stand all apart,
And let us only whisper in his ears
Some private meditations, which our order
Permits you not to hear.

[*Here, the rest being departed,* LODOVICO *and* GASPARO *discover themselves.*]

GASPARO. Brachiano.
LODOVICO. Devil Brachiano, thou art damn'd.
GASPARO. Perpetually.
LODOVICO. A slave condemn'd and given up to the gallows,
Is thy great lord and master.
GASPARO. True; for thou
Art given up to the devil.
LODOVICO. Oh, you slave!
You that were held the famous politician,
Whose art was poison.
GASPARO. And whose conscience, murder.
LODOVICO. That would have broke your wife's neck down the stairs,
Ere she was poison'd.
GASPARO. That had your villainous sallets.
LODOVICO. And fine embroider'd bottles, and perfumes,
Equally mortal with a winter plague.
GASPARO. Now there's mercury——
LODOVICO. And copperas——
GASPARO. And quicksilver——
LODOVICO. With other devilish 'pothecary stuff,
A-melting in your politic brains: dost hear?
GASPARO. This is Count Lodovico.
LODOVICO. This, Gasparo:
And thou shalt die like a poor rogue.
GASPARO. And stink
Like a dead fly-blown dog.
LODOVICO. And be forgotten

Before the funeral sermon.

BRACHIANO. Vittoria! Vittoria!

LODOVICO. Oh, the cursed devil
  Comes to himself a gain! we are undone.

GASPARO. Strangle him in private.

[*Enter* VITTORIA COROMBONA, FRANCISCO DE MEDICIS, FLAMINEO, *and* ATTENDANTS.]

What? Will you call him again to live in treble torments?
For charity, for christian charity, avoid the chamber.

[*Exeunt* VITTORIA COROMBONA, FRANCISCO DE MEDICIS, FLAMINEO, *and* ATTENDANTS.]

LODOVICO. You would prate, sir? This is a true-love knot
  Sent from the Duke of Florence.

[BRACHIANO *is strangled.*]

GASPARO. What, is it done?

LODOVICO. The snuff is out. No woman-keeper i' th' world,
  Though she had practis'd seven year at the pest-house,
  Could have done 't quaintlier. My lords, he's dead.

[*Enter* VITTORIA COROMBONA, FRANCISCO DE MEDICIS, FLAMINEO, *and* ATTENDANTS.]

OMNES. Rest to his soul!

VITTORIA. Oh me! this place is hell. [*Exit.*]

FRANCISCO. How heavily she takes it!

FLAMINEO. Oh, yes, yes;
  Had women navigable rivers in their eyes,
  They would dispend them all. Surely, I wonder
  Why we should wish more rivers to the city,
  When they sell water so good cheap. I'll tell thee
  These are but Moorish shades of griefs or fears;
  There's nothing sooner dry than women's tears.
  Why, here's an end of all my harvest; he has given me nothing.
  Court promises! let wise men count them curs'd;
  For while you live, he that scores best, pays worst.

FRANCISCO. Sure this was Florence' doing.

FLAMINEO. Very likely:
  Those are found weighty strokes which come from th' hand,
  But those are killing strokes which come from th' head.

Oh, the rare tricks of a Machiavellian!
He doth not come, like a gross plodding slave,
And buffet you to death; no, my quaint knave,
He tickles you to death, makes you die laughing,
As if you had swallow'd down a pound of saffron.
You see the feat, 'tis practis'd in a trice;
To teach court honesty, it jumps on ice.
FRANCISCO. Now have the people liberty to talk,
And descant on his vices.
FLAMINEO. Misery of princes,
That must of force be censur'd by their slaves!
Not only blam'd for doing things are ill,
But for not doing all that all men will:
One were better be a thresher.
Ud's death! I would fain speak with this duke yet.
FRANCISCO. Now he's dead?
FLAMINEO. I cannot conjure; but if prayers or oaths
Will get to th' speech of him, though forty devils
Wait on him in his livery of flames,
I'll speak to him, and shake him by the hand,
Though I be blasted. [*Exit.*]
FRANCISCO. Excellent Lodovico!
What! did you terrify him at the last gasp?
LODOVICO. Yes, and so idly, that the duke had like
T' have terrified us.
FRANCISCO. How?

[*Enter* ZANCHE.]

LODOVICO. You shall hear that hereafter.
See, yon 's the infernal, that would make up sport.
Now to the revelation of that secret
She promis'd when she fell in love with you.
FRANCISCO. You 're passionately met in this sad world.
ZANCHE. I would have you look up, sir; these court tears
Claim not your tribute to them: let those weep,
That guiltily partake in the sad cause.
I knew last night, by a sad dream I had,
Some mischief would ensue: yet, to say truth,
My dream most concern'd you.
LODOVICO. Shall 's fall a-dreaming?
FRANCISCO. Yes, and for fashion sake I'll dream with her.
ZANCHE. Methought, sir, you came stealing to my bed.
FRANCISCO. Wilt thou believe me, sweeting? by this light
I was a-dreamt on thee too; for methought

I saw thee naked.

ZANCHE. Fie, sir! as I told you,
Methought you lay down by me.

FRANCISCO. So dreamt I;
And lest thou shouldst take cold, I cover'd thee
With this Irish mantle.

ZANCHE. Verily I did dream
You were somewhat bold with me: but to come to 't——

LODOVICO. How! how! I hope you will not got to 't here.

FRANCISCO. Nay, you must hear my dream out.

ZANCHE. Well, sir, forth.

FRANCISCO. When I threw the mantle o'er thee, thou didst laugh
Exceedingly, methought.

ZANCHE. Laugh!

FRANCISCO. And criedst out, the hair did tickle thee.

ZANCHE. There was a dream indeed!

LODOVICO. Mark her, I pray thee, she simpers like the suds
A collier hath been wash'd in.

ZANCHE. Come, sir; good fortune tends you. I did tell you
I would reveal a secret: Isabella,
The Duke of Florence' sister, was empoisone'd
By a fum'd picture; and Camillo's neck
Was broke by damn'd Flamineo, the mischance
Laid on a vaulting-horse.

FRANCISCO. Most strange!

ZANCHE. Most true.

LODOVICO. The bed of snakes is broke.

ZANCHE. I sadly do confess, I had a hand
In the black deed.

FRANCISCO. Thou kept'st their counsel.

ZANCHE. Right;
For which, urg'd with contrition, I intend
This night to rob Vittoria.

LODOVICO. Excellent penitence!
Usurers dream on 't while they sleep out sermons.

ZANCHE. To further our escape, I have entreated
Leave to retire me, till the funeral,
Unto a friend i' th' country: that excuse
Will further our escape. In coin and jewels
I shall at least make good unto your use
An hundred thousand crowns.

FRANCISCO. Oh, noble wench!

LODOVICO. Those crowns we'll share.

ZANCHE. It is a dowry,
Methinks, should make that sun-burnt proverb false,

And wash the Æthiop white.
FRANCISCO. It shall; away.
ZANCHE. Be ready for our flight.
FRANCISCO. An hour 'fore day.

[*Exit* ZANCHE.]

Oh, strange discovery! why, till now we knew not
The circumstances of either of their deaths.

[*Re-enter* ZANCHE.]

ZANCHE. You'll wait about midnight in the chapel?
FRANCISCO. There.

[*Exit* ZANCHE.]

LODOVICO. Why, now our action 's justified.
FRANCISCO. Tush, for justice!
What harms it justice? we now, like the partridge,
Purge the disease with laurel; for the fame
Shall crown the enterprise, and quit the shame. [*Exeunt.*

[*Enter* FLAMINEO *and* GASPARO, *at one door; another way,*
GIOVANNI, *attended.*]

GASPARO. The young duke: did you e'er see a sweeter prince?
FLAMINEO. I have known a poor woman's bastard better favoured—this
is behind him. Now, to his face—all comparisons were hateful.
Wise was the courtly peacock, that, being a great minion, and
being compared for beauty by some dottrels that stood by to the
kingly eagle, said the eagle was a far fairer bird than herself, not in
respect of her feathers, but in respect of her long talons: his will
grow out in time. —My gracious lord.
GIOVANNI. I pray leave me, sir.
FLAMINEO. Your grace must be merry; 'tis I have cause to mourn; for
wot you, what said the little boy that rode behind his father on
horseback?
GIOVANNI. Why, what said he?
FLAMINEO. When you are dead, father, said he, I hope that I shall ride
in the saddle. Oh, 'tis a brave thing for a man to sit by himself! he
may stretch himself in the stirrups, look about, and see the whole
compass of the hemisphere. You 're now, my lord, i' th' saddle.
GIOVANNI. Study your prayers, sir, and be penitent:
'Twere fit you 'd think on what hath former been;

I have heard grief nam'd the eldest child of sin. [*Exit.*
FLAMINEO. Study my prayers! he threatens me divinely! I am falling to
pieces already. I care not, though, like Anacharsis, I were pounded
to death in a mortar: and yet that death were fitter for usurers, gold
and themselves to be beaten together, to make a most cordial cullis
for the devil.
     He hath his uncle's villainous look already,

[*Enter* COURTIER.]

In decimo-sexto.—Now, sir, what are you?
COURTIER. It is the pleasure, sir, of the young duke,
     That you forbear the presence, and all rooms
     That owe him reverence.
FLAMINEO. So the wolf and the raven are very pretty fools when they
     are young. It is your office, sir, to keep me out?
COURTIER. So the duke wills.
FLAMINEO. Verily, Master Courtier, extremity is not to be used in all
     offices: say, that a gentlewoman were taken out of her bed about
     midnight, and committed to Castle Angelo, to the tower yonder,
     with nothing about her but her smock, would it not show a cruel
     part in the gentleman-porter to lay claim to her upper garment, pull
     it o'er her head and ears, and put her in naked?
COURTIER. Very good: you are merry. [*Exit.*]
FLAMINEO. Doth he make a court-ejectment of me? a flaming fire-
     brand casts more smoke without a chimney than within 't.
          I'll smoor some of them.

[*Enter* FRANCISCO DE MEDICIS.]

How now? thou art sad.
FRANCISCO. I met even now with the most piteous sight.
FLAMINEO. Thou meet'st another here, a pitiful
     Degraded courtier.
FRANCISCO. Your reverend mother
     Is grown a very old woman in two hours.
     I found them winding of Marcello's corse;
     And there is such a solemn melody,
     'Tween doleful songs, tears, and sad elegies;
     Such as old granddames, watching by the dead,
     Were wont t' outwear the nights with that, believe me,
     I had no eyes to guide me forth the room,
     They were so o'ercharg'd with water.
FLAMINEO. I will see them.
FRANCISCO. 'Twere much uncharity in you; for your sight

Will add unto their tears.
FLAMINEO. I will see them:
 They are behind the traverse; I'll discover
 Their superstitions howling.

[CORNELIA, ZANCHE, *and three other ladies discovered winding*
 MARCELLO'*s corse. A Song.*]

CORNELIA. This rosemary is wither'd; pray, get fresh.
 I would have these herbs grow upon his grave,
 When I am dead and rotten. Reach the bays,
 I'll tie a garland here about his head;
 I have kept this twenty year, and every day
 Hallow'd it with my prayers; I did not think
 He should have wore it.
ZANCHE. Look you, who are yonder?
CORNELIA. Oh, reach me the flowers!
ZANCHE. Her ladyship 's foolish.
WOMAN. Alas, her grief
 Hath turn'd her child again!
CORNELIA. You 're very welcome: [*to* FLAMINEO.]
 There's rosemary for you, and rue for you,
 Heart's-ease for you; I pray make much of it,
 I have left more for myself.
FRANCISCO. Lady, who 's this?
CORNELIA. You are, I take it, the grave-maker.
FLAMINEO. So.
ZANCHE. 'Tis Flamineo.
CORNELIA. Will you make me such a fool? here's a white hand:
 Can blood so soon be washed out? let me see;
 When screech-owls croak upon the chimney-tops,
 And the strange cricket i' th' oven sings and hops,
 When yellow spots do on your hands appear,
 Be certain then you of a corse shall hear.
 Out upon 't, how 'tis speckled! h' 'as handled a toad sure.
 Cowslip water is good for the memory:
 Pray, buy me three ounces of 't.
FLAMINEO. I would I were from hence.
CORNELIA. Do you hear, sir?
 I'll give you a saying which my grandmother
 Was wont, when she heard the bell toll, to sing o'er
 Unto her lute.
FLAMINEO. Do, an you will, do.
CORNELIA. *Call for the robin redbreast, and the wren,*
 Since o'er shady groves they hover,

[CORNELIA *doth this in several forms of distraction.*]

And with leaves and flowers do cover
The friendless bodies of unburied men.
Call unto his funeral dole
The ant, the fieldmouse, and the mole,
To rear him hillocks that shall keep him warm,
And (when gay tombs are robb'd) sustain no harm;
But keep the wolf far thence, that's foe to men,
For with his nails he'll dig them up again.
They would not bury him 'cause he died in a quarrel;
But I have an answer for them:
Let holy Church receive him duly,
Since he paid the church-tithes truly.
His wealth is summ'd, and this is all his store,
This poor men get, and great men get no more.
Now the wares are gone, we may shut up shop.
Bless you all, good people.

[*Exeunt* CORNELIA *and* LADIES.]

FLAMINEO. I have a strange thing in me, to th' which
          I cannot give a name, without it be
          Compassion. I pray leave me.

[*Exit* FRANCISCO DE MEDICIS.]

This night I'll know the utmost of my fate;
I'll be resolv'd what my rich sister means
T' assign me for my service. I have liv'd
Riotously ill, like some that live in court,
And sometimes when my face was full of smiles,
Have felt the maze of conscience in my breast.
Oft gay and honour'd robes those tortures try:
We think cag'd birds sing, when indeed they cry.
Ha! I can stand thee: nearer, nearer yet.

[*Enter* BRACHIANO's *ghost, in his leather cassock and breeches,*
    boots, a cowl, a pot of lily flowers, with a skull in't.]

What a mockery hath death made thee! thou look'st sad.
In what place art thou? in yon starry gallery?
Or in the cursed dungeon? No? not speak?
Pray, sir, resolve me, what religion 's best

For a man to die in? or is it in your knowledge
To answer me how long I have to live?
That's the most necessary question.
Not answer? are you still, like some great men
That only walk like shadows up and down,
And to no purpose; say——

[*The* GHOST *throws earth upon him, and shows him the skull.*]

What's that? O fatal! he throws earth upon me.
A dead man's skull beneath the roots of flowers!
I pray speak, sir: our Italian churchmen
Make us believe dead men hold conference
With their familiars, and many times
Will come to bed with them, and eat with them.

[*Exit* GHOST.]

He's gone; and see, the skull and earth are vanish'd.
This is beyond melancholy. I do dare my fate
To do its worst. Now to my sister's lodging,
And sum up all those horrors: the disgrace
The prince threw on me; next the piteous sight
Of my dead brother; and my mother's dotage;
And last this terrible vision: all these
Shall with Vittoria's bounty turn to good,
Or I will drown this weapon in her blood. [*Exit.*]

[*Enter* FRANCISCO DE MEDICIS, LODOVICO, *and* HORTENSIO.]

LODOVICO. My lord, upon my soul you shall no further;
    You have most ridiculously engag'd yourself
    To far already. For my part, I have paid
    All my debts: so, if I should chance to fall,
    My creditors fall not with me; and I vow,
    To quit all in this bold assembly,
    To the meanest follower. My lord, leave the city,
    Or I'll forswear the murder. [*Exit.*]
FRANCISCO. Farewell, Lodovico:
    If thou dost perish in this glorious act,
    I'll rear unto thy memory that fame,
    Shall in the ashes keep alive thy name. [*Exit.*]
HORTENSIO. There's some black deed on foot. I'll presently
    Down to the citadel, and raise some force.
    These strong court-factions, that do brook no checks,

In the career oft break the riders' necks. [*Exit.*]

[*Enter* VITTORIA COROMBONA *with a book in her hand,* ZANCHE;
   FLAMINEO *following them.*]

FLAMINEO. What, are you at your prayers? Give o'er.
VITTORIA. How, ruffian?
FLAMINEO. I come to you 'bout worldly business.
   Sit down, sit down. Nay, stay, blowze, you may hear it:
   The doors are fast enough.
VITTORIA. Ha! are you drunk?
FLAMINEO. Yes, yes, with wormwood water; you shall taste
   Some of it presently.
VITTORIA. What intends the fury?
FLAMINEO. You are my lord's executrix; and I claim
   Reward for my long service.
VITTORIA. For your service!
FLAMINEO. Come, therefore, here is pen and ink, set down
   What you will give me.
VITTORIA. There.

[*She writes.*]

FLAMINEO. Ha! have you done already?
   'Tis a most short conveyance.
VITTORIA. I will read it:
   I give that portion to thee, and no other,
   Which Cain groan'd under, having slain his brother.
FLAMINEO. A most courtly patent to beg by.
VITTORIA. You are a villain!
FLAMINEO. Is 't come to this? they say affrights cure agues:
   Thou hast a devil in thee; I will try
   If I can scare him from thee. Nay, sit still:
   My lord hath left me yet two cases of jewels,
   Shall make me scorn your bounty; you shall see them. [*Exit.*]
VITTORIA. Sure he's distracted.
ZANCHE. Oh, he's desperate!
   For your own safety give him gentle language.

[*He enters with two cases of pistols.*]

FLAMINEO. Look, these are better far at a dead lift,
   Than all your jewel house.
VITTORIA. And yet, methinks,
   These stones have no fair lustre, they are ill set.

FLAMINEO. I'll turn the right side towards you: you shall see
    How they will sparkle.
VITTORIA. Turn this horror from me!
    What do you want? what would you have me do?
    Is not all mine yours? have I any children?
FLAMINEO. Pray thee, good woman, do not trouble me
    With this vain worldly business; say your prayers:
    Neither yourself nor I should outlive him
    The numbering of four hours.
VITTORIA. Did he enjoin it?
FLAMINEO. He did, and 'twas a deadly jealousy,
    Lest any should enjoy thee after him,
    That urged him vow me to it. For my death,
    I did propound it voluntarily, knowing,
    If he could not be safe in his own court,
    Being a great duke, what hope then for us?
VITTORIA. This is your melancholy, and despair.
FLAMINEO. Away:
    Fool thou art, to think that politicians
    DO use to kill the effects or injuries
    And let the cause live. Shall we groan in irons,
    Or be a shameful and a weighty burthen
    To a public scaffold? This is my resolve:
    I would not live at any man's entreaty,
    Nor die at any's bidding.
VITTORIA. Will you hear me?
FLAMINEO. My life hath done service to other men,
    My death shall serve mine own turn: make you ready.
VITTORIA. Do you mean to die indeed?
FLAMINEO. With as much pleasure,
    As e'er my father gat me.
VITTORIA. Are the doors lock'd?
ZANCHE. Yes, madam.
VITTORIA. Are you grown an atheist? will you turn your body,
    Which is the goodly palace of the soul,
    To the soul's slaughter-house? Oh, the cursed devil,
    Which doth present us with all other sins
    Thrice candied o'er, despair with gall and stibium;
    Yet we carouse it off;—cry out for help!—[*to* ZANCHE.]
    Makes us forsake that which was made for man,
    The world, to sink to that was made for devils,
    Eternal darkness!
ZANCHE. Help, help!
FLAMINEO. I'll stop your throat
    With winter plums.

VITTORIA. I pray thee yet remember,
    Millions are now in graves, which at last day
    Like mandrakes shall rise shrieking.
FLAMINEO. Leave your prating,
    For these are but grammatical laments,
    Feminine arguments: and they move me,
    As some in pulpits move their auditory,
    More with their exclamation than sense
    Of reason, or sound doctrine.
ZANCHE. Gentle madam,
    Seem to consent, only persuade him to teach
    The way to death; let him die first.
VITTORIA. 'Tis good, I apprehend it.—
    To kill one's self is meat that we must take
    Like pills, not chew'd, but quickly swallow it;
    The smart o' th' wound, or weakness of the hand,
    May else bring treble torments.
FLAMINEO. I have held it
    A wretched and most miserable life,
    Which is not able to die.
VITTORIA. Oh, but frailty!
    Yet I am now resolv'd; farewell, affliction!
    Behold, Brachiano, I that while you liv'd
    Did make a flaming altar of my heart
    To sacrifice unto you, now am ready
    To sacrifice heart and all. Farewell, Zanche!
ZANCHE. How, madam! do you think that I'll outlive you;
    Especially when my best self, Flamineo,
    Goes the same voyage?
FLAMINEO. O most loved Moor!
ZANCHE. Only, by all my love, let me entreat you,
    Since it is most necessary one of us
    Do violence on ourselves, let you or I
    Be her sad taster, teach her how to die.
FLAMINEO. Thou dost instruct me nobly; take these pistols,
    Because my hand is stain'd with blood already:
    Two of these you shall level at my breast,
    The other 'gainst your own, and so we'll die
    Most equally contented: but first swear
    Not to outlive me.
VITTORIA. and Zan. Most religiously.
FLAMINEO. Then here 's an end of me; farewell, daylight.
    And, O contemptible physic! that dost take
    So long a study, only to preserve
    So short a life, I take my leave of thee.

[*Showing the pistols.*]

These are two cupping-glasses, that shall draw
All my infected blood out. Are you ready?
BOTH. Ready.
FLAMINEO. Whither shall I go now? O Lucian, thy ridiculous
    purgatory! to find Alexander the Great cobbling shoes,
    Pompey tagging points, and
Julius Cæsar making hair-buttons, Hannibal selling blacking, and
Augustus crying garlic, Charlemagne selling lists by the dozen,
    and
King Pepin crying apples in a cart drawn with one horse!
Whether I resolve to fire, earth, water, air,
Or all the elements by scruples, I know not,
Nor greatly care.—Shoot! shoot!
Of all deaths, the violent death is best;
For from ourselves it steals ourselves so fast,
The pain, once apprehended, is quite past.

[*They shoot, and run to him, and tread upon him.*]

VITTORIA. What, are you dropped?
FLAMINEO. I am mix'd with earth already: as you are noble,
    Perform your vows, and bravely follow me.
VITTORIA. Whither? to hell?
ZANCHE. To most assur'd damnation?
VITTORIA. Oh, thou most cursed devil!
ZANCHE. Thou art caught——
VITTORIA. In thine own engine. I tread the fire out
    That would have been my ruin.
FLAMINEO. Will you be perjured? what a religious oath was Styx, that
    the gods never durst swear by, and violate! Oh, that we had such
    an oath to minister, and to be so well kept in our courts of justice!
VITTORIA. Think whither thou art going.
ZANCHE. And remember
    What villainies thou hast acted.
VITTORIA. This thy death
    Shall make me, like a blazing ominous star,
    Look up and tremble.
FLAMINEO. Oh, I am caught with a spring!
VITTORIA. You see the fox comes many times short home;
    'Tis here prov'd true.
FLAMINEO. Kill'd with a couple of braches!
VITTORIA. No fitter offing for the infernal furies,

Than one in whom they reign'd while he was living.
FLAMINEO. Oh, the way 's dark and horrid! I cannot see:
    Shall I have no company?
VITTORIA. Oh, yes, thy sins
    Do run before thee to fetch fire from hell,
    To light thee thither.
FLAMINEO. Oh, I smell soot,
    Most stinking soot! the chimney 's afire:
    My liver 's parboil'd, like Scotch holly-bread;
    There's a plumber laying pipes in my guts, it scalds.
    Wilt thou outlive me?
ZANCHE. Yes, and drive a stake
    Through thy body; for we'll give it out,
    Thou didst this violence upon thyself.
FLAMINEO. Oh, cunning devils! now I have tried your love,
    And doubled all your reaches: I am not wounded.

[FLAMINEO *riseth.*]

The pistols held no bullets; 'twas a plot
To prove your kindness to me; and I live
To punish your ingratitude. I knew,
One time or other, you would find a way
To give me a strong potion. O men,
That lie upon your death-beds, and are haunted
With howling wives! ne'er trust them; they 'll re-marry
Ere the worm pierce your winding-sheet, ere the spider
Make a thin curtain for your epitaphs.

    How cunning you were to discharge! do you practise at the
Artillery yard? Trust a woman? never, never; Brachiano be my
precedent. We lay our souls to pawn to the devil for a little
pleasure, and a woman makes the bill of sale. That ever man
should marry! For one Hypermnestra that saved her lord and
husband, forty-nine of her sisters cut their husbands' throats all in
one night. There was a shoal of virtuous horse leeches! Here are
two other instruments.

[*Enter* LODOVICO, GASPARO, PEDRO, *and* CARLO.]

VITTORIA. Help, help!
FLAMINEO. What noise is that? ha! false keys i' th 'court!
LODOVICO. We have brought you a mask.
FLAMINEO. A matachin it seems by your drawn swords.
    Churchmen turned revelers!

GASPARO. Isabella! Isabella!

LODOVICO. Do you know us now?

FLAMINEO. Lodovico! and Gasparo!

LODOVICO. Yes; and that Moor the duke gave pension to
    Was the great Duke of Florence.

VITTORIA. Oh, we are lost!

FLAMINEO. You shall not take justice forth from my hands,
    Oh, let me kill her!—I'll cut my safety
    Through your coats of steel. Fate 's a spaniel,
    We cannot beat it from us. What remains now?
    Let all that do ill, take this precedent:
    Man may his fate foresee, but not prevent;
    And of all axioms this shall win the prize:
    'Tis better to be fortunate than wise.

GASPARO. Bind him to the pillar.

VITTORIA. Oh, your gentle pity!
    I have seen a blackbird that would sooner fly
    To a man's bosom, than to stay the gripe
    Of the fierce sparrow-hawk.

GASPARO. Your hope deceives you.

VITTORIA. If Florence be i' th' court, would he would kill me!

GASPARO. Fool! Princes give rewards with their own hands,
    But death or punishment by the hands of other.

LODOVICO. Sirrah, you once did strike me; I'll strike you
    Unto the centre.

FLAMINEO. Thou'lt do it like a hangman, a base hangman,
    Not like a noble fellow, for thou see'st
    I cannot strike again.

LODOVICO. Dost laugh?

FLAMINEO. Wouldst have me die, as I was born, in whining?

GASPARO. Recommend yourself to heaven.

FLAMINEO. No, I will carry mine own commendations thither.

LODOVICO. Oh, I could kill you forty times a day,
    And use 't four years together, 'twere too little!
    Naught grieves but that you are too few to feed
    The famine of our vengeance. What dost think on?

FLAMINEO. Nothing; of nothing: leave thy idle questions.
    I am i' th' way to study a long silence:
    To prate were idle. I remember nothing.
    There's nothing of so infinite vexation
    As man's own thoughts.

LODOVICO. O thou glorious strumpet!
    Could I divide thy breath from this pure air
    When 't leaves thy body, I would suck it up,
    And breathe 't upon some dunghill.

VITTORIA. You, my death's-man!
    Methinks thou dost not look horrid enough,
    Thou hast too good a face to be a hangman:
    If thou be, do thy office in right form;
    Fall down upon thy knees, and ask forgiveness.
LODOVICO. Oh, thou hast been a most prodigious comet!
    But I'll cut off your train. Kill the Moor first.
VITTORIA. You shall not kill her first; behold my breast:
    I will be waited on in death; my servant
    Shall never go before me.
GASPARO. Are you so brave?
VITTORIA. Yes, I shall welcome death,
    As princes do some great ambassadors;
    I'll meet thy weapon half-way.
LODOVICO. Thou dost tremble:
    Methinks, fear should dissolve thee into air.
VITTORIA. Oh, thou art deceiv'd, I am too true a woman!
    Conceit can never kill me. I'll tell thee what,
    I will not in my death shed one base tear;
    Or if look pale, for want of blood, not fear.
GASPARO. Thou art my task, black fury.
ZANCHE. I have blood
    As red as either of theirs: wilt drink some?
    'Tis good for the falling-sickness. I am proud:
    Death cannot alter my complexion,
    For I shall ne'er look pale.
LODOVICO. Strike, strike,
    With a joint motion.

    [*They strike.*]

VITTORIA. 'Twas a manly blow;
    The next thou giv'st, murder some sucking infant;
    And then thou wilt be famous.
FLAMINEO. Oh, what blade is 't?
    A Toledo, or an English fox?
    I ever thought a culter should distinguish
    The cause of my death, rather than a doctor.
    Search my wound deeper; tent it with the steel
    That made it.
VITTORIA. Oh, my greatest sin lay in my blood!
    Now my blood pays for 't.
FLAMINEO. Th' art a noble sister!
    I love thee now; if woman do breed man,
    She ought to teach him manhood. Fare thee well.

    Know, many glorious women that are fam'd
    For masculine virtue, have been vicious,
    Only a happier silence did betide them:
    She hath no faults, who hath the art to hide them.
VITTORIA. My soul, like to a ship in a black storm,
    Is driven, I know not whither.
FLAMINEO. Then cast anchor.
    Prosperity doth bewitch men, seeming clear;
    But seas do laugh, show white, when rocks are near.
    We cease to grieve, cease to be fortune's slaves,
    Nay, cease to die by dying. Art thou gone?
    And thou so near the bottom? false report,
    Which says that women vie with the nine Muses,
    For nine tough durable lives! I do not look
    Who went before, nor who shall follow me;
    No, at my self I will begin the end.
    While we look up to heaven, we confound
    Knowledge with knowledge. Oh, I am in a mist!
VITTORIA. Oh, happy they that never saw the court,
    Nor ever knew great men but by report! [*Dies.*]
FLAMINEO. I recover like a spent taper, for a flash,
    And instantly go out.
       Let all that belong to great men remember th' old wives' tradition, to be like the lions i' th' Tower on Candlemas-day; to mourn if the sun shine, for fear of the pitiful remainder of winter to come.
       'Tis well yet there's some goodness in my death;
    My life was a black charnel. I have caught
    An everlasting cold; I have lost my voice
    Most irrecoverably. Farewell, glorious villains.
    This busy trade of life appears most vain,
    Since rest breeds rest, where all seek pain by pain.
    Let no harsh flattering bells resound my knell;
    Strike, thunder, and strike loud, to my farewell! [*Dies.*]

    [*Enter* AMBASSADORS *and* GIOVANNI.]

ENGLISH AMBASSADOR. This way, this way! break open the doors! this way!
LODOVICO. Ha! are we betray'd?
    Why then let 's constantly all die together;
    And having finish'd this most noble deed,
    Defy the worst of fate, nor fear to bleed.
ENGLISH AMBASSADOR. Keep back the prince: shoot! shoot!
LODOVICO. Oh, I am wounded!

I fear I shall be ta'en.

GIOVANNI. You bloody villains,
    By what authority have you committed
    This massacre?

LODOVICO. By thine.

GIOVANNI. Mine!

LODOVICO. Yes; thy uncle, which is a part of thee, enjoined us to 't:
    Thou know'st me, I am sure; I am Count Lodowick;
    And thy most noble uncle in disguise
    Was last night in thy court.

GIOVANNI. Ha!

LODOVICO. Yes, that Moor thy father chose his pensioner.

GIOVANNI. He turn'd murderer!
    Away with them to prison, and to torture:
    All that have hands in this shall taste our justice,
    As I hope heaven.

LODOVICO. I do glory yet,
    That I can call this act mine own. For my part,
    The rack, the gallows, and the torturing wheel,
    Shall be but sound sleeps to me: here 's my rest;
    I limn'd this night-piece, and it was my best.

GIOVANNI. Remove these bodies. See, my honour'd lord,
    What use you ought make of their punishment.
    Let guilty men remember, their black deeds
    Do lean on crutches made of slender reeds.

Instead of an Epilogue, only this of Martial supplies me:
Hæc fuerint nobis præmia, si placui.

* * * *

For the action of the play, 'twas generally well, and I dare affirm, with the joint testimony of some of their own quality (for the true imitation of life, without striving to make nature a monster,) the best that ever became them: whereof as I make a general acknowledgment, so in particular I must remember the well-approved industry of my friend Master Perkins, and confess the worth of his action did crown both the beginning and end.

THE DUCHESS OF MALFI

DRAMATIS PERSONAE

FERDINAND, *Duke of Calabria.*
CARDINAL, *his brother.*
ANTONIO BOLOGNA, *Steward of the Household to the Duchess.*
DELIO, *his friend.*
DANIEL DE BOSOLA, *Gentleman of the Horse to the Duchess.*
CASTRUCCIO, *an old Lord.*
MARQUIS OF PESCARA.
COUNT MALATESTI.
RODERIGO, *Lord.*
SILVIO, *Lord.*
GRISOLAN, *Lord.*
DOCTOR.
The Several Madmen.
DUCHESS OF MALFI.
CARIOLA, *her woman.*
JULIA, *Castruccio's wife, and the Cardinal's mistress.*
OLD LADY.
*Ladies, Three Young Children, Two Pilgrims, Executioners,
Court Officers, and Attendants.*

ACT I.

SCENE I. *Malfi. The presence-chamber in the palace of the* DUCHESS.

[*Enter* ANTONIO *and* DELIO.]

DELIO. You are welcome to your country, dear Antonio;
    You have been long in France, and you return
    A very formal Frenchman in your habit:
    How do you like the French court?
ANTONIO. I admire it:
    In seeking to reduce both state and people
    To a fix'd order, their judicious king
    Begins at home; quits first his royal palace
    Of flattering sycophants, of dissolute
    And infamous persons,—which he sweetly terms
    His master's master-piece, the work of heaven;
    Considering duly that a prince's court
    Is like a common fountain, whence should flow
    Pure silver drops in general, but if 't chance

Some curs'd example poison 't near the head,
Death and diseases through the whole land spread.
And what is 't makes this blessed government
But a most provident council, who dare freely
Inform him the corruption of the times?
Though some o' the court hold it presumption
To instruct princes what they ought to do,
It is a noble duty to inform them
What they ought to foresee.[1]—Here comes Bosola,
The only court-gall; yet I observe his railing
Is not for simple love of piety:
Indeed, he rails at those things which he wants;
Would be as lecherous, covetous, or proud,
Bloody, or envious, as any man,
If he had means to be so.—Here's the cardinal.

[*Enter* CARDINAL *and* BOSOLA]

BOSOLA. I do haunt you still.

CARDINAL. So.

BOSOLA. I have done you better service than to be slighted thus. Miserable age, where only the reward of doing well is the doing of it!

CARDINAL. You enforce your merit too much.

BOSOLA. I fell into the galleys in your service: where, for two years together, I wore two towels instead of a shirt, with a knot on the shoulder, after the fashion of a Roman mantle. Slighted thus! I will thrive some way. Black-birds fatten best in hard weather; why not I in these dog-days?

CARDINAL. Would you could become honest!

BOSOLA. With all your divinity do but direct me the way to it. I have known many travel far for it, and yet return as arrant knaves as they went forth, because they carried themselves always along with them. [*Exit* CARDINAL.] Are you gone? Some fellows, they say, are possessed with the devil, but this great fellow were able to possess the greatest devil, and make him worse.

ANTONIO. He hath denied thee some suit?

BOSOLA. He and his brother are like plum-trees that grow crooked over standing-pools; they are rich and o'erladen with fruit, but none but crows, pies, and caterpillars feed on them. Could I be one of their flattering panders, I would hang on their ears like a horseleech, till I were full, and then drop off. I pray, leave me. Who would rely upon these miserable dependencies, in expectation to be advanc'd

---

[1] Prevent.

to-morrow? What creature ever fed worse than hoping Tantalus? Nor ever died any man more fearfully than he that hoped for a pardon. There are rewards for hawks and dogs when they have done us service; but for a soldier that hazards his limbs in a battle, nothing but a kind of geometry is his last supportation.

DELIO. Geometry?

BOSOLA. Ay, to hang in a fair pair of slings, take his latter swing in the world upon an honourable pair of crutches, from hospital to hospital. Fare ye well, sir: and yet do not you scorn us; for places in the court are but like beds in the hospital, where this man's head lies at that man's foot, and so lower and lower. [*Exit.*]

DELIO. I knew this fellow seven years in the galleys
    For a notorious murder; and 'twas thought
    The cardinal suborn'd it: he was releas'd
    By the French general, Gaston de Foix,
    When he recover'd Naples.

ANTONIO. 'Tis great pity
    He should be thus neglected: I have heard
    He's very valiant. This foul melancholy
    Will poison all his goodness; for, I'll tell you,
    If too immoderate sleep be truly said
    To be an inward rust unto the soul,
    If then doth follow want of action
    Breeds all black malcontents; and their close rearing,
    Like moths in cloth, do hurt for want of wearing.

SCENE II. *Malfi. The presence-chamber in the palace of the* DUCHESS.

[ANTONIO, DELIO *are present. Enter* SILVIO, CASTRUCCIO, JULIA, RODERIGO *and* GRISOLAN.]

DELIO. The presence 'gins to fill: you promis'd me
    To make me the partaker of the natures
    Of some of your great courtiers.

ANTONIO. The lord cardinal's
    And other strangers' that are now in court?
    I shall.——Here comes the great Calabrian duke.

[*Enter* FERDINAND *and* ATTENDANTS.]

FERDINAND. Who took the ring oftenest?[2]

SILVIO. Antonio Bologna, my lord.

FERDINAND. Our sister duchess' great-master of her household? Give

---

[2] The reference is to the knightly sport of riding at the ring.

him the jewel.—When shall we leave this sportive action, and fall to action indeed?

CASTRUCCIO. Methinks, my lord, you should not desire to go to war in person.

FERDINAND. Now for some gravity.—Why, my lord?

CASTRUCCIO. It is fitting a soldier arise to be a prince, but not necessary a prince descend to be a captain.

FERDINAND. No?

CASTRUCCIO. No, my lord; he were far better do it by a deputy.

FERDINAND. Why should he not as well sleep or eat by a deputy? This might take idle, offensive, and base office from him, whereas the other deprives him of honour.

CASTRUCCIO. Believe my experience, that realm is never long in quiet where the ruler is a soldier.

FERDINAND. Thou toldest me thy wife could not endure fighting.

CASTRUCCIO. True, my lord.

FERDINAND. And of a jest she broke of[3] a captain she met full of wounds: I have forgot it.

CASTRUCCIO. She told him, my lord, he was a pitiful fellow, to lie, like the children of Ismael, all in tents.[4]

FERDINAND. Why, there's a wit were able to undo all the chirurgeons[5] o' the city; for although gallants should quarrel, and had drawn their weapons, and were ready to go to it, yet her persuasions would make them put up.

CASTRUCCIO. That she would, my lord.—How do you like my Spanish gennet?[6]

RODERIGO. He is all fire.

FERDINAND. I am of Pliny's opinion, I think he was begot by the wind; he runs as if he were ballass'd[7] with quicksilver.

SILVIO. True, my lord, he reels from the tilt often.

RODERIGO, GRISOLAN. Ha, ha, ha!

FERDINAND. Why do you laugh? Methinks you that are courtiers should be my touch-wood, take fire when I give fire; that is, laugh when I laugh, were the subject never so witty.

CASTRUCCIO. True, my lord: I myself have heard a very good jest, and have scorn'd to seem to have so silly a wit as to understand it.

FERDINAND. But I can laugh at your fool, my lord.

CASTRUCCIO. He cannot speak, you know, but he makes faces; my lady cannot abide him.

FERDINAND. No?

---

[3] At the expense of.
[4] Rolls of lint used to dress wounds.
[5] Surgeons.
[6] A small horse.
[7] Ballasted.

CASTRUCCIO. Nor endure to be in merry company; for she says too much laughing, and too much company, fills her too full of the wrinkle.

FERDINAND. I would, then, have a mathematical instrument made for her face, that she might not laugh out of compass.—I shall shortly visit you at Milan, Lord Silvio.

SILVIO. Your grace shall arrive most welcome.

FERDINAND. You are a good horseman, Antonio; you have excellent riders in France: what do you think of good horsemanship?

ANTONIO. Nobly, my lord: as out of the Grecian horse issued many famous princes, so out of brave horsemanship arise the first sparks of growing resolution, that raise the mind to noble action.

FERDINAND. You have bespoke it worthily.

SILVIO. Your brother, the lord cardinal, and sister duchess.

[*Enter* CARDINAL, *with* DUCHESS, *and* CARIOLA.]

CARDINAL. Are the galleys come about?

GRISOLAN. They are, my lord.

FERDINAND. Here's the Lord Silvio is come to take his leave.

DELIO. Now, sir, your promise: what's that cardinal?
    I mean his temper? They say he's a brave fellow,
    Will play his five thousand crowns at tennis, dance,
    Court ladies, and one that hath fought single combats.

ANTONIO. Some such flashes superficially hang on him for form; but observe his inward character: he is a melancholy churchman. The spring in his face is nothing but the engend'ring of toads; where he is jealous of any man, he lays worse plots for them than ever was impos'd on Hercules, for he strews in his way flatterers, panders, intelligencers, atheists, and a thousand such political monsters. He should have been Pope; but instead of coming to it by the primitive decency of the church, he did bestow bribes so largely and so impudently as if he would have carried it away without heaven's knowledge. Some good he hath done——

DELIO. You have given too much of him. What's his brother?

ANTONIO. The duke there? A most perverse and turbulent nature. What appears in him mirth is merely outside; If he laught heartily, it is to laugh All honesty out of fashion.

DELIO. Twins?

ANTONIO. In quality.
    He speaks with others' tongues, and hears men's suits
    With others' ears; will seem to sleep o' the bench
    Only to entrap offenders in their answers;
    Dooms men to death by information;
    Rewards by hearsay.

DELIO. Then the law to him
    Is like a foul, black cobweb to a spider,—
    He makes it his dwelling and a prison
    To entangle those shall feed him.
ANTONIO. Most true:
    He never pays debts unless they be shrewd turns,
    And those he will confess that he doth owe.
    Last, for this brother there, the cardinal,
    They that do flatter him most say oracles
    Hang at his lips; and verily I believe them,
    For the devil speaks in them.
    But for their sister, the right noble duchess,
    You never fix'd your eye on three fair medals
    Cast in one figure, of so different temper.
    For her discourse, it is so full of rapture,
    You only will begin then to be sorry
    When she doth end her speech, and wish, in wonder,
    She held it less vain-glory to talk much,
    Than your penance to hear her. Whilst she speaks,
    She throws upon a man so sweet a look
    That it were able to raise one to a galliard.[8]
    That lay in a dead palsy, and to dote
    On that sweet countenance; but in that look
    There speaketh so divine a continence
    As cuts off all lascivious and vain hope.
    Her days are practis'd in such noble virtue,
    That sure her nights, nay, more, her very sleeps,
    Are more in heaven than other ladies' shrifts.
    Let all sweet ladies break their flatt'ring glasses,
    And dress themselves in her.
DELIO. Fie, Antonio,
    You play the wire-drawer with her commendations.
ANTONIO. I'll case the picture up: only thus much;
    All her particular worth grows to this sum,—
    She stains[9] the time past, lights the time to come.
CARIOLA. You must attend my lady in the gallery,
    Some half and hour hence.
ANTONIO. I shall.

    [*Exeunt* ANTONIO *and* DELIO.]

FERDINAND. Sister, I have a suit to you.

---

[8] A lively dance.
[9] Throws into the shade.

DUCHESS. To me, sir?

FERDINAND. A gentleman here, Daniel de Bosola,
    One that was in the galleys——

DUCHESS. Yes, I know him.

FERDINAND. A worthy fellow he is: pray, let me entreat for
    The provisorship of your horse.

DUCHESS. Your knowledge of him
    Commends him and prefers him.

FERDINAND. Call him hither.

[*Exit* ATTENDANT.]

We [are] now upon[10] parting. Good Lord Silvio,
    Do us commend to all our noble friends
    At the leaguer.

SILVIO. Sir, I shall.

DUCHESS. You are for Milan?

SILVIO. I am.

DUCHESS. Bring the caroches.[11]—We'll bring you down
    To the haven.

[*Exeunt* DUCHESS, SILVIO, CASTRUCCIO, RODERIGO, GRISOLAN,
    CARIOLA, JULIA, *and* ATTENDANTS.]

CARDINAL. Be sure you entertain that Bosola
    For your intelligence.[12] I would not be seen in 't;
    And therefore many times I have slighted him
    When he did court our furtherance, as this morning.

FERDINAND. Antonio, the great-master of her household,
    Had been far fitter.

CARDINAL. You are deceiv'd in him.
    His nature is too honest for such business.—
    He comes: I'll leave you. [*Exit.*]

[*Re-enter* BOSOLA.]

BOSOLA. I was lur'd to you.

FERDINAND. My brother, here, the cardinal, could never
    Abide you.

BOSOLA. Never since he was in my debt.

FERDINAND. May be some oblique character in your face

---

[10] At the point of.
[11] Coaches.
[12] Spy.

     Made him suspect you.

BOSOLA. Doth he study physiognomy?
     There's no more credit to be given to the face
     Than to a sick man's urine, which some call
     The physician's whore, because she cozens[13] him.
     He did suspect me wrongfully.

FERDINAND. For that
     You must give great men leave to take their times.
     Distrust doth cause us seldom be deceiv'd.
     You see the oft shaking of the cedar-tree
     Fastens it more at root.

BOSOLA. Yet take heed;
     For to suspect a friend unworthily
     Instructs him the next way to suspect you,
     And prompts him to deceive you.

FERDINAND. There's gold.

BOSOLA. So:
     What follows? [*aside.*] Never rain'd such showers as these
     Without thunderbolts i' the tail of them.—Whose throat must I
       cut?

FERDINAND. Your inclination to shed blood rides post
     Before my occasion to use you. I give you that
     To live i' the court here, and observe the duchess;
     To note all the particulars of her haviour,
     What suitors do solicit her for marriage,
     And whom she best affects. She's a young widow:
     I would not have her marry again.

BOSOLA. No, sir?

FERDINAND. Do not you ask the reason; but be satisfied.
     I say I would not.

BOSOLA. It seems you would create me
     One of your familiars.

FERDINAND. Familiar! What's that?

BOSOLA. Why, a very quaint invisible devil in flesh,—
     An intelligencer.[14]

FERDINAND. Such a kind of thriving thing
     I would wish thee; and ere long thou mayst arrive
     At a higher place by 't.

BOSOLA. Take your devils,
     Which hell calls angels! These curs'd gifts would make
     You a corrupter, me an impudent traitor;
     And should I take these, they'd take me [to] hell.

---

[13] Cheats.
[14] Spy.

FERDINAND. Sir, I'll take nothing from you that I have given.
    There is a place that I procur'd for you
    This morning, the provisorship o' the horse;
    Have you heard on 't?
BOSOLA. No.
FERDINAND. 'Tis yours: is 't not worth thanks?
BOSOLA. I would have you curse yourself now, that your bounty
    (Which makes men truly noble) e'er should make me
    A villain. O, that to avoid ingratitude
    For the good deed you have done me, I must do
    All the ill man can invent! Thus the devil
    Candies all sins o'er; and what heaven terms vile,
    That names he complimental.
FERDINAND. Be yourself;
    Keep your old garb of melancholy; 'twill express
    You envy those that stand above your reach,
    Yet strive not to come near 'em. This will gain
    Access to private lodgings, where yourself
    May, like a politic dormouse——
BOSOLA. As I have seen some
    Feed in a lord's dish, half asleep, not seeming
    To listen to any talk; and yet these rogues
    Have cut his throat in a dream. What's my place?
    The provisorship o' the horse? Say, then, my corruption
    Grew out of horse-dung: I am your creature.
FERDINAND. Away! [*Exit.*]
BOSOLA. Let good men, for good deeds, covet good fame,
    Since place and riches oft are bribes of shame.
    Sometimes the devil doth preach. [*Exit.*]

SCENE III. *Malfi. Gallery in the* DUCHESS'*s palace.*

[*Enter* FERDINAND, DUCHESS, CARDINAL, *and* CARIOLA.]

CARDINAL. We are to part from you; and your own discretion
    Must now be your director.
FERDINAND. You are a widow:
    You know already what man is; and therefore
    Let not youth, high promotion, eloquence——
CARDINAL. No,
    Nor anything without the addition, honour,
    Sway your high blood.
FERDINAND. Marry! they are most luxurious[15]

---

[15] Lustful.

Will wed twice.
CARDINAL. O, fie!
FERDINAND. Their livers are more spotted
    Than Laban's sheep.[16]
DUCHESS. Diamonds are of most value,
    They say, that have pass'd through most jewellers' hands.
FERDINAND. Whores by that rule are precious.
DUCHESS. Will you hear me?
    I'll never marry.
CARDINAL. So most widows say;
    But commonly that motion lasts no longer
    Than the turning of an hour-glass: the funeral sermon
    And it end both together.
FERDINAND. Now hear me:
    You live in a rank pasture, here, i' the court;
    There is a kind of honey-dew that's deadly;
    'Twill poison your fame; look to 't. Be not cunning;
    For they whose faces do belie their hearts
    Are witches ere they arrive at twenty years,
    Ay, and give the devil suck.
DUCHESS. This is terrible good counsel.
FERDINAND. Hypocrisy is woven of a fine small thread,
    Subtler than Vulcan's engine:[17] yet, believe 't,
    Your darkest actions, nay, your privat'st thoughts,
    Will come to light.
CARDINAL. You may flatter yourself,
    And take your own choice; privately be married
    Under the eaves of night——
FERDINAND. Think 't the best voyage
    That e'er you made; like the irregular crab,
    Which, though 't goes backward, thinks that it goes right
    Because it goes its own way: but observe,
    Such weddings may more properly be said
    To be executed than celebrated.
CARDINAL. The marriage night
    Is the entrance into some prison.
FERDINAND. And those joys,
    Those lustful pleasures, are like heavy sleeps
    Which do fore-run man's mischief.
CARDINAL. Fare you well.
    Wisdom begins at the end: remember it. [*Exit.*]
DUCHESS. I think this speech between you both was studied,

---

[16] Genesis xxxi., 31-42.
[17] The net in which he caught Venus and Mars.

It came so roundly off.

FERDINAND. You are my sister;
   This was my father's poniard, do you see?
   I 'd be loth to see 't look rusty, 'cause 'twas his.
   I would have you give o'er these chargeable revels:
   A visor and a mask are whispering-rooms
   That were never built for goodness,—fare ye well—
   And women like variety of courtship.
   What cannot a neat knave with a smooth tale
   Make a woman believe? Farewell, lusty widow. [*Exit.*]

DUCHESS. Shall this move me? If all my royal kindred
   Lay in my way unto this marriage,
   I 'd make them my low footsteps. And even now,
   Even in this hate, as men in some great battles,
   By apprehending danger, have achiev'd
   Almost impossible actions (I have heard soldiers say so),
   So I through frights and threatenings will assay
   This dangerous venture. Let old wives report
   I wink'd and chose a husband.—Cariola,
   To thy known secrecy I have given up
   More than my life,—my fame.

CARIOLA. Both shall be safe;
   For I'll conceal this secret from the world
   As warily as those that trade in poison
   Keep poison from their children.

DUCHESS. Thy protestation
   Is ingenious and hearty; I believe it.
   Is Antonio come?

CARIOLA. He attends you.

DUCHESS. Good dear soul,
   Leave me; but place thyself behind the arras,
   Where thou mayst overhear us. Wish me good speed;
   For I am going into a wilderness,
   Where I shall find nor path nor friendly clue
   To be my guide.

[CARIOLA *goes behind the arras.*]

[*Enter* ANTONIO.]

I sent for you: sit down;
   Take pen and ink, and write: are you ready?

ANTONIO. Yes.

DUCHESS. What did I say?

ANTONIO. That I should write somewhat.

DUCHESS. O, I remember.
>After these triumphs and this large expense
>It's fit, like thrifty husbands,[18] we inquire
>What's laid up for to-morrow.

ANTONIO. So please your beauteous excellence.

DUCHESS. Beauteous!
>Indeed, I thank you. I look young for your sake;
>You have ta'en my cares upon you.

ANTONIO. I'll fetch your grace
>The particulars of your revenue and expense.

DUCHESS. O, you are
>An upright treasurer: but you mistook;
>For when I said I meant to make inquiry
>What's laid up for to-morrow, I did mean
>What's laid up yonder for me.

ANTONIO. Where?

DUCHESS. In heaven.
>I am making my will (as 'tis fit princes should,
>In perfect memory), and, I pray, sir, tell me,
>Were not one better make it smiling, thus,
>Than in deep groans and terrible ghastly looks,
>As if the gifts we parted with procur'd[19]
>That violent distraction?

ANTONIO. O, much better.

DUCHESS. If I had a husband now, this care were quit:
>But I intend to make you overseer.
>What good deed shall we first remember? Say.

ANTONIO. Begin with that first good deed began i' the world
>After man's creation, the sacrament of marriage;
>I'd have you first provide for a good husband;
>Give him all.

DUCHESS. All!

ANTONIO. Yes, your excellent self.

DUCHESS. In a winding-sheet?

ANTONIO. In a couple.

DUCHESS. Saint Winifred, that were a strange will!

ANTONIO. 'Twere stranger[20] if there were no will in you
>To marry again.

DUCHESS. What do you think of marriage?

ANTONIO. I take 't, as those that deny purgatory,
>It locally contains or heaven or hell;

---

[18] Housekeepers.
[19] Produced.
[20] Qq. read STRANGE.

There's no third place in 't.

DUCHESS. How do you affect it?

ANTONIO. My banishment, feeding my melancholy,
    Would often reason thus.

DUCHESS. Pray, let's hear it.

ANTONIO. Say a man never marry, nor have children,
    What takes that from him? Only the bare name
    Of being a father, or the weak delight
    To see the little wanton ride a-cock-horse
    Upon a painted stick, or hear him chatter
    Like a taught starling.

DUCHESS. Fie, fie, what's all this?
    One of your eyes is blood-shot; use my ring to 't.
    They say 'tis very sovereign. 'Twas my wedding-ring,
    And I did vow never to part with it
    But to my second husband.

ANTONIO. You have parted with it now.

DUCHESS. Yes, to help your eye-sight.

ANTONIO. You have made me stark blind.

DUCHESS. How?

ANTONIO. There is a saucy and ambitious devil
    Is dancing in this circle.

DUCHESS. Remove him.

ANTONIO. How?

DUCHESS. There needs small conjuration, when your finger
    May do it: thus. Is it fit?

[*She puts the ring upon his finger. He kneels.*]

ANTONIO. What said you?

DUCHESS. Sir,
    This goodly roof of yours is too low built;
    I cannot stand upright in 't nor discourse,
    Without I raise it higher. Raise yourself;
    Or, if you please, my hand to help you: so.

[*Raises him.*]

ANTONIO. Ambition, madam, is a great man's madness,
    That is not kept in chains and close-pent rooms,
    But in fair lightsome lodgings, and is girt
    With the wild noise of prattling visitants,
    Which makes it lunatic beyond all cure.

Conceive not I am so stupid but I aim[21]
Whereto your favours tend: but he's a fool
That, being a-cold, would thrust his hands i' the fire
To warm them.

DUCHESS. So, now the ground's broke,
You may discover what a wealthy mine
I make your lord of.

ANTONIO. O my unworthiness!

DUCHESS. You were ill to sell yourself:
This dark'ning of your worth is not like that
Which tradesmen use i' the city; their false lights
Are to rid bad wares off: and I must tell you,
If you will know where breathes a complete man
(I speak it without flattery), turn your eyes,
And progress through yourself.

ANTONIO. Were there nor heaven nor hell,
I should be honest: I have long serv'd virtue,
And ne'er ta'en wages of her.

DUCHESS. Now she pays it.
The misery of us that are born great!
We are forc'd to woo, because none dare woo us;
And as a tyrant doubles with his words,
And fearfully equivocates, so we
Are forc'd to express our violent passions
In riddles and in dreams, and leave the path
Of simple virtue, which was never made
To seem the thing it is not. Go, go brag
You have left me heartless; mine is in your bosom:
I hope 'twill multiply love there. You do tremble:
Make not your heart so dead a piece of flesh,
To fear more than to love me. Sir, be confident:
What is 't distracts you? This is flesh and blood, sir;
'Tis not the figure cut in alabaster
Kneels at my husband's tomb. Awake, awake, man!
I do here put off all vain ceremony,
And only do appear to you a young widow
That claims you for her husband, and, like a widow,
I use but half a blush in 't.

ANTONIO. Truth speak for me;
I will remain the constant sanctuary
Of your good name.

DUCHESS. I thank you, gentle love:
And 'cause you shall not come to me in debt,

---

[21] Guess.

Being now my steward, here upon your lips
I sign your Quietus est.[22] This you should have begg'd now.
I have seen children oft eat sweetmeats thus,
As fearful to devour them too soon.

ANTONIO. But for your brothers?

DUCHESS. Do not think of them:
All discord without this circumference
Is only to be pitied, and not fear'd:
Yet, should they know it, time will easily
Scatter the tempest.

ANTONIO. These words should be mine,
And all the parts you have spoke, if some part of it
Would not have savour'd flattery.

DUCHESS. Kneel.

[CARIOLA *comes from behind the arras.*]

ANTONIO. Ha!

DUCHESS. Be not amaz'd; this woman's of my counsel:
I have heard lawyers say, a contract in a chamber
Per verba [de] presenti[23] is absolute marriage.

[*She and* ANTONIO *kneel.*]

Bless, heaven, this sacred gordian[24] which let violence
Never untwine!

ANTONIO. And may our sweet affections, like the spheres,
Be still in motion!

DUCHESS. Quickening, and make
The like soft music!

ANTONIO. That we may imitate the loving palms,
Best emblem of a peaceful marriage,
That never bore fruit, divided!

DUCHESS. What can the church force more?

ANTONIO. That fortune may not know an accident,
Either of joy or sorrow, to divide
Our fixed wishes!

DUCHESS. How can the church build faster?[25]
We now are man and wife, and 'tis the church
That must but echo this.—Maid, stand apart:
I now am blind.

---

[22] The phrase used to indicate that accounts had been examined and found correct.

[23] Using words of present time; i.e., "I take," not "I will take."

[24] Knot.

[25] More firmly.

ANTONIO. What's your conceit in this?

DUCHESS. I would have you lead your fortune by the hand
    Unto your marriage-bed:
    (You speak in me this, for we now are one:)
    We 'll only lie and talk together, and plot
    To appease my humorous[26] kindred; and if you please,
    Like the old tale in ALEXANDER AND LODOWICK,
    Lay a naked sword between us, keep us chaste.
    O, let me shroud my blushes in your bosom,
    Since 'tis the treasury of all my secrets!

[*Exeunt* DUCHESS *and* ANTONIO.]

CARIOLA. Whether the spirit of greatness or of woman
    Reign most in her, I know not; but it shows
    A fearful madness. I owe her much of pity. [*Exit.*]

ACT II.

SCENE I. *Malfi. An apartment in the palace of the* DUCHESS.

[*Enter* BOSOLA *and* CASTRUCCIO.]

BOSOLA. You say you would fain be taken for an eminent courtier?

CASTRUCCIO. 'Tis the very main[27] of my ambition.

BOSOLA. Let me see: you have a reasonable good face for 't already,
    and your night-cap expresses your ears sufficient largely. I would
    have you learn to twirl the strings of your band with a good grace,
    and in a set speech, at th' end of every sentence, to hum three or
    four times, or blow your nose till it smart again, to recover your
    memory. When you come to be a president in criminal causes, if
    you smile upon a prisoner, hang him; but if you frown upon him
    and threaten him, let him be sure to scape the gallows.

CASTRUCCIO. I would be a very merry president.

BOSOLA. Do not sup o' nights; 'twill beget you an admirable wit.

CASTRUCCIO. Rather it would make me have a good stomach to
    quarrel; for they say, your roaring boys eat meat seldom, and that
    makes them so valiant. But how shall I know whether the people
    take me for an eminent fellow?

BOSOLA. I will teach a trick to know it: give out you lie a-dying, and if
    you hear the common people curse you, be sure you are taken for

---

[26] Of difficult disposition.
[27] Chief part.

one of the prime night-caps.[28] [*Enter an* OLD LADY.] You come
from painting now.

OLD LADY. From what?

BOSOLA. Why, from your scurvy face-physic. To behold thee not
painted inclines somewhat near a miracle. These in thy face here
were deep ruts and foul sloughs the last progress.[29] There was a
lady in France that, having had the small-pox, flayed the skin off
her face to make it more level; and whereas before she looked like
a nutmeg-grater, after she resembled an abortive hedge-hog.

OLD LADY. Do you call this painting?

BOSOLA. No, no, but you call [it] careening[30] of an old morphewed[31]
lady, to make her disembogue[32] again: there's rough-cast phrase to
your plastic.[33]

OLD LADY. It seems you are well acquainted with my closet.

BOSOLA. One would suspect it for a shop of witchcraft, to find in it the
fat of serpents, spawn of snakes, Jews' spittle, and their young
children's ordure; and all these for the face. I would sooner eat a
dead pigeon taken from the soles of the feet of one sick of the
plague, than kiss one of you fasting. Here are two of you, whose
sin of your youth is the very patrimony of the physician; makes
him renew his foot-cloth with the spring, and change his high-
pric'd courtesan with the fall of the leaf. I do wonder you do not
loathe yourselves.

Observe my meditation now.
What thing is in this outward form of man
To be belov'd? We account it ominous,
If nature do produce a colt, or lamb,
A fawn, or goat, in any limb resembling
A man, and fly from 't as a prodigy:
Man stands amaz'd to see his deformity
In any other creature but himself.
But in our own flesh though we bear diseases
Which have their true names only ta'en from beasts,—
As the most ulcerous wolf and swinish measle,—
Though we are eaten up of lice and worms,
And though continually we bear about us
A rotten and dead body, we delight
To hide it in rich tissue: all our fear,

---

[28] Bullies (Hazlitt); lawyers (Vaughan).

[29] Royal journey.

[30] Turning a boat on its side for repairs.

[31] Scabbed.

[32] Empty.

[33] Face-modeling (Sampson). "There's a plain statement of your practises."

Nay, all our terror, is, lest our physician
Should put us in the ground to be made sweet.—
Your wife's gone to Rome: you two couple, and get you to the
wells at Lucca to recover your aches. I have other work on foot.

[*Exeunt* CASTRUCCIO *and* OLD LADY.]

I observe our duchess
Is sick a-days, she pukes, her stomach seethes,
The fins of her eye-lids look most teeming blue,[34]
She wanes i' the cheek, and waxes fat i' the flank,
And, contrary to our Italian fashion,
Wears a loose-bodied gown: there's somewhat in 't.
I have a trick may chance discover it,
A pretty one; I have bought some apricocks,
The first our spring yields.

[*Enter* ANTONIO *and* DELIO, *talking together apart*.]

DELIO. And so long since married?
    You amaze me.
ANTONIO. Let me seal your lips forever:
    For, did I think that anything but th' air
    Could carry these words from you, I should wish
    You had no breath at all.—Now, sir, in your contemplation?
    You are studying to become a great wise fellow.
BOSOLA. O, sir, the opinion of wisdom is a foul tetter[35] that runs all
    over a man's body: if simplicity direct us to have no evil, it directs
    us to a happy being; for the subtlest folly proceeds from the
    subtlest wisdom: let me be simply honest.
ANTONIO. I do understand your inside.
BOSOLA. Do you so?
ANTONIO. Because you would not seem to appear to th' world
    Puff'd up with your preferment, you continue
    This out-of-fashion melancholy: leave it, leave it.
BOSOLA. Give me leave to be honest in any phrase, in any compliment
    whatsoever. Shall I confess myself to you? I look no higher than I
    can reach: they are the gods that must ride on winged horses. A
    lawyer's mule of a slow pace will both suit my disposition and
    business; for, mark me, when a man's mind rides faster than his
    horse can gallop, they quickly both tire.
ANTONIO. You would look up to heaven, but I think

---

[34] Blue like those of a woman with child.
[35] Scurf.

The devil, that rules i' th' air, stands in your light.

BOSOLA. O, sir, you are lord of the ascendant,[36] chief man with the
duchess: a duke was your cousin-german remov'd. Say you were
lineally descended from King Pepin, or he himself, what of this?
Search the heads of the greatest rivers in the world, you shall find
them but bubbles of water. Some would think the souls of princes
were brought forth by some more weighty cause than those of
meaner persons: they are deceiv'd, there's the same hand to them;
the like passions sway them; the same reason that makes a vicar go
to law for a tithe-pig, and undo his neighbours, makes them spoil a
whole province, and batter down goodly cities with the cannon.

[*Enter* DUCHESS *and* LADIES.]

DUCHESS. Your arm, Antonio: do I not grow fat?
    I am exceeding short-winded.—Bosola,
    I would have you, sir, provide for me a litter;
    Such a one as the Duchess of Florence rode in.

BOSOLA. The duchess us'd one when she was great with child.

DUCHESS. I think she did.—Come hither, mend my ruff:
    Here, when? thou art such a tedious lady; and
    Thy breath smells of lemon-pills: would thou hadst done!
    Shall I swoon under thy fingers? I am
    So troubled with the mother![37]

BOSOLA. [*aside.*] I fear too much.

DUCHESS. I have heard you say that the French courtiers
    Wear their hats on 'fore that king.

ANTONIO. I have seen it.

DUCHESS. In the presence?

ANTONIO. Yes.

DUCHESS. Why should not we bring up that fashion?
    'Tis ceremony more than duty that consists
    In the removing of a piece of felt.
    Be you the example to the rest o' th' court;
    Put on your hat first.

ANTONIO. You must pardon me:
    I have seen, in colder countries than in France,
    Nobles stand bare to th' prince; and the distinction
    Methought show'd reverently.

BOSOLA. I have a present for your grace.

DUCHESS. For me, sir?

BOSOLA. Apricocks, madam.

---

[36] Person of highest influence.
[37] Hysteria.

DUCHESS. O, sir, where are they?
     I have heard of none to-year[38]
BOSOLA. [*aside.*] Good; her colour rises.
DUCHESS. Indeed, I thank you: they are wondrous fair ones.
     What an unskilful fellow is our gardener!
     We shall have none this month.
BOSOLA. Will not your grace pare them?
DUCHESS. No: they taste of musk, methinks; indeed they do.
BOSOLA. I know not: yet I wish your grace had par'd 'em.
DUCHESS. Why?
BOSOLA. I forgot to tell you, the knave gardener,
     Only to raise his profit by them the sooner,
     Did ripen them in horse-dung.
DUCHESS. O, you jest.—
     You shall judge: pray, taste one.
ANTONIO. Indeed, madam,
     I do not love the fruit.
DUCHESS. Sir, you are loth
     To rob us of our dainties. 'Tis a delicate fruit;
     They say they are restorative.
BOSOLA. 'Tis a pretty art,
     This grafting.
DUCHESS. 'Tis so; a bettering of nature.
BOSOLA. To make a pippin grow upon a crab,
     A damson on a black-thorn.—[*aside.*] How greedily she eats them!
     A whirlwind strike off these bawd farthingales!
     For, but for that and the loose-bodied gown,
     I should have discover'd apparently[39]
     The young springal[40] cutting a caper in her belly.
DUCHESS. I thank you, Bosola: they were right good ones,
     If they do not make me sick.
ANTONIO. How now, madam!
DUCHESS. This green fruit and my stomach are not friends:
     How they swell me!
BOSOLA. [*aside.*] Nay, you are too much swell'd already.
DUCHESS. O, I am in an extreme cold sweat!
BOSOLA. I am very sorry. [*Exit.*]
DUCHESS. Lights to my chamber!—O good Antonio,
     I fear I am undone!
DELIO. Lights there, lights!

---

[38] This year.
[39] Clearly.
[40] Youngster.

[*Exeunt* DUCHESS *and* LADIES.]

ANTONIO. O my most trusty Delio, we are lost!
    I fear she's fall'n in labour; and there's left
    No time for her remove.
DELIO. Have you prepar'd
    Those ladies to attend her; and procur'd
    That politic safe conveyance for the midwife
    Your duchess plotted?
ANTONIO. I have.
DELIO. Make use, then, of this forc'd occasion.
    Give out that Bosola hath poison'd her
    With these apricocks; that will give some colour
    For her keeping close.
ANTONIO. Fie, fie, the physicians
    Will then flock to her.
DELIO. For that you may pretend
    She'll use some prepar'd antidote of her own,
    Lest the physicians should re-poison her.
ANTONIO. I am lost in amazement: I know not what to think on 't.

[*Exeunt.*]

    SCENE II. *Malfi. An hall in the palace of the* DUCHESS.

[*Enter* BOSOLA *and* OLD LADY.]

BOSOLA. So, so, there's no question but her techiness[41] and most
    vulturous eating of the apricocks are apparent signs of breeding,
    now?
OLD LADY. I am in haste, sir.
BOSOLA. There was a young waiting-woman had a monstrous desire to
    see the glass-house——
OLD LADY. Nay, pray, let me go. I will hear no more of the glass-
    house. You are still[42] abusing women!
BOSOLA. Who, I? No; only, by the way now and then, mention your
    frailties. The orange-tree bears ripe and green fruit and blossoms
    all together; and some of you give entertainment for pure love, but
    more for more precious reward. The lusty spring smells well; but
    drooping autumn tastes well. If we have the same golden showers
    that rained in the time of Jupiter the thunderer, you have the same
    Danaes still, to hold up their laps to receive them. Didst thou never

---

[41] Crossness.
[42] Always.

study the mathematics?

OLD LADY. What's that, sir?

BOSOLA. Why, to know the trick how to make a many lines meet in one
centre. Go, go, give your foster-daughters good counsel: tell them,
that the devil takes delight to hang at a woman's girdle, like a false
rusty watch, that she cannot discern how the time passes. [*Exit*
OLD LADY.]

[*Enter* ANTONIO, RODERIGO, *and* GRISOLAN.]

ANTONIO. Shut up the court-gates.

RODERIGO. Why, sir? What's the danger?

ANTONIO. Shut up the posterns presently, and call
    All the officers o' th' court.

GRISOLAN. I shall instantly. [*Exit.*]

ANTONIO. Who keeps the key o' th' park-gate?

RODERIGO. Forobosco.

ANTONIO. Let him bring 't presently.

[*Re-enter* GRISOLAN *with* SERVANTS.]

FIRST SERVANT. O, gentleman o' th' court, the foulest treason!

BOSOLA. [*aside.*] If that these apricocks should be poison'd now,
    Without my knowledge?

FIRST SERVANT.
    There was taken even now a Switzer in the duchess' bed-
chamber——

SECOND SERVANT. A Switzer!

FIRST SERVANT. With a pistol——

SECOND SERVANT. There was a cunning traitor!

FIRST SERVANT.
    And all the moulds of his buttons were leaden bullets.

SECOND SERVANT. O wicked cannibal!

FIRST SERVANT. 'Twas a French plot, upon my life.

SECOND SERVANT. To see what the devil can do!

ANTONIO. [Are] all the officers here?

SERVANTS. We are.

ANTONIO. Gentlemen,
    We have lost much plate, you know; and but this evening
    Jewels, to the value of four thousand ducats,
    Are missing in the duchess' cabinet.
    Are the gates shut?

SERVANT. Yes.

ANTONIO. 'Tis the duchess' pleasure
    Each officer be lock'd into his chamber

Till the sun-rising; and to send the keys
Of all their chests and of their outward doors
Into her bed-chamber. She is very sick.

RODERIGO. At her pleasure.

ANTONIO. She entreats you take 't not ill: the innocent
Shall be the more approv'd by it.

BOSOLA. Gentlemen o' the wood-yard, where's your Switzer now?

FIRST SERVANT. By this hand, 'twas credibly reported by one o' the
black guard.[43]

[*Exeunt all except* ANTONIO *and* DELIO.]

DELIO. How fares it with the duchess?

ANTONIO. She's expos'd
Unto the worst of torture, pain, and fear.

DELIO. Speak to her all happy comfort.

ANTONIO. How I do play the fool with mine own danger!
You are this night, dear friend, to post to Rome:
My life lies in your service.

DELIO. Do not doubt me.

ANTONIO. O, 'tis far from me: and yet fear presents me
Somewhat that looks like danger.

DELIO. Believe it,
'Tis but the shadow of your fear, no more:
How superstitiously we mind our evils!
The throwing down salt, or crossing of a hare,
Bleeding at nose, the stumbling of a horse,
Or singing of a cricket, are of power
To daunt whole man in us. Sir, fare you well:
I wish you all the joys of a bless'd father;
And, for my faith, lay this unto your breast,—
Old friends, like old swords, still are trusted best. [*Exit.*]

[*Enter* CARIOLA.]

CARIOLA. Sir, you are the happy father of a son:
Your wife commends him to you.

ANTONIO. Blessed comfort!—
For heaven' sake, tend her well: I'll presently[44]
Go set a figure for's nativity.[45]

---

[43] The meaner servants.

[44] At once.

[45] Cast his horoscope.

[*Exeunt.*]

SCENE III. *Malfi. The court in the palace of the* DUCHESS.

[*Enter* BOSOLA, *with a dark lantern.*]

BOSOLA. Sure I did hear a woman shriek: list, ha!
  And the sound came, if I receiv'd it right,
  From the duchess' lodgings. There's some stratagem
  In the confining all our courtiers
  To their several wards: I must have part of it;
  My intelligence will freeze else. List, again!
  It may be 'twas the melancholy bird,
  Best friend of silence and of solitariness,
  The owl, that screamed so.—Ha! Antonio!

[*Enter* ANTONIO *with a candle, his sword drawn.*]

ANTONIO. I heard some noise.—Who's there? What art thou? Speak.
BOSOLA. Antonio, put not your face nor body
  To such a forc'd expression of fear;
  I am Bosola, your friend.
ANTONIO. Bosola!—
  [*aside.*] This mole does undermine me.—Heard you not
  A noise even now?
BOSOLA. From whence?
ANTONIO. From the duchess' lodging.
BOSOLA. Not I: did you?
ANTONIO. I did, or else I dream'd.
BOSOLA. Let's walk towards it.
ANTONIO. No: it may be 'twas
  But the rising of the wind.
BOSOLA. Very likely.
  Methinks 'tis very cold, and yet you sweat:
  You look wildly.
ANTONIO. I have been setting a figure[46]
  For the duchess' jewels.
BOSOLA. Ah, and how falls your question?
  Do you find it radical?[47]
ANTONIO. What's that to you?
  'Tis rather to be question'd what design,
  When all men were commanded to their lodgings,

---

[46] Making an astrological calculation.
[47] Going to the root of the matter.

Makes you a night-walker.

BOSOLA. In sooth, I'll tell you:

Now all the court's asleep, I thought the devil

Had least to do here; I came to say my prayers;

And if it do offend you I do so,

You are a fine courtier.

ANTONIO. [*aside.*] This fellow will undo me.—

You gave the duchess apricocks to-day:

Pray heaven they were not poison'd!

BOSOLA. Poison'd! a Spanish fig

For the imputation!

ANTONIO. Traitors are ever confident

Till they are discover'd. There were jewels stol'n too:

In my conceit, none are to be suspected

More than yourself.

BOSOLA. You are a false steward.

ANTONIO. Saucy slave, I'll pull thee up by the roots.

BOSOLA. May be the ruin will crush you to pieces.

ANTONIO. You are an impudent snake indeed, sir:

Are you scarce warm, and do you show your sting?

You libel[48] well, sir?

BOSOLA. No, sir: copy it out,

And I will set my hand to 't.

ANTONIO. [*aside.*] My nose bleeds.

One that were superstitious would count

This ominous, when it merely comes by chance.

Two letters, that are wrought here for my name,[49]

Are drown'd in blood!

Mere accident.—For you, sir, I'll take order

I' the morn you shall be safe.—[*aside.*] 'Tis that must colour

Her lying-in.—Sir, this door you pass not:

I do not hold it fit that you come near

The duchess' lodgings, till you have quit yourself.—

[*aside.*] The great are like the base, nay, they are the same,

When they seek shameful ways to avoid shame. [*Exit.*]

BOSOLA. Antonio hereabout did drop a paper:— Some of your help, false friend.[50]—O, here it is. What's here? a child's nativity calculated! [*Reads.*] 'The duchess was deliver'd of a son, 'tween the hours twelve and one in the night, Anno Dom. 1504,'—that's this year—'decimo nono Decembris,'—that's this night—'taken according to the meridian of Malfi,'—that's our duchess: happy

---

[48] Write.

[49] i.e., on his handkerchief.

[50] Addressing the lantern.

discovery!—'The lord of the first house being combust in the
ascendant, signifies short life; and Mars being in a human sign,
joined to the tail of the Dragon, in the eighth house, doth threaten a
violent death. Caetera non scrutantur.'[51]

    Why, now 'tis most apparent; this precise fellow
Is the duchess' bawd:—I have it to my wish!
This is a parcel of intelligency[52]
Our courtiers were cas'd up for: it needs must follow
That I must be committed on pretence
Of poisoning her; which I'll endure, and laugh at.
If one could find the father now! but that
Time will discover. Old Castruccio
I' th' morning posts to Rome: by him I'll send
A letter that shall make her brothers' galls
O'erflow their livers. This was a thrifty[53] way!
Though lust do mask in ne'er so strange disguise,
She's oft found witty, but is never wise. [*Exit.*]

SCENE IV. *Rome. An apartment in the palace of the* CARDINAL.

[*Enter* CARDINAL *and* JULIA.]

CARDINAL. Sit: thou art my best of wishes. Prithee, tell me
    What trick didst thou invent to come to Rome
    Without thy husband?
JULIA. Why, my lord, I told him
    I came to visit an old anchorite[54]
    Here for devotion.
CARDINAL. Thou art a witty false one,—
    I mean, to him.
JULIA. You have prevail'd with me
    Beyond my strongest thoughts; I would not now
    Find you inconstant.
CARDINAL. Do not put thyself
    To such a voluntary torture, which proceeds
    Out of your own guilt.
JULIA. How, my lord!
CARDINAL. You fear
    My constancy, because you have approv'd[55]
    Those giddy and wild turnings in yourself.

---

[51] "The rest not considered."

[52] A piece of news.

[53] Cleverly contrived.

[54] Religious recluse.

[55] Experienced.

JULIA. Did you e'er find them?

CARDINAL. Sooth, generally for women,
    A man might strive to make glass malleable,
    Ere he should make them fixed.

JULIA. So, my lord.

CARDINAL. We had need go borrow that fantastic glass
    Invented by Galileo the Florentine
    To view another spacious world i' th' moon,
    And look to find a constant woman there.

JULIA. This is very well, my lord.

CARDINAL. Why do you weep?
    Are tears your justification? The self-same tears
    Will fall into your husband's bosom, lady,
    With a loud protestation that you love him
    Above the world. Come, I'll love you wisely,
    That's jealously; since I am very certain
    You cannot make me cuckold.

JULIA. I'll go home
    To my husband.

CARDINAL. You may thank me, lady,
    I have taken you off your melancholy perch,
    Bore you upon my fist, and show'd you game,
    And let you fly at it.—I pray thee, kiss me.—
    When thou wast with thy husband, thou wast watch'd
    Like a tame elephant:—still you are to thank me:—
    Thou hadst only kisses from him and high feeding;
    But what delight was that? 'Twas just like one
    That hath a little fing'ring on the lute,
    Yet cannot tune it:—still you are to thank me.

JULIA. You told me of a piteous wound i' th' heart,
    And a sick liver, when you woo'd me first,
    And spake like one in physic.[56]

CARDINAL. Who's that?——

[*Enter* SERVANT.]

    Rest firm, for my affection to thee,
    Lightning moves slow to 't.

SERVANT. Madam, a gentleman,
    That's come post from Malfi, desires to see you.

CARDINAL. Let him enter: I'll withdraw. [*Exit.*]

SERVANT. He says
    Your husband, old Castruccio, is come to Rome,

---

[56] Sick.

Most pitifully tir'd with riding post. [*Exit.*]

[*Enter* DELIO.]

JULIA. [*aside.*] Signior Delio! 'tis one of my old suitors.
DELIO. I was bold to come and see you.
JULIA. Sir, you are welcome.
DELIO. Do you lie here?
JULIA. Sure, your own experience
    Will satisfy you no: our Roman prelates
    Do not keep lodging for ladies.
DELIO. Very well:
    I have brought you no commendations from your husband,
    For I know none by him.
JULIA. I hear he's come to Rome.
DELIO. I never knew man and beast, of a horse and a knight,
    So weary of each other. If he had had a good back,
    He would have undertook to have borne his horse,
    His breech was so pitifully sore.
JULIA. Your laughter
    Is my pity.
DELIO. Lady, I know not whether
    You want money, but I have brought you some.
JULIA. From my husband?
DELIO. No, from mine own allowance.
JULIA. I must hear the condition, ere I be bound to take it.
DELIO. Look on 't, 'tis gold; hath it not a fine colour?
JULIA. I have a bird more beautiful.
DELIO. Try the sound on 't.
JULIA. A lute-string far exceeds it.
    It hath no smell, like cassia or civet;
    Nor is it physical,[57] though some fond doctors
    Persuade us seethe 't in cullises.[58] I'll tell you,
    This is a creature bred by——

[*Re-enter* SERVANT.]

SERVANT. Your husband's come,
    Hath deliver'd a letter to the Duke of Calabria
    That, to my thinking, hath put him out of his wits. [*Exit.*]
JULIA. Sir, you hear:
    Pray, let me know your business and your suit

---

[57] Medicinal.
[58] Strong broth.

As briefly as can be.

DELIO. With good speed: I would wish you,
    At such time as you are non-resident
    With your husband, my mistress.

JULIA. Sir, I'll go ask my husband if I shall,
    And straight return your answer. [*Exit.*]

DELIO. Very fine!
    Is this her wit, or honesty, that speaks thus?
    I heard one say the duke was highly mov'd
    With a letter sent from Malfi. I do fear
    Antonio is betray'd. How fearfully
    Shows his ambition now! Unfortunate fortune!
    They pass through whirl-pools, and deep woes do shun,
    Who the event weigh ere the action's done. [*Exit.*]

SCENE V. *Rome. Another apartment in the palace of the* CARDINAL.

[*Enter* CARDINAL *and* FERDINAND *with a letter.*]

FERDINAND. I have this night digg'd up a mandrake.[59]

CARDINAL. Say you?

FERDINAND. And I am grown mad with 't.

CARDINAL. What's the prodigy?

FERDINAND.
    Read there,—a sister damn'd: she's loose i' the hilts;[60]
    Grown a notorious strumpet.

CARDINAL. Speak lower.

FERDINAND. Lower!
    Rogues do not whisper 't now, but seek to publish 't
    (As servants do the bounty of their lords)
    Aloud; and with a covetous searching eye,
    To mark who note them. O, confusion seize her!
    She hath had most cunning bawds to serve her turn,
    And more secure conveyances for lust
    Than towns of garrison for service.

CARDINAL. Is 't possible?
    Can this be certain?

FERDINAND. Rhubarb, O, for rhubarb
    To purge this choler! Here's the cursed day
    To prompt my memory; and here 't shall stick
    Till of her bleeding heart I make a sponge

---

[59] The mandrake was supposed to give forth shrieks when uprooted, which drove the hearer mad.

[60] Unchaste.

    To wipe it out.
CARDINAL. Why do you make yourself
    So wild a tempest?
FERDINAND. Would I could be one,
    That I might toss her palace 'bout her ears,
    Root up her goodly forests, blast her meads,
    And lay her general territory as waste
    As she hath done her honours.
CARDINAL. Shall our blood,
    The royal blood of Arragon and Castile,
    Be thus attainted?
FERDINAND. Apply desperate physic:
    We must not now use balsamum, but fire,
    The smarting cupping-glass, for that's the mean
    To purge infected blood, such blood as hers.
    There is a kind of pity in mine eye,—
    I'll give it to my handkercher; and now 'tis here,
    I'll bequeath this to her bastard.
CARDINAL. What to do?
FERDINAND. Why, to make soft lint for his mother's wounds,
    When I have hew'd her to pieces.
CARDINAL. Curs'd creature!
    Unequal nature, to place women's hearts
    So far upon the left side![61]
FERDINAND. Foolish men,
    That e'er will trust their honour in a bark
    Made of so slight weak bulrush as is woman,
    Apt every minute to sink it!
CARDINAL. Thus ignorance, when it hath purchas'd honour,
    It cannot wield it.
FERDINAND. Methinks I see her laughing,—
    Excellent hyena! Talk to me somewhat quickly,
    Or my imagination will carry me
    To see her in the shameful act of sin.
CARDINAL. With whom?
FERDINAND. Happily with some strong-thigh'd bargeman,
    Or one o' th' wood-yard that can quoit the sledge[62]
    Or toss the bar, or else some lovely squire
    That carries coals up to her privy lodgings.
CARDINAL. You fly beyond your reason.
FERDINAND. Go to, mistress!
    'Tis not your whore's milk that shall quench my wild-fire,

---

[61] Supposed to be a sign of folly.
[62] Throw the hammer.

But your whore's blood.

CARDINAL. How idly shows this rage, which carries you,
  As men convey'd by witches through the air,
  On violent whirlwinds! This intemperate noise
  Fitly resembles deaf men's shrill discourse,
  Who talk aloud, thinking all other men
  To have their imperfection.

FERDINAND. Have not you
  My palsy?

CARDINAL. Yes, [but] I can be angry
  Without this rupture. There is not in nature
  A thing that makes man so deform'd, so beastly,
  As doth intemperate anger. Chide yourself.
  You have divers men who never yet express'd
  Their strong desire of rest but by unrest,
  By vexing of themselves. Come, put yourself
  In tune.

FERDINAND. So I will only study to seem
  The thing I am not. I could kill her now,
  In you, or in myself; for I do think
  It is some sin in us heaven doth revenge
  By her.

CARDINAL. Are you stark mad?

FERDINAND. I would have their bodies
  Burnt in a coal-pit with the ventage stopp'd,
  That their curs'd smoke might not ascend to heaven;
  Or dip the sheets they lie in in pitch or sulphur,
  Wrap them in 't, and then light them like a match;
  Or else to-boil[63] their bastard to a cullis,
  And give 't his lecherous father to renew
  The sin of his back.

CARDINAL. I'll leave you.

FERDINAND. Nay, I have done.
  I am confident, had I been damn'd in hell,
  And should have heard of this, it would have put me
  Into a cold sweat. In, in; I'll go sleep.
  Till I know who [loves] my sister, I'll not stir:
  That known, I'll find scorpions to string my whips,
  And fix her in a general eclipse.

  [*Exeunt.*]

---

[63] Boil to shreds. (Dyce.) Qq, TO BOIL.

ACT III.

SCENE I. *Malfi. An apartment in the palace of the* DUCHESS.

[*Enter* ANTONIO *and* DELIO.]

ANTONIO. Our noble friend, my most beloved Delio!
    O, you have been a stranger long at court:
    Came you along with the Lord Ferdinand?
DELIO. I did, sir: and how fares your noble duchess?
ANTONIO. Right fortunately well: she's an excellent
    Feeder of pedigrees; since you last saw her,
    She hath had two children more, a son and daughter.
DELIO. Methinks 'twas yesterday. Let me but wink,
    And not behold your face, which to mine eye
    Is somewhat leaner, verily I should dream
    It were within this half hour.
ANTONIO. You have not been in law, friend Delio,
    Nor in prison, nor a suitor at the court,
    Nor begg'd the reversion of some great man's place,
    Nor troubled with an old wife, which doth make
    Your time so insensibly hasten.
DELIO. Pray, sir, tell me,
    Hath not this news arriv'd yet to the ear
    Of the lord cardinal?
ANTONIO. I fear it hath:
    The Lord Ferdinand, that's newly come to court,
    Doth bear himself right dangerously.
DELIO. Pray, why?
ANTONIO. He is so quiet that he seems to sleep
    The tempest out, as dormice do in winter.
    Those houses that are haunted are most still
    Till the devil be up.
DELIO. What say the common people?
ANTONIO. The common rabble do directly say
    She is a strumpet.
DELIO. And your graver heads
    Which would be politic, what censure they?
ANTONIO. They do observe I grow to infinite purchase,[64]
    The left hand way; and all suppose the duchess
    Would amend it, if she could; for, say they,
    Great princes, though they grudge their officers

---

[64] Wealth.

Should have such large and unconfined means
To get wealth under them, will not complain,
Lest thereby they should make them odious
Unto the people. For other obligation
Of love or marriage between her and me
They never dream of.
DELIO. The Lord Ferdinand
    Is going to bed.

[*Enter* DUCHESS, FERDINAND, *and* ATTENDANTS.]

FERDINAND. I'll instantly to bed,
    For I am weary.—I am to bespeak
    A husband for you.
DUCHESS. For me, sir! Pray, who is 't?
FERDINAND. The great Count Malatesti.
DUCHESS. Fie upon him!
    A count! He's a mere stick of sugar-candy;
    You may look quite through him. When I choose
    A husband, I will marry for your honour.
FERDINAND. You shall do well in 't.—How is 't, worthy Antonio?
DUCHESS. But, sir, I am to have private conference with you
    About a scandalous report is spread
    Touching mine honour.
FERDINAND. Let me be ever deaf to 't:
    One of Pasquil's paper-bullets,[65] court-calumny,
    A pestilent air, which princes' palaces
    Are seldom purg'd of. Yet, say that it were true,
    I pour it in your bosom, my fix'd love
    Would strongly excuse, extenuate, nay, deny
    Faults, were they apparent in you. Go, be safe
    In your own innocency.
DUCHESS. [*aside.*] O bless'd comfort!
    This deadly air is purg'd.

[*Exeunt* DUCHESS, ANTONIO, DELIO, *and* ATTENDANTS.]

FERDINAND. Her guilt treads on
    Hot-burning coulters.[66]

[*Enter* BOSOLA.]

---

[65] Lampoons.
[66] Plowshares.

Now, Bosola,
How thrives our intelligence?[67]

BOSOLA. Sir, uncertainly:
'Tis rumour'd she hath had three bastards, but
By whom we may go read i' the stars.

FERDINAND. Why, some
Hold opinion all things are written there.

BOSOLA. Yes, if we could find spectacles to read them.
I do suspect there hath been some sorcery
Us'd on the duchess.

FERDINAND. Sorcery! to what purpose?

BOSOLA. To make her dote on some desertless fellow
She shames to acknowledge.

FERDINAND. Can your faith give way
To think there's power in potions or in charms,
To make us love whether we will or no?

BOSOLA. Most certainly.

FERDINAND. Away! these are mere gulleries,[68] horrid things,
Invented by some cheating mountebanks
To abuse us. Do you think that herbs or charms
Can force the will? Some trials have been made
In this foolish practice, but the ingredients
Were lenitive[69] poisons, such as are of force
To make the patient mad; and straight the witch
Swears by equivocation they are in love.
The witch-craft lies in her rank blood. This night
I will force confession from her. You told me
You had got, within these two days, a false key
Into her bed-chamber.

BOSOLA. I have.

FERDINAND. As I would wish.

BOSOLA. What do you intend to do?

FERDINAND. Can you guess?

BOSOLA. No.

FERDINAND. Do not ask, then:
He that can compass me, and know my drifts,
May say he hath put a girdle 'bout the world,
And sounded all her quick-sands.

BOSOLA. I do not
Think so.

FERDINAND. What do you think, then, pray?

---

[67] Spying.
[68] Deceptions.
[69] Soothing.

BOSOLA. That you
    Are your own chronicle too much, and grossly
    Flatter yourself.
FERDINAND. Give me thy hand; I thank thee:
    I never gave pension but to flatterers,
    Till I entertained thee. Farewell.
    That friend a great man's ruin strongly checks,
    Who rails into his belief all his defects.

    [*Exeunt.*]

        SCENE II. *Malfi. The bed-chamber in the apartment
            of the palace of the* DUCHESS.

[*Enter* DUCHESS, ANTONIO, *and* CARIOLA.]

DUCHESS. Bring me the casket hither, and the glass.—
    You get no lodging here to-night, my lord.
ANTONIO. Indeed, I must persuade one.
DUCHESS. Very good:
    I hope in time 'twill grow into a custom,
    That noblemen shall come with cap and knee
    To purchase a night's lodging of their wives.
ANTONIO. I must lie here.
DUCHESS. Must! You are a lord of mis-rule.
ANTONIO. Indeed, my rule is only in the night.
DUCHESS. I'll stop your mouth.

    [*Kisses him.*]

ANTONIO. Nay, that's but one; Venus had two soft doves
    To draw her chariot; I must have another.—

    [*She kisses him again.*]

    When wilt thou marry, Cariola?
CARIOLA. Never, my lord.
ANTONIO. O, fie upon this single life! forgo it.
    We read how Daphne, for her peevish [flight,][70]
    Became a fruitless bay-tree; Syrinx turn'd
    To the pale empty reed; Anaxarete
    Was frozen into marble: whereas those
    Which married, or prov'd kind unto their friends,

---

[70] Qq. read SLIGHT.

> Were by a gracious influence transhap'd
> Into the olive, pomegranate, mulberry,
> Became flowers, precious stones, or eminent stars.

CARIOLA. This is a vain poetry: but I pray you, tell me,
> If there were propos'd me, wisdom, riches, and beauty,
> In three several young men, which should I choose?

ANTONIO. 'Tis a hard question. This was Paris' case,
> And he was blind in 't, and there was a great cause;
> For how was 't possible he could judge right,
> Having three amorous goddesses in view,
> And they stark naked? 'Twas a motion
> Were able to benight the apprehension
> Of the severest counsellor of Europe.
> Now I look on both your faces so well form'd,
> It puts me in mind of a question I would ask.

CARIOLA. What is 't?

ANTONIO. I do wonder why hard-favour'd ladies,
> For the most part, keep worse-favour'd waiting-women
> To attend them, and cannot endure fair ones.

DUCHESS. O, that's soon answer'd.
> Did you ever in your life know an ill painter
> Desire to have his dwelling next door to the shop
> Of an excellent picture-maker? 'Twould disgrace
> His face-making, and undo him. I prithee,
> When were we so merry?—My hair tangles.

ANTONIO. Pray thee, Cariola, let's steal forth the room,
> And let her talk to herself: I have divers times
> Serv'd her the like, when she hath chaf'd extremely.
> I love to see her angry. Softly, Cariola.

[*Exeunt* ANTONIO *and* CARIOLA.]

DUCHESS. Doth not the colour of my hair 'gin to change?
> When I wax gray, I shall have all the court
> Powder their hair with arras,[71] to be like me.
> You have cause to love me; I ent'red you into my heart

[*Enter* FERDINAND *unseen.*]

> Before you would vouchsafe to call for the keys.
> We shall one day have my brothers take you napping.
> Methinks his presence, being now in court,
> Should make you keep your own bed; but you 'll say

---

[71] Powder of orris-root.

Love mix'd with fear is sweetest. I'll assure you,
You shall get no more children till my brothers
Consent to be your gossips. Have you lost your tongue?
'Tis welcome:
For know, whether I am doom'd to live or die,
I can do both like a prince.

FERDINAND. Die, then, quickly!

Giving her a poniard.
Virtue, where art thou hid? What hideous thing
Is it that doth eclipse thee?

DUCHESS. Pray, sir, hear me.

FERDINAND. Or is it true thou art but a bare name,
And no essential thing?

DUCHESS. Sir——

FERDINAND. Do not speak.

DUCHESS. No, sir:
I will plant my soul in mine ears, to hear you.

FERDINAND. O most imperfect light of human reason,
That mak'st [us] so unhappy to foresee
What we can least prevent! Pursue thy wishes,
And glory in them: there's in shame no comfort
But to be past all bounds and sense of shame.

DUCHESS. I pray, sir, hear me: I am married.

FERDINAND. So!

DUCHESS. Happily, not to your liking: but for that,
Alas, your shears do come untimely now
To clip the bird's wings that's already flown!
Will you see my husband?

FERDINAND. Yes, if I could change
Eyes with a basilisk.

DUCHESS. Sure, you came hither
By his confederacy.

FERDINAND. The howling of a wolf
Is music to thee, screech-owl: prithee, peace.—
Whate'er thou art that hast enjoy'd my sister,
For I am sure thou hear'st me, for thine own sake
Let me not know thee. I came hither prepar'd
To work thy discovery; yet am now persuaded
It would beget such violent effects
As would damn us both. I would not for ten millions
I had beheld thee: therefore use all means
I never may have knowledge of thy name;
Enjoy thy lust still, and a wretched life,
On that condition.—And for thee, vile woman,
If thou do wish thy lecher may grow old

In thy embracements, I would have thee build
Such a room for him as our anchorites
To holier use inhabit. Let not the sun
Shine on him till he's dead; let dogs and monkeys
Only converse with him, and such dumb things
To whom nature denies use to sound his name;
Do not keep a paraquito, lest she learn it;
If thou do love him, cut out thine own tongue,
Lest it bewray him.

DUCHESS. Why might not I marry?
I have not gone about in this to create
Any new world or custom.

FERDINAND. Thou art undone;
And thou hast ta'en that massy sheet of lead
That hid thy husband's bones, and folded it
About my heart.

DUCHESS. Mine bleeds for 't.

FERDINAND. Thine! thy heart!
What should I name 't unless a hollow bullet
Fill'd with unquenchable wild-fire?

DUCHESS. You are in this
Too strict; and were you not my princely brother,
I would say, too wilful: my reputation
Is safe.

FERDINAND. Dost thou know what reputation is?
I'll tell thee,—to small purpose, since the instruction
Comes now too late.
Upon a time Reputation, Love, and Death,
Would travel o'er the world; and it was concluded
That they should part, and take three several ways.
Death told them, they should find him in great battles,
Or cities plagu'd with plagues: Love gives them counsel
To inquire for him 'mongst unambitious shepherds,
Where dowries were not talk'd of, and sometimes
'Mongst quiet kindred that had nothing left
By their dead parents:'stay,' quoth Reputation,
'Do not forsake me; for it is my nature,
If once I part from any man I meet,
I am never found again.' And so for you:
You have shook hands with Reputation,
And made him invisible. So, fare you well:
I will never see you more.

DUCHESS. Why should only I,
Of all the other princes of the world,
Be cas'd up, like a holy relic? I have youth

And a little beauty.
FERDINAND. So you have some virgins
    That are witches. I will never see thee more. [*Exit.*]

[*Re-enter* ANTONIO *with a pistol, and* CARIOLA.]

DUCHESS. You saw this apparition?
ANTONIO. Yes: we are
    Betray'd. How came he hither? I should turn
    This to thee, for that.
CARIOLA. Pray, sir, do; and when
    That you have cleft my heart, you shall read there
    Mine innocence.
DUCHESS. That gallery gave him entrance.
ANTONIO. I would this terrible thing would come again,
    That, standing on my guard, I might relate
    My warrantable love.—

[*She shows the poniard.*]

Ha! what means this?
DUCHESS. He left this with me.
ANTONIO. And it seems did wish
    You would use it on yourself.
DUCHESS. His action seem'd
    To intend so much.
ANTONIO. This hath a handle to 't,
    As well as a point: turn it towards him, and
    So fasten the keen edge in his rank gall.

[*Knocking within.*]

How now! who knocks? More earthquakes?
DUCHESS. I stand
    As if a mine beneath my feet were ready
    To be blown up.
CARIOLA. 'Tis Bosola.
DUCHESS. Away!
    O misery! methinks unjust actions
    Should wear these masks and curtains, and not we.
    You must instantly part hence: I have fashion'd it already.

[*Exit* ANTONIO.]

[*Enter* BOSOLA.]

BOSOLA. The duke your brother is ta'en up in a whirlwind;
    Hath took horse, and's rid post to Rome.
DUCHESS. So late?
BOSOLA. He told me, as he mounted into the saddle,
    You were undone.
DUCHESS. Indeed, I am very near it.
BOSOLA. What's the matter?
DUCHESS. Antonio, the master of our household,
    Hath dealt so falsely with me in's accounts.
    My brother stood engag'd with me for money
    Ta'en up of certain Neapolitan Jews,
    And Antonio lets the bonds be forfeit.
BOSOLA. Strange!—[*aside.*] This is cunning.
DUCHESS. And hereupon
    My brother's bills at Naples are protested
    Against.—Call up our officers.
BOSOLA. I shall. [*Exit.*]

[*Re-enter* ANTONIO.]

DUCHESS. The place that you must fly to is Ancona:
    Hire a house there; I'll send after you
    My treasure and my jewels. Our weak safety
    Runs upon enginous wheels:[72] short syllables
    Must stand for periods. I must now accuse you
    Of such a feigned crime as Tasso calls
    Magnanima menzogna, a noble lie,
    'Cause it must shield our honours.—Hark! they are coming.

[*Re-enter* BOSOLA *and* OFFICERS.]

ANTONIO. Will your grace hear me?
DUCHESS. I have got well by you; you have yielded me
    A million of loss: I am like to inherit
    The people's curses for your stewardship.
    You had the trick in audit-time to be sick,
    Till I had sign'd your quietus;[73] and that cur'd you
    Without help of a doctor.—Gentlemen,
    I would have this man be an example to you all;
    So shall you hold my favour; I pray, let him;
    For h'as done that, alas, you would not think of,

---

[72] Wheels of craft.
[73] Certificate that the books were found correct.

And, because I intend to be rid of him,
I mean not to publish.—Use your fortune elsewhere.
ANTONIO. I am strongly arm'd to brook my overthrow,
As commonly men bear with a hard year.
I will not blame the cause on 't; but do think
The necessity of my malevolent star
Procures this, not her humour. O, the inconstant
And rotten ground of service! You may see,
'Tis even like him, that in a winter night,
Takes a long slumber o'er a dying fire,
A-loth to part from 't; yet parts thence as cold
As when he first sat down.
DUCHESS. We do confiscate,
Towards the satisfying of your accounts,
All that you have.
ANTONIO. I am all yours; and 'tis very fit
All mine should be so.
DUCHESS. So, sir, you have your pass.
ANTONIO. You may see, gentlemen, what 'tis to serve
A prince with body and soul. [*Exit.*]
BOSOLA. Here's an example for extortion: what moisture is drawn out
of the sea, when foul weather comes, pours down, and runs into the
sea again.
DUCHESS. I would know what are your opinions
Of this Antonio.
SECOND OFFICER. He could not abide to see a pig's head gaping:
I thought your grace would find him a Jew.
THIRD OFFICER. I would you had been his officer, for your own sake.
FOURTH OFFICER. You would have had more money.
FIRST OFFICER. He stopped his ears with black wool, and to those
came to him for money said he was thick of hearing.
SECOND OFFICER. Some said he was an hermaphrodite, for he could
not abide a woman.
FOURTH OFFICER. How scurvy proud he would look when the treasury
was full! Well, let him go.
FIRST OFFICER. Yes, and the chippings of the buttery fly after him, to
scour his gold chain.[74]
DUCHESS. Leave us.

[*Exeunt* OFFICERS.]

What do you think of these?
BOSOLA. That these are rogues that in's prosperity,

---

[74] The badge of a steward.

But to have waited on his fortune, could have wish'd
His dirty stirrup riveted through their noses,
And follow'd after's mule, like a bear in a ring;
Would have prostituted their daughters to his lust;
Made their first-born intelligencers;[75] thought none happy
But such as were born under his blest planet,
And wore his livery: and do these lice drop off now?
Well, never look to have the like again:
He hath left a sort[76] of flattering rogues behind him;
Their doom must follow. Princes pay flatterers
In their own money: flatterers dissemble their vices,
And they dissemble their lies; that's justice.
Alas, poor gentleman!

DUCHESS. Poor! he hath amply fill'd his coffers.

BOSOLA. Sure, he was too honest. Pluto,[77] the god of riches,
When he's sent by Jupiter to any man,
He goes limping, to signify that wealth
That comes on God's name comes slowly; but when he's sent
On the devil's errand, he rides post and comes in by scuttles.[78]
Let me show you what a most unvalu'd jewel
You have in a wanton humour thrown away,
To bless the man shall find him. He was an excellent
Courtier and most faithful; a soldier that thought it
As beastly to know his own value too little
As devilish to acknowledge it too much.
Both his virtue and form deserv'd a far better fortune:
His discourse rather delighted to judge itself than show itself:
His breast was fill'd with all perfection,
And yet it seemed a private whisp'ring-room,
It made so little noise of 't.

DUCHESS. But he was basely descended.

BOSOLA. Will you make yourself a mercenary herald,
Rather to examine men's pedigrees than virtues?
You shall want[79] him:
For know an honest statesman to a prince
Is like a cedar planted by a spring;
The spring bathes the tree's root, the grateful tree
Rewards it with his shadow: you have not done so.
I would sooner swim to the Bermoothes on
Two politicians' rotten bladders, tied

---

[75] Spies.
[76] Lot.
[77] For Plutus.
[78] Quick steps.
[79] Miss.

Together with an intelligencer's heart-string,
Than depend on so changeable a prince's favour.
Fare thee well, Antonio! Since the malice of the world
Would needs down with thee, it cannot be said yet
That any ill happen'd unto thee, considering thy fall
Was accompanied with virtue.

DUCHESS. O, you render me excellent music!

BOSOLA. Say you?

DUCHESS. This good one that you speak of is my husband.

BOSOLA. Do I not dream? Can this ambitious age
Have so much goodness in 't as to prefer
A man merely for worth, without these shadows
Of wealth and painted honours? Possible?

DUCHESS. I have had three children by him.

BOSOLA. Fortunate lady!
For you have made your private nuptial bed
The humble and fair seminary of peace,
No question but: many an unbenefic'd scholar
Shall pray for you for this deed, and rejoice
That some preferment in the world can yet
Arise from merit. The virgins of your land
That have no dowries shall hope your example
Will raise them to rich husbands. Should you want
Soldiers, 'twould make the very Turks and Moors
Turn Christians, and serve you for this act.
Last, the neglected poets of your time,
In honour of this trophy of a man,
Rais'd by that curious engine, your white hand,
Shall thank you, in your grave, for 't; and make that
More reverend than all the cabinets
Of living princes. For Antonio,
His fame shall likewise flow from many a pen,
When heralds shall want coats to sell to men.

DUCHESS. As I taste comfort in this friendly speech,
So would I find concealment.

BOSOLA. O, the secret of my prince,
Which I will wear on th' inside of my heart!

DUCHESS. You shall take charge of all my coin and jewels,
And follow him; for he retires himself
To Ancona.

BOSOLA. So.

DUCHESS. Whither, within few days,
I mean to follow thee.

BOSOLA. Let me think:
I would wish your grace to feign a pilgrimage

    To our Lady of Loretto, scarce seven leagues
    From fair Ancona; so may you depart
    Your country with more honour, and your flight
    Will seem a princely progress, retaining
    Your usual train about you.
DUCHESS. Sir, your direction
    Shall lead me by the hand.
CARIOLA. In my opinion,
    She were better progress to the baths at Lucca,
    Or go visit the Spa
    In Germany; for, if you will believe me,
    I do not like this jesting with religion,
    This feigned pilgrimage.
DUCHESS. Thou art a superstitious fool:
    Prepare us instantly for our departure.
    Past sorrows, let us moderately lament them,
    For those to come, seek wisely to prevent them.

    [*Exeunt* DUCHESS *and* CARIOLA.]

BOSOLA. A politician is the devil's quilted anvil;
    He fashions all sins on him, and the blows
    Are never heard: he may work in a lady's chamber,
    As here for proof. What rests[80] but I reveal
    All to my lord? O, this base quality[81]
    Of intelligencer! Why, every quality i' the world
    Prefers but gain or commendation:
    Now, for this act I am certain to be rais'd,
    And men that paint weeds to the life are prais'd. [*Exit.*]

    SCENE III. *An apartment in the* CARDINAL's *palace at Rome.*

    [*Enter* CARDINAL, FERDINAND, MALATESTI, PESCARA, DELIO, *and*
      SILVIO.]

CARDINAL. Must we turn soldier, then?
MALATESTI. The emperor,
    Hearing your worth that way, ere you attain'd
    This reverend garment, joins you in commission
    With the right fortunate soldier the Marquis of Pescara,
    And the famous Lannoy.
CARDINAL. He that had the honour

---

[80] Remains.
[81] Profession.

Of taking the French king prisoner?
MALATESTI. The same.
   Here's a plot drawn for a new fortification
   At Naples.
FERDINAND. This great Count Malatesti, I perceive,
   Hath got employment?
DELIO. No employment, my lord;
   A marginal note in the muster-book, that he is
   A voluntary lord.
FERDINAND. He's no soldier.
DELIO. He has worn gun-powder in's hollow tooth for the tooth-ache.
SILVIO. He comes to the leaguer with a full intent
   To eat fresh beef and garlic, means to stay
   Till the scent be gone, and straight return to court.
DELIO. He hath read all the late service
   As the City-Chronicle relates it;
   And keeps two pewterers going, only to express
   Battles in model.
SILVIO. Then he 'll fight by the book.
DELIO. By the almanac, I think,
   To choose good days and shun the critical;
   That's his mistress' scarf.
SILVIO. Yes, he protests
   He would do much for that taffeta.
DELIO. I think he would run away from a battle,
   To save it from taking prisoner.
SILVIO. He is horribly afraid
   Gun-powder will spoil the perfume on 't.
DELIO. I saw a Dutchman break his pate once
   For calling him pot-gun; he made his head
   Have a bore in 't like a musket.
SILVIO. I would he had made a touch-hole to 't.
   He is indeed a guarded sumpter-cloth,[82]
   Only for the remove of the court.

   [*Enter* BOSOLA.]

PESCARA. Bosola arriv'd! What should be the business?
   Some falling-out amongst the cardinals.
   These factions amongst great men, they are like
   Foxes, when their heads are divided,
   They carry fire in their tails, and all the country
   About them goes to wrack for 't.

---

[82] A decorated horse-cloth, used only when the court is traveling.

SILVIO. What's that Bosola?

DELIO. I knew him in Padua,—a fantastical scholar, like such who study to know how many knots was in Hercules' club, of what colour Achilles' beard was, or whether Hector were not troubled with the tooth-ache. He hath studied himself half blear-eyed to know the true symmetry of Caesar's nose by a shoeing-horn; and this he did to gain the name of a speculative man.

PESCARA. Mark Prince Ferdinand:
A very salamander lives in's eye,
To mock the eager violence of fire.

SILVIO. That cardinal hath made more bad faces with his oppression than ever Michael Angelo made good ones. He lifts up's nose, like a foul porpoise before a storm.

PESCARA. The Lord Ferdinand laughs.

DELIO. Like a deadly cannon
That lightens ere it smokes.

PESCARA. These are your true pangs of death,
The pangs of life, that struggle with great statesmen.

DELIO. In such a deformed silence witches whisper their charms.

CARDINAL. Doth she make religion her riding-hood
To keep her from the sun and tempest?

FERDINAND. That, that damns her. Methinks her fault and beauty,
Blended together, show like leprosy,
The whiter, the fouler. I make it a question
Whether her beggarly brats were ever christ'ned.

CARDINAL. I will instantly solicit the state of Ancona
To have them banish'd.

FERDINAND. You are for Loretto:
I shall not be at your ceremony; fare you well.—
Write to the Duke of Malfi, my young nephew
She had by her first husband, and acquaint him
With's mother's honesty.

BOSOLA. I will.

FERDINAND. Antonio!
A slave that only smell'd of ink and counters,
And never in's life look'd like a gentleman,
But in the audit-time.—Go, go presently,
Draw me out an hundred and fifty of our horse,
And meet me at the foot-bridge.

[*Exeunt.*]

SCENE IV.

[*Enter* TWO PILGRIMS *to the Shrine of our Lady of Loretto.*

FIRST PILGRIM. I have not seen a goodlier shrine than this;
Yet I have visited many.
SECOND PILGRIM. The Cardinal of Arragon
Is this day to resign his cardinal's hat:
His sister duchess likewise is arriv'd
To pay her vow of pilgrimage. I expect
A noble ceremony.
FIRST PILGRIM. No question.—They come.

[*Here the ceremony of the* CARDINAL's *installment, in the habit of a soldier, perform'd in delivering up his cross, hat, robes, and ring, at the shrine, and investing him with sword, helmet, shield, and spurs; then* ANTONIO, *the* DUCHESS *and their children, having presented themselves at the shrine, are, by a form of banishment in dumb-show expressed towards them by the* CARDINAL *and the state of Ancona, banished: during all which ceremony, this ditty is sung, to very solemn music, by divers churchmen: and then exeunt all except the* TWO PILGRIMS.]

Arms and honours deck thy story,
To thy fame's eternal glory!
Adverse fortune ever fly thee;
No disastrous fate come nigh thee!
I alone will sing thy praises,
Whom to honour virtue raises,
And thy study, that divine is,
Bent to martial discipline is,
Lay aside all those robes lie by thee;
Crown thy arts with arms, they 'll beautify thee.
O worthy of worthiest name, adorn'd in this manner,
Lead bravely thy forces on under war's warlike banner!
O, mayst thou prove fortunate in all martial courses!
Guide thou still by skill in arts and forces!
Victory attend thee nigh, whilst fame sings loud thy powers;
Triumphant conquest crown thy head, and blessings pour down showers![83]

---

[83] The first quarto has in the margin: "The Author disclaims this Ditty to be his."

FIRST PILGRIM. Here's a strange turn of state! who would have thought
    So great a lady would have match'd herself
    Unto so mean a person? Yet the cardinal
    Bears himself much too cruel.
SECOND PILGRIM. They are banish'd.
FIRST PILGRIM. But I would ask what power hath this state
    Of Ancona to determine of a free prince?
SECOND PILGRIM. They are a free state, sir, and her brother show'd
    How that the Pope, fore-hearing of her looseness,
    Hath seiz'd into th' protection of the church
    The dukedom which she held as dowager.
FIRST PILGRIM. But by what justice?
SECOND PILGRIM. Sure, I think by none,
    Only her brother's instigation.
FIRST PILGRIM. What was it with such violence he took
    Off from her finger?
SECOND PILGRIM. 'Twas her wedding-ring;
    Which he vow'd shortly he would sacrifice
    To his revenge.
FIRST PILGRIM. Alas, Antonio!
    If that a man be thrust into a well,
    No matter who sets hand to 't, his own weight
    Will bring him sooner to th' bottom. Come, let's hence.
    Fortune makes this conclusion general,
    All things do help th' unhappy man to fall.

[*Exeunt.*]

SCENE V. *Near Loretto.*

[*Enter* DUCHESS, ANTONIO, CHILDREN, CARIOLA, *and* SERVANTS.]

DUCHESS. Banish'd Ancona!
ANTONIO. Yes, you see what power
    Lightens in great men's breath.
DUCHESS. Is all our train
    Shrunk to this poor remainder?
ANTONIO. These poor men
    Which have got little in your service, vow
    To take your fortune: but your wiser buntings,[84]
    Now they are fledg'd, are gone.
DUCHESS. They have done wisely.
    This puts me in mind of death: physicians thus,

---

[84] Small birds.

With their hands full of money, use to give o'er
Their patients.

ANTONIO. Right the fashion of the world:
From decay'd fortunes every flatterer shrinks;
Men cease to build where the foundation sinks.

DUCHESS. I had a very strange dream to-night.

ANTONIO. What was 't?

DUCHESS. Methought I wore my coronet of state,
And on a sudden all the diamonds
Were chang'd to pearls.

ANTONIO. My interpretation
Is, you 'll weep shortly; for to me the pearls
Do signify your tears.

DUCHESS. The birds that live i' th' field
On the wild benefit of nature live
Happier than we; for they may choose their mates,
And carol their sweet pleasures to the spring.

[*Enter* BOSOLA *with a letter.*]

BOSOLA. You are happily o'erta'en.

DUCHESS. From my brother?

BOSOLA. Yes, from the Lord Ferdinand your brother
All love and safety.

DUCHESS. Thou dost blanch mischief,
Would'st make it white. See, see, like to calm weather
At sea before a tempest, false hearts speak fair
To those they intend most mischief.

[*Reads.*]

'send Antonio to me; I want his head in a business.'

A politic equivocation!
He doth not want your counsel, but your head;
That is, he cannot sleep till you be dead.
And here's another pitfall that's strew'd o'er
With roses; mark it, 'tis a cunning one:

[*Reads.*]

'I stand engaged for your husband for several debts at Naples:let
not that trouble him; I had rather have his heart than his money':—

And I believe so too.

BOSOLA. What do you believe?

DUCHESS. That he so much distrusts my husband's love,
     He will by no means believe his heart is with him
     Until he see it: the devil is not cunning enough
     To circumvent us In riddles.

BOSOLA. Will you reject that noble and free league
     Of amity and love which I present you?

DUCHESS. Their league is like that of some politic kings,
     Only to make themselves of strength and power
     To be our after-ruin; tell them so.

BOSOLA. And what from you?

ANTONIO. Thus tell him; I will not come.

BOSOLA. And what of this?

ANTONIO. My brothers have dispers'd
     Bloodhounds abroad; which till I hear are muzzl'd,
     No truce, though hatch'd with ne'er such politic skill,
     Is safe, that hangs upon our enemies' will.
     I'll not come at them.

BOSOLA. This proclaims your breeding.
     Every small thing draws a base mind to fear,
     As the adamant draws iron. Fare you well, sir;
     You shall shortly hear from's. [*Exit.*]

DUCHESS. I suspect some ambush;
     Therefore by all my love I do conjure you
     To take your eldest son, and fly towards Milan.
     Let us not venture all this poor remainder
     In one unlucky bottom.

ANTONIO. You counsel safely.
     Best of my life, farewell. Since we must part,
     Heaven hath a hand in 't; but no otherwise
     Than as some curious artist takes in sunder
     A clock or watch, when it is out of frame,
     To bring 't in better order.

DUCHESS. I know not which is best,
     To see you dead, or part with you.—Farewell, boy:
     Thou art happy that thou hast not understanding
     To know thy misery; for all our wit
     And reading brings us to a truer sense
     Of sorrow.—In the eternal church, sir,
     I do hope we shall not part thus.

ANTONIO. O, be of comfort!
     Make patience a noble fortitude,
     And think not how unkindly we are us'd:
     Man, like to cassia, is prov'd best, being bruis'd.

DUCHESS. Must I, like to slave-born Russian,

Account it praise to suffer tyranny?
And yet, O heaven, thy heavy hand is in 't!
I have seen my little boy oft scourge his top,
And compar'd myself to 't: naught made me e'er
Go right but heaven's scourge-stick.

ANTONIO. Do not weep:
Heaven fashion'd us of nothing; and we strive
To bring ourselves to nothing.—Farewell, Cariola,
And thy sweet armful.—If I do never see thee more,
Be a good mother to your little ones,
And save them from the tiger: fare you well.

DUCHESS. Let me look upon you once more, for that speech
Came from a dying father. Your kiss is colder
Than that I have seen an holy anchorite
Give to a dead man's skull.

ANTONIO. My heart is turn'd to a heavy lump of lead,
With which I sound my danger: fare you well.

[*Exeunt* ANTONIO *and his son.*]

DUCHESS. My laurel is all withered.

CARIOLA. Look, madam, what a troop of armed men
Make toward us!

[*Re-enter* BOSOLA, *visarded, with a* GUARD.]

DUCHESS. O, they are very welcome:
When Fortune's wheel is over-charg'd with princes,
The weight makes it move swift: I would have my ruin
Be sudden.—I am your adventure, am I not?

BOSOLA. You are: you must see your husband no more.

DUCHESS. What devil art thou that counterfeit'st heaven's thunder?

BOSOLA. Is that terrible? I would have you tell me whether
Is that note worse that frights the silly birds
Out of the corn, or that which doth allure them
To the nets? You have heark'ned to the last too much.

DUCHESS. O misery! like to a rusty o'ercharg'd cannon,
Shall I never fly in pieces?—Come, to what prison?

BOSOLA. To none.

DUCHESS. Whither, then?

BOSOLA. To your palace.

DUCHESS. I have heard
That Charon's boat serves to convey all o'er
The dismal lake, but brings none back again.

BOSOLA. Your brothers mean you safety and pity.

DUCHESS. Pity!
    With such a pity men preserve alive
    Pheasants and quails, when they are not fat enough
    To be eaten.
BOSOLA. These are your children?
DUCHESS. Yes.
BOSOLA. Can they prattle?
DUCHESS. No:
    But I intend, since they were born accurs'd,
    Curses shall be their first language.
BOSOLA. Fie, madam!
    Forget this base, low fellow——
DUCHESS. Were I a man,
    I 'd beat that counterfeit face[85] into thy other.
BOSOLA. One of no birth.
DUCHESS. Say that he was born mean,
    Man is most happy when's own actions
    Be arguments and examples of his virtue.
BOSOLA. A barren, beggarly virtue.
DUCHESS. I prithee, who is greatest? Can you tell?
    Sad tales befit my woe: I'll tell you one.
    A salmon, as she swam unto the sea,
    Met with a dog-fish, who encounters her
    With this rough language; 'Why art thou so bold
    To mix thyself with our high state of floods,
    Being no eminent courtier, but one
    That for the calmest and fresh time o' th' year
    Dost live in shallow rivers, rank'st thyself
    With silly smelts and shrimps? And darest thou
    Pass by our dog-ship without reverence?'
    'O,' quoth the salmon,'sister, be at peace:
    Thank Jupiter we both have pass'd the net!
    Our value never can be truly known,
    Till in the fisher's basket we be shown:
    I' th' market then my price may be the higher,
    Even when I am nearest to the cook and fire.'
    So to great men the moral may be stretched;
    Men oft are valu'd high, when they're most wretched.——
    But come, whither you please. I am arm'd 'gainst misery;
    Bent to all sways of the oppressor's will:
    There's no deep valley but near some great hill.

[*Exeunt.*]

---

[85] His vizard.

ACT IV.

SCENE I. *Malfi. An apartment in the palace of the* DUCHESS.

[*Enter* FERDINAND *and* BOSOLA.]

FERDINAND. How doth our sister duchess bear herself
    In her imprisonment?
BOSOLA. Nobly: I'll describe her.
    She's sad as one long us'd to 't, and she seems
    Rather to welcome the end of misery
    Than shun it; a behaviour so noble
    As gives a majesty to adversity:
    You may discern the shape of loveliness
    More perfect in her tears than in her smiles:
    She will muse for hours together; and her silence,
    Methinks, expresseth more than if she spake.
FERDINAND. Her melancholy seems to be fortified
    With a strange disdain.
BOSOLA. 'Tis so; and this restraint,
    Like English mastives that grow fierce with tying,
    Makes her too passionately apprehend
    Those pleasures she is kept from.
FERDINAND. Curse upon her!
    I will no longer study in the book
    Of another's heart. Inform her what I told you. [*Exit.*]

[*Enter* DUCHESS *and* ATTENDANTS.]

BOSOLA. All comfort to your grace!
DUCHESS. I will have none.
    Pray thee, why dost thou wrap thy poison'd pills
    In gold and sugar?
BOSOLA. Your elder brother, the Lord Ferdinand,
    Is come to visit you, and sends you word,
    'Cause once he rashly made a solemn vow
    Never to see you more, he comes i' th' night;
    And prays you gently neither torch nor taper
    Shine in your chamber. He will kiss your hand,
    And reconcile himself; but for his vow
    He dares not see you.
DUCHESS. At his pleasure.—
    Take hence the lights.—He's come.

[*Exeunt* ATTENDANTS *with lights.*]

[*Enter* FERDINAND.]

FERDINAND. Where are you?

DUCHESS. Here, sir.

FERDINAND. This darkness suits you well.

DUCHESS. I would ask you pardon.

FERDINAND. You have it;
    For I account it the honorabl'st revenge,
    Where I may kill, to pardon.—Where are your cubs?

DUCHESS. Whom?

FERDINAND. Call them your children;
    For though our national law distinguish bastards
    From true legitimate issue, compassionate nature
    Makes them all equal.

DUCHESS. Do you visit me for this?
    You violate a sacrament o' th' church
    Shall make you howl in hell for 't.

FERDINAND. It had been well,
    Could you have liv'd thus always; for, indeed,
    You were too much i' th' light:—but no more;
    I come to seal my peace with you. Here's a hand

[*Gives her a dead man's hand.*]

    To which you have vow'd much love; the ring upon 't
    You gave.

DUCHESS. I affectionately kiss it.

FERDINAND. Pray, do, and bury the print of it in your heart.
    I will leave this ring with you for a love-token;
    And the hand as sure as the ring; and do not doubt
    But you shall have the heart too. When you need a friend,
    Send it to him that ow'd it; you shall see
    Whether he can aid you.

DUCHESS. You are very cold:
    I fear you are not well after your travel.—
    Ha! lights!——O, horrible!

FERDINAND. Let her have lights enough. [*Exit.*]

DUCHESS. What witchcraft doth he practise, that he hath left
    A dead man's hand here?

[*Here is discovered, behind a traverse,*[86] *the artificial figures of* ANTONIO *and his* CHILDREN, *appearing as if they were dead.*]

BOSOLA. Look you, here's the piece from which 'twas ta'en.
 He doth present you this sad spectacle,
 That, now you know directly they are dead,
 Hereafter you may wisely cease to grieve
 For that which cannot be recovered.
DUCHESS. There is not between heaven and earth one wish
 I stay for after this. It wastes me more
 Than were 't my picture, fashion'd out of wax,
 Stuck with a magical needle, and then buried
 In some foul dunghill; and yon's an excellent property
 For a tyrant, which I would account mercy.
BOSOLA. What's that?
DUCHESS. If they would bind me to that lifeless trunk,
 And let me freeze to death.
BOSOLA. Come, you must live.
DUCHESS. That's the greatest torture souls feel in hell,
 In hell, that they must live, and cannot die.
 Portia,[87] I'll new kindle thy coals again,
 And revive the rare and almost dead example
 Of a loving wife.
BOSOLA. O, fie! despair? Remember
 You are a Christian.
DUCHESS. The church enjoins fasting:
 I'll starve myself to death.
BOSOLA. Leave this vain sorrow.
 Things being at the worst begin to mend: the bee
 When he hath shot his sting into your hand,
 May then play with your eye-lid.
DUCHESS. Good comfortable fellow,
 Persuade a wretch that's broke upon the wheel
 To have all his bones new set; entreat him live
 To be executed again. Who must despatch me?
 I account this world a tedious theatre,
 For I do play a part in 't 'gainst my will.
BOSOLA. Come, be of comfort; I will save your life.
DUCHESS. Indeed, I have not leisure to tend so small a business.
BOSOLA. Now, by my life, I pity you.
DUCHESS. Thou art a fool, then,

---

[86] Curtain.
[87] The wife of Brutus, who died by swallowing fire.

To waste thy pity on a thing so wretched
As cannot pity itself. I am full of daggers.
Puff, let me blow these vipers from me.

[*Enter* SERVANT.]

What are you?
SERVANT. One that wishes you long life.
DUCHESS. I would thou wert hang'd for the horrible curse
     Thou hast given me: I shall shortly grow one
     Of the miracles of pity. I'll go pray;—

[*Exit* SERVANT.]

No, I'll go curse.
BOSOLA. O, fie!
DUCHESS. I could curse the stars.
BOSOLA. O, fearful!
DUCHESS. And those three smiling seasons of the year
     Into a Russian winter; nay, the world
     To its first chaos.
BOSOLA. Look you, the stars shine still.
DUCHESS. O, but you must
     Remember, my curse hath a great way to go.—
     Plagues, that make lanes through largest families,
     Consume them!—
BOSOLA. Fie, lady!
DUCHESS. Let them, like tyrants,
     Never be remembered but for the ill they have done;
     Let all the zealous prayers of mortified
     Churchmen forget them!—
BOSOLA. O, uncharitable!
DUCHESS. Let heaven a little while cease crowning martyrs,
     To punish them!—
     Go, howl them this, and say, I long to bleed:
     It is some mercy when men kill with speed. [*Exit.*]

[*Re-enter* FERDINAND.]

FERDINAND. Excellent, as I would wish; she's plagu'd in art.[88]
     These presentations are but fram'd in wax
     By the curious master in that quality,[89]

---

[88] By artificial means.
[89] Profession.

> Vincentio Lauriola, and she takes them
> For true substantial bodies.

BOSOLA. Why do you do this?

FERDINAND. To bring her to despair.

BOSOLA. Faith, end here,
> And go no farther in your cruelty:
> Send her a penitential garment to put on
> Next to her delicate skin, and furnish her
> With beads and prayer-books.

FERDINAND. Damn her! that body of hers.
> While that my blood run pure in 't, was more worth
> Than that which thou wouldst comfort, call'd a soul.
> I will send her masques of common courtezans,
> Have her meat serv'd up by bawds and ruffians,
> And, 'cause she 'll needs be mad, I am resolv'd
> To move forth the common hospital
> All the mad-folk, and place them near her lodging;
> There let them practise together, sing and dance,
> And act their gambols to the full o' th' moon:
> If she can sleep the better for it, let her.
> Your work is almost ended.

BOSOLA. Must I see her again?

FERDINAND. Yes.

BOSOLA. Never.

FERDINAND. You must.

BOSOLA. Never in mine own shape;
> That's forfeited by my intelligence[90]
> And this last cruel lie: when you send me next,
> The business shall be comfort.

FERDINAND. Very likely;
> Thy pity is nothing of kin to thee, Antonio
> Lurks about Milan: thou shalt shortly thither,
> To feed a fire as great as my revenge,
> Which nev'r will slack till it hath spent his fuel:
> Intemperate agues make physicians cruel.

[*Exeunt.*]

---

[90] Spying.

SCENE II. *Another room in the lodging of the* DUCHESS.

[*Enter* DUCHESS *and* CARIOLA.]

DUCHESS. What hideous noise was that?
CARIOLA. 'Tis the wild consort[91]
    Of madmen, lady, which your tyrant brother
    Hath plac'd about your lodging. This tyranny,
    I think, was never practis'd till this hour.
DUCHESS. Indeed, I thank him. Nothing but noise and folly
    Can keep me in my right wits; whereas reason
    And silence make me stark mad. Sit down;
    Discourse to me some dismal tragedy.
CARIOLA. O, 'twill increase your melancholy!
DUCHESS. Thou art deceiv'd:
    To hear of greater grief would lessen mine.
    This is a prison?
CARIOLA. Yes, but you shall live
    To shake this durance off.
DUCHESS. Thou art a fool:
    The robin-red-breast and the nightingale
    Never live long in cages.
CARIOLA. Pray, dry your eyes.
    What think you of, madam?
DUCHESS. Of nothing;
    When I muse thus, I sleep.
CARIOLA. Like a madman, with your eyes open?
DUCHESS. Dost thou think we shall know one another
    In th' other world?
CARIOLA. Yes, out of question.
DUCHESS. O, that it were possible we might
    But hold some two days' conference with the dead!
    From them I should learn somewhat, I am sure,
    I never shall know here. I'll tell thee a miracle:
    I am not mad yet, to my cause of sorrow:
    Th' heaven o'er my head seems made of molten brass,
    The earth of flaming sulphur, yet I am not mad.
    I am acquainted with sad misery
    As the tann'd galley-slave is with his oar;
    Necessity makes me suffer constantly,
    And custom makes it easy. Who do I look like now?
CARIOLA. Like to your picture in the gallery,

---

[91] Band.

    A deal of life in show, but none in practice;
    Or rather like some reverend monument
    Whose ruins are even pitied.
DUCHESS. Very proper;
    And Fortune seems only to have her eye-sight
    To behold my tragedy.—How now!
    What noise is that?

[*Enter* SERVANT.]

SERVANT. I am come to tell you
    Your brother hath intended you some sport.
    A great physician, when the Pope was sick
    Of a deep melancholy, presented him
    With several sorts[92] of madmen, which wild object
    Being full of change and sport, forc'd him to laugh,
    And so the imposthume[93] broke: the self-same cure
    The duke intends on you.
DUCHESS. Let them come in.
SERVANT. There's a mad lawyer; and a secular priest;
    A doctor that hath forfeited his wits
    By jealousy; an astrologian
    That in his works said such a day o' the month
    Should be the day of doom, and, failing of 't,
    Ran mad; an English tailor craz'd i' the brain
    With the study of new fashions; a gentleman-usher
    Quite beside himself with care to keep in mind
    The number of his lady's salutations
    Or 'How do you,' she employ'd him in each morning;
    A farmer, too, an excellent knave in grain,[94]
    Mad 'cause he was hind'red transportation:[95]
    And let one broker that's mad loose to these,
    You'd think the devil were among them.
DUCHESS. Sit, Cariola.—Let them loose when you please,
    For I am chain'd to endure all your tyranny.

[*Enter* MADMEN.]

Here by a Madman this song is sung to a dismal kind of music
    O, let us howl some heavy note,
    Some deadly dogged howl,

---

[92] Bands.
[93] Boil.
[94] Punning on the two senses of "dye" and "corn."
[95] From exporting his grain.

Sounding as from the threatening throat
Of beasts and fatal fowl!
As ravens, screech-owls, bulls, and bears,
We 'll bell, and bawl our parts,
Till irksome noise have cloy'd your ears
And corrosiv'd your hearts.
At last, whenas our choir wants breath,
Our bodies being blest,
We 'll sing, like swans, to welcome death,
And die in love and rest.

FIRST MADMAN. Doom's-day not come yet! I'll draw it nearer by a perspective,[96] or make a glass that shall set all the world on fire upon an instant. I cannot sleep; my pillow is stuffed with a litter of porcupines.

SECOND MADMAN. Hell is a mere glass-house, where the devils are continually blowing up women's souls on hollow irons, and the fire never goes out.

FIRST MADMAN. I have skill in heraldry.

SECOND MADMAN. Hast?

FIRST MADMAN. You do give for your crest a woodcock's head with the brains picked out on 't; you are a very ancient gentleman.

THIRD MADMAN. Greek is turned Turk: we are only to be saved by the Helvetian translation.[97]

FIRST MADMAN. Come on, sir, I will lay the law to you.

SECOND MADMAN. O, rather lay a corrosive: the law will eat to the bone.

THIRD MADMAN. He that drinks but to satisfy nature is damn'd.

FOURTH MADMAN. If I had my glass here, I would show a sight should make all the women here call me mad doctor.

FIRST MADMAN. What's he? a rope-maker?

SECOND MADMAN. No, no, no, a snuffling knave that, while he shows the tombs, will have his hand in a wench's placket.[98]

THIRD MADMAN. Woe to the caroche[99] that brought home my wife from the masque at three o'clock in the morning! It had a large feather-bed in it.

FOURTH MADMAN. I have pared the devil's nails forty times, roasted them in raven's eggs, and cured agues with them.

THIRD MADMAN. Get me three hundred milch-bats, to make possets[100] to procure sleep.

FOURTH MADMAN. All the college may throw their caps at me:

---

[96] Optical glass.
[97] The Geneva Bible.
[98] Petticoat.
[99] Coach.
[100] A warm drink containing milk, wine, etc.

I have made a soap-boiler costive; it was my masterpiece.

Here the dance, consisting of Eight Madmen, with music answerable thereunto; after which, BOSOLA, like an old man, enters.

DUCHESS. Is he mad too?

SERVANT. Pray, question him. I'll leave you.

[*Exeunt* SERVANT *and* MADMEN.]

BOSOLA. I am come to make thy tomb.

DUCHESS. Ha! my tomb!
   Thou speak'st as if I lay upon my death-bed,
   Gasping for breath. Dost thou perceive me sick?

BOSOLA.
   Yes, and the more dangerously, since thy sickness is insensible.

DUCHESS. Thou art not mad, sure: dost know me?

BOSOLA. Yes.

DUCHESS. Who am I?

BOSOLA. Thou art a box of worm-seed, at best but a salvatory[101] of green mummy.[102] What's this flesh? a little crudded[103] milk, fantastical puff-paste. Our bodies are weaker than those paper-prisons boys use to keep flies in; more contemptible, since ours is to preserve earth-worms. Didst thou ever see a lark in a cage? Such is the soul in the body: this world is like her little turf of grass, and the heaven o'er our heads like her looking-glass, only gives us a miserable knowledge of the small compass of our prison.

DUCHESS. Am not I thy duchess?

BOSOLA. Thou art some great woman, sure, for riot begins to sit on thy forehead (clad in gray hairs) twenty years sooner than on a merry milk-maid's. Thou sleepest worse than if a mouse should be forced to take up her lodging in a cat's ear: a little infant that breeds its teeth, should it lie with thee, would cry out, as if thou wert the more unquiet bedfellow.

DUCHESS. I am Duchess of Malfi still.

BOSOLA. That makes thy sleep so broken:
   Glories, like glow-worms, afar off shine bright,
   But, look'd to near, have neither heat nor light.

DUCHESS. Thou art very plain.

BOSOLA. My trade is to flatter the dead, not the living;
   I am a tomb-maker.

DUCHESS. And thou comest to make my tomb?

---

[101] Receptacle.
[102] A drug supposed to ooze from embalmed bodies.
[103] Curdled.

BOSOLA. Yes.

DUCHESS. Let me be a little merry:—of what stuff wilt thou make it?

BOSOLA. Nay, resolve me first, of what fashion?

DUCHESS. Why, do we grow fantastical on our deathbed?
      Do we affect fashion in the grave?

BOSOLA. Most ambitiously. Princes' images on their tombs do not lie,
      as they were wont, seeming to pray up to heaven; but with their
      hands under their cheeks, as if they died of the tooth-ache. They
      are not carved with their eyes fix'd upon the stars, but as their
      minds were wholly bent upon the world, the selfsame way they
      seem to turn their faces.

DUCHESS. Let me know fully therefore the effect
      Of this thy dismal preparation,
      This talk fit for a charnel.

BOSOLA. Now I shall:—

[*Enter* EXECUTIONERS, *with a coffin, cords, and a bell.*]

      Here is a present from your princely brothers;
      And may it arrive welcome, for it brings
      Last benefit, last sorrow.

DUCHESS. Let me see it:
      I have so much obedience in my blood,
      I wish it in their veins to do them good.

BOSOLA. This is your last presence-chamber.

CARIOLA. O my sweet lady!

DUCHESS. Peace; it affrights not me.

BOSOLA. I am the common bellman
      That usually is sent to condemn'd persons
      The night before they suffer.

DUCHESS. Even now thou said'st
      Thou wast a tomb-maker.

BOSOLA. 'Twas to bring you
      By degrees to mortification. Listen.
      Hark, now everything is still,
      The screech-owl and the whistler shrill
      Call upon our dame aloud,
      And bid her quickly don her shroud!
      Much you had of land and rent;
      Your length in clay's now competent:
      A long war disturb'd your mind;
      Here your perfect peace is sign'd.
      Of what is 't fools make such vain keeping?
      Sin their conception, their birth weeping,
      Their life a general mist of error,

Their death a hideous storm of terror.
Strew your hair with powders sweet,
Don clean linen, bathe your feet,
And (the foul fiend more to check)
A crucifix let bless your neck.
'Tis now full tide 'tween night and day;
End your groan, and come away.

CARIOLA. Hence, villains, tyrants, murderers! Alas!
What will you do with my lady?—Call for help!

DUCHESS. To whom? To our next neighbours? They are mad-folks.

BOSOLA. Remove that noise.

DUCHESS. Farewell, Cariola.
In my last will I have not much to give:
A many hungry guests have fed upon me;
Thine will be a poor reversion.

CARIOLA. I will die with her.

DUCHESS. I pray thee, look thou giv'st my little boy
Some syrup for his cold, and let the girl
Say her prayers ere she sleep.

[CARIOLA *is forced out by the* EXECUTIONERS.]

Now what you please:
What death?

BOSOLA. Strangling; here are your executioners.

DUCHESS. I forgive them:
The apoplexy, catarrh, or cough o' th' lungs,
Would do as much as they do.

BOSOLA. Doth not death fright you?

DUCHESS. Who would be afraid on 't,
Knowing to meet such excellent company
In th' other world?

BOSOLA. Yet, methinks,
The manner of your death should much afflict you:
This cord should terrify you.

DUCHESS. Not a whit:
What would it pleasure me to have my throat cut
With diamonds? or to be smothered
With cassia? or to be shot to death with pearls?
I know death hath ten thousand several doors
For men to take their exits; and 'tis found
They go on such strange geometrical hinges,
You may open them both ways: any way, for heaven-sake,
So I were out of your whispering. Tell my brothers
That I perceive death, now I am well awake,

Best gift is they can give or I can take.
I would fain put off my last woman's-fault,
I 'd not be tedious to you.

FIRST EXECUTIONER. We are ready.

DUCHESS. Dispose my breath how please you; but my body
Bestow upon my women, will you?

FIRST EXECUTIONER. Yes.

DUCHESS. Pull, and pull strongly, for your able strength
Must pull down heaven upon me:—
Yet stay; heaven-gates are not so highly arch'd
As princes' palaces; they that enter there
Must go upon their knees [Kneels].—Come, violent death,
Serve for mandragora to make me sleep!—
Go tell my brothers, when I am laid out,
They then may feed in quiet.

They strangle her.

BOSOLA. Where's the waiting-woman??
Fetch her: some other strangle the children.

[*Enter* CARIOLA.]

Look you, there sleeps your mistress.

CARIOLA. O, you are damn'd
Perpetually for this! My turn is next;
Is 't not so ordered?

BOSOLA. Yes, and I am glad
You are so well prepar'd for 't.

CARIOLA. You are deceiv'd, sir,
I am not prepar'd for 't, I will not die;
I will first come to my answer,[104] and know
How I have offended.

BOSOLA. Come, despatch her.—
You kept her counsel; now you shall keep ours.

CARIOLA. I will not die, I must not; I am contracted
To a young gentleman.

FIRST EXECUTIONER. Here's your wedding-ring.

CARIOLA. Let me but speak with the duke. I'll discover
Treason to his person.

BOSOLA. Delays:—throttle her.

FIRST EXECUTIONER. She bites and scratches.

CARIOLA. If you kill me now,
I am damn'd; I have not been at confession
This two years.

---

[104] Trial.

BOSOLA. [*to* EXECUTIONERS.] When?[105]
CARIOLA. I am quick with child.
BOSOLA. Why, then,
　　Your credit's saved.

　　[EXECUTIONERS *strangle* CARIOLA.]

　　Bear her into the next room;
　　Let these lie still.

　　[*Exeunt the* EXECUTIONERS *with the body of* CARIOLA.]

　　[*Enter* FERDINAND.]

FERDINAND. Is she dead?
BOSOLA. She is what
　　You 'd have her. But here begin your pity:
　　Shows the Children strangled.
　　Alas, how have these offended?
FERDINAND. The death
　　Of young wolves is never to be pitied.
BOSOLA. Fix your eye here.
FERDINAND. Constantly.
BOSOLA. Do you not weep?
　　Other sins only speak; murder shrieks out.
　　The element of water moistens the earth,
　　But blood flies upwards and bedews the heavens.
FERDINAND. Cover her face; mine eyes dazzle: she died young.
BOSOLA. I think not so; her infelicity
　　Seem'd to have years too many.
FERDINAND. She and I were twins;
　　And should I die this instant, I had liv'd
　　Her time to a minute.
BOSOLA. It seems she was born first:
　　You have bloodily approv'd the ancient truth,
　　That kindred commonly do worse agree
　　Than remote strangers.
FERDINAND. Let me see her face
　　Again. Why didst thou not pity her? What
　　An excellent honest man mightst thou have been,
　　If thou hadst borne her to some sanctuary!
　　Or, bold in a good cause, oppos'd thyself,
　　With thy advanced sword above thy head,

---

[105] An exclamation of impatience.

Between her innocence and my revenge!
I bade thee, when I was distracted of my wits,
Go kill my dearest friend, and thou hast done 't.
For let me but examine well the cause:
What was the meanness of her match to me?
Only I must confess I had a hope,
Had she continu'd widow, to have gain'd
An infinite mass of treasure by her death:
And that was the main cause,—her marriage,
That drew a stream of gall quite through my heart.
For thee, as we observe in tragedies
That a good actor many times is curs'd
For playing a villain's part, I hate thee for 't,
And, for my sake, say, thou hast done much ill well.

BOSOLA. Let me quicken your memory, for I perceive
You are falling into ingratitude: I challenge
The reward due to my service.

FERDINAND. I'll tell thee
What I'll give thee.

BOSOLA. Do.

FERDINAND. I'll give thee a pardon
For this murder.

BOSOLA. Ha!

FERDINAND. Yes, and 'tis
The largest bounty I can study to do thee.
By what authority didst thou execute
This bloody sentence?

BOSOLA. By yours.

FERDINAND. Mine! was I her judge?
Did any ceremonial form of law
Doom her to not-being? Did a complete jury
Deliver her conviction up i' the court?
Where shalt thou find this judgment register'd,
Unless in hell? See, like a bloody fool,
Thou'st forfeited thy life, and thou shalt die for 't.

BOSOLA. The office of justice is perverted quite
When one thief hangs another. Who shall dare
To reveal this?

FERDINAND. O, I'll tell thee;
The wolf shall find her grave, and scrape it up,
Not to devour the corpse, but to discover
The horrid murder.

BOSOLA. You, not I, shall quake for 't.

FERDINAND. Leave me.

BOSOLA. I will first receive my pension.

FERDINAND. You are a villain.

BOSOLA. When your ingratitude
Is judge, I am so.

FERDINAND. O horror,
That not the fear of him which binds the devils
Can prescribe man obedience!—
Never look upon me more.

BOSOLA. Why, fare thee well.
Your brother and yourself are worthy men!
You have a pair of hearts are hollow graves,
Rotten, and rotting others; and your vengeance,
Like two chain'd-bullets, still goes arm in arm:
You may be brothers; for treason, like the plague,
Doth take much in a blood. I stand like one
That long hath ta'en a sweet and golden dream:
I am angry with myself, now that I wake.

FERDINAND. Get thee into some unknown part o' the world,
That I may never see thee.

BOSOLA. Let me know
Wherefore I should be thus neglected. Sir,
I serv'd your tyranny, and rather strove
To satisfy yourself than all the world:
And though I loath'd the evil, yet I lov'd
You that did counsel it; and rather sought
To appear a true servant than an honest man.

FERDINAND. I'll go hunt the badger by owl-light:
'Tis a deed of darkness. [*Exit.*]

BOSOLA. He's much distracted. Off, my painted honour!
While with vain hopes our faculties we tire,
We seem to sweat in ice and freeze in fire.
What would I do, were this to do again?
I would not change my peace of conscience
For all the wealth of Europe.—She stirs; here's life:—
Return, fair soul, from darkness, and lead mine
Out of this sensible hell:—she's warm, she breathes:—
Upon thy pale lips I will melt my heart,
To store them with fresh colour.—Who's there?
Some cordial drink!—Alas! I dare not call:
So pity would destroy pity.—Her eye opes,
And heaven in it seems to ope, that late was shut,
To take me up to mercy.

DUCHESS. Antonio!

BOSOLA. Yes, madam, he is living;
The dead bodies you saw were but feign'd statues.
He's reconcil'd to your brothers; the Pope hath wrought

The atonement.

DUCHESS. Mercy! [*Dies.*]

BOSOLA. O, she's gone again! there the cords of life broke.
    O sacred innocence, that sweetly sleeps
    On turtles' feathers, whilst a guilty conscience
    Is a black register wherein is writ
    All our good deeds and bad, a perspective
    That shows us hell! That we cannot be suffer'd
    To do good when we have a mind to it!
    This is manly sorrow;
    These tears, I am very certain, never grew
    In my mother's milk. My estate is sunk
    Below the degree of fear: where were
    These penitent fountains while she was living?
    O, they were frozen up! Here is a sight
    As direful to my soul as is the sword
    Unto a wretch hath slain his father.
    Come, I'll bear thee hence,
    And execute thy last will; that's deliver
    Thy body to the reverend dispose
    Of some good women: that the cruel tyrant
    Shall not deny me. Then I'll post to Milan,
    Where somewhat I will speedily enact
    Worth my dejection.

[*Exit with the body.*]

ACT V.

SCENE I. *Milan. A public place.*

[*Enter* ANTONIO *and* DELIO.]

ANTONIO. What think you of my hope of reconcilement
    To the Arragonian brethren?

DELIO. I misdoubt it;
    For though they have sent their letters of safe-conduct
    For your repair to Milan, they appear
    But nets to entrap you. The Marquis of Pescara,
    Under whom you hold certain land in cheat,[106]
    Much 'gainst his noble nature hath been mov'd
    To seize those lands; and some of his dependants
    Are at this instant making it their suit

---

[106] In escheat; here, in fee.

To be invested in your revenues.
I cannot think they mean well to your life
That do deprive you of your means of life,
Your living.
ANTONIO. You are still an heretic[107]
To any safety I can shape myself.
DELIO. Here comes the marquis: I will make myself
Petitioner for some part of your land,
To know whither it is flying.
ANTONIO. I pray, do.

[*Withdraws.*]

[*Enter* PESCARA.]

DELIO. Sir, I have a suit to you.
PESCARA. To me?
DELIO. An easy one:
There is the Citadel of Saint Bennet,
With some demesnes, of late in the possession
Of Antonio Bologna,—please you bestow them on me.
PESCARA. You are my friend; but this is such a suit,
Nor fit for me to give, nor you to take.
DELIO. No, sir?
PESCARA. I will give you ample reason for 't
Soon in private:—here's the cardinal's mistress.

[*Enter* JULIA.]

JULIA. My lord, I am grown your poor petitioner,
And should be an ill beggar, had I not
A great man's letter here, the cardinal's,
To court you in my favour.

[*Gives a letter.*]

PESCARA. He entreats for you
The Citadel of Saint Bennet, that belong'd
To the banish'd Bologna.
JULIA. Yes.
PESCARA. I could not have thought of a friend I could rather
Pleasure with it: 'tis yours.
JULIA. Sir, I thank you;

---

[107] Disbeliever.

And he shall know how doubly I am engag'd
Both in your gift, and speediness of giving
Which makes your grant the greater. [*Exit.*]

ANTONIO. How they fortify
Themselves with my ruin!

DELIO. Sir, I am
Little bound to you.

PESCARA. Why?

DELIO. Because you deni'd this suit to me, and gave 't
To such a creature.

PESCARA. Do you know what it was?
It was Antonio's land; not forfeited
By course of law, but ravish'd from his throat
By the cardinal's entreaty. It were not fit
I should bestow so main a piece of wrong
Upon my friend; 'tis a gratification
Only due to a strumpet, for it is injustice.
Shall I sprinkle the pure blood of innocents
To make those followers I call my friends
Look ruddier upon me? I am glad
This land, ta'en from the owner by such wrong,
Returns again unto so foul an use
As salary for his lust. Learn, good Delio,
To ask noble things of me, and you shall find
I'll be a noble giver.

DELIO. You instruct me well.

ANTONIO. Why, here's a man now would fright impudence
From sauciest beggars.

PESCARA. Prince Ferdinand's come to Milan,
Sick, as they give out, of an apoplexy;
But some say 'tis a frenzy: I am going
To visit him. [*Exit.*]

ANTONIO. 'Tis a noble old fellow.

DELIO. What course do you mean to take, Antonio?

ANTONIO. This night I mean to venture all my fortune,
Which is no more than a poor ling'ring life,
To the cardinal's worst of malice. I have got
Private access to his chamber; and intend
To visit him about the mid of night,
As once his brother did our noble duchess.
It may be that the sudden apprehension
Of danger,—for I'll go in mine own shape,—
When he shall see it fraight[108] with love and duty,

---

[108] Fraught.

    May draw the poison out of him, and work
    A friendly reconcilement. If it fail,
    Yet it shall rid me of this infamous calling;
    For better fall once than be ever falling.
DELIO. I'll second you in all danger; and howe'er,
    My life keeps rank with yours.
ANTONIO. You are still my lov'd and best friend.

    [*Exeunt.*]

SCENE II. *A gallery in the residence of the*
CARDINAL *and* FERDINAND.

[*Enter* PESCARA *and* DOCTOR.]

PESCARA. Now, doctor, may I visit your patient?
DOCTOR. If 't please your lordship; but he's instantly
    To take the air here in the gallery
    By my direction.
PESCARA. Pray thee, what's his disease?
DOCTOR. A very pestilent disease, my lord,
    They call lycanthropia.
PESCARA. What's that?
    I need a dictionary to 't.
DOCTOR. I'll tell you.
    In those that are possess'd with 't there o'erflows
    Such melancholy humour they imagine
    Themselves to be transformed into wolves;
    Steal forth to church-yards in the dead of night,
    And dig dead bodies up: as two nights since
    One met the duke 'bout midnight in a lane
    Behind Saint Mark's church, with the leg of a man
    Upon his shoulder; and he howl'd fearfully;
    Said he was a wolf, only the difference
    Was, a wolf's skin was hairy on the outside,
    His on the inside; bade them take their swords,
    Rip up his flesh, and try. Straight I was sent for,
    And, having minister'd to him, found his grace
    Very well recover'd.
PESCARA. I am glad on 't.
DOCTOR. Yet not without some fear
    Of a relapse. If he grow to his fit again,
    I'll go a nearer way to work with him
    Than ever Paracelsus dream'd of; if
    They 'll give me leave, I'll buffet his madness out of him.

Stand aside; he comes.

[*Enter* FERDINAND, CARDINAL, MALATESTI, *and* BOSOLA.]

FERDINAND. Leave me.

MALATESTI. Why doth your lordship love this solitariness?

FERDINAND. Eagles commonly fly alone: they are crows, daws, and
    starlings that flock together. Look, what's that follows me?

MALATESTI. Nothing, my lord.

FERDINAND. Yes.

MALATESTI. 'Tis your shadow.

FERDINAND. Stay it; let it not haunt me.

MALATESTI. Impossible, if you move, and the sun shine.

FERDINAND. I will throttle it.

[*Throws himself down on his shadow.*]

MALATESTI. O, my lord, you are angry with nothing.

FERDINAND. You are a fool: how is 't possible I should catch my
    shadow, unless I fall upon 't? When I go to hell, I mean to carry a
    bribe; for, look you, good gifts evermore make way for the worst
    persons.

PESCARA. Rise, good my lord.

FERDINAND. I am studying the art of patience.

PESCARA. 'Tis a noble virtue.

FERDINAND. To drive six snails before me from this town to Moscow;
    neither use goad nor whip to them, but let them take their own
    time; —the patient'st man i' th' world match me for an
    experiment:—an I'll crawl after like a sheep-biter.[109]

CARDINAL. Force him up.

[*They raise him.*]

FERDINAND. Use me well, you were best. What I have done, I have
    done: I'll confess nothing.

DOCTOR. Now let me come to him.—Are you mad, my lord? are you
    out of your princely wits?

FERDINAND. What's he?

PESCARA. Your doctor.

FERDINAND. Let me have his beard saw'd off, and his eye-brows fil'd
    more civil.

DOCTOR. I must do mad tricks with him, for that's the only way on
    't.—I have brought your grace a salamander's skin to keep you

---

[109] A dog which worries sheep.

from sun-burning.

FERDINAND. I have cruel sore eyes.

DOCTOR. The white of a cockatrix's[110] egg is present remedy.

FERDINAND. Let it be a new-laid one, you were best.
Hide me from him: physicians are like kings,—
They brook no contradiction.

DOCTOR. Now he begins to fear me: now let me alone with him.

CARDINAL. How now! put off your gown!

DOCTOR. Let me have some forty urinals filled with rosewater: he and
I'll go pelt one another with them.—Now he begins to fear me.—
Can you fetch a frisk,[111] sir?—Let him go, let him go, upon my
peril: I find by his eye he stands in awe of me; I'll make him as
tame as a dormouse.

FERDINAND. Can you fetch your frisks, sir!—I will stamp him into a
cullis,[112] flay off his skin to cover one of the anatomies[113] this
rogue hath set i' th' cold yonder in Barber-Chirurgeon's-hall.
—Hence, hence! you are all of you like beasts for sacrifice.

[*Throws the* DOCTOR *down and beats him.*]

There's nothing left of you but tongue and belly, flattery and
lechery. [*Exit.*]

PESCARA. Doctor, he did not fear you thoroughly.

DOCTOR. True; I was somewhat too forward.

BOSOLA. Mercy upon me, what a fatal judgment
Hath fall'n upon this Ferdinand!

PESCARA. Knows your grace
What accident hath brought unto the prince
This strange distraction?

CARDINAL. [*aside.*] I must feign somewhat.—Thus they say it grew.
You have heard it rumour'd, for these many years
None of our family dies but there is seen
The shape of an old woman, which is given
By tradition to us to have been murder'd
By her nephews for her riches. Such a figure
One night, as the prince sat up late at's book,
Appear'd to him; when crying out for help,
The gentleman of's chamber found his grace
All on a cold sweat, alter'd much in face
And language: since which apparition,
He hath grown worse and worse, and I much fear

---

[110] A fabulous serpent that killed by its glance.

[111] Cut a caper.

[112] Broth.

[113] Skeletons.

He cannot live.

BOSOLA. Sir, I would speak with you.

PESCARA. We 'll leave your grace,
Wishing to the sick prince, our noble lord,
All health of mind and body.

CARDINAL. You are most welcome.

[*Exeunt* PESCARA, MALATESTI, *and* DOCTOR.]

Are you come? so.—[*aside.*] This fellow must not know
By any means I had intelligence
In our duchess' death; for, though I counsell'd it,
The full of all th' engagement seem'd to grow
From Ferdinand.—Now, sir, how fares our sister?
I do not think but sorrow makes her look
Like to an oft-dy'd garment: she shall now
Take comfort from me. Why do you look so wildly?
O, the fortune of your master here the prince
Dejects you; but be you of happy comfort:
If you 'll do one thing for me I'll entreat,
Though he had a cold tomb-stone o'er his bones,
I 'd make you what you would be.

BOSOLA. Any thing;
Give it me in a breath, and let me fly to 't.
They that think long small expedition win,
For musing much o' th' end cannot begin.

[*Enter* JULIA.]

JULIA. Sir, will you come into supper?

CARDINAL. I am busy; leave me.

JULIA [*aside.*] What an excellent shape hath that fellow! [*Exit.*]

CARDINAL. 'Tis thus. Antonio lurks here in Milan:
Inquire him out, and kill him. While he lives,
Our sister cannot marry; and I have thought
Of an excellent match for her. Do this, and style me
Thy advancement.

BOSOLA. But by what means shall I find him out?

CARDINAL. There is a gentleman call'd Delio
Here in the camp, that hath been long approv'd
His loyal friend. Set eye upon that fellow;
Follow him to mass; may be Antonio,
Although he do account religion
But a school-name, for fashion of the world
May accompany him; or else go inquire out

Delio's confessor, and see if you can bribe
Him to reveal it. There are a thousand ways
A man might find to trace him; as to know
What fellows haunt the Jews for taking up
Great sums of money, for sure he's in want;
Or else to go to the picture-makers, and learn
Who bought[114] her picture lately: some of these
Happily may take.

BOSOLA. Well, I'll not freeze i' th' business:
I would see that wretched thing, Antonio,
Above all sights i' th' world.

CARDINAL. Do, and be happy. [*Exit.*]

BOSOLA. This fellow doth breed basilisks in's eyes,
He's nothing else but murder; yet he seems
Not to have notice of the duchess' death.
'Tis his cunning: I must follow his example;
There cannot be a surer way to trace
Than that of an old fox.

[*Re-enter* JULIA, *with a pistol.*]

JULIA. So, sir, you are well met.

BOSOLA. How Now!

JULIA. Nay, the doors are fast enough:
Now, sir, I will make you confess your treachery.

BOSOLA. Treachery!

JULIA. Yes, confess to me
Which of my women 'twas you hir'd to put
Love-powder into my drink?

BOSOLA. Love-powder!

JULIA. Yes, when I was at Malfi.
Why should I fall in love with such a face else?
I have already suffer'd for thee so much pain,
The only remedy to do me good
Is to kill my longing.

BOSOLA. Sure, your pistol holds
Nothing but perfumes or kissing-comfits.[115]
Excellent lady!
You have a pretty way on 't to discover
Your longing. Come, come, I'll disarm you,
And arm you thus: yet this is wondrous strange.

JULIA. Compare thy form and my eyes together,

---

[114] So Dyce. Qq. BROUGHT.
[115] Perfumed sweetmeats for the breath.

You 'll find my love no such great miracle.
Now you 'll say
I am wanton: this nice modesty in ladies
Is but a troublesome familiar
That haunts them.

BOSOLA. Know you me, I am a blunt soldier.

JULIA. The better:
Sure, there wants fire where there are no lively sparks
Of roughness.

BOSOLA. And I want compliment.

JULIA. Why, ignorance
In courtship cannot make you do amiss,
If you have a heart to do well.

BOSOLA. You are very fair.

JULIA. Nay, if you lay beauty to my charge,
I must plead unguilty.

BOSOLA. Your bright eyes
Carry a quiver of darts in them sharper
Than sun-beams.

JULIA. You will mar me with commendation,
Put yourself to the charge of courting me,
Whereas now I woo you.

BOSOLA. [*aside.*] I have it, I will work upon this creature.—
Let us grow most amorously familiar:
If the great cardinal now should see me thus,
Would he not count me a villain?

JULIA. No; he might count me a wanton,
Not lay a scruple of offence on you;
For if I see and steal a diamond,
The fault is not i' th' stone, but in me the thief
That purloins it. I am sudden with you.
We that are great women of pleasure use to cut off
These uncertain wishes and unquiet longings,
And in an instant join the sweet delight
And the pretty excuse together. Had you been i' th' street,
Under my chamber-window, even there
I should have courted you.

BOSOLA. O, you are an excellent lady!

JULIA. Bid me do somewhat for you presently
To express I love you.

BOSOLA. I will; and if you love me,
Fail not to effect it.
The cardinal is grown wondrous melancholy;
Demand the cause, let him not put you off
With feign'd excuse; discover the main ground on 't.

JULIA. Why would you know this?

BOSOLA. I have depended on him,
And I hear that he is fall'n in some disgrace
With the emperor: if he be, like the mice
That forsake falling houses, I would shift
To other dependance.

JULIA. You shall not need
Follow the wars: I'll be your maintenance.

BOSOLA. And I your loyal servant: but I cannot
Leave my calling.

JULIA. Not leave an ungrateful
General for the love of a sweet lady!
You are like some cannot sleep in feather-beds,
But must have blocks for their pillows.

BOSOLA. Will you do this?

JULIA. Cunningly.

BOSOLA. To-morrow I'll expect th' intelligence.

JULIA. To-morrow! get you into my cabinet;
You shall have it with you. Do not delay me,
No more than I do you: I am like one
That is condemn'd; I have my pardon promis'd,
But I would see it seal'd. Go, get you in:
You shall see my wind my tongue about his heart
Like a skein of silk.

[*Exit* BOSOLA.]

[*Re-enter* CARDINAL.]

CARDINAL. Where are you?

[*Enter* SERVANTS.]

SERVANTS. Here.

CARDINAL. Let none, upon your lives, have conference
With the Prince Ferdinand, unless I know it.—
[*aside.*] In this distraction he may reveal
The murder.

[*Exeunt* SERVANTS.]

Yond's my lingering consumption:
I am weary of her, and by any means
Would be quit of.

JULIA. How now, my lord! what ails you?

CARDINAL. Nothing.

JULIA. O, you are much alter'd:
    Come, I must be your secretary, and remove
    This lead from off your bosom: what's the matter?

CARDINAL. I may not tell you.

JULIA. Are you so far in love with sorrow
    You cannot part with part of it? Or think you
    I cannot love your grace when you are sad
    As well as merry? Or do you suspect
    I, that have been a secret to your heart
    These many winters, cannot be the same
    Unto your tongue?

CARDINAL. Satisfy thy longing,—
    The only way to make thee keep my counsel
    Is, not to tell thee.

JULIA. Tell your echo this,
    Or flatterers, that like echoes still report
    What they hear though most imperfect, and not me;
    For if that you be true unto yourself,
    I'll know.

CARDINAL. Will you rack me?

JULIA. No, judgment shall
    Draw it from you: it is an equal fault,
    To tell one's secrets unto all or none.

CARDINAL. The first argues folly.

JULIA. But the last tyranny.

CARDINAL. Very well: why, imagine I have committed
    Some secret deed which I desire the world
    May never hear of.

JULIA. Therefore may not I know it?
    You have conceal'd for me as great a sin
    As adultery. Sir, never was occasion
    For perfect trial of my constancy
    Till now: sir, I beseech you——

CARDINAL. You 'll repent it.

JULIA. Never.

CARDINAL. It hurries thee to ruin: I'll not tell thee.
    Be well advis'd, and think what danger 'tis
    To receive a prince's secrets. They that do,
    Had need have their breasts hoop'd with adamant
    To contain them. I pray thee, yet be satisfi'd;
    Examine thine own frailty; 'tis more easy
    To tie knots than unloose them. 'Tis a secret
    That, like a ling'ring poison, may chance lie
    Spread in thy veins, and kill thee seven year hence.

JULIA. Now you dally with me.

CARDINAL. No more; thou shalt know it.
By my appointment the great Duchess of Malfi
And two of her young children, four nights since,
Were strangl'd.

JULIA. O heaven! sir, what have you done!

CARDINAL. How now? How settles this? Think you your bosom
Will be a grave dark and obscure enough
For such a secret?

JULIA. You have undone yourself, sir.

CARDINAL. Why?

JULIA. It lies not in me to conceal it.

CARDINAL. No?
Come, I will swear you to 't upon this book.

JULIA. Most religiously.

CARDINAL. Kiss it.

[*She kisses the book.*]

Now you shall never utter it; thy curiosity
Hath undone thee; thou 'rt poison'd with that book.
Because I knew thou couldst not keep my counsel,
I have bound thee to 't by death.

[*Re-enter* BOSOLA.]

BOSOLA. For pity-sake, hold!

CARDINAL. Ha, Bosola!

JULIA. I forgive you
This equal piece of justice you have done;
For I betray'd your counsel to that fellow.
He over-heard it; that was the cause I said
It lay not in me to conceal it.

BOSOLA. O foolish woman,
Couldst not thou have poison'd him?

JULIA. 'Tis weakness,
Too much to think what should have been done. I go,
I know not whither.

[*Dies.*]

CARDINAL. Wherefore com'st thou hither?

BOSOLA. That I might find a great man like yourself,
Not out of his wits, as the Lord Ferdinand,
To remember my service.

CARDINAL. I'll have thee hew'd in pieces.

BOSOLA. Make not yourself such a promise of that life
    Which is not yours to dispose of.

CARDINAL. Who plac'd thee here?

BOSOLA. Her lust, as she intended.

CARDINAL. Very well:
    Now you know me for your fellow-murderer.

BOSOLA. And wherefore should you lay fair marble colours
    Upon your rotten purposes to me?
    Unless you imitate some that do plot great treasons,
    And when they have done, go hide themselves i' th' grave
    Of those were actors in 't?

CARDINAL. No more; there is
    A fortune attends thee.

BOSOLA. Shall I go sue to Fortune any longer?
    'Tis the fool's pilgrimage.

CARDINAL. I have honours in store for thee.

BOSOLA. There are a many ways that conduct to seeming
    Honour, and some of them very dirty ones.

CARDINAL. Throw to the devil
    Thy melancholy. The fire burns well;
    What need we keep a stirring of 't, and make
    A greater smother?[116] Thou wilt kill Antonio?

BOSOLA. Yes.

CARDINAL. Take up that body.

BOSOLA. I think I shall
    Shortly grow the common bier for church-yards.

CARDINAL. I will allow thee some dozen of attendants
    To aid thee in the murder.

BOSOLA. O, by no means. Physicians that apply horse-leeches to any rank swelling use to cut off their tails, that the blood may run through them the faster: let me have no train when I go to shed blood, less it make me have a greater when I ride to the gallows.

CARDINAL. Come to me after midnight, to help to remove
    That body to her own lodging. I'll give out
    She died o' th' plague; 'twill breed the less inquiry
    After her death.

BOSOLA. Where's Castruccio her husband?

CARDINAL. He's rode to Naples, to take possession
    Of Antonio's citadel.

BOSOLA. Believe me, you have done a very happy turn.

CARDINAL. Fail not to come. There is the master-key
    Of our lodgings; and by that you may conceive

---

[116] Smoke.

What trust I plant in you.
BOSOLA. You shall find me ready.

[*Exit* CARDINAL.]

O poor Antonio, though nothing be so needful
To thy estate as pity, yet I find
Nothing so dangerous! I must look to my footing:
In such slippery ice-pavements men had need
To be frost-nail'd well, they may break their necks else;
The precedent's here afore me. How this man
Bears up in blood! seems fearless! Why, 'tis well;
Security some men call the suburbs of hell,
Only a dead wall between. Well, good Antonio,
I'll seek thee out; and all my care shall be
To put thee into safety from the reach
Of these most cruel biters that have got
Some of thy blood already. It may be,
I'll join with thee in a most just revenge.
The weakest arm is strong enough that strikes
With the sword of justice. Still methinks the duchess
Haunts me: there, there!—'Tis nothing but my melancholy.
O Penitence, let me truly taste thy cup,
That throws men down only to raise them up! [*Exit.*]

SCENE III. *A fortification.*

[*Enter* ANTONIO *and* DELIO. *Echo from the* DUCHESS'*s Grave.*]

DELIO. Yond's the cardinal's window. This fortification
    Grew from the ruins of an ancient abbey;
    And to yond side o' th' river lies a wall,
    Piece of a cloister, which in my opinion
    Gives the best echo that you ever heard,
    So hollow and so dismal, and withal
    So plain in the distinction of our words,
    That many have suppos'd it is a spirit
    That answers.
ANTONIO. I do love these ancient ruins.
    We never tread upon them but we set
    Our foot upon some reverend history;
    And, questionless, here in this open court,
    Which now lies naked to the injuries
    Of stormy weather, some men lie interr'd
    Lov'd the church so well, and gave so largely to 't,

> They thought it should have canopied their bones
> Till dooms-day. But all things have their end;
> Churches and cities, which have diseases like to men,
> Must have like death that we have.

ECHO. Like death that we have.

DELIO. Now the echo hath caught you.

ANTONIO. It groan'd methought, and gave
> A very deadly accent.

ECHO. Deadly accent.

DELIO. I told you 'twas a pretty one. You may make it
> A huntsman, or a falconer, a musician,
> Or a thing of sorrow.

ECHO. A thing of sorrow.

ANTONIO. Ay, sure, that suits it best.

ECHO. That suits it best.

ANTONIO. 'Tis very like my wife's voice.

ECHO. Ay, wife's voice.

DELIO. Come, let us walk further from t.
> I would not have you go to the cardinal's to-night:
> Do not.

ECHO. Do not.

DELIO. Wisdom doth not more moderate wasting sorrow
Than time. Take time for 't; be mindful of thy safety.

ECHO. Be mindful of thy safety.

ANTONIO. Necessity compels me.
> Make scrutiny through the passages
> Of your own life, you 'll find it impossible
> To fly your fate.

ECHO. O, fly your fate!

DELIO. Hark! the dead stones seem to have pity on you,
> And give you good counsel.

ANTONIO. Echo, I will not talk with thee,
> For thou art a dead thing.

ECHO. Thou art a dead thing.

ANTONIO. My duchess is asleep now,
> And her little ones, I hope sweetly. O heaven,
> Shall I never see her more?

ECHO. Never see her more.

ANTONIO. I mark'd not one repetition of the echo
> But that; and on the sudden a clear light
> Presented me a face folded in sorrow.

DELIO. Your fancy merely.

ANTONIO. Come, I'll be out of this ague,
> For to live thus is not indeed to live;
> It is a mockery and abuse of life.

I will not henceforth save myself by halves;
Lose all, or nothing.
DELIO. Your own virtue save you!
I'll fetch your eldest son, and second you.
It may be that the sight of his own blood
Spread in so sweet a figure may beget
The more compassion. However, fare you well.
Though in our miseries Fortune have a part,
Yet in our noble sufferings she hath none.
Contempt of pain, that we may call our own.

[*Exeunt.*]

SCENE IV. *Milan. An apartment in the*
residence of the CARDINAL *and* FERDINAND.

[*Enter* CARDINAL, PESCARA, MALATESTI, RODERIGO, *and*
GRISOLAN.]

CARDINAL. You shall not watch to-night by the sick prince;
His grace is very well recover'd.
MALATESTI. Good my lord, suffer us.
CARDINAL. O, by no means;
The noise, and change of object in his eye,
Doth more distract him. I pray, all to bed;
And though you hear him in his violent fit,
Do not rise, I entreat you.
PESCARA. So, sir; we shall not.
CARDINAL. Nay, I must have you promise
Upon your honours, for I was enjoin'd to 't
By himself; and he seem'd to urge it sensibly.
PESCARA. Let our honours bind this trifle.
CARDINAL. Nor any of your followers.
MALATESTI. Neither.
CARDINAL. It may be, to make trial of your promise,
When he's asleep, myself will rise and feign
Some of his mad tricks, and cry out for help,
And feign myself in danger.
MALATESTI. If your throat were cutting,
I 'd not come at you, now I have protested against it.
CARDINAL. Why, I thank you.
GRISOLAN. 'Twas a foul storm to-night.
RODERIGO. The Lord Ferdinand's chamber shook like an osier.
MALATESTI. 'Twas nothing put pure kindness in the devil
To rock his own child.

[*Exeunt all except the* CARDINAL.]

CARDINAL. The reason why I would not suffer these
    About my brother, is, because at midnight
    I may with better privacy convey
    Julia's body to her own lodging. O, my conscience!
    I would pray now; but the devil takes away my heart
    For having any confidence in prayer.
    About this hour I appointed Bosola
    To fetch the body. When he hath serv'd my turn,

[*He dies.*]

[*Exit.*]

[*Enter* BOSOLA.]

BOSOLA. Ha! 'twas the cardinal's voice; I heard him name
    Bosola and my death. Listen; I hear one's footing.

[*Enter* FERDINAND.]

FERDINAND. Strangling is a very quiet death.
BOSOLA. [*aside.*] Nay, then, I see I must stand upon my guard.
FERDINAND. What say to that? Whisper softly: do you agree to 't?
    So; it must be done i' th' dark; the cardinal would not for a
    thousand pounds the doctor should see it. [*Exit.*]
BOSOLA. My death is plotted; here's the consequence of murder.
    We value not desert nor Christian breath,
    When we know black deeds must be cur'd with death.

[*Enter* ANTONIO *and* SERVANT.]

SERVANT. Here stay, sir, and be confident, I pray;
    I'll fetch you a dark lantern. [*Exit.*]
ANTONIO. Could I take him at his prayers,
    There were hope of pardon.
BOSOLA. Fall right, my sword!—

[*Stabs him.*]

    I'll not give thee so much leisure as to pray.
ANTONIO. O, I am gone! Thou hast ended a long suit
    In a minute.

BOSOLA. What art thou?

ANTONIO. A most wretched thing,

> That only have thy benefit in death,
> To appear myself.

[*Re-enter* SERVANT *with a lantern.*]

SERVANT. Where are you, sir?

ANTONIO. Very near my home.—Bosola!

SERVANT. O, misfortune!

BOSOLA. Smother thy pity, thou art dead else.—Antonio!

> The man I would have sav'd 'bove mine own life!
> We are merely the stars' tennis-balls, struck and banded
> Which way please them.—O good Antonio,
> I'll whisper one thing in thy dying ear
> Shall make thy heart break quickly! Thy fair duchess
> And two sweet children——

ANTONIO. Their very names

> Kindle a little life in me.

BOSOLA. Are murder'd.

ANTONIO. Some men have wish'd to die

> At the hearing of sad tidings; I am glad
> That I shall do 't in sadness.[117] I would not now
> Wish my wounds balm'd nor heal'd, for I have no use
> To put my life to. In all our quest of greatness,
> Like wanton boys whose pastime is their care,
> We follow after bubbles blown in th' air.
> Pleasure of life, what is 't? Only the good hours
> Of an ague; merely a preparative to rest,
> To endure vexation. I do not ask
> The process of my death; only commend me
> To Delio.

BOSOLA. Break, heart!

ANTONIO. And let my son fly the courts to princes. [*Dies.*]

BOSOLA. Thou seem'st to have lov'd Antonio.

SERVANT. I brought him hither,

> To have reconcil'd him to the cardinal.

BOSOLA. I do not ask thee that.

> Take him up, if thou tender thine own life,
> And bear him where the lady Julia
> Was wont to lodge.—O, my fate moves swift!
> I have this cardinal in the forge already;
> Now I'll bring him to th' hammer. O direful misprision![118]

---

[117] Reality.

I will not imitate things glorious.
No more than base; I'll be mine own example.—
On, on, and look thou represent, for silence,
The thing thou bear'st.[119]

[*Exeunt.*]

SCENE V. *Milan. Another apartment in the residence of
the* CARDINAL *and* FERDINAND.

[*Enter* CARDINAL, *with a book.*]

CARDINAL. I am puzzl'd in a question about hell;
He says, in hell there's one material fire,
And yet it shall not burn all men alike.
Lay him by. How tedious is a guilty conscience!
When I look into the fish-ponds in my garden,
Methinks I see a thing arm'd with a rake,
That seems to strike at me.

[*Enter* BOSOLA, *and* SERVANT *bearing* ANTONIO's *body.*]

Now, art thou come?
Thou look'st ghastly;
There sits in thy face some great determination
Mix'd with some fear.
BOSOLA. Thus it lightens into action:
I am come to kill thee.
CARDINAL. Ha!—Help! our guard!
BOSOLA. Thou art deceiv'd; they are out of thy howling.
CARDINAL. Hold; and I will faithfully divide
Revenues with thee.
BOSOLA. Thy prayers and proffers
Are both unseasonable.
CARDINAL. Raise the watch!
We are betray'd!
BOSOLA. I have confin'd your flight:
I'll suffer your retreat to Julia's chamber,
But no further.
CARDINAL. Help! we are betray'd!

[*Enter, above,* PESCARA, MALATESTI, RODERIGO, *and* GRISOLAN.]

---

[118] Mistake.
[119] i.e., the dead body.

MALATESTI. Listen.

CARDINAL. My dukedom for rescue!

RODERIGO. Fie upon his counterfeiting!

MALATESTI. Why, 'tis not the cardinal.

RODERIGO. Yes, yes, 'tis he:
  But, I'll see him hang'd ere I'll go down to him.

CARDINAL. Here's a plot upon me; I am assaulted! I am lost,
  Unless some rescue!

GRISOLAN. He doth this pretty well;
  But it will not serve to laugh me out of mine honour.

CARDINAL. The sword's at my throat!

RODERIGO. You would not bawl so loud then.

MALATESTI. Come, come, let's go to bed: he told us this much aforehand.

PESCARA. He wish'd you should not come at him; but, believe 't,
  The accent of the voice sounds not in jest:
  I'll down to him, howsoever, and with engines
  Force ope the doors.

  [*Exit above.*]

RODERIGO. Let's follow him aloof,
  And note how the cardinal will laugh at him.

  [*Exeunt, above,* MALATESTI, RODERIGO, *and* GRISOLAN.]

BOSOLA. There's for you first,
  'Cause you shall not unbarricade the door
  To let in rescue.

  [*Kills the* SERVANT.]

CARDINAL. What cause hast thou to pursue my life?

BOSOLA. Look there.

CARDINAL. Antonio!

BOSOLA. Slain by my hand unwittingly.
  Pray, and be sudden. When thou kill'd'st thy sister,
  Thou took'st from Justice her most equal balance,
  And left her naught but her sword.

CARDINAL. O, mercy!

BOSOLA. Now it seems thy greatness was only outward;
  For thou fall'st faster of thyself than calamity
  Can drive thee. I'll not waste longer time; there!

[*Stabs him.*]

CARDINAL. Thou hast hurt me.
BOSOLA. Again!
CARDINAL. Shall I die like a leveret,
    Without any resistance?—Help, help, help!
    I am slain!

[*Enter* FERDINAND.]

FERDINAND. Th' alarum! Give me a fresh horse;
    Rally the vaunt-guard, or the day is lost,
    Yield, yield! I give you the honour of arms
    Shake my sword over you; will you yield?
CARDINAL. Help me; I am your brother!
FERDINAND. The devil!
    My brother fight upon the adverse party!

[*He wounds the* CARDINAL, *and, in the scuffle, gives* BOSOLA *his death-wound.*]

    There flies your ransom.
CARDINAL. O justice!
    I suffer now for what hath former bin:
    Sorrow is held the eldest child of sin.
FERDINAND. Now you 're brave fellows. Caesar's fortune was harder
    than Pompey's; Caesar died in the arms of prosperity, Pompey at
    the feet of disgrace. You both died in the field. The pain's nothing;
    pain many times is taken away with the apprehension of greater, as
    the tooth-ache with the sight of a barber that comes to pull it out.
    There's philosophy for you.
BOSOLA. Now my revenge is perfect.—Sink, thou main cause

[*Kills* FERDINAND.]

    Of my undoing!—The last part of my life
    Hath done me best service.
FERDINAND. Give me some wet hay; I am broken-winded.
    I do account this world but a dog-kennel:
    I will vault credit and affect high pleasures
    Beyond death.
BOSOLA. He seems to come to himself,
    Now he's so near the bottom.
FERDINAND. My sister, O my sister! there's the cause on 't.

Whether we fall by ambition, blood, or lust,
Like diamonds, we are cut with our own dust. [*Dies.*]
CARDINAL. Thou hast thy payment too.
BOSOLA. Yes, I hold my weary soul in my teeth;
  'Tis ready to part from me. I do glory
  That thou, which stood'st like a huge pyramid
  Begun upon a large and ample base,
  Shalt end in a little point, a kind of nothing.

[*Enter, below*, PESCARA, MALATESTI, RODERIGO, *and* GRISOLAN.]

PESCARA. How now, my lord!
MALATESTI. O sad disaster!
RODERIGO. How comes this?
BOSOLA. Revenge for the Duchess of Malfi murdered
  By the Arragonian brethren; for Antonio
  Slain by this hand; for lustful Julia
  Poison'd by this man; and lastly for myself,
  That was an actor in the main of all
  Much 'gainst mine own good nature, yet i' the end
  Neglected.
PESCARA. How now, my lord!
CARDINAL. Look to my brother:
  He gave us these large wounds, as we were struggling
  Here i' th' rushes. And now, I pray, let me
  Be laid by and never thought of. [*Dies.*]
PESCARA. How fatally, it seems, he did withstand
  His own rescue!
MALATESTI. Thou wretched thing of blood,
  How came Antonio by his death?
BOSOLA. In a mist; I know not how:
  Such a mistake as I have often seen
  In a play. O, I am gone!
  We are only like dead walls or vaulted graves,
  That, ruin'd, yield no echo. Fare you well.
  It may be pain, but no harm, to me to die
  In so good a quarrel. O, this gloomy world!
  In what a shadow, or deep pit of darkness,
  Doth womanish and fearful mankind live!
  Let worthy minds ne'er stagger in distrust
  To suffer death or shame for what is just:
  Mine is another voyage. [*Dies.*]
PESCARA. The noble Delio, as I came to th' palace,
  Told me of Antonio's being here, and show'd me
  A pretty gentleman, his son and heir.

[*Enter* DELIO, *and* ANTONIO'*s Son.*]

MALATESTI. O sir, you come too late!
DELIO. I heard so, and
    Was arm'd for 't, ere I came. Let us make noble use
    Of this great ruin; and join all our force
    To establish this young hopeful gentleman
    In's mother's right. These wretched eminent things
    Leave no more fame behind 'em, than should one
    Fall in a frost, and leave his print in snow;
    As soon as the sun shines, it ever melts,
    Both form and matter. I have ever thought
    Nature doth nothing so great for great men
    As when she's pleas'd to make them lords of truth:
    Integrity of life is fame's best friend,
    Which nobly, beyond death, shall crown the end.

[*Exeunt.*]

THE DEVIL'S LAW-CASE

DRAMATIS PERSONAE

ROMELIO, *a merchant.*
CONTARINO, *a nobleman, and suitor to Jolenta.*
ERCOLE, *a Knight of Malta, also suitor to Jolenta.*
CRISPIANO, *a lawyer.*
JULIO, *son to Crispiano.*
PROSPERO, *a merchant, and colleage of Romelio.*
ARIOSTO, *a lawyer, and afterwards a judge.*
CONTILUPO, *a lawyer, representing Leonora at the trial.*
SANITONELLA, *a law-clerk, assisting Contilupo.*
A CAPUCHIN FRIAR.
BAPTISTA, *a merchant (ghost character.)*
LEONORA, *mother of Romelio and of Jolenta.*
JOLENTA, *sister of Romelio, and sought in marriage by Contarino
    and Ercole.*
WINIFRID, *her waiting woman.*
ANGIOLELLA, *a nun, pregnant by Romelio.*
*Two Surgeons, Judges, Lawyers, Bellmen, Registrar, Marshal,
    Herald, and Servants.*

THE DEVIL'S LAW-CASE

ACT I.

SCENE I. *The action takes place at Naples.*

[*Enter* ROMELIO, *and* PROSPERO.]

PROSPERO. You have shown a world of wealth; I did not think
    There had been a merchant liv'd in Italy
    Of half your substance.
ROMELIO. I'll give the King of Spain
    Ten thousand ducats yearly, and discharge
    My yearly custom. The Hollanders scarce trade
    More generally than I: my factors' wives
    Wear chaperons of velvet, and my scriveners
    Merely through my employment, grow so rich,
    They build their palaces and belvederes
    With musical water-works: never in my life
    Had I loss at sea. They call me on th'Exchange,
    The fortunate young man, and make great suit
    To venture with me. Shall I tell you sir,
    Of a strange confidence in my way of trading?
    I reckon it as certain as the gain
    In erecting a lottery.
PROSPERO. I pray, sir, what do you think
    Of Signor Baptista's estate?
ROMELIO. A mere beggar:
    He's worth some fifty thousand ducats.
PROSPERO. Is not that well?
ROMELIO. How, well? For a man to be melted to snow-water,
    With toiling in the world from three and twenty,
    Till threescore, for poor fifty thousand ducats!
PROSPERO. To your estate 'tis little I confess:
    You have the spring tide of gold.
ROMELIO. Faith, and for silver,
    Should I not send it packing to th'East Indies,
    We should have a glut on't.

[*Enter* SERVANT.]

SERVANT. Here's the great Lord Contarino.
PROSPERO. O, I know
    His business, he's a suitor to your sister.

ROMELIO. Yes sir, but to you—
    As my most trusted friend, I utter it—
    I will break the alliance.
PROSPERO. You are ill-advis'd then;
    There lives not a completer gentleman
    In Italy, nor of a more ancient house.
ROMELIO. What tell you me of gentry? 'Tis nought else
    But a superstitious relic of time past:
    And sift it to the true worth, it is nothing
    But ancient riches: and in him you know
    They are pitifully in the wane. He makes his colour
    Of visiting us so often, to sell land,
    And thinks if he can gain my sister's love,
    To recover the treble value.
PROSPERO. Sure he loves her
    Entirely, and she deserves it.
ROMELIO. Faith, though she were
    Crook'd-shoulder'd, having such a portion,
    She would have noble suitors. But truth is,
    I would wish my noble venturer take heed;
    It may be whiles he hopes to catch a gilthead,
    He may draw up a gudgeon.

    [*Enter* CONTARINO.]

PROSPERO. He's come. Sir I will leave you.

    [*Exeunt* PROSPERO *and* SERVANT.]

CONTARINO. I sent you the evidence of the piece of land
    I motioned to you for the sale.
ROMELIO. Yes
CONTARINO. Has your counsel perus'd it?
ROMELIO. Not yet my Lord. Do you
    Intend to travel?
CONTARINO. No.
ROMELIO. O then you lose
    That which makes a man most absolute.
CONTARINO. Yet I have heard
    Of divers, that in passing of the Alps,
    Have but exchang'd their virtues at dear rate
    For other vices.
ROMELIO. O my Lord, lie not idle;
    The chiefest action for a man of great spirit,
    Is never to be out of action. We should think

The soul was never put into the body,
Which has so many rare and curious pieces
Of mathematical motion, to stand still.
Virtue is ever sowing of her seeds:
In the trenches for the soldier; in the wakeful study
For the scholar; in the furrows of the sea
For men of our profession: of all which
Arise and spring up honour. Come, I know
You have some noble great design in hand,
That you levy so much money.

CONTARINO. Sir, I'll tell you,
The greatest part of it I mean to employ
In payment of my debts, and the remainder
Is like to bring me into greater bonds,
As I aim it.

ROMELIO. How sir?

CONTARINO. I intend it
For the charge of my wedding.

ROMELIO. Are you to be married, my Lord?

CONTARINO. Yes sir; and I must now entreat your pardon,
That I have conceal'd from you a business
Wherein you had at first been call'd to counsel,
But that I thought it a less fault in friendship,
To engage myself thus far without your knowledge,
Than to do it against your will: another reason
Was that I would not publish to the world,
Nor have it whisper'd, scarce, what wealthy voyage
I went about, till I had got the mine
In mine own possession.

ROMELIO. You are dark to me yet.

CONTARINO. I'll now remove the cloud. Sir, your sister and I
Are vow'd each other's, and there only wants
Her worthy mother's, and your fair consents
To style it marriage. This is a way,
Not only to make a friendship, but confirm it
For our posterities. How do you look upon't?

ROMELIO. Believe me sir, as on the principal column
To advance our house: why you bring honour with you,
Which is the soul of wealth. I shall be proud
To live to see my little nephews ride
O'th upper hand of their uncles; and the daughters
Be rank'd by heralds at solemnities
Before the mother: all this deriv'd
From your nobility. Do not blame me sir,
If I be taken with't exceedingly:

For this same honour with us citizens,
Is a thing we are mainly fond of, especially
When it comes without money, which is very seldom.
But as you do perceive my present temper,
Be sure I am yours—fir'd with scorn and laughter
At your over-confident purpose—and no doubt
My mother will be of your mind.
CONTARINO. 'Tis my hope sir.

[*Exit* ROMELIO.]

I do observe how this Romelio
Has very worthy parts, were they not blasted
By insolent vainglory. There rests now
The mother's approbation to the match,
Who is a woman of that state and bearing,
Though she be city-born, both in her language,
Her garments, and her table, she excels
Our ladies of the Court: she goes not gaudy,
Yet I have seen her wear one diamond,
Would have bought twenty gay ones out of their clothes,
And some of them, without the greater grace,
Out of their honesties.

[*Enter* LEONORA.]

She comes, I will try
How she stands affected to me, without relating
My contract with her daughter.
LEONORA. Sir, you are nobly welcome, and presume
You are in a place that's wholly dedicated
To your service.
CONTARINO. I am ever bound to you
For many special favours.
LEONORA. Sir, your fame
Renders you most worthy of it.
CONTARINO. It could never have got
A sweeter air to fly in, than your breath.
LEONORA. You have been strange a long time; you are weary
Of our unseasonable time of feeding:
Indeed, th'exchange bell makes us dine so late.
I think the ladies of the Court from us
Learn to lie so long abed.
CONTARINO. They have a kind of exchange among them too.
Marry, unless it be to hear of news, I take it,

Theirs is like the New Burse,[120] Thinly furnish'd
With tires and new fashions. I have a suit to you.
LEONORA. I would not have you value it the less,
    If I say, 'tis granted already.
CONTARINO. You are all bounty.
    'Tis to bestow your picture on me.
LEONORA. O sir,
    Shadows are coveted in summer; and with me,
    'Tis fall o'th' leaf.
CONTARINO. You enjoy the best of time:
    This latter spring of yours shows in my eye,
    More fruitful and more temperate withall,
    Than that whose date is only limited
    By the music of the cuckoo.
LEONORA. Indeed sir, I dare tell you,
    My looking glass is a true one, and as yet
    It does not terrify me. Must you have my picture?
CONTARINO. So please you lady, and I shall preserve it
    As a most choice object.
LEONORA. You will enjoin me to a strange punishment:
    With what a compell'd face a woman sits
    While she is drawing! I have noted divers,
    Either to feign smiles, or suck in the lips,
    To have a little mouth; ruffle the cheeks,
    To have the dimple seen, and so disorder
    The face with affectation, at next sitting
    It has not been the same. I have known others
    Have lost the entire fashion of their face,
    In half an hour's sitting.
CONTARINO. How?
LEONORA. In hot weather,
    The painting on their face has been so mellow,
    They have left the poor man harder work by half,
    To mend the copy he wrought by. But indeed,
    If ever I would have mine drawn to th' life,
    I would have a painter steal it, at such a time
    I were devoutly kneeling at my prayers;
    There is then a heavenly beauty in't; the soul
    Moves in the superficies.
CONTARINO. Excellent lady,
    Now you teach beauty a preservative,

---

[120] i.e. the New Exchange in the Strand, where were shops in which female finery and trinkets of every description were sold. Our old dramatics do not scruple to attribute to a foreign country the peculiarities of their own.

More than 'gainst fading colours; and your judgement
Is perfect in all things.

LEONORA. Indeed sir, I am a widow,
And want the addition to make it so:
For man's experience has still been held
Woman's best eyesight. I pray sir tell me,
You are about to sell a piece of land
To my son, I hear.

CONTARINO. 'Tis truth.

LEONORA. Now I could rather wish,
That noblemen would ever live i'th' country,
Rather than make their visits up to th' city
About such business. O sir, noble houses
Have no such goodly prospects any way,
As into their own land: the decay of that,
Next to their begging church land, is a ruin
Worth all men's pity. Sir, I have forty thousand crowns
Sleep in my chest, shall waken when you please,
And fly to your commands. Will you stay supper?

CONTARINO. I cannot, worthy lady.

LEONORA. I would not have you come hither sir, to sell,
But to settle your estate. I hope you understand
Wherefore I make this proffer: so I leave you. [*Exit.*]

CONTARINO. What a treasury have I perch'd [on]![121] 'I hope
You understand wherefore I make this proffer.'
She has got some intelligence, how I intend to marry
Her daughter, and ingenuously perceiv'd
That by her picture, which I beg'd of her,
I meant the fair Jolenta. Here's a letter,
Which gives express charge, not to visit her
Till midnight: *fail not to come, for 'tis a business that concerns*
    both our honours.
Yours, in danger to be lost, Jolenta.
'Tis a strange injuction; what should be the business?
She is not chang'd I hope. I'll thither straight:
For women's resolutions in such deeds,
Like bees, light oft on flowers, and oft on weeds. [*Exit.*]

---

[121] The old copy "pearch'd."

SCENE II.

[*Enter* ERCOLE, ROMELIO, *and* JOLENTA.]

ROMELIO. O sister, come, the tailor must to work,
    To make your wedding clothes.
JOLENTA. The tomb-maker,
    To take measure of my coffin.
ROMELIO. Tomb-maker?
    Look you, the King of Spain greets you.
JOLENTA. What does this mean?
    Do you serve process on me?
ROMELIO. Process? Come,
    You would be witty now.
JOLENTA. Why, what's this, I pray?
ROMELIO. Infinite grace to you: it is a letter
    From his Catholic Majesty, for the commends
    Of this gentleman for your husband.
JOLENTA. In good season:
    I hope he will not have my allegiance stretch'd
    To the undoing of myself.
ROMELIO. Undo yourself? He does proclaim him here—
JOLENTA. Not for a traitor, does he?
ROMELIO. You are not mad?
    For one of the noblest gentlemen.
JOLENTA. Yet kings many times
    Know merely but men's outsides. Was this commendation
    Voluntary, think you?
ROMELIO. Voluntary: what mean you by that?
JOLENTA. Why I do not think but he beg'd it of the King,
    And it may fortune to be out of's way:
    Some better suit, that would have stood his Lordship
    In far more stead. Letters of commendations;
    Why 'tis reported that they are grown stale,
    When places fall i'th' university.
    I pray you return his pass: for to a widow
    That longs to be a courtier, this paper
    May do knight's service.
ERCOLE. Mistake not excellent mistress, these commends
    Express, his Majesty of Spain has given me
    Both addition of honour, as you may perceive
    By my habit, and a place here to command
    O'er thirty galleys: this your brother shows,
    As wishing that you would be partner

In my good fortune.

ROMELIO. I pray come hither.
    Have I any interest in you?

JOLENTA. You are my brother

ROMELIO. I would have you then use me with that respect
    You may still keep me so, and to be sway'd
    In this main business of life, which wants
    Greatest consideration, your marriage,
    By my direction. Here's a gentleman—

JOLENTA. Sir: I have often told you,
    I am so little my own to dispose that way,
    That I can never be his.

ROMELIO. Come, too much light
    Makes you moo-eyed: are you in love with title?
    I will have a herald, whose continual practice
    Is all in pedigree, come a-wooing to you,
    Or an antiquary in old buskins.

ERCOLE. Sir, you have done me the mainest wrong
    That e'er was off'red to a gentleman
    Of my breeding.

ROMELIO. Why sir?

ERCOLE. You have led me
    With a vain confidence, that I should marry
    Your sister, have proclaim'd it to my friends,
    Employ'd the greatest lawyers of our state
    To settle her a jointure; and the issue
    Is, that I must become ridiculous
    Both to my friends and enemies: I will leave you
    Till I call to you for a strict account
    Of your unmanly dealing.

ROMELIO. Stay my Lord.—
    Do you long to have my throat cut?—Good my Lord,
    Stay but a little, till I have remov'd
    This court-mist from her eyes, till I wake her
    From this dull sleep, wherein she'll dream herself
    To a deformed beggar.—You would marry
    The great Lord Contarino—

[*Enter* LEONORA.]

LEONORA. Contarino
    Were you talking of? He lost last night at dice
    Five thousand ducats; and when that was gone,
    Set at one throw a lordship, that twice trebled
    The former loss.

ROMELIO. And that flew after.

LEONORA. And most carefully
 Carried the gentleman in his caroche
 To a lawyer's chaber, there most legally
 To put him in possession: was this wisdom?

ROMELIO. O yes, their credit in the way of gaming
 Is the main thing they stand on; that must be paid,
 Though the brewer bawl for's money. And this lord
 Does she prefer i'th' way of marriage,
 Before our choice here, noble Ercole!

LEONORA. You'll be advis'd, I hope. Know for your sakes
 I married, that I might have children;
 And for your sakes, if you'll be rul'd by me,
 I will never marry again. Here's a gentleman
 Is noble, rich, well featur'd, but 'bove all,
 He loves you entirely; his intents are aim'd
 For an expedition 'gainst the Turk,
 Which makes the contract cannot be delayed.

JOLENTA. Contract? You must do this without my knowledge;
 Give me some potion to make me mad,
 And happily not knowing what I speak,
 I may then consent to't.

ROMELIO. Come, you are mad already,
 And I shall never hear you speak good sense,
 Till you name him for husband.

ERCOLE. Lady, I will do
 A manly office for you. I will leave you,
 To the freedom of your own soul; may it mothe whither
 Heaven and you please.

JOLENTA. Now you express yourself,
 Most nobly.

ROMELIO. Stay sir, what do you mean to do?

LEONORA. Hear me: if ever thou dost marry Contarino,
 All the misfortune that did ever dwell
 In a parent's curse, light on thee!

ERCOLE. O rise lady, certainly heaven never
 Intended kneeling to this fearful purpose.

JOLENTA. Your imprecation has undone me for ever.

ERCOLE. Give me your hand.

JOLENTA. No sir.

ROMELIO. Give't me then:
 O what rare workmanship have I seen this
 To finish with your needle, what excellent music
 Have these struck upon the viol! Now I'll teach
 A piece of art.

JOLENTA. Rather a damnable cunning,
    To have me go about to give't away,
    Without consent of my soul.
ROMELIO. Kiss her my lord.
    If crying had been regarded, maidenheads
    Had ne'er been lost; at least some apprearance of crying
    As an April shower i'th' sunshine—
LEONORA. She is yours.
ROMELIO. Nay, continue your station, and deal you in dumb show;
    Kiss this doggedness out of her.
LEONORA. To be contracted
    In tears, is but fashionable.
ROMELIO. Yet suppose
    That they were hearty—
LEONORA. Virgins must seem unwilling.
ROMELIO. O what else? And you remember, we observe
    The like in greater ceremonies than these contracts:
    At the consecration of prelates, the ever use
    Twice to say nay, and take it.
JOLENTA. O brother!
ROMELIO. Keep your possession, you have the door by th'ring,
    That's livery and seasin in England:[122]
    But my lord, kiss that tear from her lip;
    You'll find the rose the sweeter for the dew.
JOLENTA. Bitter as gall.
ROMELIO. Aye, aye, all you women,
    Although you be of never so low stature,
    Have gall in you most abundant; it exceeds
    Your brains by two ounces. I was saying somewhat:
    O, do but observe i'th' city, and you'll find
    The thriftiest bargains that were ever made,
    What a deal of wrangling ere they could be brought
    To an upshot!
LEONORA. Great persons do not ever come together—
ROMELIO. With revelling faces, nor is it necessary
    They should; the strangeness and unwillingness
    Wears the greater state, and gives occasion that
    The people may buzz and talk of't, though the bells
    Be tongue-tied at the wedding.
LEONORA. And truly I have heard say,
    To be a little strange to one another,

---

[122] The allusion here is to a ceremony used in the common law, on conveyance of lands, houses, &c. when the ring or latch of the door is delivered to the feoffee: *livery* and *seisin* are delivery and possession.

Will keep your longing fresh.

ROMELIO. Aye, and make you beget
    More children when y'are married: some doctors
    Are of that opinion. You see, my lord, we are merry
    At the contract; your sport is to come hereafter.

ERCOLE. I will leave you excellent lady, and withal
    Leave heart with you so entirely yours,
    That I protest, had I the least of hope
    To enjoy you, though I were to wait the time
    That scholars do in taking their degree
    In the noble arts, 'twere nothing. Howsoe'er,
    He parts from you, that will depart from life,
    To do you any service, and so humbly
    I take my leave.

JOLENTA. Sir, I will pray for you.

    [*Exit* ERCOLE.]

ROMELIO. Why, that's well; 'twill make your prayer complete,
    To pray for your husband.

JOLENTA. Husband!

LEONORA. This is
    The happiest hour that I ever arriv'd at. [*Exit.*]

ROMELIO. Husband, ay, husband! Come you peevish thing,
    Smile me a thank for the pains I have ta'en.

JOLENTA. I hate myself for being thus enforc'd;
    You may soon judge then what I think of you
    Which are the cause of it.

    [*Enter* WINIFRID.]

ROMELIO. You lady of the laundry, come hither.

WINIFRID. Sir?

ROMELIO. Look as you love your life, you have an eye
    Upon your mistress: I do henceforth bar her
    All visitansts. I do hear there are bawds abroad,
    That bring cut-works, and mantoons,[123] and convey letters
    To such young gentlewomen, and there are others
    That deal in corn-cutting, and fortune-telling:
    Let none of these come at her on your life,
    Nor Deuce-ace the wafer woman, that prigs abroad
    With musk melons, and malakatoons;[124]

---

[123] Qy. If from "*mantone*, a great robe or mantle." Florio's *Ital. Diet.* 1611.

[124] The malakatoone, melicotton, malecotoon, malecotone, or maligatoon, (for so

Nor the Scotchwoman with the cittern, do you mark,
Nor a dancer by any means, though he ride on's footcloth,
Nor a hackney coachman, if he can speak French.

WINIFRID. Why Sir?

ROMELIO. By no means: no more words;
Nor the woman with marrow-bone puddings. I have heard
Strange juggling tricks have been convey'd to a woman
In a pudding. You are apprehensive?

WINIFRID. O good sir, I have travell'd.

ROMELIO. When you had a bastard, you travell'd indeed:
But, my precious chaperones,
I trust thee the better for that; for I have heard
There is no warier keeper of a park,
To prevent stalkers, or your night-walkers,
That such a man, as in his youth has been
A most notorious deer-stealer.

WINIFRID. Very well sir,
You may use me at your pleasure.

ROMELIO. By no means, Winifrid, that were the way
To make thee travel again. Come, be not angry,
I do but jest; thou knowest, wit and a woman
Are two very frail things, and so I leave you. [*Exit.*]

WINIFRID. I could weep with you, but 'tis no matter,
I can do that at any time; I have now
A greater mind to rail a little. Plague of these
Unsanctified matches: they make us loathe
The most natural desire our grandame Eve ever left us.
Force one to marry against their will! Why 'tis
A more ungodly work than enclosing the commons.

JOLENTA. Prithee, peace.
This is indeed an argument so common,
I cannot think of matter new enough,
To express it bad enough.

WINIFRID. Here's one, I hope
Will put you out of't.

[*Enter* CONTARINO.]

---

variously do old writers spell the word,) was a sort of late peach. Gerard in his *Herball*, enumerating different kinds of peaches, mentions "the Blacke Peach; the *Melacotone*; the White," &c. 1446. ed. 1633.

"Pine are much after the Figure of a Sceth Thistle, and in my minde taste most like a Peach, or *Maligatoon*." Note on a poem (p. 10) entitled *A Description of the Last Voyage to Bermudas, in the Ship Mary Gold*, by J. H. [ardy]. 1671, 4to.

CONTARINO. How now, sweet mistress?
    You have made sorrow look lovely of late,
    You have wept.

WINIFRID. She has done nothing else these three days. Had you stood behind the arras, to have heard her shed so much salt water as I have done, you would have thought she had been turn'd fountain.

CONTARINO. I would fain know the cause can be worthy this
    Thy sorrow.

JOLENTA. Reach me the caskanet.[125] I am studying, sir,
    To take an inventory of all that's mine.

CONTARINO. What to do with it, lady?

JOLENTA. To make you a deed of gift.

CONTARINO. That's done already. You are all mine.

WINIFRID. Yes, but the devil would fain put in for's share,
    In likeness of a separation.

JOLENTA. O sir, I am bewitch'd.

CONTARINO. Ha?

JOLENTA. Most certain. I am forespoken,
    To be married to another: can you ever think
    That I shall ever thrive in't? Am I not then bewitch'd?
    All comfort I can teach myself is this:
    There is a time left for me to die nobly,
    When I cannot live so.

CONTARINO. Give me in a word, to whom, or by whose means,
    Are you thus torn from me?

JOLENTA. By Lord Ercole, my mother, and my[126] brother.

CONTARINO. I'll make his bravery[127] fitter far for a grave,
    Than for a wedding.

JOLENTA. So you will beget
    A far more dangerous and strange disease
    Out of the cure. You must love him again
    For my sake: for the noble Ercole
    Had such a true compassion of my sorrow,—
    Hark in your ear, I'll show you his right worthy
    Demeanour to me.

WINIFRID. O you pretty ones!
    I have seen this lord many a time and oft
    Set her in's lap, and talk to her of love
    So feelingly, I do protest it has mede me

---

[125] A word not found in dictionaries. I meet with it in a formidable list of articles necessary for a lady's toilette in *Lingua*; "such stirre with Stickes and Combes, *Cascanets*, Dressings, Purles, Falles, Squares, Buskes, Bodies, Scarffes, Neck-laces, Carcanets," &c. Sig. I. 2. Ed. 1607.

[126] The old copy "*by*."

[127] i.e. finery.

Run out of my self to think on't.
O sweet-breath'd monkey; how they grow together!
Well, 'tis my opinion, he was no woman's friend
That did invent a punishment for kissing.

CONTARINO. If he bear himself so nobly,
The manliest office I can do for him,
Is to afford him my pity, since he's like
To fail of so dear a purchase. For your mother,
Your goodness quits her ill; for your brother,
He that vows friendship to a man, and proves
A traitor, deserves rather to be hang'd,
Than he that counterfeits money. Yet for your sake
I must sign his pardon too. Why do you tremble?
Be safe, you are now free from him.

JOLENTA. O but sir,
The intermission from a fit of an ague
Is grievous; for indeed it doth prepare us
To entertain torment next morning.

CONTARINO. Why, he's gone to sea.

JOLENTA. But he may return too soon.

CONTARINO. To avoid which, we will instantly be married.

WINIFRID. To avoid which, get you instantly to bed together,
Do, and I think no civil lawyer for his fee
Can give you better counsel.

JOLENTA. Fie upon thee, Prithee leave us.

CONTARINO. Be of comfort, sweet mistress.

JOLENTA. Upon one condition, we may have no quarrel
About this

CONTARINO. Upon my life, none.

JOLENTA. None,
Upon your honour?

CONTARINO. With whom? With Ercole?
You have delivered him guiltless.
With your brother? He's part of yourself.
With your complemental mother?
I use no fight with women.
Tomorrow we'll be married.[128]
Let those that would oppose this union,
Grow ne'er so subtle, and entangle themselves
In their own work like spiders, while we two
Haste to our noble wishes, and presume

---

[128] So far the rhythm of this speech is imperfect, nor is it to be improved by clipping words from one line and tacking them on to the next. How often in Webster's plays have we to complain of passages of blank verse scarcely metrical!

The hindrance of it will breed more delight,
As black copartaments shows gold more bright.

[*Exeunt.*]

ACT II.

SCENE I.

[*Enter* CRISPIANO *and* SANITONELLA.]

CRISPIANO. Am I well habited?

SANITONELLA. Exceeding well. Any man would take you for a merchant: but pray sir, resolve me what should be the reason, that you being one of the most eminent civil lawyers in Spain, and but newly arriv'd from the East Indies, should take this habit of a merchant upon you?

CRISPIANO. Why my son lives here in Naples, and in's riot doth far exceed the exhibition I allow'd him.

SANITONELLA. So then, and in this disguise you mean to trace him?

CRISPIANO. Partly for that, but there is other business
    Of greater consequence.

SANITONELLA. Faith, for his expense, 'tis nothing to your estate: what, to Don Crispiano, the famous Corregidor of Seville, who by his mere practice of the law, in less time than half a Jubilee, hath gotten thirty thousand ducats a year!

CRISPIANO. Well, I will give him line,
    Let him run on in's course of spending.

SANITONELLA. Freely?

CRISPIANO. Freely.
    For I protest, if that I could conceive
    My son would take more pleasure or content,
    By any course of riot, in the expense,
    Than I took joy, nay soul's felicity,
    In the getting of it, should all the wealth I have
    Waste to as small an atomy as flies
    I'th' sun, I do protest on that condition,
    It should not move me.

SANITONELLA. How's this? Cannot he take more pleasure in spending it riotously than you have done by scraping it together? O ten thousand times more, and I make no question, five hundred young gallants will be of my opinion.
    Why all the time of your collectionship,
    Has been a perpetual calendar. Begin first
    With your melancholy study of the law

Before you came to finger the ruddocks; after that,
The tiring importunity of clients,
To rise so early, and sit up so late,
You made yourself half ready in a dream,[129]
And never pray'd but in your sleep. Can I think
That you have half your lungs left with crying out
For judgements, and days of trial? Remember sir,
How often have I borne you on my shoulder,
Among a shoal or swarm of reeking night-caps,
When that your worship has bepiss'd yourself,
Either with vehemency or argument,
Or being out from the matter. I am merry.

CRISPIANO. Be so.

SANITONELLA. You could not eat like a gentleman, at leissure;
    But swallow'd it like flap-dragons,[130] as if you liv'd
    With chewing the cud after.

CRISPIANO. No pleasure in the world was comparable to't.

SANITONELLA. Possible?

CRISPIANO. He shall never taste the like,
    Unless he study law.

SANITONELLA. What, not in wenching, sir?
    'Tis a court game believe it, as familiar
    As gleek,[131] or any other.

CRISPIANO. Wenching! O fie, the disease follows it:
    Beside, can the fing'ring taffetas, or lawns,
    Or a painted hand, or a breast, be like the pleasure
    In taking clients' fees, and piling them
    In several goodly rows before my desk?
    An according to the bigness of each heap,
    Which I took by a leer (for lawyers do not tell them)
    I vail'd my cap, and withal gave great hope
    The cause should go on their sides.

SANITONELLA. What think you then
    Of a good cry of hounds? I has been known
    Dogs have hunted lordships to a fault.

CRISPIANO. Cry of curs!
    The noise of clients at my chamber door

---

[129] To *make* ones-self *ready* is the old expression for *dressing* ones-self.

[130] Raisins, plums, *candles' ends!* &c. made to float in a dish of ardent spirits, from which, when set on fire, they were to be snatched by the mouth and swallowed. The amorous youths of olden time delighted in drinking off flap-dragons to the health of their mistresses. This nasty sport, still common in Holland, I have seen practised in our own country by boys during Christmas holidays.

[131] A fashionable game at cards in our author's time. Full instructions how to play at "this noble and delightful Game or Recreation" may be found in *The Compleat Gamester*, p. 67, et seq. ed. 1709.

Was sweeter music far, in my conceit,
Than all the hunting in Europe.
SANITONELLA. Pray stay sir,
Say he should spend it in good housekeeping?
CRISPIANO. Aye, marry sir, to have him keep a good house,
And not sell't away; I'd find no fault with that:
But his kitchen, I'd have no bigger than a sawpit;
For the smallness of a kitchen, without question,
Makes many noblemen in France and Spain
Build the rest of the house the bigger.
SANITONELLA. Yes, mock-beggars.
CRISPIANO. Some sevenscore chimneys,
But half of them have no tunnels.
SANITONELLA. A pox upon them, cuckshaws, that beget
Such monsters without fundaments.
CRISPIANO. Come, come, leave citing other vanities;
For neither wine, nor lust, nor riotous feasts,
Rich clothes, nor all the pleasure that the devil
Has ever practis'd with, to raise a man
To a devil's likeness, e'er brought man that pleasure
I took in getting my wealth: so I conclude.
If he can outvie me, let it fly to th' devil.
Yon's my son, what company keeps he?

[*Enter* ROMELIO, JULIO, ARIOSTO, *and* BAPTISTA.]

The gentleman he talks with, is Romelio
The merchant.
CRISPIANO. I never saw him till now.
A has a brave sprightly look; I knew his father,
And sojourn'd in his house two years together,
Before this young man's birth. I have news to tell him
Of certain losses happened him at sea,
That will not please him.
SANITONELLA. What's[132] that dapper fellow
In the long stocking? I do think 'twas he
Came to your lodging this morning.
CRISPIANO. 'Tis the same.
There he stands, but a little piece of flesh,
But he is the very miracle of a lawyer,
One that persuades men to peace and compounds quarrels,
Among his neighbours, without going to law.
SANITONELLA. And is he a lawyer?

---

[132] The old copy "What."

CRISPIANO. Yes, and will give counsel
    In honest causes gratis, never in his life
    Took fee, but he came a spake for't, is a man
    Of extreme practice, and yet all his longing
    Is to become a judge.

SANITONELLA. Indeed, tha's a rare longing with men of his profession.
    I think he'll prove the miracle of a lawyer indeed.

ROMELIO. Here's the man brought word your father died i'th' Indies.

JULIO. He died in perfect memory I hope,
    And made me his heir,

CRISPIANO. Yes sir.

JULIO. He's gone the right way then without question. Friend, in time
    of mourning we must not use any action, that is but accessory to
    the making men merry. I do therefore give you nothing for your
    good tidings.

CRISPIANO. Nor do I look for it sir.

JULIO. Honest fellow, give me thy hand. I do not think but thou hast
    carried New Year's gift to th' Court in thy days, and learned'st
    there to be so free of thy painstaking.

ROMELIO. Here's an old gentleman says he was chamber-fellow to your
    father, when they studied the law together at Barcelona.

JULIO. Do you know him?

ROMELIO. Not I, he's newly come to Naples.

JULIO. And what's his business?

ROMELIO. A says he's come to read you good counsel.

CRISPIANO. To him: rate him soundly.

    [*This is spoke aside.*]

JULIO. And what's your counsel?

ARIOSTO. Why, I would have you leave your whoring.

JULIO. He comes hotly upon me at first. Whoring?

ARIOSTO. O young quat,[133] incontinence is plagu'd
    In all the creatures of the world.

JULIO. When did you ever hear that a cock-sparrow
    Had the French pox?

ARIOSTO. When did you ever know any of them fat, but in the nest?
    Ask all your Cantaride-mongers that question: remember your self
    sir.

JULIO. A very fine naturalist, a physician, I take you, by your round
    slop; for 'tis just of the bigness, and no more, of the case for a

---

[133] *Quat* means originally a pimple: compare Shakespeare;
    "I have rubb'd this *young quat* almost to the sense."
                        Othello, Act V. Sc. I.

urinal: 'tis concluded, you are a physician. What do you mean sir,
you'll take cold.

ARIOSTO. 'Tis concluded, you are a fool, a precious one; you are a
mere stick of sugar candy, a man may look quite thorough you.

JULIO. You are a very bold gamester.

ARIOSTO. I can play at chess, and know how to handle a rook.

JULIO. Pray preserve your velvet from the dust.

ARIOSTO. Keep your hat upon the block sir, 'twill continue fashion the
longer.

JULIO. I was never so abus'd with the hat in the hand
In my life.

ARIOSTO. I will put on; why look you,
Those lands that were the client's are now become
The lawyer's; and those tenements that were
The country gentleman's, are now grown
To be his tailor's.

JULIO. Tailor's?

ARIOSTO. Yes, tailors in France, they grow to great abominable
purchase, and become great officers. How many ducats think you
he has spent within a twelve-month, besides his father's
allowance?

JULIO. Besides my father's allowance? Why gentleman, do you think
an auditor begat me? Would you have me make even at year's
end?

ROMELIO. A hundred ducats a month in breaking Venice glasses.

ARIOSTO. He learnt that of an English drunkard, and a knight too, as I
take it. This comes of your numerous wardrobe.

ROMELIO. Aye, and wearing cut-work, a pound a purl.

ARIOSTO. Your dainty embroidered stockings, with overblown roses, to
hide your gouty ankles.

ROMELIO. And wearing more taffeta for a garter, than would serve the
galley dung-boat for streamers.

ARIOSTO. Your switching up at the horse-race, with the illustrissimi.

ROMELIO. And studying a puzzling arithmetic at the cock-pit.

ARIOSTO. Shaking your elbow at the Table-board.[134]

ROMELIO. And resorting to your whore in hired velvet, with a spangled
copper fringe at her netherlands.

ARIOSTO. Whereas if you had stay'd at Padua, and fed upon cow-
trotters, and fresh beef to supper.

JULIO. How I am baited!

ARIOSTO. Nay, be not you so forward with him neither, for 'tis thought,

---

[134] The old copy "Taule-boord."—Tables (Lat. *Tabularum lusus*, Fr. Tables,) is the
old name for backgammon: but other games were played with the same board. On the
back of the title page of the old play of *Arden of Feversluim*, ed. 1638, is a representation
of a table-board.

you'll prove a main part of this undoing.

JULIO. I think this fellow is a witch.

ROMELIO. Who, I sir?

ARIOSTO. You have certain rich city choughs, that when they have no acres of their own, they will go and plough up fools, and turn them into excellent meadow; besides some enclosures for the first cherries in the spring, and apricots to pleasure a friend at Court with. You have 'pothecaries deal in selling commodities to young gallants, will put four or five coxcombs into a sieve, and so drum with them upon their counter; they'll searse them through like Guinea pepper. They cannot endure to find a man like a pair of tarriers, they would undo him in a trice.

ROMELIO. Maybe there are such.

ARIOSTO. O terrible exactors, fellows with six hands, and three heads.

JULIO. Aye, those are hell-hounds.

ARIOSTO. Take heed of them, they'll rend thee like tenterhooks. Hark in your ear, there is intelligence upon you; the report goes, there has been gold convey'd beyond the sea in hollow anchors. Farewell, you shall know me better, I will do thee more good, than thou art aware of. [*Exit.*]

JULIO. He's a mad fellow.

SANITONELLA. He would have made an excellent barber, he does so curry it with his tongue. [*Exit.*]

CRISPIANO. Sir, I was directed to you.

ROMELIO. From whence?

CRISPIANO. From the East Indies.

ROMELIO. You are very welcome.

CRISPIANO. Please you walk apart,
    I shall acquaint you with particulars
    Touching your trading i'th' East Indies.

ROMELIO. Willingly, pray walk sir.

[*Exit* CRISPIANO *and* ROMELIO.]

[*Enter* ERCOLE.]

ERCOLE. O my right worthy friends, you have stay'd me long:
    One health, and then aboard; for all the galleys
    Are come about.

[*Enter* CONTARINO.]

CONTARINO. Signor Ercole,
    The wind has stood my friend sir, to prevent
    Your putting to sea.

ERCOLE. Pray why sir?
CONTARINO. Only love sir;
    That I might take my leave sir, and withal
    Entreat from you a private recommends
    To a friend in Malta; 'twould be deliver'd
    To your bosom, for I had not time to writw.
ERCOLE. Pray leave us gentlemen.

[*Exeunt* JULIO *and* BAPTISTA.]

Wilt please you sit?

[*They sit down.*]

CONTARINO. Sir, my love to you has proclaim'd you one,
    Whose word was still lead by a noble thought,
    And that thought follow'd by as fair a deed:
    Deceive not that opinion. We were students
    At Padua together, and have long
    To'th' worlds's eye shown like friends;
    Was it hearty on your part to me?
ERCOLE. Unfeign'd.
CONTARINO. You are false
    To the good thought I held of you, and now
    Join the worst part of man to you, your malice,
    To uphold that falsehood; sacred innocence
    Is fled your bosom. Signor, I must tell you,
    To draw the picture of unkindness truly,
    Is to express two that have dearly lov'd,
    And fallen at variance. 'Tis a wonder to me,
    Knowing my interest in the fair Jolenta,
    That you should love her.
ERCOLE. Compare her beauty, and my youth together,
    And you will find the fair effects of love
    No miracle at all.
CONTARINO. Yes, it will prove
    Prodigious to you. I must stay your voyage.
ERCOLE. Your warrant must be mighty.
CONTARINO. 'T'as a seal
    From heaven to do it, since you would ravish from me
    What's there entitl'ed mine: and yet I vow,
    By the essential front of spotless virtue,
    I have compassion of both our youths:
    To approve which, I have not tane the way,
    Like an Italian, to cut your throat

  By practice, that had given you now for dead,
  And never frown'd upon.

ERCOLE. You deal fair, sir.

CONTARINO. Quit me of one doubt, pray sir.

ERCOLE. Move it.

CONTARINO. 'Tis this.
  Whether her brother were a main instrument
  In her design for marriage.

ERCOLE. If I tell truth,
  You will not credit me.

CONTARINO. Why?

ERCOLE. I will tell you truth,
  Yet show some reason you have not to believe me:
  Her brother had no hand in't: is't not hard
  For you to credit this? For you may think
  I count it baseness to engage another
  Into my quarrel; and for that take leave
  To dissemble the truth. Sir, If you will fight
  With any but myself, fight with her mother,
  She was the motive.

CONTARINO. I have no enemy
  In the world them, but yourself:
  You must fight with me.

ERCOLE. I will sir.

CONTARINO. And instantly.

ERCOLE. I will haste before you; point whither.

CONTARINO. Why, you speak nobly, and for this fair dealing,
  Were the rich jewel which we vary for,
  A thing to be divided; by my life,
  I would be well content to give you half.
  But since 'tis vain to think we can be friends,
  'Tis needful one of us be tane away,
  From being the other's enemy.

ERCOLE. Yet methinks,
  This looks not like a quarrel.

CONTARINO. Not a quarrel?

ERCOLE. You have not apparell'd your fury well,
  It goes too plain, like a scholar.

CONTARINO. It is an ornament
  Makes it more terrible, and you shall find it
  A weighty injury, and attended on
  By discreett valour. Because I do not strike you,
  Or give you the lie—such foul preparatives
  Would show like the stale injury of wine—
  I reserve my rage to sit on my sword's point,

  Which a great quantity of your best blood
  Cannot satisfy.
ERCOLE. You promise well to yourself.
  Shall's have no seconds?
CONTARINO. None, for fear of prevention.
ERCOLE. The length of our weapons?
CONTARINO. We'll fit them by the way.
  So whether our time calls us to live or die,
  Let us do both like noble gentlemen,
  And true Italians.
ERCOLE. For that let me embrace you.
CONTARINO. Methinks, being an Italian, I trust you
  To come somewhat too near me:
  But your jealousy gave that embrace to try
  If I were arm'd, did it not?
ERCOLE. No, believe me,
  I take heart to be sufficient proof,
  Without a privy coat; and for my part,
  A taffeta is all the shirt of mail
  I am arm'd with.
CONTARINO. You deal equally.[135]

  [*Exeunt.*]

  [*Enter* JULIO, *and* SERVANT.]

JULIO. Where are these gallants, the brave Ercole,
  And noble Contarino?
SERVANT. They are newly gone, sir,
  And bade me tell you that they will return
  Within this half hour.

  [*Enter* ROMELIO.]

JULIO. Met you the Lord Ercole?
ROMELIO. No, but I met the devil in villainous tidings.
JULIO. Why, what's the matter?
ROMELIO. O, I am pour'd out
  Like water: the greatest rivers i'th' world
  Are lost in the sea, and so am I. Pray leave me.
  Where's Lord Ercole?
JULIO. You were scarce gone hence,

---

[135] Mr. Lamb calls this scene between Contarino and Ercole "the model of a well-managed and gentlemanlike difference." *Spec. of Eng. Dram. Poets*, p. 199.

But in came Contarino.

ROMELIO. Contarino?

JULIO. And entreated some private conference with Ercole,
    And on the sudden they have giv'n's the slip.

ROMELIO. One mischief never comes alone: they are gone to fight.

JULIO. To fight?

ROMELIO. And you be gentlemen,
    Do not talk, but make haste after them.

JULIO. Let's take several ways then,
    And if't be possible, for women's sakes,
    For they are proper men, use our endeavours,
    That the prick do not spoil them.

[*Exeunt.*]

SCENE II.

[*Enter* ERCOLE *and* CONTARINO.]

CONTARINO. You'll not forgo your interest in my mistress?

ERCOLE. My sword shall answer that: come, are you ready?

CONTARINO. Before you fight sir, think upon your cause
    It is a wondrous foul one, and I wish
    That all your exercise these four days past
    Had been employ'd in a most fervent prayer,
    And the foul sin for which your are to fight
    Chiefly remembered in't.

ERCOLE. I'd as soon take
    Your counsel in divinity at this present,
    As I would take a kind direction from you
    For the managing my weapon: and indeed,
    Both would show much alike.
    Come, are you ready?

CONTARINO. Bethink yourself,
    How fair the object is that we conted for.

ERCOLE. O, I cannot forget it.

[*They fight.*]

CONTARINO. You are hurt.

ERCOLE. Did you come hither only to tell me so,
    Or to do it? I mean well, but 'twill not thrive.

CONTARINO. Your cause, your cause, sir:
    Will you yet be a man of conscience, and make
    Restitution for your rage upon your death-bed?

ERCOLE. Never, till the grave father one of us.

[*Fight.*]

CONTARINO. That was fair, and home I think.
ERCOLE. You prate as if you were in a fence-school.
CONTARINO. Spare your youth, have compassion on yourself.
ERCOLE. When I am all in pieces; I am now unfit
    For any lady's bed; take the rest with you.

[CONTARINO *wounded, falls upon* ERCOLE.]

CONTARINO. I am lost in too much daring; yield your sword.
ERCOLE. To the pangs of death I shall, but not to thee.
CONTARINO. You are now at my rapairing, or confusion:
    Beg your life.
ERCOLE. O, most foolishly demanded,
    To bid me beg that which thou canst not give.

[*Enter* ROMELIO, PROSPERO, BAPTISTA, ARIOSTO, *and* JULIO.]

PROSPERO. See both of them are lost: we come too late.
ROMELIO. Take up the body, and convey it
    To Saint Sebstian's monastery.
CONTARINO. I will not part with his sword, I have won't.
JULIO. You shall not: take him up gently; so:
    And bow his body, for fear of bleeding inward.
    Well, these are perfect lovers.
PROSPERO. Why, I pray?
JULIO. It has ever been my opinion,
    That there are none love perfectly indeed,
    But those that hang or drown themselves for love:
    Now these have chose a death next to beheading;
    They have cut one another's throats,
    Brave valiant lads.
PROSPERO. Come, you do ill, to set the name of valour
    Upon a violent and mad despair.
    Hence may all learn, that count such actions well,
    The roots of fury shoot themselves to hell.

[*Exeunt.*]

SCENE III.

[*Enter* ROMELIO *and* ARIOSTO.]

ARIOSTO. Your losses, I confess, are infinite,
    Yet sir, you must have patience.
ROMELIO. Sir, my losses
    I know, but you I do not.
ARIOSTO. 'Tis most true,
    I am but a stranger to you, but am wish'd
    By some of your best friends, to visit you,
    And out of my experience in the world,
    To instruct you patience.
ROMELIO. Of what profession are you?
ARIOSTO. Sir I am a lawyer.
ROMELIO. Of all men living,
    You lawyers I account the only men
    To confirm patience in us; your delays
    Would make three parts of this little Christian world
    Run out of their wits else. Now I remember,
    You read lectures to Julio: are you such a leech
    For patience?
ARIOSTO. Yes sir, I have had some crosses.
ROMELIO. You are married then, I am certain.
ARIOSTO. That I am sir.
ROMELIO. And have you studied patience?
ARIOSTO. You shall find I have.
ROMELIO. Did you ever see your wife make you cuckold?
ARIOSTO. Make me cuckold?
ROMELIO. I ask it seriously: and you have not seen that,
    Your patience has not tane the right degree
    Of wearing scarlet; I should rather take you
    For a Bachelor in the Art, than for a Doctor.
ARIOSTO. You are merry.
ROMELIO. No sir, with leave of your patience,
    I am horrible angry.
ARIOSTO. What should move you
    Put forth that harsh interrogatory, if these eyes,
    Ever saw my wife do the thing you wot of?
ROMELIO. Why, I'll tell you,
    Most radically to try your patience,
    And the mere question shows you but a dunce in't.
    It has made you angry; there's another lawyer's beard
    In your forehead, you do bristle.

ARIOSTO. You are very conceited.[136]
> But come, this is not the right way to cure you.
> I must talk to you like a divine.

ROMELIO. I have heard
> Some talk of it very much, and many times
> To their auditors' impatience; but I pray,
> What practice do they make of't in their lives?
> They are too full of choler with living honest,
> And some of them not only impatient
> Of their own slightest injuries, but stark mad
> At one another's preferment. Now to you sir;
> I have lost three goodly carracks.[137]

ARIOSTO. So I hear.

ROMELIO. The very spice in them,
> Had they been shipwreck'd here upon our coast,
> Would have made all our sea a drench.

ARIOSTO. All the sick horses in Italy
> Would have been glad of your loss then.

ROMELIO. You are conceited too.

ARIOSTO. Come, come, come,
> You gave those ships most strange, most dreadful, and
> Unfortunate names: I never look'd they'd prosper.

ROMELIO. Is there any ill omen in giving names to ships?

ARIOSTO. Did you not call one, *The storms defiance*,
> Another, *The scourge of the sea*; and the third,
> *The great leviathan*?

ROMELIO. Very right, sir.

ARIOSTO. Very devilish names, all three of them:
> And surely I think they were curs'd
> In their very cradles; I do mean, when they were
> Upon their stocks.

ROMELIO. Come, you are superstitious.
> I'll give you my opinion, and 'tis serious:
> I am persuaded there came not cuckolds enough
> To the first launching of them, and 'twas that
> Made them thrive the worse for't. O, your cuckold's handsel
> Is pray'd for i'th' City.

ARIOSTO. I will hear no more.
> Give me thy hand. My intent of coming hither,
> Was to persuade you to patience: as I live,
> If ever I do visit you again,
> It shall be to entreat you to be angry; sure it will,

---

[136] i.e. disposed to jest, to be merry.
[137] i.e. large ships of burthen.

I'll be as good as my word, believe it.
ROMELIO. So sir. How now?

[*Exit* ARIOSTO.]

[*Enter* LEONORA.]

Are the screech owls abroad already?
LEONORA. What a dismal noise yon bell makes;
    Sure, some great person's dead.
ROMELIO. No such matter,
    I is the common bellman goes about,
    To publish the sale of goods.
LEONORA. Why do they ring
    Before my gate thus? Let them into th' court,
    I cannot understand what they say.

[*Enter* TWO BELLMEN *and a* CAPUCHIN.]

CAPUCHIN. For pity's sake, you that have tears to shed,
    Sigh a soft requiem, and let fall a bead
    For two unfortunate nobles, whose sad fate
    Leaves them both death, and excommunicate:
    No churchman's prayer to comfort their last groans,
    No sacred sod of earth to hide their bones;
    But as their fury wrought them out of breath,
    The canon speaks them guilty of their own death.
LEONORA. What noblemen, I pray sir?
CAPUCHIN. The Lord Ercole,
    And the noble Contarino, both of them
    Slain in single combat.
LEONORA. O, I am lost forever.
ROMELIO. Denied Christian burial—I pray, what does that,
    Or the dead lazy march in the funeral,
    Or the flattery in the epitaphs, which shows
    More sluttish far than all the spider's webs
    Shall ever grow upon it; what do these
    Add to our well-being after death?
CAPUCHIN. Not a scruple.
ROMELIO. Very well then,
    I have a certain meditation,
    If I can think of't,[138] somewhat to this purpose;
    I'll say it to you, while my mother there

---

[138] The old copy "*of.*"

Numbers her beads.
You that dwell near these graves and vaults,
Which oft do hide physicians' faults,
Note what a small room does suffice,
To express men's good; their vanities
Would fill more volume in small hand,
Than all the evidence of church land.
Funerals hide men in civil wearing,
And are to the drapers a good hearing,
Make the heralds laugh in their black raiment,
And all die worthies die worth payment
To the altar offerings; though their fame,
And all the charity of their name,
'Tween heaven and this yield no more light,
Than rotten trees, which shine i'th' night.
O, look the last act be the best i'th' play,
And then rest gentle bones; yet pray
That when by the precise you are view'd,
A supersedeas be not sued,
To remove you to a place more airy,
That in your stead they make keep chary
Stockfish, or sea-coal, for the abuses
Of sacrilege have turn'd graves to viler uses.
How then can any monument say,
Here rest these bones, till the last day,
When time swift both of foot and feather,
May bear them the sexton kens not whither?
What care I then,[139] though my last sleep
Be in the desert, or in the deep;
No lamp, nor taper, day and night,
To give my charnel chargeable light?
I have there like quantity of ground,
And at the last day I shall be found.
Now I pray leave me.
CAPUCHIN. I am sorry for your losses.
ROMELIO. Um sir, the more spacious that the tennis
Court is, the more large is the hazard.
I dare the spiteful Fortune do her worst,
I can now fear nothing.
CAPUCHIN. O sir, yet consider,
He that is without fear, is without hope,

---

[139] Compare the splendid conclusion of Sir Thomas Brown's *Urn-Burial*; "'Tis all one to lie in St. Innocent's Church-yard as in the sands of Egypt; ready to be anything in the ectasie of being ever; as content with six foot as the Moles of Adrianus."

And sins from presumption. Better thoughts attend you.

[*Exeunt* CAPUCHIN *and* BELLMEN.]

ROMELIO. Poor Jolente, should she hear of this!
    She would not after the report keep fresh,
    So long as flowers in graves.

[*Enter* PROSPERO.]

    How now Prospero?
PROSPERO. Contarino has sent you here his will,
    Wherein a has made your sister his sole heir.
ROMELIO. Is he not dead?
PROSPERO. He's yet living.
ROMELIO. Living? The worse luck.
LEONORA. The worse? I do protest it is the best
    That ever came to disturb my prayers.
ROMELIO. How?
LEONORA. Yet I would have him live
    To satisfy public justice for the death
    Of Ercole. O, go visit him for heaven's sake.
    I have within my closet a choice relic,
    Preservative 'gainst swounding, and some earth,
    Brought from the Holy Land, right sovereign
    To staunch blood. Has he skilful surgeons, think you?
PROSPERO. The best in Naples.
ROMELIO. How oft has he been dress'd?
PROSPERO. But once.
LEONORA. I have some skill this way.
    The second or third dressing will show clearly,
    Whether there be hope of life. I pray be near him,
    If there be any soul can bring me word,
    That there is hope of life.
ROMELIO. Do you prize his life so?
LEONORA. That he may live, I mean, to come to his trial,
    To satisfy the law.
ROMELIO. O, is't nothing else?
LEONORA. I shall be the happiest woman.

[*Exeunt* LEONORA *and* PROSPERO.]

ROMELIO. Here is cruelty apparell'd in kindness.
    I am full of thoughts, strange ones, but they're no good ones.
    I must visit Contarino; upon that

Depends an engine shall weigh up my losses,
Were they sunk as low as hell: yet let me think,
How I am impair'd in an hour, and the cause of't:
Lost in security. O how this wicked world bewitches,
Especially made insolent with riches!
So sails with force-winds stretch'd, do soonest break,
And pyramids a'th' top are still most weak. [*Exit.*]

SCENE IV.

[*Enter* CAPUCHIN, ERCOLE *led between two.*]

CAPUCHIN. Look up, sir:
    You are preserved beyond natural reason;
    You were brought dead out a'th' field, the surgeons
    Ready to have embalm'd you.
ERCOLE. I do look on my action with a thought of terror;
    To do ill and dwell in't, is unmanly.
CAPUCHIN. You are divinely informed sir.
ERCOLE. I fought for one, in whom I have no more right,
    Than false executors have in orphans' goods
    They cozen them of; yet though my cause were naught,
    I rather chose the hazard of my soul,
    Than forgo the compliment of a choleric man.
    I pray continue the report of my death, and give out,
    'Cause the Church denied me Christian burial,
    The vice-admiral of my galleys took my body,
    With purpose to commit it to the earth,
    Either in Sicil, or Malta.
CAPUCHIN. What aim you at
    By this rumour of your death?
ERCOLE. There is hope of life
    In Contarino, and he has my prayers,
    That he may live to enjoy what is his own,
    The fair Jolenta; where,[140] should it be thought
    That I were breathing, happily her friends
    Would oppose it still.
CAPUCHIN. But if you be suppos'd dead,
    The law will strictly prosecute his life
    For your murder.
ERCOLE. That's prevented thus:
    There does belong a noble privilege
    To all his family, ever since his father

---

[140] i.e. whereas.

> Bore from the worthy Emperor Charles the Fith
> An answer to the French King's challenge, at such time
> The two noble princes were engag'd to fight
> Upon a frontier arm o'th' sea in a flat-bottomed boat,
> That if any of his family should chance
> To kill a man i'th' field, in a noble cause,
> He should have his pardon: now, sir, for his cause,
> The world may judge if it were not honest.
> Pray help me in speech, 'tis very painful to me.

CAPUCHIN. Sir I shall.

ERCOLE. The guilt of this lies in Romelio,
> And as I hear, to second this good contract,
> He has got a nun with child.

CAPUCHIN. These are crimes
> That either must make work for speedy repentance,
> Or for the devil.

ERCOLE. I have much compassion on him,
> For sin and shame are ever tied together,
> With Gordian knots, of such a strong thread spun,
> They cannot without violence be undone.

[*Exeunt.*]

ACT III.

SCENE I.

[*Enter* ARIOSTO, CRISPIANO.]

ARIOSTO. Well sir, now I must claim your promise,
> To reveal to me the cause why you live
> Thus clouded.

CRISPIANO. Sir, the King of Spain
> Suspects that your Romelio here, the merchant,
> Has discover'd some gold mine to his own use,
> In the West Indies, and for that employs me
> To discover in what part of Christendom
> He vents this treasure. Besides, he is inform'd
> What mad tricks have[141] been played of late by ladies.

ARIOSTO. Most true, and I am glad the King has heard on't.
> Why, they use their lords as if they were their wards;
> And as your Dutchwomen in the Low Countries,
> Take all and pay all, and do keep their husbands

---

[141] The old copy "*has*."

So silly all their lives of their own estates,
That when they are sick, and come to make their will,
They know not precisely what to give away
From their wives, because they know not what they are worth:
So here should I repeat what factions,
What bat-fowling for offices,
As you must conceive their game is all i'th' night,
What calling in question one another's honesties,
Withal what sway they bear i'th' Viceroy's court,
You'd wonder at it: 'twill do well shortly,
Can we keep them off being of our
Council of War.
CRISPIANO. Well, I have vow'd
That I will never sit upon the bench more,
Unless it be to curb the insolencies
Of these women.
ARIOSTO. Well, take it on my word then,
Your place will not long be empty.

[*Exeunt.*]

SCENE II.

[*Enter* ROMELIO *in the habit of a Jew.*]

ROMELIO. Excellently well habited! Why, methinks
That I could play with mine own shadow now,
And be a rare Italianated Jew;
To have as many several change of faces,
As I have seen carv'd upon one cherry stone;
To wind about a man like rotten ivy,
Eat into him like quicksilver, poison a friend
With pulling but a loose hair from's beard, or give a drench,
He should linger of't nine years, and ne'er complain,
But in the spring and fall, and so the cause
Imputed to the disease natural. For slight villainies,
As to coin money, corrupt ladies' honours,
Betray a town to th' Turk, or make a bonfire
A'th' Christian navy, I could settle to't,
As if I had eat a politician,
And digested[142] him to nothing but pure blood.
But stay, I lose myself, this is the house.
Within there.

---

[142] By old writers *digest* is frequently used for *digest*.

[*Enter* TWO SURGEONS.]

FIRST SURGEON: Now sir.

ROMELIO. You are the men of art, that as I hear,
      Have the Lord Contarino under cure.

SECOND SURGEON. Yes sir, we are his surgeons,
      But he is past all cure.

ROMELIO. Why, is he dead?

FIRST SURGEON: He is speechless sir, and we do find this wound
      So fester'd near the vitals, all our art
      By warm drinks, cannot clear th'imposthumation;
      And he's so weak, to make [incision]¹⁴³
      By the orifix were present death to him.

ROMELIO. He has made a will I hear.

FIRST SURGEON: Yes sir.

ROMELIO. And deputed Jolenta his heir.

SECOND SURGEON. He has, we are witness to't.

ROMELIO. Has not Romelio been with you yet,
      To give you thanks, and ample recompense
      For the pains you have tane.

FIRST SURGEON. Not yet.

ROMELIO. Listen to me gentlemen, for I protest
      If you will seriously mind your own good,
      I am come about a business shall convey
      Large legacies from Contarino's will
      To both of you.

SECOND SURGEON. How sir? Why Romelio
      Has the will, and in that he has given us nothing.

ROMELIO. I pray attend me: I am a physician.

SECOND SURGEON. A physician? Where do you practise?

ROMELIO. In Rome.

FIRST SURGEON. O then you have store of patients.

ROMELIO. Store? Why look you, I can kill my twenty a month
      And work but i'th' forenoons: you will give me leave
      To jest and be merry with you; but as I said,
      All my study has been physic; I am sent
      From a noble Roman that is near akin
      To Contarino, and that ought indeed,
      By the law of alliance, be his only heir,
      To practise his good and yours.

BOTH. How, I pray sir?

ROMELIO. I can by an extraction which I have,

---

¹⁴³ A word has here dropt out from the old copy.

Though he were speechless, his eyes set in's head,
His pulse without motion, restore to him
For half an hour's space, the use of sense,
And perhaps a little speech: having done this,
If we can work him, as no doubt we shall,
To make another will, and therein assign
This gentleman his heir, I will assure you,
'Fore I depart this house, ten thousand ducats,
And then we'll pull the pillow from his head,
And let him e'en go whither the religion sends him that he died in.
FIRST SURGEON. Will you give's ten thousand ducats?
ROMELIO. Upon my Jewism.

[CONTARINO *in a bed.*[144]]

SECOND SURGEON. 'Tis a bargain sir, we are yours:
　　Here is the subject you must work on.
ROMELIO. Well said, you are honest men,
　　And go to the business roundly: but gentlemen,
　　I must use my art singly.
FIRST SURGEON. Osir, you shall have all privacy.
ROMELIO. And the doors lock'd to me.
SECOND SURGEON. At your best pleasure.
　　Yet for all this, I will not trust this Jew.
FIRST SURGEON. Faith, to say truth,
　　I do not like him neither, he looks like a rogue.
　　This is a fine toy, fetch a man to life,
　　To make a new will! There's some trick in't.
　　I'll be near you, Jew.

[*Exeunt* SURGEONS.]

ROMELIO. Excellent, as I would wish, these credulous fools
　　Have given me freely what I would have bought
　　With a great deal of money. -Softly, here's breath yet;
　　Now Ercole, for part of the revenge,
　　Which I have vow'd for thy untimely death:
　　Besides this politic working of my own,
　　That scorns precedent. Why, should this graet man live,

---

[144] Here, perhaps, the actor who played Contarino lay down on a bed behind a traverse or curtain, which was drawn back by the second surgeon when he said, "Here is the subject you must work on:" or, perhaps, the audience of those days was content with seeing a bed, containing Contarino, thrust upon the stage.—In Heywood's *If you know not me, you know nobody*, we find "*Enter Elizabeth in her bed,*" Sig. A 4, ed. 1623; and similar stage directions occur in other old plays.

And not enjoy my sister, as I have vow'd
He never shall? O, he may alter's will
Every new moon if he please; to prevent which,
I must put in a strong caveat. Come forth then,
My desperate stiletto, that may be worn
In a woman's hair, and ne'er discover'd,
And either would be taken for a bodkin,
Or a curling iron at most; why 'tis an engine
That's only fit to put in execution
Barmotho pigs,[145] a most unmanly weapon,
That steals into a man's life he knows not how.
O that great Caesar, he that pass'd the shock
Of so many armed pikes, and poison'd darts,
Swords, slings, and battleaxes, should at length,
Sitting at ease on a cushion, come to die
By such a shoemaker's awl as this, his soul let forth
At a hole no bigger than the incision
Made for a Wheal! 'Uds foot, I am horribly angry
That he should die so scurvily: yet wherefore
Do I condemn thee thereof so cruelly,
Yet shake him by the hand? 'Tis to express
That I would never have such weapons us'd,
But in a plot like this, that's treacherous:
Yet this shall prove most merciful to thee,
For it shall preserve thee from dying
On public scaffold, and withal
Bring thee an absolute cure, thus. So, 'tis done:

[*stabs him.*]

And now for my escape.

[*Enter* SURGEONS.]

FIRST SURGEON. You rogue mountebank,
    I will try whether your inwards can endure
    To be wash'd in scalding lead.
ROMELIO. Hold, I turn Christian.

---

[145] i.e. pigs of the Bermudas, or (as the word was also written,) Bermoothes: "theile
send me of a voiage to *the yland of Hogs* and Devil's, *the Barmudas.*" Dekker's *If It Be
Not Good, the Devil is in it*, 1612, Sig. K 3. "Tis the Land of Peace, where *Hogs* and
Tobacco yield fair increase - - - - I am for *the Bermudas.*" Middleton's *Any Thing for a
Quiet* Life, 1662, Sig. G 3. In *Odcomb's Complaint* by Taylor, the water-poet, is an
"Epitaph in the *Barmooda* tongue, *which must be pronounced* with *the accent of the
grunting of a hogge.*"

SECOND SURGEON. Nay, prithee be a Jew still;
I would not have a Christian be guilty
Of such a villainous act as this is.
ROMELIO. I am Romelio the merchant.
FIRST SURGEON. Romelio!
You have prov'd yourself a cunning merchant indeed.
ROMELIO. You may read why I came hither.
SECOND SURGEON. Yes,
In a bloody Roman letter.
ROMELIO. I did hate this man,
Each minute of his breath was torture to me.
FIRST SURGEON. Had you forborne this act, he had not liv'd
This two hours.
ROMELIO. But he had died then,
And my revenge unsatisfied. Here's gold;
Never did wealthy man purchase the silence
Of a terrible scolding wife at a dearer rate,
Than I will pay for your. Here's your earnest
In a bag of double ducats.
SECOND SURGEON. Why look you sir, as I do weigh this business,
This cannot be counted murder in you by no means.
Why, 'tis no more than should I go and choke
An Irishman that were three quartes drown'd,
With pouring usquebath in's throat.
ROMELIO. You will be secret?
FIRST SURGEON. As your soul.
ROMELIO. The West Indies shall sooner want gold, than you yhen.
SECOND SURGEON. That protestation has the music of the Mint in't.
ROMELIO. [*aside.*] How unfortunately was I surpris'd!
I have made myself a slave perpetually
To these two beggars. [*Exit.*]
FIRST SURGEON. Excellent.
By this act he has made his estate ours.
SECOND SURGEON. I'll presently grow a lazy surgeon, and ride on my
footcloth. I'll fetch from him every eight days a policy for a
hundred double ducats; if he grumble, I'll peach.
FIRST SURGEON. But let's take heed he do not poison us.
SECOND SURGEON. O, I will never eat nor drink with him,
Without unicorn's horn in a hollow tooth.
CONTARINO. O!
FIRST SURGEON. Did he not groan?
SECOND SURGEON. I s the wind in that door still?
FIRST SURGEON. Ha! Come hither, note a strange accident:
His steel has lighted in the former wound,
And made free passage for the congealed blood.

    Observe in what abundance it delivers
    The putrefaction.
SECOND SURGEON. Methinks he fetches
    His breath very lively.
FIRST SURGEON. The hand of heaven is in't,
    That his intent to kill him should become
    The very direct way to save his life.
SECOND SURGEON. Why this is like one I have heard of in England,
    Was cur'd a'th' gout, by being rack'd i'th' Tower.
    Well, if we can recover him, here's reward
    On both sides. Howsoever, we must be secret.
FIRST SURGEON. We are tied to't.
    When we cure gentlemen of foul diseases,
    They give us so much for the cure, and twice as much
    That we do not blab on't. Come, let's to work roundly,
    Heat the lotion, and bring the searing.

    [*Exeunt.*]

                        SCENE III.

    [*A table set forth with two tapers, a death's-head, a book.* JOLENTA
    in mourning, ROMELIO *sits by her.*]

ROMELIO. Why do you grieve thus? Take a looking glass,
    And see if this Sorrow become you; that pale face
    Will make men think you us'd Some art before,
    Some odious painting: Contarino's dead.
JOLENTA. O that he should die so soon!
ROMELIO. Why, I pray tell me,
    Is not the shortest fever the best? And are not bad plays
    The Worse for their length?
JOLENTA. Add not to th' ill y'ave done
    An odious slander. He stuck i'th' eyes a'th' Court
    As the most choice jewel there.
ROMELIO. O be not angry.
    Indeed the Court to well composed nature
    Adds much to perfection; for it is, or should be,
    As a bright crystal mirror to the World,
    To dress itself; but I must tell you sister,
    If th 'excellency of the place could have
    Wrought salvation, the devil had ne'er fallen
    From heaven; he was proud. Leave us, leave us?
    Come, take your seat again, I have a plot,
    If you will listen to it seriously,

    That goes beyond example; it shall breed
    Out of the death of these two noblemen,
    The advancement of our house.
JOLENTA. O take heed,
    A grave is a rotten foundation.
ROMELIO. Nay, nay, hear me.
    'Tis somewhat indirectly, I confess:
    But there is much advancement in the world,
    That comes in indirectly. I pray mind me:
    You are already made by absolute will,
    Contarino's heir: now, if it can be prov'd
    That you have issue by Lord Ercole,
    I will make you inherit his land too.
JOLENTA. How's this?
    Issue by him, he dead, and I a virgin?
ROMELIO. I knew you would wonder how it could be done,
    But I have laid the case so radically,
    Not all the lawyers in Christendom
    Shall find any the least flaw in't. I have a mistress
    Of the Order of St Clare, a beauteous nun,
    Who being cloister'd ere she knew the heat
    Her blood would arrive to, had only time enough
    To repent, and idleness sufficient
    To fall in love with me; and to be short,
    I have so much disorder'd the holy Order,
    I have got this nun with child.
JOLENTA. Excellent work, made for a dumb midwife!
ROMELIO. I am glad you grow thus pleasant.
    Now will I have you presently give out,
    That you are full t'vvo months quick'ned with child
    By Ercole: which rumour can beget
    No scandal to you, since we will affirm,
    The precontract was so exactly done,
    By the same words used in the form of marriage,
    That with a little dispensation,
    A money matter, it shall be register'd
    Absolute matrimony.
JOLENTA. So, then I conceive you,
    My child must prove your bastard.
ROMELIO. Right;
    For at such time my mistress fall in labour,
    You must feign the like.
JOLENTA. 'Tis a pretty feat this,
    But I am not capable of it.
ROMELIO. Not capable?

JOLENTA. No, for the thing you would have me counterfeit,
    Is most essentially put in practice: nay, 'tis done,
    I am with child already.
ROMELIO. Ha, by whom?
JOLENTA. By Contarino. Do not knit the brow,
    The precontract shall justify it, it shall:
    Nay, I will get some singular fine churchman,
    Or though he be a plural one, shall affirm
    He coupl'd us together.
ROMELIO. O misfortune!
    Your child must then be reputed Ercole's.
JOLENTA. Your hopes are dash'd then, since your votary's Issue
    Must not inherit the land.
ROMELIO. No matter for that,
    So I preserve her fame. I am strangely puzzl'd:
    Why, suppose that she be brought abed before you,
    And we conceal her issue till the time
    Of your delivery, and then give out
    That you have two at a birth. Ha, were't not excellent?
JOLENTA. And what resemblance think you, would they have
    To one another? Twins are still alike:
    But this is not your aim; you would have your child
    Inherit Ercole's land —O my sad soul,
    Have you not made me yet wretched enough,
    But after all this frosty age in youth,
    Which you have witch' d upon me, you will seek
    To poison my fame?
ROMELIO. That's done already.
JOLENTA. No sir, I did but feign it, to a fatal
    Purpose, as I thought.
ROMELIO. What purpose?
JOLENTA. If you had lov'd or tend'red my dear honour,
    You would have locked your poniard in my heart,
    When I nam'd I was with child. But I must live
    To linger out, till the consumption
    Of my own sorrow kill me.
ROMELIO. This will not do.
    The devil has on the sudden furnish'd me
    With a rare charm, yet a most unnatural
    Falsehood: no matter, so 'twill take.
    Stay sister, I would utter to you a business,
    But I am very loath: a thing indeed,
    Nature would have compassionately conceal'd,
    Till my mother's eyes be clos'd.
JOLENTA. Pray what's that sir?

ROMELIO. You did observe
    With what a dear regard our mother tend'red
    The Lord Contarino, yet how passionately
    She sought to cross the match: why this was merely
    To blind the eye o'th' world; for she did know
    That you would marry him, and he was capable.
    My mother doted upon him, and it was plotted
    Cunningly between them, after you were married,
    Living all three together in one house,
    A thing I cannot whisper without horror:
    Why the malice scarce of devils would suggest
    Incontinence 'tween them two.
JOLENTA. I remember since his hurt,
    She has been very passionately enquiring
    After his health.
ROMELIO. Upon my soul, this jewel
    With a piece of the holy cross in't, this relic,
    Valued at many thousand crowns, she would
    Have sent him, lying upon his death-bed.
JOLENTA. Professing, as you say, love to my mother:
    Wherefore did he make me his heir?
ROMELIO. His will was made afore he went to fight,
    When he was first a suitor to you.
JOLENTA. To fight: O well rememb'red!
    If he lov'd my mother, wherefore did he lose
    His life in my quarrel?
ROMELIO. For the affront sake, a word you understand not;
    Because Ercole was pretended rival to him,
    To clear your suspicion: I was gulled in't too.
    Should he not have fought upon't,
    He had undergone the censure of a coward.
JOLENTA. How came you by this wretched knowledge?
ROMELIO. His surgeon overheard it,
    As he did sigh it out to his confessor,
    Some half hour 'fore he died.
JOLENTA. I would have the surgeon hang'd
    For abusing confession, and for making me
    So wretched by'th' report. Can this be truth?
ROMELIO. No, but direct falsehood,
    As ever was banish'd the Court. Did you ever hear
    Of a mother that has kept her daughter's husband
    For her own tooth? He fancied you in one kind,
    For his lust, and he lov'd our mother
    In another kind, for her money;
    The gallant's fashion right. But come, ne'er think on't,

Throw the fowl to the devil that hatch' d it, and let this
Bury all ill that's in't; she is our mother.

JOLENTA. I never did find anything i'th' world,
Turn my blood so much as this: here's such a conflict
Between apparent presumption, and unbelief,
That I shall die in't.
O, if there be another world i'th' moon,
As some fantastics dream,[146] I could wish all men,
The whole race of them, for their inconstancy,
Sent thither to people that. Why, I protest
I now affect the Lord Ercole's memory
Better than the other's.

ROMELIO. But were Contarino living?

JOLENTA. I do call anything to witness,
That the divine law prescribed[147] us to strengthen
An oath, were he living and in health, I would never
Marry with him. Nay, since I have found the world
So false to me, I'll be as false to it;
I will mother this child for you.

ROMELIO. Ha?

JOLENTA. Most certainly it will beguile part of my sorrow.

ROMELIO. O most assuredly; make you smile to think
How many times i'th' world lordships descend
To divers men that might, and truth were known,
Be heir, for anything that belongs to th' flesh,
As well to the Turk's richest eunuch.

JOLENTA. But do you not think
I shall have a horrible strong breath now?

ROMELIO. Why?

JOLENTA. O, with keeping your counsel, 'tis so terrible foul.

ROMELIO. Come, come, come, you must leave these bitter flashes.

JOLENTA. Must I dissemble dishonesty? You Have divers
Counterfeit honesty: but I hope here's none
Will take exceptions; I now must practise
The art of a great-bellied woman, and go feign
Their qualms and swoundings.

ROMELIO. Eat unripe fruit, and oatmeal,
To take away your colour.

---

[146] Compare Milton;

"Not in *the* neighbouring *moon, as* same *hate dream'd.*"

Par. Lost, Book iii. v. 459.

[147] Perhaps we should read "*hath* prescribed." In this speech the measure is sadly defective.

JOLENTA. Dine in my bed
    Some two hours after noon.
ROMELIO. And when you are up,
    Make to your petticoat a quilted preface,
    To advance your belly.
JOLENTA. I have a strange conceit now.
    I have known some women when they were with child,
    Have long'd to beat their husbands: what if I,
    To keep decorum, exercise my longing
    Upon my tailor that way, and noddle him soundly?
    He'll make the larger bill for't.
ROMELIO. I'll get one shall be as tractable to't as stockfish.
JOLENTA. O my fantastical sorrow! Cannot I now
    Be miserable enough, unless I wear
    A pied fool's coat? Nay worse, for when our passions
    Such giddy and uncertain changes breed,
    We are never well, till we are mad indeed. [*Exit.*]
ROMELIO. So, nothing in the world could have done this,
    But to beget in her a strong distaste
    Of the Lord Contarino. O jealousy,
    How violent, especially in women,
    How often has it rais'd the devil up
    In form of a law-case! My especial care
    Must be, to nourish craftily this fiend,
    'Tween the mother and the daughter, that the deceit
    Be not perceiv'd. My next task, that my sister,
    After this suppos'd childbirth, be persuaded
    To enter into religion: 'tis concluded
    She must never marry; so I am left guardian
    To her estate: and lastly, that my two surgeons
    Be wag'd to tlle East Indies. Let them prate
    When they are beyond the line: the callenture,
    Or the scurvy, or the Indian pox, I hope,
    Will take ordcr for their coming back.

    [*Enter* LEONORA.]

    O here's my mother. I ha' strange news for you,
    My sister is with child.
LEONORA. I do look now
    For some great misfortunes to follow.
    For indeed mischiefs are like the visits
    Of Franciscan friars, they never come
    To prey upon us single. In what estate
    Left you Contarino?

ROMELIO. Strange that you
  Can skip from the former sorrow to such a question?
  I'll tell you: in the absence of his surgeon,
  My charity did that for him in a trice,
  They would have done at leisure, and been paid for't.
  I have kill'd him.

LEONORA. I am twenty years elder
  Since you last opened your lips.

ROMELIO. Ha?

LEONORA. You have given him the wound you speak of,
  Quite thorough your mother's heart.

ROMELIO. I will heal it presently mother; for this sorrow
  Belongs to your error. You would have him live
  Because you think he's father of the child;
  But Jolenta vows by all the rights of truth,
  'Tis Ercole's. It makes me smile to think
  How cunningly my sister could be drawn
  To the contract, and yet how familiarly
  To his bed. Doves never couple without
  A kind of murmur.

LEONORA. O I am very sick!

ROMELIO. Your old disease; when you are griev'd,
  You are troubled with the mother.

LEONORA. [*aside.*] I am rapt with the mother indeed,
  That I ever bore such a son.

ROMELIO. Pray tend my sister,
  I am infinitely full of business.

LEONORA. Stay, you will mourn for Contarino?

ROMELIO. O by all means, 'tis fit; my sister is his heir. [*Exit.*

LEONORA. I will make you chief mourner, believe it.
  Never was woe like mine: O that my care
  And absolute study to preserve his life,
  Should be his absolute ruin! Is he gone then?
  There is no plague i'th' world can be compar'd
  To impossible desire, for they are plagu'd
  In the desire itself: never, O never
  Shall I behold him living, in whose life
  I liv'd far sweetlier than in mine own.
  A precise curiosity[148] has undone me: why did I not
  Make my love known directly? 'T had not been
  Beyond example, for a matron to affect
  I'th' honourable way of marriage,
  So youthful a person. O I shall run mad:

---

[148] i.e. niceness, scrupulousness.

For as we love our youngest children best,
So the last fruit of our affection,
Wherever we bestow it, is most strong,
Most violent, most unresistable,
Since 'tis indeed our latest harvest-home,
Last merriment 'fore winter. And we widows,
As men report of our best picture makers,
We love the piece we are in hand with better
Than all the excellent work we have done before:
And my son has depriv'd me of all this. Ha, my son!
I'll be a fury to him; like an Amazon lady,
I'd cut off this right pap, that gave him suck,
To shoot him dead. I'll no more tender him,
Than had a wolf stol'n to my teat i'th' night,
And robb'd me of my milk: nay, such a creature
I should love better far.—Ha, ha, what say you?
I do talk to somewhat, methinks: it may be
My evil genius. Do not the bells ring?
I have a strange noise in my head. O, fly in pieces!
Come age, and wither me into the malice
Of those that have been happy; let me have
One more property more than the Devil of Hell,
Let me envy the pleasure of youth heartily,
Let me in this life fear no kind of ill,
That have no good to hope for: let me die
In the distraction of that worthy princess,
Who loathed food,[149] and sleep, and ceremony,
For thought of losing that brave gentleman,
She would fain have sav'd, had not a false conveyance
Express'd him stubborn-hearted. Let me sink,
Where neither man, nor memory may ever find me.

[*Falls down.*]

[*Enter* CAPUCHIN *and* ERCOLE.]

CAPUCHIN. This is a private way which I command,
As her confessor. I would not have you seen yet,
Till I prepare her. Peace to you lady.
LEONORA. Ha?
CAPUCHIN. You are well employ'd, I hope; the best pillow i'th' world

---

[149] Here, I think, there is a manifest allusion to the closing scene of Queen Elizabeth's life, and to what Mr. Lodge calls "the well-known, but weakly authenticated tale of the Countess of Nottingham and the ring."

> For this your contemplation, Is the earth,
> And the best object, heaven.

LEONORA. I am whispering to a dead friend.

CAPUCHIN. And I am come
> To bring you tidings of a friend was dead,
> Restor'd to life again.

LEONORA. Say sir?

CAPUCHIN. One whom I dare presume, next to your children,
> You tend'red above life.

LEONORA. Heaven will not suffer me
> Utterly to be lost.

CAPUCHIN. For he should have been
> Your son-in-law; miraculously sav'd,
> When surgery gave him o'er.

LEONORA. O may you live
> To win many souls to heaven, worthy sir,
> That your crown may be the greater. Why my son
> Made me believe he stole into his chamber,
> And ended that which Ercole began
> By a deadly stab in's heart.

ERCOLE. Alas, she mistakes,
> 'Tis Contarino she wishes living; but I must fasten
> On her last words, for my own safety.

LEONORA. Where,
> O where shall I meet this comfort?

ERCOLE. Here in the vow'd comfort of your daughter.

LEONORA. O I am dead again; instead of the man,
> You present me the grave swallowed him.

ERCOLE. Collect yourself, good lady
> Would you behold brave Contarino living?
> There cannot be a nobler chronicle
> Of his good than myself: if you would view him dead,
> I will present him to you bleeding fresh,
> In my penitency.

LEONORA. Sir, you do only live
> To redeem another ill you have committed,
> That my poor innocent daughter perish not
> By your vile sin, whom you have got: with child.

ERCOLE. Here begin all my compassion: O poor soul!
> She is with child by Contarino, and he dead;
> By whom should she preserve her fame to'th' world,
> But by myself that lov'd her 'bove the world?
> There never was a way more honourable
> To exercise my virtue, than to father it,
> And preserve her credit, and to marry her.

I'll suppose her Contarino's widow, bequeath'd to me
Upon his death: for sure she was his wife,
But that the ceremony a'th' Church was wanting.
Report this to her, madam, and withal,
That never father did conceive more joy
For the birth of an heir, than I to understand
She had such confidence in me. I will not now
Press a visit upon her, till you have prepar'd her:
For I do read in your distraction,
Should I be brought a'th' sudden to her presence,
Either the hasty fright, or else the shame
May blast the fruit within her. I will leave you
To commend as loyal faith and service to her,
As e'er heart harbour'd. By my hope of bliss,
I never liv'd to do good act but this.
CAPUCHIN. Withal, and you be wise,
Remember what the mother has reveal'd
Of Romelio's treachery.

[*Exeunt* ERCOLE, CAPUCHIN.]

LEONORA. A most noble fellow! In his loyalty
I read what worthy comforts I have lost
In my dear Contarino, and all adds
To my despair. Within there!

[*Enter* WINIFRID.]

Fetch the picture
Hangs in my inner closet. I remember,

[*Exit* WINIFRID.]

I let a word slip of Romelio's practice
At the surgeons': no matter, I can salve it,
I have deeper vengeance that's preparing for him:
To let him live and kill him, that's revenge
I meditate upon.

[*Enter* WINIFRID *and the Picture.*]

So, hang it up.
I was enjoin'd by the party ought that picture,
Forty years since, ever when I was vex'd,
To look upon that. What was his meaning in't,

> I know not, but methinks upon the sudden
> It has furnish'd me with mischief; such a plot
> As never mother dreamt of. Here begins
> My part i'th' play: my son's estate is sunk
> By loss at sea, and he has nothing left
> But the land his father left him. 'Tis concluded,
> The law shall undo him. Come hither,
> I have a weighty secret to impart,
> But I would have thee first confirm to me,
> How I may trust that thou canst keep my counsel
> Beyond death.

WINIFRID. Why mistress, 'tis your only way
> To enjoin me first that I reveal to you
> The worst act I e'er did in all my life:
> So one secret shall bind another.

LEONORA. Thou instruct'st me
> Most ingeniously, for indeed it is not fit,
> Where any act is plotted, that is nought,
> Any of counsel to it should be good;
> And in a thousand ills have happ'd i'th' world,
> The intelligence of one another's shame
> Have wrought far more effectually than the tie
> Of conscience, or religion.

WINIFRID. But think not, mistress,
> That any sin which ever I committed
> Did concern you; for proving false in one thing,
> You were a fool if ever you would trust me
> In the least matter of weight.

LEONORA. Thou hast liv'd with me
> These forty years; we have grown old together,
> As many ladies and their women do,
> With talking nothing, and with doing less:
> We have spent our life in that which least concerns life,
> Only in putting on our clothes. And now I think on't,
> I have been a very courtly mistress to thee,
> I have given thee good words, but no deeds;
> Now's the time to requite all. My son has
> Six lordships left him.

WINIFRID. 'Tis truth.

LEONORA. But he cannot
> Live four days to enjoy them.

WINIFRID. Have you poison'd him?

LEONORA. No, the poison is yet but brewing.

WINIFRID. You must minister it to him with all privacy.

LEONORA. Privacy? It shall be given him

In open court. I'll make him swallow it
Before the judge's face. If he be master
Of poor ten arpines[150] of land forty hours longer,
Let the world repute me an honest woman.
WINIFRID. So 'twill I hope.
LEONORA. O thou canst not conceive
My inimitable plot. Let's to my ghostly father,
Where first I will have thee make a promise
To keep my counsel, and then I will employ thee
In such a subtle combination,
Which will require to make the practice fit,
Four devils, five advocates, to one woman's wit.

[*Exeunt.*]

ACT IV.

SCENE I.

[*Enter* LEONORA, SANITONELLA, WINIFRID *and* REGISTER *at one door: at the other,* ARIOSTO.]

SANITONELLA. Take her into your office sir, she has that in her belly
will dry up your ink, I can tell you.—
This is the man that is your learned counsel,
A fellow that will trowel it off with tongue:
He never goes without restorative powder
Of the lungs of fox in's pocket, and Malligo raisins
To make him long-winded. Sir, this gentlewoman
Entreats your counsel in an honest cause,
Which please you sir, this brief, my own poor labour
Will give you light of.
ARIOSTO. Do you call this a brief?
Here's as I weigh them, some fourscore sheets of paper.
What would they weigh if there were cheese wrapt in them,
Or figdates?
SANITONELLA. Joy come to you, you are merry;
We call this but a brief in our office.
The scope of the business lies i'th' margent.
ARIOSTO. Methinks you prate too much.
I never could endure an honest cause
With a long prologue to't.
LEONORA. You trouble him.

---

[150] Fr. Arpent, an acre.

ARIOSTO. What's here? O strange. I have liv'd this sixty years,
    Yet in all my practice never did shake hands
    With a cause so odious. Sirrah, are you her knave?
SANITONELLA. No sir, I am a clerk.
ARIOSTO. Why you whoreson fogging rascal,
    Are there not whores enough for presentations,
    Of overseers, wrong the will o'th' dead,
    Oppressions of widows, or young orphans,
    Wicked divorces, or your vicious cause
    Of *plus quam satis*, to content a woman,
    But you must find new stratagems, new pursenets?
    O Woman, as the ballad lives to tell you,
    What will you shortly come to?
SANITONELLA. Your fee is ready sir.
ARIOSTO. The devil take such fees,
    And all such suits i'th' tail of them; see the slave
    Has written false Latin: sirrah Ignoramus,
    Were you ever at the university?
SANITONELLA. Never sir: but 'tis well known to divers
    I nave commenc'd in a pew of our office.
ARIOSTO. Where? In a pew of your office!
SANITONELLA. I have been dry-founder;d in't this four years,
    Seldom found non-resident from my desk.
ARIOSTO. Non-resident subsumner!
    I'll tear your libel for abusing that word,
    By virtue of the clergy.
SANITONELLA. What do you mean sir?
    It cost me four nights'labour.
ARIOSTO. Hadst thou been drunk
    So long, th'adst done our court better service.
LEONORA. Sir, you do forget your gravity, methinks.
ARIOSTO. Cry ye mercy, do I so?
    And as I take it, you do very little
    Remember either womanhood
    Or Christianity: why do ye meddle
    With that seducing knave, that's good for naught,
    Unless 't be to fill the office full of fleas,
    Or a winter itch, wears that spacious inkhorn
    All a vacation only to cure tetters,
    And his penknife to weed corns from the splay toes
    Of the right worshipful of the office?
LEONORA. You make bold with me sir.
ARIOSTO. Woman, y'are mad, I'll swear it, and have more need
    Of a physician than a lawyer.
    The melancholy humour flows in your face,

Your painting cannot hide it. Such vile suits
Disgrace our courts, and these make honest lawyers
Stop their own ears whilst they plead, and that's the reason
Your younger men that have good conscience,
Wear such large nightcaps. Go old woman, go pray,
For lunacy, or else the devil himself
Has tane possession of thee. May like cause
In any Christian court never find name:
Bad suits, and not the law, bred the law's shame. [*Exit.*]

LEONORA. Sure the old man's frantic.

SANITONELLA. Plague on's gouty fingers.
Were all of his mind, to entertain no suits
But such they thought were honest, sure our lawyers
Would not purchase[151] half so fast. But here's the man,

[*Enter* CONTILUPO, *a spruce lawyer.*]

Learned Signior Contilupo, here's a fellow
Of another piece, believe't; I must make shift
With the foul copy.

CONTILUPO. Business to me?

SANITONELLA. To you sir, from this lady.

CONTILUPO. She is welcome.

SANITONELLA. 'Tis a foul copy sir, you'll hardly read it.
There's twenty double ducats, can you read sir?

CONTILUPO. Exceeding well; very, very exceeding well

SANITONELLA. [*aside.*] This man will be sav'd, he can read.
Lord, lord, to see
What money can do! Be the hand never so foul,
Somewhat will be pick'd out on't.

CONTILUPO. Is not this *Vivere honeste*?

SANITONELLA. No, that's struck out sir;
And wherever you find *vivere honeste* in these papers,
Give it a dash sir.

CONTILUPO. I shall be mindful of it.
In truth you write a pretty secretary;
Your secretary hand ever takes best
In mine opinion.

SANITONELLA. Sir, I have been in France,
And there, believe't, your court hand generally,
Takes beyond thought.

CONTILUPO. Even as a man is traded in't.

SANITONELLA. That I could not think of this virtuous gentleman

---

[151] i.e. acquire wealth.

Before I went to'th' other hog-rubber![152]
Why this was wont to give young clerks half fees,
To help him to clients. Your opinion in the case sir?

CONTILUPO. I am struck with wonder, almost extasied,
With this most goodly suit.

LEONORA. It is the fruit
Of a most hearty penitence.

CONTILUPO. 'Tis a case
Shall leave a precedent to all the world,
In our succeeding annals, and deserves
Rather a spacious public theatre
Than a pent court for audience: it shall teach
All ladies the right path to rectify
Their issue.

SANITONELLA. Lo you, here's a man of comfort.

CONTILUPO. And you shall go unto a peaceful grave,
Discharg'd of such a guilt, as would have lain
Howling for ever at your wounded heart,
And rose with you to Judgement.

SANITONELLA. O give me
Such a lawyer, as will think of the day
Of Judgement!

LEONORA. You must urge the business
Against him as spitefully as may be.

CONTILUPO. Doubt not. What, is he summon'd?

SANITONELLA. Yes, and the court
Will sit within this half hour. Peruse your notes,
You have very short warning.

CONTILUPO. Never fear you that.
Follow me worthy lady, and make account
This suit is ended already.

[*Exeunt.*]

SCENE II.

[*Enter officers preparing seats for the judges; to them* ERCOLE,
muffled.]

FIRST OFFICER: You would have a private seat sir?

ERCOLE. Yes sir.

SECOND OFFICER: Here's a closet belongs to'th' court,

---

[152] Not a "dictionary word;" but old Burton uses it; "The very rusticks and *hog-rubbers*, Menalcas and Coridon, &c." *Anat. of Melancholy*, p. 540, ed. 1660.

Where you may hear all unseen.
ERCOLE. I thank you;
    There's money.
SECOND OFFICER: I give your thanks again sir.

[*Enter* CONTARINO, *the two surgeons, disguised.*]

CONTARINO. Is't possible Romelio's persuaded
    You are gone to the East Indies?
FIRST SURGEON. Most confidently.
CONTARINO. But do you mean to go?
SECOND SURGEON. How? Go to the East Indies? And so many
    Hollanders gone to fetch sauce for their pickled herrings: some
    have been pepper'd there too, lately.[153] But I pray, being thus well
    recover'd of your wound, why do you not reveal yourself?
CONTARINO. That my fair Jolenta should be rumour'd
    To be with child by noble Ercole,
    Makes me expect to what a violent issue
    These passages will come. I hear her brother
    Is marrying the infant she goes with,
    'Fore it be born, as, if it be a daughter,
    To the Duke of Austria's nephew; if a son,
    Into the noble ancient family
    Of the Palavafini.[154] He's a subtle devil.
    And I do wonder what strange suit in law
    Has happ'd between him and's mother.
FIRST SURGEON. 'Tis whispered 'mong the lawyers,
    'Twill undo him for ever.

[*Enter* SANITONELLA, WINIFRID.]

SANITONELLA. Do you hear, officers?
    You must take special care, that you let in
    No brachigraphy[155] men, to take notes.
FIRST OFFICER: No sir?
SANITONELLA. By no means;
    We cannot have a cause of any fame,
    But you must have scurvy pamphlets, and lewd ballads

---

[153] Webster alludes to the massacre of the English by the Dutch at Amboyna, in February, 1622. The *True Relation* of the atrocity has been several times reprinted. Dryden wrote an execrable play on the subject.

[154] Qy. "*Pallavicini.*"

[155] i.e. short-hand writers:—no great favourites of our old dramatists, who had sometimes to complain of their plays being printed without their consent, in a mutilated state, from copies taken down by brachygraphy during the representation.

Engend'red of it presently. Have you broke fast yet?

WINIFRID. Not I sir.

SANITONELLA. 'Twas very ill done of you:
 For this cause will be long a-pleading; but no[156] matter,
 I have a modicum in my buckram bag,
 To stop your stomach.

WINIFRID. What is't? Green ginger?

SANITONELLA. Green ginger, nor pellitory of Spain
 Neither, yet 'twill stop a hollow tooth better
 Than either of them.

WINIFRID. Pray what is't?

SANITONELLA. Look you,
 It is a very lovely pudding-pie,
 Which we clerks find great relief in.

WINIFRID. I shall have no stomach.

SANITONELLA. No matter and you have not, I may pleasure
 Some of our learned counsel with't; I have done it
 Many a time and often, when a cause
 Has proved like an after-game at Irish.[157]

[*Enter* CRISPIANO *like a judge, with another judge*; CONTILUPO
 and another lawyer at one bar; ROMELIO, ARIOSTO *at
 another*; LEONORA *with a black veil over her, and* JULIO.]

CRISPIANO. 'Tis a strange suit; is Leonora come?

CONTILUPO. She's here my lord; make way there for the lady.

CRISPIANO. Take off her veil: it seems she is asham'd
 To look her cause i'th' face.

CONTILUPO. She's sick, my lord.

ARIOSTO. She's mad my lord, and would be kept more dark.
 By your favour sir, I have now occasion
 To be at your elbow, and within this half hour
 Shall entreat you to be angry, very angry.

CRISPIANO. Is Romelio come?

ROMELIO. I am here my lord, and call'd, I do protest,
 To answer what I know not, for as yet
 I am wholly ignorant of what the court
 Will charge me with.

---

[156] The old copy "not."

[157] Irish, "a game within the tables," differed very little from back-gammon. "Irish,"
says *The Compleat Gamester*, "is an ingenious game, and requires a great deal of skill to
play it well, *especially the After-game:.........* for *an After-game* I know not what
instructions to give you: you must herein trust to your own judgment and the chance of
the dice, and if they run low for some time, it will be so much the better." pp. 111, 112.
ed. 1709.

CRISPIANO. I assure you, the proceeding
   Is most unequal then, for I perceive
   The counsel of the adverse party furnish' d
   With full instruction.
ROMELIO. Pray my lord,
   Who is my accuser?
CRISPIANO. 'Tis your mother.
ROMELIO. She has discover'd Contarino's murder:
   If she prove so unnatural, to call
   My life in question, I am arm'd to suffer
   This to end all my losses.
CRISPIANO. Sir, we will do you
   This favour: you shall hear the accusation,
   Which being known, we will adjourn the court
   Till a fortnight hence, you may provide your counsel.
ARIOSTO. I advise you, take their proffer,
   Or else the lunacy runs in a blood,
   You are more mad than she.
ROMELIO. What are you sir?
ARIOSTO. An angry fellow that would do thee good,
   For goodness' sake itself, I do protest,
   Neither for love nor money.
ROMELIO. Prithee stand further, I shall gall your gout else.
ARIOSTO. Come, come, I know you for an East Indy merchant,
   You have a spice of pride in you still.
ROMELIO. My lord,
   I am so strength'ned in my innocence,
   For any the least shadow of a crime,
   Committed 'gainst my mother, or the world,
   That she can charge me with, here do I make it
   My humble suit, only this hour and place
   May give it as full hearing, and as free,
   And unrestrain'd a sentence.
CRISPIANO. Be not too confident; you have cause to fear.
ROMELIO. Let fear dwell with earthquakes,
   Shipwrecks at sea, or prodigies in heaven;
   I cannot set myself so many fathom
   Beneath the height of my true heart, as fear.
ARIOSTO. Very fine words, I assure you, if they were
   To any purpose.
CRISPIANO. Well, have your entreaty:
   And if your own credulity undo you,
   Blame not the court hereafter. Fall to your plea.
CONTILUPO. May it please your lordship and the reverend court,
   To give me leave to open to you a case

So rare, so altogether void of precedent,
That I do challenge all the spacious volumes
Of the whole civil law to show the like.
We are of counsel for this gentlewoman,
We have receiv'd our fee, yet the whole course
Of what we are to speak, is quite against her,
Yet we'll deserve our fee too. There stands one,
Romelio the merchant; I will name him to you
Without either title or addition:
For those false beams of his supposed honour,
As void of true heat as are all painted fires,
Or glow-worms in the dark, suit him all basely,
As if he had bought his gentry from the herald,
With money got by extortion: I will first
Produce this Aesop's crow as he stands forfeit
For the long use of his gay borrowed plumes,
And then let him hop naked. I come to'th' point:
'T'as been a dream in Naples, very near
This eight and thirty years, that this Romelio
Was nobly descended; he has rank'd himself
With the nobility, shamefully usurp'd
Their place, and in a kind of saucy pride,
Which like to mushrooms, ever grow most rank
When they do spring from dunghills, sought to o'ersway
The *Fliski*,[158] the *Grimaldi, Dori,*
And all the ancient pillars of our state.
View now what he is come to: this poor thing
Without a name, this cuckoo hatch'd i'th'nest
Of a hedge-sparrow.
ROMELIO. Speaks he all this to me?
ARIOSTO. Only to you sir.
ROMELIO. I do not ask thee,
    Prithee hold thy prating.
ARIOSTO. Why very good!
    You will be presently as angry as I could wish.
CONTILUPO. What title shall I set to this base coin?
    He has no name, and for's aspect he seems
    A giant in a May-game, that within
    Is nothing but a porter: I'll undertake
    He had as good have travell'd all his life
    With gypsies: I will sell him to any man
    For an hundred chickeens, and he that buys him of me
    Shall lose by th' hand too.

---

[158] Qy. "Fieschi."

ARIOSTO. Lo, what are you come to:
    You that did scorn to trade in anything
    But gold or spices, or your cochineal,
    He rates you now at poor John.
ROMELIO. Out upon thee,
    I would thou wert of his side.
ARIOSTO. Would you so?
ROMELIO. The devil and thee together on each hand,
    To prompt the lawyer's memory when he founders.
CRISPIANO. Signor Contilupo, the court holds it fit,
    You leave this stale declaiming 'gainst the person,
    And come to the matter.
CONTILUPO. Now I shall my lord.
CRISPIANO. It shows a poor malicious eloquence,
    And it is strange men of your gravity
    Will not forgo it. Verily, I presume,
    If you but heard yourself speaking with my ears,
    Your phrase would be more modest.
CONTILUPO. Good my lord, be assured,
    I will leave all circumstance, and come to th' purpose:
    This Romelio is a bastard.
ROMELIO. How, a bastard?
    O mother, now the day begins grow hot
    On your side.
CONTILUPO. Why she is your accuser.
ROMELIO. I had forgot that; was my father married
    To any other woman, at the time
    Of my begetting?
CONTILUPO. That's not the business.
ROMELIO. I turn me then to you that were my mother,
    But by what name I am to call you now,
    You must instruct me: were you ever married
    To my father?
LEONORA. To my shame I speak it, never.
CRISPIANO. Not to Francisco Romelio?
LEONORA. May it please your lordships,
    To him I was, but he was not his father.
CONTILUPO. Good my lord, give us leave in a few words
    To expound the riddle, and to make it plain
    Without the least of scruple: for I take it,
    There cannot be more lawful proof i'th' world,
    Than the oath of the mother.
CRISPIANO. Well then, to your proofs,
    And be not tedious.
CONTILUPO. I'll conclude in a word:

Some nine and thirty years since, which was the time
This woman was married, Francisco Romelio,
This gentleman's putative father, and her husband,
Being not married to her past a fortnight,
Would needs go travel; did so, and continued
In France and the Low Countries eleven months:
Take special note o'th' time, I beseech your lordship,
For it makes much to'th' business. In his absence
He left behind to sojourn at his house
A Spanish gentleman, a fine spruce youth
By the ladies' confession, and you may be sure
He was no eunuch neither; he was one
Romelio loved very dearly, as oft haps,
No man alive more welcome to the husband
Than he that makes him cuckold. This gentleman
I say, breaking all laws of hospitality,
Got his friend's wife with child, a full two months
'Fore the husband returned.

SANITONELLA. Good sir, forget not the lamb-skin.

CONTILUPO. I warrant thee.

SANITONELLA. I will pinch by the buttock, to put you in mind of't.

CONTILUPO. Prithee hold thy prating.

What's to be practis'd now, my lord? Marry this:
Romelio being a young novice, not acquainted
With this precedence, very innocently
Returning home from travel, finds his wife
Grown an excellent good huswife, for she had set
Her women to spin flax, and to that use,
Had in a study which was built of stone,
Stor'd up at least an hundredweight of flax:
Marry such a thread as was to be spun from the flax,
I think the like was never heard of.

CRISPIANO. What was that?

CONTILUPO. You may be certain, she would lose no time
In bragging that her husband had got up
Her belly: to be short, at seven months' end,
Which was the time of her delivery,
And when she felt her self to fall in travail,
She makes her waiting woman, as by mischance,
Set fire to the flax, the fright[159] whereof,
As they pretend, causes this gentlewoman
To fall in pain, and be delivered
Eight weeks afore her reckoning.

---

[159] The old copy "flight."

SANITONELLA. Now sir, remember the lambskin.

CONTILUPO. The midwife straight howls out, there was no hope
    Of th'infant's life, swaddles it in a flay'd lambskin,
    As a bird hatch'd too early, makes it up
    With three quarters of a face, that made it look
    Like a changeling, cries out to Romelio
    To have it christ'ned, lest it should depart
    Without that it came for: and thus are many serv'd,
    That take care to get gossips for those children,
    To which they might be godfathers themselves,
    And yet be no arch-puritans neither.

CRISPIANO. No more!

ARIOSTO. Pray my lord, give him way, you spoil
    His oratory else: thus would they jest
    Were they feed to open their sister's cases.

CRISPIANO. You have urg'd enough; you first affirm,
    Her husband was away from her eleven Months?

CONTILUPO. Yes my lord.

CRISPIANO. And at seven months' end,
    After his return she was delivered
    Of this Romelio, and had gone her full time?

CONTILUPO. True my lord.

CRISPIANO. So by this account this gentleman was begot
    In his suppos'd father's absence.

CONTILUPO. You have it fully.

CRISPIANO. A most strange suit this, 'tis beyond example,
    Either time past, or present, for a woman
    To publish her own dishonour voluntarily,
    Without being call'd in question, some forty years
    After the sin committed, and her counsel
    To enlarge the offence with as much oratory
    As ever I did hear them in my life
    Defend a guilty woman; 'tis most strange:
    Or why with such a poison'd violence
    Should she labour her son's undoing? We observe
    Obedience of creatures to the Law of Nature
    Is the stay of the whole world: here that Law is broke,
    For though our civil law makes difference
    'Tween the base, and the legitimate,
    Compassionate Nature makes them equal;
    Nay, she many times prefers them. I pray
    Resolve me sir, have not you and your mother
    Had some suit in law together lately?

ROMELIO. None my lord.

CRISPIANO. No? No contention about parting your goods?

ROMELIO. Not any.

CRISPIANO. No flaw, no unkindness?

ROMELIO. None that ever arriv'd at my knowledge.

CRISPIANO. Bethink yourself, this cannot choose but savour
 Of a woman's malice deeply; and I fear
 Y' are practis'd upon most devilishly.
 How happ'd gentlewoman, you revealed this no sooner?

LEONORA. While my husband lived, my lord, I durst not.

CRISPIANO. I should rather ask you, why you reveal it now?

LEONORA. Because my lord, I loath'd that such a sin
 Should lie smother'd with me in my grave; my penitence,
 Though to my shame, prefers the revealing of it
 'Bove worldly reputation.

CRISPIANO. Your penitence?
 Might not your penitence have been as hearty,
 Though it had never summon'd to the court
 Such a conflux of people?

LEONORA. Indeed, I might have confess'd it,
 Privately to'th' Church, I grant; but you know repentance
 Is nothing without satisfaction.

CRISPIANO. Satisfaction? Why your husband's dead,
 What satisfaction can you make him?

LEONORA. The greatest satisfaction in the world, my lord,
 To restore the land to'th' right heir, and that's
 My daughter.

CRISPIANO. O she's straight begot then?

ARIOSTO. Very well, may it please this honourable court,
 If he be a bastard, and must forfeit his land for't,
 She has prov'd herself a strumpet, and must lose
 Her dower; let them go a-begging together.

SANITONELLA. Who shall pay us our fees then?

CRISPIANO. Most just.

ARIOSTO. You may see now what an old house
 You are like to pull over your head, dame.

ROMELIO. Could I conceive this publication
 Grew from a hearty penitence, I could bear
 My undoing the more patiently; but my lord,
 There is no reason, as you said even now,
 To satisfy me but this suit of hers
 Springs from a devilish malice, and her pretence,
 Of a grieved conscience, and religion,
 Like to the horrid powder-treason in England,
 Has a most bloody unnatural revenge
 Hid under it. O the violencies of women!
 Why, they are creatures made up and compounded

Of all monsters, poisoned minerals,
And sorcerous herbs that grow.[160]

ARIOSTO. Are you angry yet?

ROMELIO. Would man[161] express a bad one, let him forsake
All natural example, and compare
One to another; they have no more mercy
Than ruinous fires in great tempests.

ARIOSTO. Take heed you do not crack your voice sir.

ROMELIO. Hard-hearted creatures, good for nothing else,
But to wind dead bodies.

ARIOSTO. Yes, to weave seaming lace
With the bones of their husbands that were long since buried,
And curse them when they tangle.

ROMELIO. Yet why do I
Take bastardy so distastefully, when i'th' world,
A many things that are essential parts
Of greatness, are but by-slips, and are father'd
On the wrong parties?
Preferment in the world a many times,
Basely begotten? Nay, I have observ'd
The immaculate justice of a poor man's cause,
In such a court as this, has not known whom
To call father, which way to direct itself
For compassion: but I forget my temper:
Only that I may stop that lawyer's throat,
I do beseech the court, and the whole world,
They will not think the baselier of me,
For the vice of a mother: for that woman's sin,
To which you all dare swear when it was done,
I would not give my consent.

CRISPIANO. Stay, here's an accusation,
But here's no proof; what was the Spaniard's name
You accuse of adultery?

CONTILUPO. Don Crispiano, my lord.

CRISPIANO. What part of Spain was he born in?

CONTILUPO. In Castile.

JULIO. This may prove my father.

SANITONELLA. And my master; my client's spoil'd then.

CRISPIANO. I knew that Spaniard well: if you be a bastard,
Such a man being your father, I dare vouch you
A gentleman; and in that, Signior Contilupo,
Your oratory went a little too far.

---

[160] The old copy "growes."
[161] The old copy "men."

When do we name Don John of Austria..
The Emperor's son, but with reverence?
And I have known in divers families,
The bastards the greater spirits. But to th' purpose;
What time was this gentleman begot? And be sure
You lay your time right.

ARIOSTO. Now the metal comes
    To the touchstone.

CONTILUPO. In anno seventy-one, my lord.

CRISPIANO. Very well, seventy-one;
    The battle of Lepanto was fought in't;
    A most remarkable time, 'twill lie
    For no man's pleasure: and what proof is there
    More than the affirmation of the mother,
    Of this corporal dealing?

CONTILUPO. The deposition of a waiting-woman
    Serv'd her the same time.

CRISPIANO. Where is she?

CONTILUPO. Where is our solicitor with the waiting-woman?

ARIOSTO. Room for the bag and baggage!

SANITONELLA. Here my lord, *ore tenus*.

CRISPIANO. And what can you say gentlewoman?

WINIFRID. Please your lordship, I was the party that dealt in the business, and brought them together.

CRISPIANO. Well.

WINIFRID. And convey'd letters between them.

CRISPIANO. What needed letters, when 'tis said he lodged in her house?

WINIFRID. A running ballad now and then to her viol, for he was never well, but when he was fiddling.

CRISPIANO. Speak to the purpose, did you ever know them bed together?

WINIFRID. No my lord, but I have brought him to the bed-side.

CRISPIANO. That was somewhat near to the business;
    And what, did you help him off with his shoes?

WINIFRID. He wore no shoes, an't please you my lord.

CRISPIANO. No? What then, pumps?

WINIFRID. Neither.

CRISPIANO. Boots were not fit for his journey.

WINIFRID. He wore tennis-court woollen slippers, for fear of creaking sir, and making a noise, to wake the rest o'th' house.

CRISPIANO. Well, and what did he there, in his tennis-court woollen slippers?

WINIFRID. Please your lordship, question me in Latin, for the cause is very foul; the Examiner o'th' court was fain to get it out of me alone i'th' counting house, 'cause he would not spoil the youth o'th' office.

ARIOSTO. Here's a latin spoon, and a long one, to feed with the devil.[162]

WINIFRID. I'd be loath to be ignorant that way, for I hope to marry a proctor, and take my pleasure abroad at the Commencements with him.

ARIOSTO. Come closer to the business.

WINIFRID. I will come as close as modesty will give me leave. Truth is, every morning when he lay with her, I made a caudle for him, by the appointment of my mistress, which he would still refuse, and call for small drink.

CRISPIANO. Small drink?

ARIOSTO. For a julep.

WINIFRID. And said he was wondrous thirsty.

CRISPIANO. What's this to the purpose?

WINIFRID. Most effectual, my lord; I have heard them laugh together extremely, and the curtain rods fall from the tester of the bed, and he ne'er came from her, but he thrust money in my hand; and once in truth, he would have had some dealing with me; which I took he thought 'twould be the only way i'th' world to make me keep counsel the better.

SANITONELLA. That's a stinger, 'tis a good wench, be not daunted.

CRISPIANO. Did you ever find the print of two in the bed?

WINIFRID. What a question that to be ask'd! May it please your lordship, 'tis to be thought he lay nearer to her than so.

CRISPIANO. What age are you of, gentlewoman?

---

[162] Latten a mixed kind of metal: lexicographers have variously explained its composition, but they seem agreed that it was brass, though old Gower certainly distinguishes it from that metal;

"The craft whiche thylk tyme was
To worken in *laton* & in *bras*,
He lerneth," &c.

Confessio *Amantis*, Lib. sec. fol. 41. ed.
Caxton, 1483.

Webster alludes here to the proverb; "he had need of a long spoon, that eats with the devil." The following anecdote, which fathers upon Shakespeare a pun similar to that in the text, has been repeated in several books: I now transcribe it from the MS. volume where it was originally discovered,—a collection of *Merry Passages and Jeasts* by L'Estrange, Sir Roger's nephew, among the Harleian MSS. 6395. Plut. LIX. A. "Shakespeare was godfather to one of Ben Jonson's children, and after the christning being in a deepe study Jonson came to cheere him up, and askt him why he was so melancholy 1 no faith Ben (sayes he) not I, but I have been considering a great while what should be the fittest gift for me to bestow upon my God-child, and I have resolved at last; I pry'the what sayes he? I faith Ben I'le e'en give him a dozen good *Lattin* spoones, and thou shall translate them." At the end of the vol. the writer gives a list of his authorities, from which we learn, that the story just quoted was told to him by "Dun:"— Qy. Donne?

WINIFRID. About six and forty, my lord.

CRISPIANO. Anno seventy-one,
And Romelio is thirty-eight: by that reckoning,
You were a bawd at eight year old: now verily,
You fell to the trade betimes.

SANITONELLA. There y'are from the bias.

WINIFRID. I do not know my age directly: sure I am elder, I can
remember two great frosts, and three great plagues, and the loss of
Calais, and the first coming up of the breeches with the great
codpiece; and I pray what age do you take me of then?

SANITONELLA. Well come off again!

ARIOSTO. An old hunted hare,
She has all her doubles.

ROMELIO. For your own gravities,
And the reverence of the court, I do beseech you,
Rip up the cause no further, but proceed
To sentence.

CRISPIANO. One question more and I have done:
Might not this Crispiano, this Spaniard,
Lie with your mistress at some other time,
Either afore or after, than i'th' absence
Of her husband?

LEONORA. Never.

CRISPIANO. Are you certain of that?

LEONORA. On my soul, never.

CRISPIANO. That's well - he never lay with her,
But in anno seventy-one, let that be remembered.
Stand you aside a while. Mistress, the truth is,
I knew this Crispiano, lived in Naples
At the same time, and loved the gentleman
As my bosom friend; and as I do remember,
The gentleman did leave his picture with you,
If age or neglect have not in so long time ruin'd it.

LEONORA. I preserve it still my lord.

CRISPIANO. I pray let me see't,
Let me see the face I then loved so much to look on.

LEONORA. Fetch it.

WINIFRID. I shall, my lord.

CRISPIANO. No, no, gentlewoman,
I have other business for you.

[*Exit one for the picture.*]

FIRST SURGEON. Now were the time to cut Romelio's throat,
And accuse him for your murder.

CONTARINO. By no means.
SECOND SURGEON. Will you not let us be men of fashion,
    And down with him now he's going?
CONTARINO. Peace,
    Let's attend the sequel.
CRISPIANO. I commend you lady,
    There was a main matter of conscience;
    How many ills spring from adultery !
    First, the supreme law that is violated,
    Nobility oft stain'd with bastardy,
    Inheritance of land falsely possess'd,
    The husband scorn'd, wife sham'd, and babes unbless'd.

[*The picture is brought in.*]

    So, hang it up i'th' court. You have heard
    What has been urged 'gainst Romelio.
    Now my definitive sentence in this cause,
    Is, I will give no sentence at all.
ARIOSTO. No?
CRISPIANO. No, I cannot, for I am made a party.
SANITONELLA. How, a party? Here are fine cross tricks,
    What the devil will he do now?
CRISPIANO. Signior Ariosto, his Majesty of Spain
    Confers my place upon you by this patent,
    Which till this urgent hour I have kept
    From your knowledge: may you thrive in't, noble sir,
    And do that which but few in our place do;
    Go to their grave uncurs'd!
ARIOSTO. This law business
    Will leave me so small leisure to serve God,
    I shall serve the King the worse.
SANITONELLA. Is he a judge?
    We must then look for all conscience, and no law;
    He'll beggar all his followers.
CRISPIANO. Sir,
    I am of your counsel, for the cause in hand
    Was begun at such a time, 'fore you could speak;
    You had need therefore have one speak for you.
ARIOSTO. Stay, I do here first make protestation,
    I ne'er took fee of this Romelio,
    For being of his counsel; which may free me,
    Being now his judge, for the imputation
    Of taking a bribe. Now sir, speak your mind.
CRISPIANO. I do first entreat, that the eyes of all

Here present, may be fixed upon this.

LEONORA. O I am confounded: this is Crispiano.

JULIO. This is my father; how the judges have blear'd him!

WINIFRID. You may see truth will out in spite of the devil.

CRISPIANO. Behold, I am the shadow of this shadow,
    Age has made me so; take from me forty years,
    And I was such a summer fruit as this,
    At least the painter feigned so: for indeed,
    Paintings and epitaphs are both alike,
    They flatter us, and say we have been thus.
    But I am the party here, that stands accus'd
    For adultery with this woman, in the year
    Seventy-one. Now I call you my lord to witness,
    Four years before that time I went to'th' Indies,
    And till this month, did never set my foot since
    In Europe; and for any former incontinence,
    She has vow'd there was never any. What remains then,
    But this is a mere practice 'gainst her son?
    And I beseech the court it may be sifted,
    And most severely punish'd.

SANITONELLA. 'Uds foot, we are spoiled;
    Why my client's proved an honest woman.

WINIFRID. What do you think will become of me now?

SANITONELLA. You'll be made dance *lachrymæ*,[163] I fear at a cart's tail.

ARIOSTO. You mistress, where are you now?
    Your tennis-court slippers,[164] and your tane drink
    In a morning for your hot liver; where's the man
    Would have had some dealing with you, that you might
    Keep counsel the better?

WINIFRID. May it please the court, I am but a young thing, and was
    drawn arsy varsy into the business.

ARIOSTO. How young? Of five and forty?

WINIFRID. Five and forty! And shall please you, I am not five and
    twenty: she made me colour my hair with bean flour, to seem elder
    than I was; and then my rotten teeth, with eating sweet-meats;—
    why, should a farrier look in my mouth, he might mistake my age.
    O mistress, mistress, you are an honest woman, and you may be
    ashamed on't, to abuse the court thus.

---

[163] One of the allusions, so frequent in our old dramatists, to a musical work by John Dowland, the famous lutanist, "the rarest musician" according to A. Wood, (*Fasti Oxon.* Part I. p.242. ed. Bliss,) "that his age did behold:" it is dedicated to Anne, the Queen of James I. and entitled *Lacrims, or seaven Teares jigured in leaven passionate Paiumt, with divers other* Puuans, *Galiards, and* Almands, *set forth for the Lute, Viols, or Violons, infiue* ports.

[164] The old copy "slips."

LEONORA. Whatso'er I have attempted,
 'Gainst my own fame, or the reputation
 Of that gentleman my son, the Lord Contarino
 Was cause of it.

CONTARINO. Who, I?

ARIOSTO. He that should have married your daughter?
 It was a plot belike then to confer
 The land on her that should have been his wife?

LEONORA. More than I have said already, all the world
 Shall ne'er extract from me; I entreat from both
 Your equal pardons.

JULIO. And I from you sir.

CRISPIANO. Sirrah, stand you aside,
 I will talk with you hereafter.

JULIO. I could never away with[165] after reckonings.

LEONORA. And now my lords, I do most voluntarily
 Confine myself unto a stricter prison,
 And a severer penance, than this court
 Can impose; I am ent'red into religion.

CONTARINO. I the cause of this practice! This ungodly woman
 Has sold herself to falsehood. I will now
 Reveal myself.

ERCOLE. Stay my lord, here's a window
 To let in more light to the court.

CONTARINO. Mercy upon me! O that thou art living
 Is mercy indeed!

FIRST SURGEON. Stay, keep in your shell
 A little longer.

ERCOLE. I am Ercole.

ARIOSTO. A guard upon him for the death of Contarino!

ERCOLE. I obey the arrest o'th' court.

ROMELIO. O sir, you are happily restor'd to life,
 And to us your friends!

ERCOLE. Away, thou art the traitor
 I only live to challenge; this former suit
 Touch'd but thy fame; this accusation
 Reaches to thy fame and life: the brave Contarino
 Is generally suppos'd slain by this hand—

CONTARINO. How knows he the contrary?

ERCOLE. But truth is,
 Having receiv'd from me some certain wounds,
 Which were not mortal, this vile murderer,
 Being by will deputed overseer

---

[165] i.e. endure.

Of the nobleman's estate, to his sister's use,
That he might make him sure from[166] surviving,
To revoke the will, stole to him in's bed,
And kill'd him.

ROMELIO. Strange, unheard of! More practice yet!

ARIOSTO. What proof of this?

ERCOLE. The report of his mother deliver'd to me,
    In distraction for Contarino's death.

CONTARINO. For my death? I begin to apprehend,
    That the violence of this woman's love to me
    Might practise the disinheriting of her son.

ARIOSTO. What say you to this, Leonora?

LEONORA. Such a thing I did utter out of my distraction:
    But how the court will censure that report,
    I leave to their wisdoms.

ARIOSTO. My opinion is,
    That this late slander urg'd against her son,
    Takes from her all manner of credit:
    She that would not stick to deprive him of his living,
    Will as little tender his life.

LEONORA. I beseech the court,
    I may retire myself to my place of penance,
    I have vowed myself and my woman.

ARIOSTO. Go when you please. What should move you be

[*Exeunt* LEONORA, *and* WINIFRID.]

Thus forward in the accusation?

ERCOLE. My love to Contarino.

ARIOSTO. O, it bore very bitter fruit at your last meeting.

ERCOLE. 'Tis true: but I begun to love him
    When I had most cause to hate him; when our bloods
    Embrac'd each other, then I pitied
    That so much valour should be hazarded
    On the fortune of a single rapier,
    And not spent against the Turk.

ARIOSTO. Stay sir,
    Be well advis'd, there is no testimony
    But your own, to approve you slew him,
    Therefore no other way to decide it,
    But by duel.

CONTARINO. Yes my lord, I dare affirm
    'Gainst all the world, this nobleman speaks truth.

---

[166] In some of the old copies this word is omitted.

ARIOSTO. You will make yourself a party in the duel.

ROMELIO. Let him, I will fight with them both, sixteen of them.

ERCOLE. Sir, I do not know you.

CONTARINO. Yes, but you have forgot me,
    You and I have sweat in the breach together at Malta.

ERCOLE. Cry you mercy, I have known
    Of your nation brave soldiers.

JULIO. Now if my father
    Have any true spirit in him, I'll recover
    His good opinion. Do you hear? Do not swear sir,
    For I dare swear, that you will swear a lie,
    A very filthy, stinking, rotten lie:
    And if the lawyers think not this sufficient,
    I'll give the lie in the stomach,
    That's somewhat deeper than the throat:
    Both here, and all France over and over,
    From Marseilles, or Bayonne, to Calais sands,
    And there draw my sword upon thee,
    And new scour it in the gravel of thy kidneys.

ARIOSTO. You the defendant charg'd with the murder,
    And you second there, must be committed
    To the custody of the Knight-Marshal;
    And the court gives charge, they be tomorrow
    Ready in the lists before the sun be risen.

ROMELIO. I do entreat the court, there be a guard
    Placed o'er my sister, that she enter not
    Into religion: she's rich, my lords,
    And the persuasions of friars, to gain
    All her possessions to their monasteries,
    May do much upon her.

ARIOSTO. We'll take order for her.

CRISPIANO. There's a nun too you have got with child,
    How will you dispose of her?

ROMELIO. You question me, as if l were grav'd already,
    When I have quench'd this wild-fire in Ercole's
    Tame blood, I'll tell you. [*Exit.*]

ERCOLE. You have judg'd today
    A most confused practice, that takes end
    In as bloody a trial; and we may observe
    By these great persons, and their indirect
    Proceedings, shadow'd in a veil of state,
    Mountains are deform'd heaps, swell'd up aloft;
    Vales wholesomer, though lower, and trod on oft.

SANITONELLA. Well, I will put up my papers,
    And send them to France for a precedent,

That they may not say yet, but, for one strange law-suit,
We come somewhat near them.

[*Exeunt.*]

ACT V.

SCENE I.

[*Enter* JOLENTA, *and* ANGIOLELLA *great-bellied.*]

JOLENTA. How dost thou friend? Welcome, thou and I
　　Were playfellows together, little children,
　　So small a while ago, that I presume
　　We are neither of us wise yet.
ANGIOLELLA. A most sad truth on my part.
JOLENTA. Why do you pluck your veil
　　Over your face?
ANGIOLELLA. If you will believe truth,
　　There's nought more terrible to a guilty heart
　　Than the eye of a respected friend.
JOLENTA. Say friend, are you quick with child?
ANGIOLELLA. Too sure.
JOLENTA. How could you know
　　Of your first when you quickened?
ANGIOLELLA. How could you know friend?
　　'Tis reponed you are in the same taking.
JOLENTA. Ha, ha, ha, so 'tis given out:
　　But Ercole's coming to life again has shrunk,
　　And made invisible my great belly; yes faith,
　　My being with child was merely in supposition,
　　Not practice.
ANGIOLELLA. You are happy; what would I give,
　　To be a maid again!
JOLENTA. Would you? To what purpose?
　　I would never give great purchase for that thing
　　Is in danger every hour to be lost:
　　Pray thee laugh. A boy or a girl for a wager?
ANGIOLELLA. What heaven please.
JOLENTA. Nay, nay, will you venture
　　A chain of pearl with me whether?
ANGIOLELLA. I'll lay nothing,
　　I have ventur'd too much for't already; my fame.
　　I make no question sister, you have heard
　　Of the intended combat.

JOLENTA. O what else?

    I have a sweetheart in't, against a brother.

ANGIOLELLA. And I a dead friend, I fear; what good counsel

    Can you minister unto me?

JOLENTA. Faith only this

    Since there's no means i'th' world to hinder it,

    Let thou and I, wench, get as far as we can

    From the noise of it.

ANGIOLELLA. Whither?

JOLENTA. No matter, any whither.

ANGIOLELLA. Any whither, so you go not by sea:

    I cannot abide salt[167] water.

JOLENTA. Not endure to be tumbled? Say no more then,

    We'll be land-soldiers for that trick: take heart,

    Thy boy shall be born a brave Roman.

ANGIOLELLA. O you mean

    To go to Rome then.

JOLENTA. Within there. Bear this letter

    [*Enter a* SERVANT.]

    To the Lord Ercole. Now wench, I am for thee

    All the world over.

ANGIOLELLA. I like your shade pursue you.

    [*Exeunt.*]

SCENE II.

    [*Enter* PROSPERO *and* SANITONELLA.]

PROSPERO. Well, I do not think but to see you as pretty a piece of law-flesh.

SANITONELLA. In time I may; marry I am resolv'd to take a new way for't. You have lawyers take their clients' fees, and their backs are no sooner turn'd, but they call them fools, and laugh at them.

PROSPERO. That's ill done of them.

SANITONELLA. There's one thing too that has a vile abuse in't.

PROSPERO. What's that?

SANITONELLA. Marry this; that no proctor in the term time be tolerated to go to the tavern above six times i'th' forenoon.

PROSPERO. Why, man?

SANITONELLA. O sir, it makes their clients overtaken, and become

---

[167] Some of the old copies "rough."

friends sooner than they would be.

[*Enter* ERCOLE *with a letter, and* CONTARINO, *coming in Friars'
    habits, as having been at the Bathanites, a ceremony used
    afore these combats.*]

ERCOLE. Leave the room, gentlemen.

[*Exeunt* PROSPERO *and* SANITONELLA.]

CONTARINO. Wherefore should I with such an obstinacy,
    [*aside.*] Conceal myself any longer? I am taught
    That all the blood which will be shed tomorrow,
    Must fall upon my head: one question
    Shall fix or untie it.—Noble brother,
    I would fain know how it is possible,
    When it appears you love the fair Jolenta
    With such a height of fervour, you were ready
    To father another's child, and marry her,
    You would so suddenly engage yourself
    To kill her brother, one that ever stood,
    Your loyal and firm friend?
ERCOLE. Sir, I'll tell you:
    My love, as I have formerly protested,
    To Contarino, whose unfortunate end
    The traitor wrought: and here is one thing more,
    Dead's all good thoughts of him, which I now receiv'd
    From Jolenta.
CONTARINO. In a letter?
ERCOLE. Yes, in this letter:
    For having sent to her to be resolv'd
    Most truly, who was father of the child,
    She writes back, that the shame she goes withal,
    Was begot by her brother.
CONTARINO. O most incestuous villain!
ERCOLE. I protest,
    Before I thought 'twas Contarino's issue,
    And for that would have veil'd her dishonour.
CONTARINO. No more. Has the armourer brought the weapons?
ERCOLE. Yes sir.
CONTARINO. I will no more think of her.
ERCOLE. Of whom?
CONTARINO. Of my mother; I was thinking
    Of my mother. Call the armourer.

[*Exeunt.*]

SCENE III.

[*Enter* SURGEON *and* WINIFRID.]

WINIFRID. You do love me sir, you say?

FIRST SURGEON. O most entirely.

WINIFRID. And you will marry me?

FIRST SURGEON. Nay, I'll do more than that.
 The fashion of the world is many times
 To make a woman naught, and afterwards
 To marry her: but I a'th' contrary,
 Will make you honest first, and afterwards
 Proceed to the wedlock.

WINIFRID. Honest! What mean you by that?

FIRST SURGEON. I mean, that your suborning the late law-suit
 Has got you a filthy report. Now there's no way
 But to do some excellent piece of honesty,
 To recover your good name.

WINIFRID. How sir?

FIRST SURGEON. You shall straight go, and reveal to your old mistress
 For certain truth, Contarino is alive.

WINIFRID. How, living?

FIRST SURGEON. Yes, he is living.

WINIFRID. No, I must not tell her of it.

FIRST SURGEON. No? Why?

WINIFRID. For she did bind me yesterday by oath,
 Never more to speak of him .

FIRST SURGEON. You shall reveal it then
 To Ariosto the judge.

WINIFRID. By no means, he has heard me
 Tell so many lies i'th' court, he'll ne'er believe me.
 What if I told it to the Capuchin?

FIRST SURGEON. You cannot
 Think of a better; as for[168] your young mistress,
 Who as you told me, has persuaded you
 To run away with her: let her have her humour.
 I have a suit Romelio left i'th' house,
 The habit of a Jew, that I'll put on,
 And pretending I am robbed, by break of day
 Procure all passengers to be brought back,
 And by the way reveal myself, and discover

---

[168] The old copy "for us."

The comical event. They say she's a little mad;
This will help to cure her. Go, go presently,
And reveal it to the Capuchin.
WINIFRID. Sir, I shall.

[*Exeunt.*]

SCENE IV.

[*Enter* JULIO, PROSPERO, *and* SANITONELLA.]

JULIO. A pox on't,
I have undertaken the challenge very foolishly:
What if I do not appear to answer it?
PROSPERO. It would be absolute conviction
Of cowardice, and perjury; and the Dane
May to your public shame, reverse your arms,
Or have them ignominiously fastened
Under his horse tail.
JULIO. I do not like that so well.
I see then I must fight whether I will or no.
PROSPERO. How does Romelio bear himself? They say
He has almost brain'd one of our cunning'st fencers,
That practis'd with him.
JULIO. Very certain: and now you talk of fencing,
Do you not remember the Welsh gentleman,
That was travelling to Rome upon return?
PROSPERO. No, what of him?
JULIO. There was a strange experiment of a fencer.
PROSPERO. What was that?
JULIO. The Welshman in's play, do what the fencer could,
Hung still an arse; he could not for's life
Make him come on bravely: till one night at supper,
Observing what a deal of Parma cheese
His scholar devoured, goes ingeniously
The next morning, and makes a spacious button
For his foil, of toasted cheese, and as sure as you live,
That made him come on the braveliest.
PROSPERO. Possible!
JULIO. Marry it taught him an ill grace in's play,
It made him gape still, gape as he put in for't,
As I have seen some hungry usher.
SANITONELLA. The toasting of it belike,
Was to make it more supple, had he chanc'd
To have hit him a'th' chaps.

JULIO. Not unlikely.
    Who can tell me if we may breathe in the duel?
PROSPERO. By no means.
JULIO. Nor drink?
PROSPERO. Neither.
JULIO. That's scurvy, anger will make me very dry.
PROSPERO. You mistake sir, 'tis sorrow that is very dry.
SANITONELLA. Not always sir, I have known sorrow very wet.
JULIO. In rainy weather?
SANITONELLA. No, when a woman has come dropping wet.
    Out of a cuckingstool.
JULIO. Then 'twas wet indeed sir.

[*Enter* ROMELIO, *very melancholy, and the* CAPUCHIN.]

CAPUCHIN. Having from Leonora's waiting-woman
    Deliver'd a most strange intelligence
    Of Contarino's recovery, I am come
    To sound Romelio's penitence; that perform'd;
    To end these errors by discovering
    What she related to me. Peace to you sir. [*to* ROMELIO.]
    Pray gentlemen, let the freedom of this room
    Be mine a little. Nay sir, you may stay. [*to* JULIO.]

[*Exeunt* PROSPERO *and* SANITONELLA.]

    Will you pray with me?
ROMELIO. No, no, the world and I
    Have not made up our accounts yet.
CAPUCHIN. Shall I pray for you?
ROMELIO: Whether you do or no, I care not.
CAPUCHIN. O you have a dangerous voyage to take.
ROMELIO. No matter, I will be mine own pilot:
    Do not you trouble your head with the business.
CAPUCHIN. Pray tell me, do not you meditate of death?
ROMELIO. Phew, I took out that lesson
    When I once lay sick of an ague: I do now
    Labour for life, for life! Sir, can you tell me
    Whether your Toledo, or your Milan blade
    Be best temper'd?
CAPUCHIN. These things you know,
    Are out of my practice.
ROMELIO. But these are things you know,
    I must practise with tomorrow.
CAPUCHIN. Were I in your case,

    I should present to myself strange shadows.
ROMELIO. Turn you, were I in your case, I should laugh
    At mine own shadow. Who has hired you
    To make me coward?
CAPUCHIN. I would make you
    A good Christian.
ROMELIO. Withal, let me continue
    An honest man, which I am very certain,
    A coward can never be: you take upon you
    A physician's place, rather than a divine's.
    You go about to bring my body so low,
    I should fight i'th' lists tomorrow like a dormouse,
    And be made away in a slumber.
CAPUCHIN. Did you murder Contarino?
ROMELIO. That's a scurvy question now.
CAPUCHIN. Why sir?
ROMELIO. Did you ask it as a confessor, or as a spy?
CAPUCHIN. As one that fain would jostle the devil
    Out of your way.
ROMELIO. Um, you are but weakly made for't:
    He's a cunning wrestler, I can tell you, and has broke
    Many a man's neck.
CAPUCHIN. But to give him the foil
    Goes not by strength.
ROMELIO. Let it go by what it will,
    Get me some good victuals to breakfast,
    I am hungry.
CAPUCHIN. Here's food for you.

    [*Offering him a book.*]

ROMELIO. Pew, I am not to commence Doctor:
    For then the word, devour that book, were proper.
    I am to fight, to fight sir, and I'll do't,
    As I would feed, with a good stomach.
CAPUCHIN. Can you feed,
    And apprehend death?
ROMELIO. Why sir? Is not Death
    A hungry companion? Say? Is not the grave
    Said to be a great devourer? Get me some victuals.
    I knew a man that was to lose his head,
    Feed with an excellent good appetite,
    To strengthen his heart, scarce half an hour before.
    And if he did it, that only was to speak,
    What should I, that am to do?

CAPUCHIN. This confidence,
   If it be grounded upon truth, 'tis well.
ROMELIO. You must understand, that resolution
   Should ever wait upon a noble death,
   As captains bring their soldiers out o'th' field,
   And come off last: for, I pray, what is death?
   The safest trench i'th' world to keep man free
   From fortune's gunshot; to be afraid of that
   Would prove me weaker than a teeming woman,
   That does endure a thousand times more pain
   In bearing of a child.
CAPUCHIN. O, I tremble for you:
   For I do know you have a storm within you,
   More terrible than a sea fight, and your soul
   Being heretofore drown'd in security,
   You know not how to live, nor how to die:
   But I have an object that shall startle you,
   And make you know whither you are going.
ROMELIO. I am arm'd for't.

[*Enter* LEONORA *with two coffins borne by her servants, and two
   winding sheets stuck with flowers; presents one to her son, and
   the other to* JULIO.]

'Tis very welcome, this is a decent garment
Will never be out of fashion. I will kiss it.
All the flowers of the spring
Meet to perfume our burying:
These have but their growing prime,
And man does flourish but his time.
Survey our progress from our birth,
We are set, we grow, we turn to earth.
Courts adieu, and all delights, [*Soft music.*
All bewitching appetites;
Sweetest breath, and clearest eye,
Like perfumes go out and die;
And consequently this is done,
As shadows wait upon the sun.
Vain the ambition of kings,
Who seek by trophies and dead things,
To leave a living name behind,
And weave but nets to catch the wind.
O you have wrought a miracle, and melted
A heart of adamant: you have compris'd
In this dumb pageant, a right excellent form

Of penitence.
CAPUCHIN. I am glad you so receive it.
ROMELIO. This object does persuade me to forgive
    The wrong she has done me, which I count the way
    To be forgiven yonder: and this shroud
    Shows me how rankly we do smell of earth
    When we are in all our glory. Will it please you [*to* LEONORA.]
    Enter that closet, where I shall confer
    'Bout matters of most weighty consequence,
    Before the duel?

        [*Exit* LEONORA.]

JULIO. Now I am right in the bandoleer
    For th' gallows. What a scurvy fashion 'tis,
    To hang one's coffin in a scarf!
CAPUCHIN. Why this is well:
    And now that I have made you fit for death,
    And brought you even as low as is the grave,
    I will raise you up again, speak comforts to you
    Beyond your hopes, turn this intended duel
    To a triumph.
ROMELIO. More divinity yet?
    Good sir, do one thing first, there's in my closet
    A prayer book that is cover'd with gilt vellum;
    Fetch it, and pray you certify my mother,
    I'll presently come to her.

        [ROMELIO *locks the* CAPUCHIN *into the closet.*]

So now you are safe.
JULIO. What have you done?
ROMELIO. Why I have lock'd them up
    Into a turret of the castle, safe enough
    For troubling us this four hours; and he please,
    He may open a casement, and whistle out to'th' sea,
    Like a bosun, not any creature can hear him.
    Wast not thou a-weary of his preaching?
JULIO. Yes, if he had had an hour-glass by him,
    I would have wish'd he would have jogg'd it a little.
    But your mother, your mother's lock'd in too.
ROMELIO. So much the better,
    I am rid of her howling at parting.
JULIO. Hark, he knocks to be let out and he were mad.
ROMELIO. Let him knock till his sandals fly in pieces.

JULIO. Ha, what says he? Contarino living?

ROMELIO. Aye, aye,
 He means he would have Contarino's living
 Bestow'd upon his monastery, 'tis that
 He only fishes for. So, 'tis break of day,
 We shall be call'd to the combat presently.

JULIO. I am sorry for one thing.

ROMELIO. What's that?

JULIO. That I made not mine own ballad: I do fear
 I shall be roguishly abused in metre,
 If I miscarry. Well, if the young Capuchin
 Does not talk a'th' flesh as fast now to your mother,
 As he did to us a'th' spirit! If he do,
 'Tis not the first time that the prison royal
 Has been guilty of close committing.

ROMELIO. Now to'th' combat.

 [*Exeunt.*]

SCENE V.

[*Enter* CAPUCHIN *and* LEONORA *above at a window.*]

LEONORA. Contarino living?

CAPUCHIN. Yes madam, he is living and Ercole's second.

LEONORA. Why has he lock'd us up thus?

CAPUCHIN. Some evil angel
 Makes him deaf to his own safety; we are shut
 Into a turret, the most desolate prison
 Of all the castle, and his obstinacy,
 Madness, or secret fate, has thus prevented
 The saving of his life.

LEONORA. O the saving Contarino's,
 His is worth nothing: for heaven's sake call louder.

CAPUCHIN. To little purpose.

LEONORA. I will leap these battlements,
 And may I be found dead time enough,
 To hinder the combat!

CAPUCHIN. O look upwards rather,
 Their deliverance must come thence: to see how heaven
 Can invert man's firmest purpose! His intent
 Of murdering Contarino, was a mean
 To work his safety, and my coming hither
 To save him, is his ruin: wretches turn
 The tide of their good fortune, and being drench'd

In some presumptuous and hidden sins,
    While they aspire to do themselves most right,
    The devil that rules i'th' air, hangs in their light.
LEONORA. O they must not be lost thus: some good Christian
    Come within our hearing! Ope the other casettlent
    That looks into the city.
CAPUCHIN. Madam, I shall.

[*Exeunt.*]

SCENE VI.

[*The lists set up. Enter the* MARSHAL, CRISPIANO, *and* ARIOSTO *as*
    JUDGES, *they sit.*]

MARSHAL. Give the appellant his summons, do the like to the
    defendant.

[*Two tuckets sounded by several trumpets. Enter at one door,*
    ERCOLE *and* CONTARINO, *at the other,* ROMELIO *and* JULIO.]

Can any of you allege aught, why the combat
    Should not proceed?
COMBATANTS. Nothing.
ARIOSTO. Have the knights weigh'd
    And measur'd their weapons?
MARSHAL. They have.
ARIOSTO. Proceed then to the battle,
    And may heaven determine the right.
HERALD: *Soit la bataille, et victoire à ceux qui ont droit.*
ROMELIO. Stay, I do not well know whither I am going:
    'Twere needful therefore, though at the last gasp,
    To have some churchman's prayer. Run I pray thee,
    To Castle Novo; this key will release
    A Capuchin and my mother, whom I shut
    Into a turret; bid them make haste, and pray,
    I may be dead ere he comes. Now, *victoire à ceux qui ont droit!*
ALL THE CHAMP. *Victoire à ceux qui ont droit!*

[*The combat continued to a good length, when enters* LEONORA,
    and the CAPUCHIN.]

LEONORA. Hold, hold, for heaven's sake hold!
ARIOSTO. What are these that interrupt the combat?
    Away to prison with them.

CAPUCHIN. We have been prisoners too long:
    O sir, what mean you? Contarino's living.
ERCOLE. Living!
CAPUCHIN. Behold him living.
ERCOLE. You were but now my second, now I make you
    Myself for ever.
LEONORA. O here's one between,
    Claims to be nearer.
CONTARINO. And to you, dear lady,
    I have entirely vowed my life.
ROMELIO. If I do not
    Dream, I am happy too.
ARIOSTO. How insolently
    Has this high court of honour been abus'd!

[*Enter* ANGIOLELLA, *veil'd, and* JOLENTA, *her face colour'd like a
    Moor, the two* SURGEONS, *one of them like a Jew.*]

How now, who are these?
SECOND SURGEON. A couple of strange fowl, and I the falconer,
    That have sprung them. This is a white nun,
    Of the Order of Saint Clare; and this a black one,
    You'll take my word for't.

[*Discovers* JOLENTA.]

ARIOSTO. She's a black one indeed.
JOLENTA. Like or dislike me, choose you whether;
    The down upon the raven's feather
    Is as gentle and as sleek,
    As the mole on Venus' cheek.
    Hence vain show! I only care,
    To preserve my soul most fair.
    Never mind the outward skin,
    But the jewel that's within:
    And though I want the crimson blood,
    Angels boast my sisterhood.
    Which of us now judge you whiter,
    Her whose credit proves the lighter,
    Or this black, and ebon hue,
    That unstain'd, keeps fresh and true?
    For I proclaim't without control,
    There's no true beauty, but i'th' soul.
ERCOLE. O 'tis the fair Jolenta; to what purpose
    Are you thus eclips'd?

JOLENTA. Sir, I was running away
  From the rumour of this combat: I fled likewise,
  From the untrue report my brother spread
  To his politic ends, that I was got with child.
LEONORA. Cease here all further scrutiny, this paper
  Shall give unto the court each circumstance,
  Of all these passages.
ARIOSTO. No more: attend the sentence of the court.
  Rareness and difficulty give estimation
  To all things are i'th' world: you have met both
  In these several passages: now it does remain,
  That these so comical events be blasted
  With no severity of sentence. You Romelio,
  Shall first deliver to that gentleman,
  Who stood your second, all those obligations
  Wherein he stands engag'd to you, receiving
  Only the principal.
ROMELIO. I shall my lord.
JULIO. I thank you,
  I have an humour now to go to sea
  Against the pirates; and my only ambition
  Is to have my ship furnish'd with a rare consort[169]
  Of music; and when I am pleased to be mad,
  They shall play me Orlando.
SANITONELLA. You must lay in wait for the fiddlers,
  They'll flyaway from the press like watermen.
ARIOSTO. Next, you shall marry that nun.
ROMELIO. Most willingly.
ANGIOLELLA. O sir, you have been unkind,
  But I do only wish, that this my shame
  May warn all honest virgins, not to seek
  The way to heaven, that is so wondrous steep,
  Thorough those vows they are too frail to keep.
ARIOSTO. Contarino, and Romelio, and yourself:
  Shall for seven years maintain against the Turk
  Six galleys. Leonora, Jolenta,
  And Angiolella there, the beauteous nun,
  For their vows' breach unto the monastery,
  Shall build a monastery. Lastly, the two surgeons,
  For concealing Contarino's recovery,
  Shall exercise their art at their own charge,
  For a twelvemonth in the galleys: so we leave you,
  Wishing your future life may make good use

---

[169] See note on *Northward Ho*, act ii., scene 1.

Of these events, since that these passages,
Which threat'ned ruin, built on rotten ground,
Are with Success beyond our wishes crown'd.

[*Exeunt omnes.*]

A CURE FOR A CUCKOLD

By JOHN WEBSTER and WILLIAM ROWLEY

A CURE FOR A CUCKOLD.

This play, although not printed till 1661, when, as narrated in the General Introduction to these volumes, Mr. Kirkman published it, must have been acted many years before that time, and before 1649. The story, as summarized by Mr. Genest, runs thus:—" Lessingham is in love with Clare; she sends him a letter, in which she says,

'Prove all thy friends, find out the best and nearest,
Kill for my sake that friend that loves thee dearest.'

Lessingham debates the matter in a soliloquy; he tells four of his friends that he has a duel on his hands, and that he wants a second, who is himself to fight: they decline his proposal, under various pretences. Bonvile agrees to accompany him to the appointed place, notwithstanding that it is his wedding-day. When they arrive at Calais Sands, Lessingham tells Bonvile that he is come thither on purpose to kill him. Bonvile refuses to fight him, and adds, that he may boast to Clare that he has killed his friend, as all friendship between them is dead.

"In Massinger's *Parliament of Love*, Leonora says to Cleremond:—

'I have heard thee boast,
That of all blessings in the earth next me,
The number of thy trusty, faithful friends
Made up thy happiness: out of these, I charge thee,
To kill the best deserver.'

"Cleremond has a soliloquy; all his friends refuse to take a part in the duel, except Montrose. When they come to the spot, they fight, and Cleremond is worsted.

"It seems more prohable (observes Mr. Genest) that Webster and Massinger should both have borrowed from the same story, than that either of them should have been guilty of flagrant plagiarism. As they were contemporaries, and as neither of the plays was printed till after the author's death, it is impossible to determine which was the first written.

"In the *Cure for a Cuckold*, Compass returns from sea, after an absence of four years; he finds that his wife (who had supposed him dead) has a child about a quarter of a year old. Instead of being angry, he claims the child: the real father refuses to resign him. A friend recommends Compass to make a divorce between himself and his wife:—'Within two hours you may wed again, and then the cuckold's blotted.' This gives the title to the play. Compass calls his second marriage 'the shedding of horns.' Lessingham marries Clare, and requests Bonvile's forgiveness.

"In 1696, at the Lincoln's Inn Fields Theatre, Harris brought out a Comedy, entitled, *The City Bride, or the Merry Cuckold*, which is a mere alteration of Webster's play. The names in this alteration are *Bonvile, Friendly, Compass, Justice Merryman* (father to *Arabella)*, *Summerfield, Venter, Spruce, Arabella* (the Bride), *Clara, Compass' wife, Nurse, Mrs. Venter*. The alterations, in other respects, are not material, but they are all for the worse. In particular, the writer has omitted Compass in the last scene, and consequently the best joke in the play."—*Account of the English Stage*, ii. 91.

The copy of this play in the British Museum, from which the present edition has been prepared, is throughout corrected in pencil by some critic, who has applied himself to restore that blank verse which the author manifestly contemplated, but which the printers, whether from ignorance, carelessness, or the desire to economize space, have converted into prose. These emendations have been, for the most part, adopted.

THE STATIONER TO THE JUDICIOUS READER.

Gentlemen,

It was not long since I was only a book-reader, and not a bookseller, which quality (my former employment somewhat failing, and I being unwilling to be idle,) I have now lately taken on me. It hath been my fancy and delight, ever since I knew anything, to converse with books; and the pleasure I have taken in those of this nature, viz. Plays, hath been so extraordinary, that it hath been much to my cost, for I have been, as we term it, a gatherer of plays for some years, and I am confident I have move of several sorts than any man in England, bookseller or other: I can at any time show seven hundred in number, which is within a small matter all that were ever printed. Many of these I have several times over, and intend, as I sell, to purchase more; all, or any of which, I shall be ready either to sell or lend to you upon reasonable considerations.

In order to the encreasing of my store, I have now this term printed and published three, viz. this called *A Cure for a Cuckold*, and another called *The Thracian Wonder*, and the third called *Gammer Gurfon's Needle*. Two of these three were never printed, the third, viz. *Gammer Gurion's Needle*, hath been formerly printed, but it is almost an hundred years since. As for this play, I need not speak anything in its commendation, the authors' names, Webster and Rowley, are (to knowing men) sufficient to declare its worth: several persons remember the acting of it, and say that it then pleased generally well; and let me tell you in my judgment" it is an excellent old play. The expedient of curing a cuckold, after the manner set down in this play, hath been Aried to my knowledge, and therefore I may say *probatum est.* I should, I doubt, be too tedious, or else I would say somewhat in defence of this, and in commendation of plays in general, but I question not but you have read what abler pens than mine have writ in their vindication. Gentlemen, I hope you will so encourage me in my beginnings, that I may be induced to proceed to do you service, and that I may frequently have occasion in this nature, to subscribe myself

Your servant,

Francis Kirkman.

DRAMATIS PERSONAE

WOODROFF, *a Justice of the Peace, Father to Annabel.*
FRANCKFORD, *a Merchant, Brother-in-law to Woodroff.*
LESSINGHAM, *a Gentleman, in love with Clare.*
BONVILE, *a Gentleman, the Bridegroom and Husband to Annabel.*
RAYMOND, *Gallant invited to the wedding.*
EUSTACE, *Gallant invited to the wedding.*
LIONEL, *Gallant invited to the wedding.*
GROVER, *Gallant invited to the wedding.*
ROCHFIELD, *a young Gentleman and a thief.*
COMPASS, *a Seaman.*
PETTIFOG, *an attorney*
DODGE, *an attorney.*
A Counsellor, Two Clients, Two Boys, and A Sailor.
LUCE, *Wife to Franckford, and Sister to Woodroff.*
ANNABEL, *the Bride and Wife to Bonvile.*
CLARE, *Lessingham's Mistress.*
URSE, *Wife to Compass.*
Nurse and a Waitingwoman.

A CURE FOR A CUCKOLD

ACT I.

SCENE I.

[*Enter* LESSINGHAM *and* CLARE.]

LESSINGHAM. This is a place of feasting and of joy,
    And, as in triumphs and ovations, here
    Nothing save state and pleasure.
CLARE. Tis confest.
LESSINGHAM. A day of mirth and solemn jubilee—
CLARE. For such as can be merry.
LESSINGHAM. A happy nuptial,
    Since a like pair of fortunes suitable,
    Equality in birth, parity in years,
    And in affection no way different,
    Are this day sweetly coupled.
CLARE. 'Tis a marriage—
LESSINGHAM. True, lady, and a noble precedent
    Methinks for us to follow. Why should these
    Outstrip us in our loves, that have not yet
    Outgone us in our time? if we thus lose
    Our best and not to be recover'd hours
    Unprofitably spent, we sball be held
    Mere truants in love's school.
CLARE. That's a study
    In which I never shall ambition have
    To become graduate.
LESSINGHAM. Lady, you are sad:
    This jovial meeting puts me in a spirit
    To be made such. We two are guests invited,
    And meet by purpose, not by accident.
    Where's, then, a place more opportunely fit,
    In which we may solicit our own loves,
    Than before this example?
CLARE. In a word,
    I purpose not to marry.
LESSINGHAM. By your favour,—
    For as I ever to this present hour
    Have studied your observance, so from henceforth
    I now will study plainness,—I have lov'd you
    Beyond myself, misspended for your sake

Many a fair hour which might have been employ'd
To pleasure or to profit; have neglected
Duty to them from whom my being came,
My parents, but my hopeful studies most.
I have stolen time from all my choice delights
And robb'd myself, thinking to enrich you.
Matches I have had offer'd, some have told me
As fair, as rich—I never thought 'em so;
And lost all these in hope to find out you.
Resolve me, then, for Christian charity;
Think you an answer of that frozen nature
Is a sufficient satisfaction for
So many more than needful services?

CLARE. I have said, sir.

LESSINGHAM. Whence might this distaste arise?
Be at least so kind to perfect nie in that.
Is it of some dislike lately conceiv'd
Of this my person, which perhaps may grow
From calumny and scandal? if not that,
Some late received melancholy in you?
If neither, your perverse and peevish will—
To which I most imply it.

CLARE. Be it what it can, or may be, thus it is;
And with this answer pray rest satisfied
In all these travels, windings, and indents,
Paths, and by-paths, which many have sought out,
There's but one only road, and that alone,
To my fruition; which whoso finds out,
'Tis like he may enjoy me, but that failing,
I ever am mine own.

LESSINGHAM. O, name it, sweet!
I am already in a labyrinth,
Until you guide me out.

CLARE. I'll to my chamber.
May you be pleas'd unto your mis-spent time
To add but some few minutes; by my maid
You shall hear further from me. [*Exit.*]

LESSINGHAM. I'll attend you.
What more can I desire than be resolv'd
Of such a long suspense? Here's now the period
Of much expectation.

[*Enter* RAYMOND, EUSTACE, LIONEL, *and* GROVER, *gallants.*]

RAYMOND. What, you alone retir'd to privacy,
    Of such a goodly confluence, all prepar'd
    To grace the present nuptials!
LESSINGHAM. I have heard some say,
    Men are ne'er less alone than when alone,
    Such power hath meditation.
EUSTACE. O, these choice beauties!
    That are this day assembled! but of all
    Fair Mistress Clare, the bride excepted still,
    She bears away the prize.
LIONEL. And worthily,
    For, setting off her present melancholy,
    She is without taxation.[170]
GROVER. I conceive
    The cause of her so sudden discontent.
RAYMOND. 'Tis far out of my way.
GROVER. I'll speak it, then.
    In all estates, professions, or degrees,
    In arts or sciences, there is a kind
    Of emulation, likewise so in this.
    There's a maid this day married, a choice beauty;
    Now, Mistress Clare, a virgin of like age,
    And fortunes correspondent, apprehending
    Time lost in her that's in another gain'd,
    May upon this—for who knows women's thoughts—
    Grow into this deep sadness.
RAYMOND. Like enough.
LESSINGHAM. You are pleasant, gentlemen, or else perhaps Though I
    know many have pursu'd her love
GROVER. And you amongst the rest, with pardon, sir,
    Yet she might cast some more peculiar eye
    On some that not respects her.
LESSINGHAM. That's my fear,
    Which you now make your sport.

[*Enter* WAITINGWOMAN.]

WAITINGWOMAN. A letter, sir.
LESSINGHAM. From whom?
WAITINGWOMAN. My mistress.
LESSINGHAM. She has kept her promise,
    And I will read it, though I in the same

---

[170] i.e. her merits are so unquestionable that none of them are capable, in legal phrase, of being *taxed off.*

Know my own death included.

WAITINGWOMAN. Fare you well, sir. [*Exit.*]

LESSINGHAM. *Prove all thy friends, find out the best and nearest,*
  Kill for my sake that friend that loves thee dearest.
  Her servant, nay, her hand and character,
  All meeting in my ruin! Read again:
  Prove all thy friends, find out the best and nearest,
  Kill *for* my sake that friend that loves thee dearest.
  And what might that one be? 'tis a strange difficulty,
  And it will ask much counsel. [*Exit.*]

RAYMOND. Lessingham hath left us on a sudden.

EUSTACE. Sure, the occasion was of that letter sent him.

LIONEL. It may be it was some challenge.

GROVER. Challenge! never dream it: Are such things sent by women?

RAYMOND. 'Twere an heresy
  To conceive but such a thought.

LIONEL. Tush, all the difference
  Begot this day must be at night decided
  Betwixt the bride and bridegroom. Here both come.

[*Enter* WOODROFF, ANNABEL, BONVILE, FRANCKFORD, LUCE, *and*
  NURSE.]

WOODROFF. What did you call the gentleman we met
  But now in some distraction?

BONVILLE. Lessingham;
  A most approv'd and noble friend of mine,
  And one of our prime guests.

WOODROFF. He seeni'd to me
  Somewhat in mind distemper'd. What concern
  Those private humours our so public mirth,
  In such a time of revels? Mistress Clare,
  I miss her, too; why, gallants, have you suffer'd her
  Thus to be lost amongst you?

ANNABEL. Dinner done, unknown to any, she retir'd herself.

WOODROFF. Sick of the maid, perhaps, because she sees
  You, mistress bride, her school and playfellow,
  So suddenly turn'd wife.

FRANCKFORD. 'Twas shrewdly guess'd.

WOODROFF. Go, find her out. Fie, gentlemen, within
  The music plays unto the silent walls,
  And no man there to grace it: when I was young,
  At such a meeting, I have so bestirr'd me,
  Till I have made the pale green-sickness girls
  Blush like the ruby, and drop pearls apace

Down from their ivory foreheads; in those days
I have cut capers thus high. Nay, in, gentlemen,
And single out the ladies.

RAYMOND. Well advis'd.
Nay, mistress bride, you shall along with us,
For without you all's nothing.

ANNABEL. Willingly,
With master bridegroom's leave.

BONVILLE. O, my best joy!
This day I am your servant.

WOODROFF. True, this day;
She his, her whole life after, so it should be;
Only this day a groom to do her service,
For which, the full remainder of his age,
He may write master. I have done it yet,
And so, I hope, still shall do. Sister Luce,
May I presume my brother Franckford can
Say as much and truly?

LUCE. Sir, he may; I freely give him leave.

WOODROFF. Observe that, brother; she freely gives you leave:
But who gives leave, the master or the servant?

FRANCKFORD. You're pleasant,
And it becomes you well, but this day most,
That having but one daughter, have bestow'd her
To your great hope and comfort.

WOODROFF. I have one:
Would you could say so, sister; but your barrenness
Hath given your husband freedom, if he please,
To seek his pastime elsewhere.

LUCE. Well, well, brother,
Though you may taunt me, that have never yet
Been blest with issue, spare my husband, pray,
For he may have a by-blow, or an heir,
That you never heard of.

FRANCKFORD. [*aside.*] O fie, wife, make not my fault too public.

LUCE. Yet himself keep within compass.

FRANCKFORD. [*aside.*] If you love me, sweet—

LUCE. Nay, I have done.

WOODROFF. But if he have not, wench,
I would he had the hurt I wish you both.
Prithee, thine ear a little.

NURSE. Your boy grows up, and 'tis a chopping lad, A man even in the
cradle.

FRANCKFORD. Softly, nurse.

NURSE. One of the forward'st infants! how it will crow,

And chirrup like a sparrow! I fear shortly
It will breed teeth: you must provide him, therefore,
A coral, with a whistle and a chain.
FRANCKFORD. He shall have anything.
NURSE. He's now quite out of blankets.
FRANCKFORD. There's a piece, provide him what he wants;
    Only, good nurse, prithee at this time be silent.
NURSE. A charm to bind
    Any nurse's tongue that's living.
WOODROFF. Come, we are miss'd
    Among the younger fry: gravity ofttimes
    Becomes the sports of youth, especially
    At such solemnities: and it were sin
    Not in our age to show what we have bin.[171]

[*Exeunt.*]

SCENE II.

[*Enter* LESSINGHAM, *sad, with a letter in his hand.*]

LESSINGHAM. *Amicitia nihil dedit natura majus nec rarius*;
    So saith my author. If, then, powerful nature,
    In all her bounties shower'd upon mankind,
    Found none more rare and precious than this one
    We call friendship, O, to what a monster
    Would this transshape me; to be made that he
    To violate such goodness! To kill any,
    Had been a sad injunction; but a friend,
    Nay, of all friends the most approv'd! A task
    Hell, till this day, could never parallel.
    And yet this woman has a power of me
    Beyond all virtue,—virtue! almost grace.
    What might her hidden purpose be in this?
    Unless she apprehend some fantasy,
    That no such thing has being; and as kindred
    And claims to crowns are worn out of the world,
    So the name friend: 't may be 'twas her conceit.
    I have tried those that have professed much
    For coin, nay, sometimes, slighter courtesies,
    Yet found 'em cold enough; so, perhaps, she,
    Which makes her thus opinion'd. If in the former,
    And therefore better days, 'twas held so rare.

---

[171] For been, to suit the rhyme.

Who knows but in these last and worser times
It may be now with justice banish'd th' earth?
I'm full of thoughts, and this my troubled breast
Distemper'd with a thousand fantasies.
Something I must resolve. I'll first make proof
If such a thing there be, which having found,
'Twixt love and friendship 'twill be a brave fight,
To prove in man which claims the greatest right.

[*Enter* RAYMOND, EUSTACE, LIONEL, *and* GROVER.]

RAYMOND. What, Master Lessingham!
    You that were wont to be compos'd of mirth,
    All spirit and fire, alacrity itself,
    Like the lustre of a late bright-shining sun,
    Now wrapt in clouds and darkness!
LIONEL. Prithee, be merry;
    Thy dulness sads the half part of the house,
    And deads that spirit which thou wast wont to quicken,
    And, half spent, to give life to.
LESSINGHAM. Gentlemen,
    Such as have cause for sport, I shall wish ever
    To make of it the present benefit,
    While it exists: content is still short-breath'd;
    When it was mine, I did so; if now yours,
    I pray make your best use on't.
LIONEL. Riddles and paradoxes:
    Come, come, some crotchet's come into thy pate,
    And I will know the cause on't.
GROVER. So will I,
    Or I protest ne'er leave thee.
LESSINGHAM. 'Tis a business
    Proper to myself, one that concerns
    No second person.
GROVER. How's that? not a friend?
LESSINGHAM. Why, is there any such?
GROVER. Do you question that? what do you take me for?
EUSTACE. Ay, sir, or me? Tis many months ago
    Since we betwixt us interchang'd that name,
    And, of my part, ne'er broken.
LIONEL. Troth, nor mine.
RAYMOND. If you make question of a friend, I pray,
    Number not me the last in your account,
    That would be crown'd in your opinion first.
LESSINGHAM. You all speak nobly; but amongst you all

Can such a one be found?

RAYMOND. Not one amongst us but would be proud
To wear the character of noble friendship:
In the name of which,
And of all us here present, I entreat,
Expose to us the grief that troubles you.

LESSINGHAM. I shall, and briefly. If ever gentleman
Sunk beneath scandal, or his reputation,
Never to be recover'd, suffer'd, and
For want of one whom I may call a friend,
Then mine is now in danger.

RAYMOND. I'll redeem't,
Though with my life's dear hazard.

EUSTACE. I pray, sir,
Be to us open-breasted.

LESSINGHAM. Then 'tis thus.
There is to be perform'd a monomachy,
Combat or duel, time, place, and weapon,
Agreed betwixt us. Had it touch'd myself,
And myself only, I had then been happy,
But I by composition am engag'd
To bring with me my second, and he too,
Not as the law of combat is, to stand
Aloof and see fair play, bring off his friend,
But to engage his person: both must fight,
And either of them dangerous.

EUSTACE. Of all things
I do not like this fighting.

LESSINGHAM. Now, gentlemen,
Of this so great a courtesy I am
At this instant merely[172] destitute.

RAYMOND. The time?

LESSINGHAM. By eight o'clock to-morrow.

RAYMOND. How unhappily
Things may fall out! I am just at that hour
Upon some late conceived discontents
To atone[173] me to my father, otherwise
Of all the rest you had commanded me
Your second and your servant.

LIONEL. Pray, the place?

LESSINGHAM. Calais sands.

LIONEL. It once was fatal to a friend of mine,

---

[172] Wholly, absolutely.
[173] Reconcile.

And a near kinsman, for which I vow'd then,
And deeply too, never to see that ground:
But if it had been elsewhere, one of them
Had before nine been worms-meat.

GROVER. What's the weapon?

LESSINGHAM. Single sword.

GROVER. Of all that you could name,
A thing I never practis'd: had it been
Rapier, or that and poniard, where men use
Rather sleight than force, I had been then your man.
Being young, I strain'd the sinews of my arm,
Since then to me 'twas never serviceable.

EUSTACE. In troth, sir, had it been a money-matter,
I could have stood your friend; but as for fighting,
I was ever out at that.

LESSINGHAM. Well, farewell, gentlemen. [*Exeunt gallants.*
But where's the friend in all this? Tush, she's wise,
And knows there's no such thing beneath the moon;
I now applaud her judgment.

[*Enter* BONVILE.]

BONVILLE. Why, how now, friend? This discontent, which now
Is so unseason'd, makes me question what
I ne'er durst doubt before, your love to me:
Doth it proceed from envy of my bliss,
Which this day crowns me with? or have you been
A secret rival in my happiness,
And grieve to see me owner of those joys,
Which you could wish your own?

LESSINGHAM. Banish such thoughts,
Or you shall wrong the truest faithful friendship
Man e'er could boast of. O, mine honour, sir!
'Tis that which makes me wear this brow of sorrow:
Were that free from the power of calumny—
But pardon me, that being now a-dying
Which is so near to man, if part we cannot
With pleasant looks.

BONVILLE. Do but speak the burden,
And I protest to take it off from you,
And lay it on myself.

LESSINGHAM. 'Twere a request,
Impudence without blushing could not ask,
It bears with it such injury.

BONVILLE. Yet must I know't.

LESSINGHAM. Receive it, then—but I entreat you, sir,
    Not to imagine that I apprehend
    A thought to further my intent by you;
    From you 'tis least suspected—'twas my fortune
    To entertain a quarrel with a gentleman,
    The field betwixt us challeng'd, place and time,
    And these to be perform'd not without seconds:
    I have relied on many seeming friends,
    But cannot bless my memory with one
    Dares venture in my quarrel.
BONVILLE. Is this all?
LESSINGHAM. It is enough to make all temperature
    Convert to fury. Sir, my reputation,
    The life and soul of honour, is at stake,
    In danger to be lost, the word of coward
    Still printed in the name of Lessingham.
BONVILLE. Not while there is a Bonvile. May I live poor,
    And die despis'd, not having one sad friend
    To wait upon my hearse, if I survive
    The ruin of that honour. Sir, the time?
LESSINGHAM. Above all spare me [that],[174] for that once known
    You'll cancel this your promise, and unsay
    Your friendly proffer; neither can I blame you:
    Had you confirm'd it with a thousand oaths,
    The heavens would look with mercy, not with justice[175]
    On your offence, should you infringe 'em all.
    Soon after sun-rise, upon Calais sands,
    To-morrow we should meet; now to defer
    Time one half hour, I should but forfeit all.
    But, sir, of all men living, this, alas,
    Concerns you least! for shall I he the man
    To rob you of this night's felicity,
    And make your bride a widow, her soft bed
    No witness of those joys this night expects?
BONVILLE. I still prefer my friend before my pleasure,
    Which is not lost for ever, but adjourn'd
    For more mature employment.
LESSINGHAM. Will you go then?
BONVILLE. I am resolv'd, I will.
LESSINGHAM. And instantly?
BONVILLE. With all the speed celerity can make.
LESSINGHAM. You do not weigh those inconveniences

---

[174] Supplied by Mr. Dyce.
[175] i.e. not with the rigour of strict justice.

This action meets with: your departure hence
Will breed a strange distraction in your friends,
Distrust of love in your fair virtuous bride,
Whose eyes perhaps may never more be blest
With your dear sight, since you may meet a grave,
And that not amongst your noble ancestors,
But amongst strangers, almost enemies.

BONVILLE. This were enough to shake a weak resolve,
It moves not me. Take horse as secretly
As you well may: my groom shall make mine ready
With all speed possible, unknown to any.

LESSINGHAM. But, sir, the bride.

[*Enter* ANNABEL.]

ANNABEL. Did you not see the key, that's to unlock
My carcanet and bracelets; now, in troth,
I am afraid 'tis lost.

BONVILLE. No, sweet, I ha't;
I found it lie at random in your chamber,
And knowing you would miss it, laid it by:
'Tis safe, I warrant you.

ANNABEL. Then my fear's past:
But till you give it back, my neck and arms
Are still your prisoners.

BONVILLE. But you shall find they have a gentle jailor,

ANNABEL. So I hope': within y' are much enquir'd of.

BONVILLE. Sweet, I follow. [*Exit* ANNABEL.] Dover?

LESSINGHAM. Yes, that's the place.

BONVILLE. If you be there before me, hire a bark:
I shall not fail to meet you. [*Exit.*]

LESSINGHAM. Was ever known
A man so miserably blest as I?
I have no sooner found the greatest good
Man in this pilgrimage of life can meet,
But I must make the womb where 'twas conceiv'd
The tomb to bury it, and the first hour it lives
The last it must breathe. Yet there is a fate
That sways and governs above woman's hate. [*Exit.*]

ACT II.

SCENE I.

[*Enter* ROCHFIELD, *a young gentleman.*]

ROCHFIELD. Younger brother? 'tis a poor calling,
    Though not unlawful, very hard to live on
    The elder fool inherits all the lands,
    And we that follow, legacies of wit,
    And get 'em when we can too. Why should law,
    If we be lawful and legitimate,
    Leave us without an equal dividend?
    Or why compels it not our fathers else
    To cease from getting, when they want[176] to give?
    No sure, our mothers will ne'er agree to that;
    They love to groan, although the gallows echo
    And groan together for us; from the first[177]
    We travel forth, t' other's[178] our journey's end.
    I must forward. To beg is out of my way,
    And borrowing is out of date. The old road,
    The old high-way't must be, and I am in't.
    The place will serve for a young beginner,
    For this is the first day I set ope shop.
    Success, then, sweet Laverna! I have heard
    That thieves adore thee for a deity:
    I would not purchase by thee but to eat,
    And 'tis too churlish to deny me meat.
    Soft, here may be a booty.

[*Enter* ANNABEL *and a* SERVANT.]

ANNABEL. Hors'd, say'st thou?
SERVANT. Yes, mistress, with Lessingham.
ANNABEL. Alack, I know not what to doubt or fear!
    I know not well whether't be well or ill:
    But sure it is no custom for the groom
    To leave his bride upon the nuptial day.
    I am so young and ignorant a scholar—
    Yes, and it proves so; I talk away perhaps

---

[176] i.e. are in want of the means.
[177] i.e. the groaning.
[178] The gallows.

That might be yet recover'd. Prithee, run:
The forepath may advantage thee to meet 'em,
Or the ferry, which is not two miles before,
May trouble 'em, until thou com'st in ken,
And if thou dost, prithee, enforce thy voice
To overtake thine eyes; cry out, and crave
For me but one word 'fore his departure;
I will not stay him, say, beyond his pleasure,
Nor rudely ask the cause, if he be willing
To keep it from me. Charge him by all the love—
But I stay thee too long: run, run.

SERVANT. If I had wings, I would spread 'em now, mistress. [*Exit.*]

ANNABEL. I'll make the best speed after that I can,
    Yet I am not well acquainted with the path:
    My fears, I fear me, will misguide me too. [*Exit.*]

ROCHFIELD. There's good movables, I perceive, whate'er the ready
coin be: whoever owns her, she's mine now; the next ground has a
most pregnant hollow for the purpose. [*Exit.*]

SCENE II.

[*Enter* SERVANT, *running over*; *enter* ANNABEL, *after her*
ROCHFIELD.]

ANNABEL. I'm at a doubt already where I am.

ROCHFIELD. I'll help you, mistress; well overtaken.

ANNABEL. Defend me, goodness! What are you?

ROCHFIELD. A man.

ANNABEL. An honest man, I hope.

ROCHFIELD. In some degrees hot, not altogether cold,
    So far as rank poison,[179] yet dangerous,
    As I may be drest. I am an honest thief.

ANNABEL. Honest and thief hold small affinity,
    I never heard they were akin before:
    Pray heaven I find it now.

ROCHFIELD. I tell you my name.

ANNABEL. Then, honest thief, since you have taught me so,
    For I'll enquire no other, use me honestly.

ROCHFIELD. Thus then I'll use you. First, then, to prove me honest,
    I will not violate your chastity,
    (That's no part yet of my profession,)
    Be you wife or virgin.

ANNABEL. I am both, sir.

---

[179] Dangerous if not well treated.

ROCHFIELD. This then it seems should be your wedding day,
    And these the hours of interim to keep you
    In that double state: come, then, I'll be brief,
    For I'll not hinder your desired hymen.
    You have about you some superfluous toys,
    Which my lank hungry pockets would contrive[180]
    With much more profit and more privacy;
    You have an idle chain which keeps your neck
    A prisoner; a manacle, I take it,
    About your wrist too. If these prove emblems
    Of the combined hemp to halter mine,
    The fates take their pleasure! these are set down
    To be your ransom, and there the thief is prov'd.
ANNABEL. I will confess both, and the last forget.
    You shall be only honest in this deed.
    Pray you take it, I entreat you to it,
    And then you steal 'em not.
ROCHFIELD. You may deliver 'em.
ANNABEL. Indeed I cannot. If you observe, sir,
    They are both lock'd about me, and the key
    I have not: happily you are furnish'd
    With some instrument that may unloose 'em.
ROCHFIELD. No, in troth, lady, I am but a freshman;
    I never read further than this book you see,
    And this very day is my beginning too:
    These picking-laws I am to study yet.
ANNABEL. O, do not show me that, sir, 'tis too frightful!
    Good, hurt me not, for I do yield 'em freely;
    Use but your hands, perhaps their strength will serve
    To tear 'em from me without much detriment:
    Somewhat I will endure.
ROCHFIELD. Well, sweet lady,
    Y' are the best patient for a young physician,
    That I think e'er was practis'd on. I'll use you
    As gently as I can, as I'm an honest thief.
    No? will't not do? do I hurt you, lady?
ANNABEL. Not much, sir.
ROCHFIELD. I'd be loath at all. I cannot do't.
ANNABEL. Nay, then, you shall not, sir. You a thief,

[*She draws his sword.*]

---

[180] Qy. "contain."—Dyce.

And guard yourself no better? no further read?
Yet out in your own book? a bad clerk, are you not?
ROCHFIELD. Ay, by Saint Nicholas,[181] lady, sweet lady.
ANNABEL. Sir, I have now a masculine vigour,
    And will redeem myself with purchase too.
    What money have you?
ROCHFIELD. Not a cross, by this foolish hand of mine.
ANNABEL. No money? 'twere pity, then, to take this from thee;
    I know thou'lt use me ne'er the worse for this;
    Take it again, I know not how to use it:
    A frown had taken't from me, which thou had'st not.
    And now hear, and believe me—on my knees
    I make the protestation—forbear
    To take what violence and danger must
    Dissolve, if I forego 'em now. I do assure
    You would not strike my head off for my chain,
    Nor my hand for this: how to deliver 'em
    Otherwise, I know not. Accompany
    Me back unto my house, 'tis not far off:
    By all the vows which this day I have tied
    Unto my wedded husband, the honour
    Yet equal with my cradle purity,
    (If you will tax me,) to the hoped joys,
    The blessings of the bed, posterity,
    Or what aught else by woman may be pledg'd,
    I will deliver you in ready coin
    The full and dearest esteem[182] of what you crave.
ROCHFIELD. Ha! ready money is the prize I look for:
    It walks without suspicion anywhere,
    When chains and jewels may be stay'd and call'd
    Before the constable; but—
ANNABEL. But? can you doubt?
    You saw I gave you my advantage up:
    Did you e'er think a woman to be true?
ROCHFIELD. Thought's free; I have heard of some few, lady,
    Very few indeed.
ANNABEL. Will you add one more to your belief?
ROCHFIELD. They were fewer than the articles of my belief,
    Therefore I have room for you, and will believe you.
    Stay, you'll ransom your jewels with ready coin;
    So may you do, and then discover me.
ANNABEL. Shall I reiterate the vows I made

---

[181] St. Nicholas was the patron of thieves.
[182] Estimate, value.

To this injunction, or new ones coin?
ROCHFIELD. Neither; I'll trust you: if you do destroy
  A thief that never yet did robbery,
  Then farewell I, and mercy fall upon me.
  I knew one once fifteen years courtier old,
  And he was buried ere he took a bribe.
  It may be my case in the worser way.
  Come, you know your path back.
ANNABEL. Yes, I shall guide you.
ROCHFIELD. Your arm: I'll lead with greater dread than will,
  Nor do you fear, though in thief's handling still.

[*Exeunt.*]

SCENE III.

[*Enter* TWO BOYS, *one with a* CHILD *in his arms.*]

FIRST BOY. I say 'twas fair play.
SECOND BOY. To snatch up stakes! I say you should not say so if the
  child were out of mine arms.
FIRST BOY. Ay, then thoud'st lay about like a man; but the child will
  not be out of thine arms this five years, and then thou hast a
  prenticeship to serve to a boy afterwards.
SECOND BOY. So, sir! you know you have the advantage of me.
FIRST BOY. I'm sure you have the odds of me, you are two to one.

[*Enter* COMPASS.]

But soft, Jack, who comes here? if a point will make us friends,
  we'll not fall out.
SECOND BOY. O, the pity! 'tis Gaffer Compass: they said he was dead
  three years ago.
FIRST BOY. Did not he dance the Hobby-horse in Hackney Morrice[183]
  once?
SECOND BOY. Yes, yes, at Green-goose fair; as honest and as poor a
  man.
COMPASS. Blackwall, sweet Blackwall, do I see thy white cheeks
  again? I have brought some brine from sea for thee; tears that
  might be tied in a true-love knot, for they're fresh salt indeed. O,
  beautiful Blackwall! if Urse, my wife, be living to this day, though
  she die to-morrow, sweet fates!
SECOND BOY. Alas! let's put him out of his dumps, for pity's sake !—

---

[183] The Morris-dance at Hackney.

Welcome home, Gaffer Compass welcome home, Gaffer.

COMPASS. My pretty youths, I thank you. Honest Jack, what a little man art thou grown, since I saw thee! Thou hast got a child, since, methinks.

SECOND BOY. I am fain to keep it, you see, whosoever got it, Gaffer: it may be another man's case as well as mine.

COMPASS. Sayest true, Jack: and whose pretty knave is it?

SECOND BOY. One that I mean to make a younger brother, if he live to't, Gaffer. But I can tell you news: you have a brave boy of your own wife's; O, 'tis a shote[184] to this pig!

COMPASS. Have I, Jack? I'll owe thee a dozen of points[185] for this news.

SECOND BOY. O, 'tis a chopping boy! it cannot choose, you know, Gaffer, it was so long a breeding.

COMPASS. How long, Jack?

SECOND BOY. You know 'tis four year ago since you went to sea, and your child is but a quarter old yet.

COMPASS. What plaguy boys are bred, now-a-days!

FIRST BOY. Pray, Gaffer, how long may a child be breeding, before 'tis born?

COMPASS. That is as things are and prove, child; the soil has a great hand in't, too, the horizon, and the clime: these things you'll understand when you go to sea. In some parts of London hard by, you shall have a bride' married to-day, and brought to bed within a month after, sometimes within three weeks, a fortnight.

FIRST BOY. O, horrible!

COMPASS. True, as I tell you, lads. In another place you shall have a couple of drones, do what they can, shift lodgings, beds, bed-fellows, yet not a child in ten years.

SECOND BOY. O, pitiful!

COMPASS. Now it varies again by that time you come at Wapping, Radcliff, Limehouse, and here with us at Blackwall; our children come uncertainly, as the wind serves. Sometimes here we are supposed to be away three or four years together: 'tis nothing so, we are at home and gone again, when nobody knows on't. If you'll believe me, I have been at Surat, as this day; I have taken the long-boat, (a fair gale with me,) been here a-bed with my wife by twelve a clock at night, up and gone again i' th' morning, and no man the wiser, if you'll believe me.

SECOND BOY. Yes, yes, Gaffer, I have thought so many times that you or somebody else have been at home; I lie at next wall, and I have heard a noise in your chamber all night long.

---

[184] *Shote*, a half-grown hog.
[185] Tagged laces used in the dress of the period.

COMPASS. Right, why that was I, yet thou never sawest me.

SECOND BOY. No indeed, Gaffer.

COMPASS. No, I warrant thee; I was a thousand leagues off, ere thou wert up. But, Jack, I have been loth to ask all this while, for discomforting myself, how does my wife? is she living?

SECOND BOY. O, never better, Gaffer, never so lusty! and truly she wears better clothes than she was wont in your days, especially on holidays; fair gowns, brave petticoats, and fine smocks, they say that have seen 'em, and some of the neighbours reports that they were taken up at London.

COMPASS. Like enough: they must be paid for, Jack.

SECOND BOY. And good reason, Gaffer.

COMPASS. Well, Jack, thou shalt have the honour on't: go, tell my wife the joyful tidings of my return.

SECOND BOY. That I will, for she heard you were dead long ago. [*Exit.*

FIRST BOY. Nay, sir, I'll be as forward as you, by your leave. [*Exit.*

COMPASS. Well, wife, if I be one of the livery, I thank thee. The horners are a great company; there may be an alderman amongst us one day; 'tis but changing our copy, and then we are no more to be called by our old brotherhood.

[*Enter* COMPASS'*s* WIFE.]

WIFE. O my sweet Compass, art thou come again!

COMPASS. O, Urse, give me leave to shed! The fountains of love will have their course: though I cannot sing at first sight, yet I can cry before I see. I am new come into the world, and children cry before they laugh, a fair while.

WIFE. And so thou art, sweet Compass, new born indeed, for rumour laid thee out for dead long since. I never thought to see this face again: I heard thou wert div'd to th' bottom of the sea, and taken up a lodging in the sands, never to come to Blackwall again.

COMPASS. I was going, indeed, wife, but I turn'd back: I heard an ill report of my neighbours, sharks and sword-fishes, and the like, whose companies I did not like. Come kiss my tears, now, sweet Urse: sorrow begins to ebb.

WIFE. A thousand times welcome home, sweet Compass.

COMPASS. An ocean of thanks, and that will hold 'em. And, Urse, how goes all at home? or cannot all go yet? lank still! will't never be full sea at our wharf?

WIFE. Alas, husband!

COMPASS. A lass, or a lad, wench, I should be glad of both: I did look for a pair of compasses before this day.

WIFE. And you from home!

COMPASS. I from home! why, though I be from home, and other of our neighbours from home, it is not fit all should be from home; so the town might be left desolate, and our neighbours of Bow might come further from the Itacus,[186] and inhabit here.

WIFE. I'm glad y'are merry, sweet husband.

COMPASS. Merry! nay, I'll be merrier yet: why should I be sorry? I hope my boy's well, is he not? I looked for another by this time.

WIFE. What boy, husband?

COMPASS. What boy! why the boy I got when I came home in the cock-boat one night about a year ago: you have not forgotten't, I hope. I think I left behind for a boy, and a boy I must be answer'd: I'm sure I was not drunk; it could be no girl.

WIFE. Nay, then, I do perceive my fault is known: dear man, your pardon.

COMPASS. Pardon! why, thou hast not made away my boy, hast thou? I'll hang thee, if there were ne'er a whore in London more, if thou hast hurt but his little toe.

WIFE. Your long absence, with rumourof yourdeath—after long battery, I was surpris'd.

COMPASS. Surpris'd! I cannot blame thee: Black wall, if it were double black-wall'd, can't hold out always, no more than Limehouse, or Shad well, or the strongest suburbs about London; and when it comes to that, woe be to the city, too.

WIFE. Pursu'd by gifts and promises, I yielded: consider, husband, I am a woman, neither the first nor last of such offenders. Tis true I have a child.

COMPASS. Ha' you? and what shall I have then, I pray? Will not you labour for me, as I shall do for you? Because I was out o' th' way when 'twas gotten, shall I lose my share? There's better law amongst the players yet, for a fellow shall have his share,[187] though he do not play that day. If you look for any part of my four years' wages, I will have half the boy.

WIFE. If you can forgive me, I shall be joy'd at it.

COMPASS. Forgive thee! for what? for doing me a pleasure? And what is he that would seem to father my child?

WIFE. A man, sir, whom in better courtesies we have been beholding to, the merchant Master Franckford.

COMPASS. I'll acknowledge no other courtesies: for this I am beholding to him, and I would requite it, if his wife were young enough. Though he be one of our merchants at sea, he shall give me leave to be owner at home. And where's my boy? shall I see him?

---

[186] Equally with Mr. Dyce, I am unable to divine how this, probably, misprint should be corrected.

[187] The performers at our earlier theatres were distinguished into whole sharers, three-quarter sharers, half-sharers, and hired men, and all but the last were in the favourable position indicated by Compass.

WIFE. He's nurs'd at Bednal Green; 'tis now too late; to-morrow I'll
    bring you to it, if you please.
COMPASS. I would thou could'st bring me another by tomorrow. Come,
    we'll eat, and to bed, and if a fair gale come, we'll hoist sheets, and
    set forwards.
        Let fainting fools lie sick upon their scorns,
    I'll teach a cuckold how to hide his horns. [*Exeunt.*

SCENE IV.

[*Enter* WOODROFF, FRANCKFORD, RAYMOND, EUSTACE, GROVER,
    LIONEL, CHARE, LUCE.]

WOODROFF. This wants a precedent, that a bridegroom
    Should so discreet and decently observe
    His forms, postures, all customary rites
    Belonging to the table, and then hide himself
    From his expected wages in the bed.
FRANCKFORD. Let this be forgotten too, that it remains not
    A first example.
RAYMOND. Keep it amongst us,
    Lest it beget too much unfruitful sorrow.
    Most likely 'tis, that love to Lessingham
    Hath fastened on him, we all denied.
EUSTACE. 'Tis more certain than likely: I know 'tis so.
GROVER. Conceal then: the event may be well enough.
WOODROFF. The bride, my daughter, she's hidden too;
    This last hour she hath not been seen with us.
RAYMOND. Perhaps they are together.
EUSTACE. And then we make too strict an inquisition.
    Under correction of fair modesty,
    Should they be stol'n away to bed together,
    What would you say to that?
WOODROFF. I would say, speed 'em well;
    And if no worse news comes, I'll never weep for't.

[*Enter* NURSE.]

    How now! hast thou any tidings?
NURSE. Yes, forsooth, I have tidings.
WOODROFF. Of any one that's lost?
NURSE. Of one that's found again, forsooth.
WOODROFF. O, he was lost, it seems then.
FRANCKFORD. This tidings comes to me, I guess, sir.
NURSE. Yes, truly, does it, sir.

RAYMOND. Ay, have old lads work for young nurses?

EUSTACE. Yes, when they groan towards their second infancy.

CLARE. I fear myself most guilty for the absence
    Of the bridegroom. What our wills will do
    With overrash and headlong peevishness
    To bring our calm discretions to repentance!
    Lessingham's mistaken, quite out of the way
    Of my purpose too.

FRANCKFORD. Return'd!

NURSE. And all discover'd.

FRANCKFORD. A fool rid him further off! let him not come near the child.

NURSE. Nor see't, if it be your charge.

FRANCKFORD. It is, and strictly.

NURSE. To-morrow morning, as I hear, he purposeth to come to Bednal
    Green, his wife with him.

FRANCKFORD. He shall be met there; yet, if lie forestall my coming,
    keep the child safe.

NURSE. If he be the earlier up, he shall arrive at the proverb.[188] [*Exit.*]

[*Enter* ROCHFIELD *and* ANNABEL.]

WOODROFF. So, so,
    There's some good luck yet, the bride's in sight again.

ANNABEL. Father, and gentlemen all, beseech you
    Entreat this gentleman with all courtesy,
    He is a loving kinsman of my Bonvile's,
    That kindly came to gratulate our wedding;
    But as the day falls out, you see alone
    I personate both groom and bride, only
    Your help to make this welcome better.

WOODROFF. Most dearly.

RAYMOND. To all, assure you, sir.

WOODROFF. But where's the bridegroom, girl?
    "We are all at a nonplus, here, at a stand,
    Quite out, the music ceas'd, and dancing surbated,[189]
    Not a light heel amongst us; my cousin Clare, too,
    As cloudy here as on a washing. day.

CLARE. It is because you will not dance with me;
    I should then shake it off.

ANNABEL. 'Tis I have cause

---

[188] "Early up and never the nearer."—Ray's *Proverbs.*
[189] *Surbated*—meaning *bruised in the feet,* wearied. *Dancing* should, probably, be read *dancers.*

To be the sad one now, if any be:
But I have question'd with my meditations,
And they have render'd well and comfortably
To the worst fear I found. Suppose this day
He had long since appointed to his foe
To meet, and fetch a reputation from him,
Which is the dearest jewel unto man:
Say he do fight, I know his goodness such,
That all those powers that love it are his guard,
And ill cannot betide him.

WOODROFF. Prithee, peace,
Thoul't make us all cowards to hear a woman
Instruct so valiantly. Come, the music,
I'll dance myself rather than[190] thus put down.
What! I am rife a little yet.

ANNABEL. Only this gentleman
Pray you be free in welcome to; I tell you
I was in fear when first I saw him.

ROCHFIELD. [*aside.*] Ha! she'll tell.

ANNABEL. I had quite lost my way in
My first amazement, but he so fairly came
To my recovery, in his kind conduct
Gave me such loving comforts to my fears,
'Twas he instructed me in what I spake,
And many better than I have told you yet;
You shall hear more anon.

ROCHFIELD. [*aside.*] So, she will out with't.

ANNABEL. I must, I see, supply both places still.
Come, when I have seen you back to your pleasure,
I will return to you, sir; we must discourse
More of my Bonvile yet.

OMNES. A noble bride, faith.

CLARE. You have your wishes, and you may be merry:
Mine have overgrown me.

[*Exeunt.* ROCHFIELD *remains alone.*]

ROCHFIELD. It is the trembling'st trade to be a thief!
H'ad need have all the world bound to the peace!
Besides the bushes and the vanes of houses,
Everything that moves, he goes in fear of's life on;
A fur-gown'd cat, and I meet her in the night,
She stares with a constable's eye upon him,

---

[190] [Be].

And every dog's a watchman; a black cow,
And a calf with a white face after her,
Shows like a surly justice and his clerk;
And if the baby go but to the bag,
Tis ink and paper for a mittimus.
Sure, I shall never thrive on't; and it may be
I shall need take no care, I may be now
At my journey's end, or but the gaol's distance,
And so to the other place. I trust a woman
With a secret worth a hanging; is that well?
I could find in my heart to run away yet:
And that were base, too, to run from a woman:
I can lay claim to nothing but her vows,
And they shall strengthen me.

[*Enter* ANNABEL.]

ANNABEL. See, sir, my promise:
    There's twenty pieces, the full value, I vow,
    Of what they cost.
ROCHFIELD. Lady, do not trap me
    Like a sumpter-horse, and then spur-gall me
    Till I break my wind. If the constable
    Be at the door, let his fair staff appear:
    Perhaps I may corrupt him with this gold.
ANNABEL. Nay, then, if you mistrust me, father, gentlemen,
    Master Raymond, Eustace!

[*Enter* ALL, *as before, and a* SAILOR.]

WOODROFF. How now, what's the matter, girl?
ANNABEL. For shame, will you hid your kinsman welcome?
    No one but I will lay a hand on him:
    Leave him alone, and all a revelling!
WOODROFF. O, is that it? Welcome, welcome heartily!
    I thought the bridegroom had been return'd: but
    I have news, Annabel; this fellow brought it.
    Welcome, sir! why, you tremble methinks, sir.
ANNABEL. Some agony of anger, 'tis, believe it,
    His entertainment is so cold and feeble.
RAYMOND. Pray, be cheer'd, sir.
ROCHFIELD. I'm wondrous well, sir; 'twas the gentleman's mistake.
WOODROFF. 'Twas my hand shook belike, then ; you must pardon
    Age, I was stiffer once. But as I was saying,
    I should by promise see the sea to-morrow

('Tis meant for physic) as low as Lee or Margate,
I have a vessel riding forth, gentlemen,
'Tis call'd the God-speed, too,
Though I say't, a brave one, well and richly fraughted;
And I can tell you she carries a Letter of Mart
In her mouth, too, and twenty roaring boys
On both sides on her, starboard and larboard.
What say you, now, to make you all adventurers?
You shall have fair dealing, that I'll promise you.
RAYMOND. A very good motion, sir, I begin,
　There's my ten pieces.
EUSTACE. I second 'em with these.
GROVER. My ten in the third place.
ROCHFIELD. And, sir, if you refuse not a proffer'd love,
　Take my ten pieces with you, too.
WOODROFF. Your's above all the rest, sir.
ANNABEL. Then make 'em above, venture ten more.
ROCHFIELD. Alas, lady, 'tis a younger brother's portion,
　And all in one bottom!
ANNABEL. At my encouragement, sir,
　Your credit if you want, sir, shall not sit down
　Under that sum return'd.
ROCHFIELD. With all my heart, lady. There, sir.
　So, she has fish'd for her gold back, and caught it;
　I am no thief now.
WOODROFF. I shall make here a pretty assurance.
ROCHFIELD. Sir, I shall have a suit to you.
WOODROFF. You are likely to obtain it, then, sir.
ROCHFIELD. That I may keep you company to sea,
　And attend you back; I am a little travell'd.
WOODROFF. And heartily thank you, too, sir.
ANNABEL. Why, that's well said.
　Pray you be merry: though your kinsman be absent,
　I am here the worst part of him, yet that shall serve
　To give you welcome; to-morrow may show you
　What this night will not, and be full assur'd,
　Unless your twenty pieces be ill-lent,
　Nothing shall give you cause of discontent.
　There's ten more, sir.
ROCHFIELD. Why should I fear? Foutre[191] on't,
　I'll be merry now, spite of the hangman.

[Exeunt.]

---

[191] A French oath, not susceptible of explanation here.

ACT III.

SCENE I.

[*Enter* LESSINGHAM *and* BONVILE.]

BONVILE. We are first i' th' field: I think your enemy
    Is stay'd at Dover, or some other port,
    We hear not of his landing.
LESSINGHAM. I am confident he is come over.
BONVILLE. You look, methinks, fresh colour'd.
LESSINGHAM. Like a red morning, friend, that still foretells
    A stormy day to follow: but, methinks,
    Now I observe your face, that you look pale,
    There's death in't already.
BONVILLE. I could chide your error.
    Do you take me for a coward? A coward
    Is not his own friend, much less can he be
    Another man's. Know, sir, I am come hither
    To instruct you, by my generous example,
    To kill your enemy, whose name as yet
    I never question'd.
LESSINGHAM. Nor dare I name him yet
    For disheartening you.
BONVILLE. I do begin to doubt The goodness of your quarrel.
LESSINGHAM. Now you hav't:
    For I protest that I must fight with one
    From whom, in the whole course of our acquaintance,
    I never did receive the least injury.
BONVILLE. It may be the forgetful wine begot
    Some sudden blow, and thereupon this challenge.
    Howe'er, you are engag'd; and for my part
    I will not take your course, my unlucky friend,
    To say your conscience grows pale and heartless,
    Maintaining a bad cause. Fight, as lawyers plead,
    Who gain the best of reputation
    When they can fetch a bad cause smoothly off:
    You are in and must through.
LESSINGHAM. O my friend,
    The noblest ever man had! when my fate
    Threw me upon this business, I made trial
    Of divers had profess'd to me much love,
    And found their friendship, like the effects that kept
    Our company together—wine and riot—

Giddy and sinking; I had found 'em oft,
Brave seconds at pluralities of healths;
But when it came to th' proof, my gentlemen
Appear'd to me as promising and failing
As cozening lotteries. But then I found
This jewel worth a thousand counterfeits:
I did but name my-engagement, and you flew
Unto my succour with that cheerfulness,
As a great general hastes to a battle,
When that the chief of the adverse part
Is a man glorious but of ample fame.
You left your bridal-bed to find your death-bed.
And herein you most nobly express'd
That the affection 'tween two loyal friends
Is far beyond the love of man to woman,
And is more near allied to eternity.
What better friend's part could be show'd i' the world!
It transcends all: my father gave me life,
But you stand by my honour when 'tis falling,
And nobly underprop it with your sword.
But now you have done me all this service,
How, how shall I requite this? how return
My grateful recompense for all this love?
For it am I come hither with full purpose
To kill you.

BONVILLE. Ha!

LESSINGHAM. Yes, I have no opposite i' th' world but
    Yourself: there, read the warrant for your death.

BONVILLE. 'Tis a woman's hand.

LESSINGHAM. And 'tis a bad hand too:
    The most of 'em speak fair, write foul, mean worse.

BONVILLE. Kill me! away, you jest.

LESSINGHAM. Such jest as your sharp-witted gallants use
    To utter, and lose their friends. Bead there how
    I'm fetter'd in a woman's proud command:
    I do love madly, and must do madly.
    Deadliest hellebore or vomit of a toad
    Is qualified poison to the malice of a woman.

BONVILLE. *And kill that friend?* strange!

LESSINGHAM. You may see, sir,
    Although the tenure by which land was held
    In villanage be quite extinct in England,
    Yet you have women there at this day living
    Make a number of slaves.

BONVILLE. *And kill that friend!*

She mocks you upon my life, she does equivocate:
Her meaning is, you cherish in your breast
Either self-love, or pride, as your best friend,
And she wishes you'd kill that.
LESSINGHAM. Sure, her command
Is more bloody; for she loathes me, and has put,
As she imagines, this impossible task,
For ever to be quit and free from me:
But such is the violence of my affection,
That I must undergo it. Draw your sword,
And guard yourself! though I fight in fury
I shall kill you in cold blood, for I protest
'Tis done in heart-sorrrow.
BONVILLE. I'll not fight with you,
For I have much advantage: the truth is,
I wear a privy[192] coat.
LESSINGHAM. Prithee put it off then,
If thou beest manly.
BONVILLE. The defence I mean, is the justice of my cause;
That would guard me, and fly to thy destruction.
What confidence thou wear'st in a bad cause!
I am likely to kill thee if I fight,
And then you fail to effect your mistress' bidding,
Or to enjoy the fruit oft. I have ever
Wished thy happiness, and vow I now
So much affect it, in compassion
Of my friend's sorrow: make thy way to it[193]
LESSINGHAM. That were a cruel murder.
BONVILLE. Believ't, 'tis ne'er intended otherwise,
When 'tis a woman's bidding.
LESSINGHAM. O, the necessity of my fate!
BONVILLE. You shed tears.
LESSINGHAM. And yet must on in my cruel purpose:
A judge, methinks, looks loveliest when he weeps
Pronouncing of death's sentence. How I stagger
In my resolve! Guard thee, for I came hither
To do and not to suffer: wilt not yet
Be persuaded to defend thee? turn the point,
Advance it from the ground above thy head,
And let it underprop thee otherwise
In a bold resistance.
BONVILLE. Stay; thy injunction

---

[192] A secret coat of mail.
[193] A line seems to have dropped out here.—Dyce.

Was thou should'st kill thy friend.

LESSINGHAM. It was.

BONVILLE. Observe me:

He wrongs me most, ought to offend me least,
And they that study man say of a friend,
There's nothing in the world that's harder found,
Nor sooner lost. Thou cam'st to kill thy friend,
And thou may'st brag thou'st done't; for here for ever
All friendship dies between us, and my heart,
For bringing forth any effects of love,
Shall be as barren to thee as this sand
We tread on, cruel and inconstant as
The sea that beats upon this beach. We now
Are severed: thus hast thou slain thy friend,
And satisfied what the witch, thy mistress, bade thee.
Go, and report that thou hast slain thy friend.

LESSINGHAM. I am serv'd right.

BONVILLE. And now that I do cease "to be thy friend,
I will fight with thee as thine enemy:
I came not over idly to do nothing.

LESSINGHAM. O, friend!

BONVILLE. Friend!

The naming of that word shall be the quarrel.
What do I know but that thou lov'st my wife,
And feign'st this plot to divide me from her bed,
And that this letter here is counterfeit?
Will you advance, sir?

LESSINGHAM. Not a blow:

'Twould appear ill in either of us to fight,
In you unmanly; for believe it, sir,
You have disarm'd me already, done away
All power of resistance in me. It would show
Beastly to do wrong to the dead: to me, you say,
You are dead for ever, lost on Calais sands
By the cruelty of a woman. Yet remember
You had a noble friend, whose love to you
Shall continue after death. Shall I go over
In the same bark with you?

BONVILLE. Not for yon town of Calais:

You know 'tis dangerous living
At sea with a dead body.

LESSINGHAM. O, you mock me!

May you enjoy all your noble wishes!

BONVILLE. And may you find a better friend than I,
And better keep him!

[*Exeunt.*]

SCENE II.

[*Enter* NURSE, COMPASS, *and his* WIFE.]

NURSE. Indeed you must pardon me, goodman Compass; I have no
authority to deliver, no, not to let you see the child: to tell you true,
I have command unto the contrary.
COMPASS. Command? from whom?
NURSE. By the father of it.
COMPASS. The father! who am I?
NURSE. Not the father sure: the civil law has found it otherwise.
COMPASS. The civil law! why then the uncivil law shall make it mine
again. I'll be as dreadful as a Shrove-Tuesday[194] to thee: I will tear
thy cottage, but I will see my child.
NURSE. Speak but half so much again, I'll call the constable, and lay
burglary to thy charge.
WIFE. My good husband, be patient. And prithee, Nurse, let him see the
child.
NURSE. Indeed I dare not. The father first delivered me the child: he
pays me well and weekly for my pains, and to his use I keep it.
COMPASS. Why, .thou white bastard-breeder, is not this the mother?
NURSE. Yes, I grant you that.
COMPASS. Dost thou? and I grant it too: and is not the child mine own,
then, by the wife's copyhold?
NURSE. The law must try that.
Camp. Law! dost think I'll be but a father-in-law? All the law betwixt
Blackwall and Tothill-street, and there's a pretty deal, shall not
keep it from me, mine own flesh and blood: who does use to get
my children but myself?
NURSE. Nay, you must look to that: I ne'er knew you get any.
COMPASS. Never? Put on a clean smock and try me if thou darest; three
to one I get a bastard on thee to-morrow morning between one and
three.
NURSE. I'll see thee hang'd first.
COMPASS. So thou shalt too.

[*Enter* FRANCKFORD *and* LUCE.]

NURSE. O, here's the father: now pray talk with him.

---

[194] The London apprentices were wont, on Shrove Tuesday, to assemble together to
storm and devastate the houses of ill fame in the city.

FRANCKFORD. Good morrow, neighbour: morrow to you both.

COMPASS. Both! morrow to you and your wife too.

FRANCKFORD. I would speak calmly with you.

COMPASS. I know what belongs to a calm and a storm too. A cold word with you: you have tied your mare in my ground.

FRANCKFORD. No, 'twas my nag.

COMPASS. I will cut off your nag's tail, and make his rump make hair-buttons, if e'er I take him there again.

FRANCKFORD. "Well, sir, but to the main.

COMPASS. Main! yes, and I'll clip his mane too, and crop his ears, too, do you mark? and backgall him, and spur-gall him, do you note? and slit his nose, do you smell me now, sir? unbreech his barrel, and discharge his bullets; I'll gird him till he stinks: you smell me now I'm sure.

FRANCKFORD. You are too rough, neighbour. To maintain—

COMPASS. Maintain! you shall not maintain no child of mine: my wife does not bestow her labour to that purpose.

FRANCKFORD. You are too speedy. I will not maintain—

COMPASS. No, marry, shall you not.

FRANCKFORD.—the deed to be lawful: I have repented it, and to the law given satisfaction; my purse has paid for't.

COMPASS. Your purse! 'twas my wife's purse: you brought in the coin indeed, but it was found base and counterfeit.

FRANCKFORD. I would treat colder with you, if you be pleased.

COMPASS. Pleased! yes, I am pleased well enough, serve me so still. I am going again to sea one of these days: you know where I dwell. Yet you'll but lose your labour: get as many children as you can, you shall keep none of them.

FRANCKFORD. You are mad.

COMPASS. If I be horn-mad, what's that to you?

FRANCKFORD. I leave off milder phrase, and then tell you plain, you are a—

COMPASS. A what? what am I?

FRANCKFORD. A coxcomb.

COMPASS. A coxcomb! I knew 'twould begin with a C.

FRANCKFORD. The child is mine, I am the father of it. As it is past the deed, 'tis past the shame; I do acknowledge and will enjoy it.

COMPASS. Yes, when you can get it again. Is it not my wife's labour? I'm sure she's the mother: you may be as far off the father as I am, for my wife's acquainted with more whoremasters besides yourself, and crafty merchants too.

WIFE. No, indeed, husband, to make my offence both least and most, I knew no other man; he's the begetter, but the child is mine; I bred and bore it, and I will not lose it.

LUCE. The child's my husband's, dame, and he must have it. I do allow

         my sufferance to the deed, in lieu I never yet was fruitful to him,
         and in my barrenness excuse my wrong.

COMPASS. Let him dung his own ground better at home, then: if he
         plant his radish roots in my garden, I'll eat 'em with bread and salt,
         though I get no mutton to 'em. What though your husband lent my
         wife your distaff, shall not the yarn be mine? I'll have the head ; let
         him carry the spindle home again.

FRANCKFORD. Forbear more words then; let the law try it. Meantime,
         nurse, keep the child, and to keep it better Here take more pay
         beforehand: there's money for thee.

COMPASS. There's money for me too: keep it for me, nurse. Give him
         both thy dugs at once: I pay for thy right dug.

NURSE. I have two hands, you see: gentlemen, this does but show how
         the law will hamper you; even thus you must be used.

FRANCKFORD. The law shall show which is the worthier gender: A
         schoolboy can do't.

COMPASS. I'll whip that schoolboy that declines the child from my wife
         and her heirs: do not I know my wife's case, the genitive case, and
         that's *hujus*, as great a case as can be?

FRANCKFORD. Well, fare you well: we shall meet in another place.
         Come, Luce.

[*Exit, with* LUCE.]

COMPASS. Meet her in the same place again, if you dare, and do you
         worst. Must we go to law for our children now-a-days? No marvel
         if the lawyers grow rich; but ere the law shall have a limb, a leg, a
         joint, a nail, I will spend more than a whole child in getting; "Some
         win by play, and others by bye-getting.[195]

[*Exeunt.*]

SCENE III.

[*Enter* RAYMOND, EUSTACE, LIONEL, GROVER, ANNABEL, *and*
     CLARE.]

LIONEL. Whence was that letter sent?

ANNABEL. From Dover, sir?

LIONEL. And does that satisfy you what was the cause
       Of his going over?

ANNABEL. It does: yet had he
       Only sent this, it had been sufficient.

---

[195] i.e. perhaps, as *betters* standing by.

RAYMOND. Why, what's that?

ANNABEL. His will, wherein
    He has estated me in all his land.

EUSTACE. He's gone to fight.

LIONEL. Lessingham's second, certain.

ANNABEL. And I am lost, lost in't for ever.

CLARE. [*aside.*] O fool Lessingham,
    Thou hast mistook my injunction utterly,
    Utterly mistook it! and I am mad, stark mad
    With my own thoughts, not knowing what event
    Their going o'er will come to. Tis too late
    Now for my tongue to cry my heart mercy.
    Would I could be senseless till I hear
    Of their return! I fear me both are lost.

RAYMOND. Who should it be Lessingham's gone to fight with?

EUSTACE. Faith, I cannot possibly conjecture.

ANNABEL. Miserable creature! a maid, a wife,
    And widow in the compass of two days.

RAYMOND. Are you sad, too?

CLARE. I am not very well, sir.

RAYMOND. I must put life in you.

CLARE. Let me go, sir.

RAYMOND. I do love you in spite of your heart.

CLARE. Believe it,
    There was never a fitter time to express it,
    For my heart has a great deal of spite in't.

RAYMOND. I will discourse to you fine fancies.

CLARE. Fine fooleries, will you not?

RAYMOND. By this hand, I love you and will court you.

CLARE. Fie!
    You can command your tongue, and I my ears
    To hear you no further.

RAYMOND. On my reputation,
    She's off o' th' hinges strangely.

[*Enter* WOODROFF, ROCHFIELD, *and a* SAILOR.]

WOODROFF. Daughter, good news.

ANNABEL. What, is my husband heard of?

WOODROFF. That's not the business: but you have here a cousin
    You may be mainly proud of, and I am sorry
    'Tis by your husband's kindred, not your own,
    That we might boast to have so brave a man
    In our alliance.

ANNABEL. What, so soon return'd?

You have made but a short voyage: howsoever
You are to me most welcome.

ROCHFIELD. Lady, thanks;
'Tis you have made me your own creature;
Of all my being, fortunes, and poor fame,
(If I have purchas'd[196] any, and of which
I no way boast,) next the high providence,
You have been the sole creatress.

ANNABEL. O dear cousin,
You are gratefid above merit! What occasion
Drew you so soon from sea?

WOODROFF. Such an occasion,
As I may bless heaven for, you thank their bounty,
And all of lis be joyful.

ANNABEL. Tell us how.

WOODROFF. Nay, daughter, the discourse will best appear
In his relation: where he fails, I'll help.

ROCHFIELD. Not to molest your patience with recital
Of every vain and needless circumstance,
'Twas briefly thus: scarce having reach'd to Margate,
Bound on our voyage, suddenly in view
Appear'd to us three Spanish men of war.
These, having spied the English cross advance,
Salute us with a piece to have us strike:
Ours, better spirited, and no way daunted
At their unequal odds, though but one bottom,
Return'd 'em fire for fire. The fight begins,
And dreadful on the sudden: still they proffer'd
To board us, still we bravely beat 'em off.

WOODROFF. But, daughter, mark the event.

ROCHFIELD. Sea-room we got: our ship being swift of sail,
It help'd us much. Yet two unfortunate shot,
One struck the captain's head off, and the other,
With an unlucky splinter, laid the master
Dead on the hatches: all our spirits then fail'd us.

WOODROFF. Not all: you shall hear further, daughter.

ROCHFIELD. For none was left to manage: nothing now
Was talk'd of but to yield up ship and goods,
And mediate for our peace.

WOODROFF. Nay, coz, proceed.

ROCHFIELD. Excuse me, I entreat you, for what's more
Hath already past my memory.

WOODROFF. But mine it never can. Then he stood up,

---

[196] For *acquired.*

And with his oratory made us again
To recollect our spirits, so late dejected.
ROCHFIELD. Pray, sir.
WOODROFF. I'll speak't out. By unite consent
Then the command was his, and 'twas his place
Now to bestir him; down he went below,
And put the linstocks in the gunners' hands;
They ply their ordnance bravely: then again
Up to the decks; courage is there renew'd,
Fear now not found amongst us. Within less
Than four hours' fight two of their ships were sunk,
Both founder'd, and soon swallow'd. Not long after
The third begins to wallow, lies on the lee
To stop her leaks: then boldly we come on,
Boarded, and took her, and she's now our prize.
SAILOR. Of this we were eye-witness.
WOODROFF. And many more brave boys of us, besides;
Myself, for one. Never was, gentlemen,
A sea-fight better manag'd.
ROCHFIELD. Thanks to heaven
We have sav'd our own, damag'd the enemy,
And, to our nation's glory, we bring home
Honour and profit.
WOODROFF. In which, cousin Rochfield,
You, as a venturer, have a double share,
Besides the name of captain, and in that
A second benefit; but, most of all,
Way to more great employment.
ROCHFIELD. Thus your bounty [*to* ANNABEL.]
Hath been to me a blessing.
RAYMOND. Sir, we are all
Indebted to your valour: this beginning
May make us of small venturers to become
Hereafter wealthy merchants.
WOODROFF. Daughter, and gentlemen,
This is the man was born to make us all.
Come, enter, enter! we will in and feast:
He's in the bridegroom's absence my chief guest.

[*Exeunt.*]

ACT IV.

SCENE I.

[*Enter* COMPASS, WIFE, LIONEL, *and* PETTIFOG *the Attorney, and one* BOY.]

COMPASS. Three Tuns do you call this tavern? It has a good neighbour of Guildhall, Master Pettifog. Show a room, boy.

BOY. Welcome, gentlemen.

COMPASS. What, art thou here, Hodge?

BOY. I am glad you are in health, sir.

COMPASS. This was the honest crack-rope first gave me tidings of my wife's fruitfulness. Art bound prentice?

BOY. Yes, sir.

COMPASS. Mayest thou long jumble bastard[197] most artificially, to the profit of thy master and pleasure of thy mistress.

BOY. What wine drink ye, gentlemen?

LIONEL. What wine relishes your palate, good Master Pettifog?

PETTIFOG. Nay, ask the woman.

COMPASS. Elegant[198] for her: I know her diet.

PETTIFOG. Believe me, I con her thank for't:[199] I am of her side.

COMPASS. Marry, and reason, sir: we have entertained you for our attorney.

BOY. A cup of neat Allegant?

COMPASS. Yes, but do not make it speak Welsh, boy.

BOY. How mean you?

COMPASS. Put no metheglin in't, ye rogue.

BOY. Not a drop, as I am true Briton.

[*They sit down*: PETTIFOG *pulls out papers.*]

---

[197] *Bastard,*—a kind of sweet Spanish wine; of which there were two sorts—white and brown. Ritson calls it a wine of Corsica. It approached the Muscadel wine in flavour, and was, perhaps, made from a bastard species of Muscadine grape; but the term, in more ancient times, seems to have been applied to all mixed and sweetened wines.—Halliwell.

[198] A pun seems intended here: *Allegant* or *Alligant* (for our old poets write it both ways) is wine of Alicant; or perhaps the following lines may illustrate Compass's meaning:—

"In dreadful darkenesse *Alligant* lies drown'd,
Which marryed men invoke for procreation."
Pasquil's Palinodia. 1634, Sig. C 3.—Dyce.

[199] *Con,*—the Ang. Sax. *connan,* to know. "To con thanks" answers to the French *sçavoir grè.*

[*Enter* FRANCKFORD, EUSTACE, LUCE, *and* MASTER DODGE, *a lawyer, to another table; and a* DRAWER.]

FRANCKFORD. Show a private room, Drawer.

DRAWER. Welcome, gentlemen.

EUSTACE. As far as you can from noise, boy.

DRAWER. Further this way, then, sir, for in the next room there are three or four fishwives taking up a brabbling business.

FRANCKFORD. Let's not sit near them by any means.

DODGE. Fill canary, sirrali.

FRANCKFORD. And what do you think of my cause, Master Dodge?

DODGE. O, we shall carry it most indubitably. You have money to go through with the business, and ne'er fear it but we'll trounce 'em; you are the true father.

LUCE. The mother will confess as much.

DODGE. Yes, mistress, we have taken her affidavit. Look, you, sir, here's the answer to his declaration.

FRANCKFORD. You may think strange, sir, that I am at charge
　　To call a charge upon me; but 'tis truth
　　I made a purchase lately, and in that
　　I did estate the child, 'bout which I'm sued,
　　Joint-purchaser in all the land I bought.
　　Now that's one reason that I should have care,
　　Besides the tie of blood, to keep the child
　　Under my wing, and see it carefully
　　Instructed in those fair abilities
　　May make it worthy hereafter to be mine,
　　And enjoy the land I have provided for 't.

LUCE. Right: and I counsell'd you to make that purchase;
　　And therefore I'll not have the child brought up
　　By such a coxcomb as now sues for him.
　　He'd bring him up only to be a swabber:
　　He was born a merchant and a gentleman,
　　And he shall live and die so.

DODGE. Worthy mistress, I drink to you: you are a good woman, and but few of so noble a patience.

[*Enter* BOY.]

BOY. Score a quart of Allegant to the Woodcock.

[*Enter* BOY,[200] *like a musician.*]

---

[200] In the original, First Boy; corrected to Second Boy by Mr. Dyce. The First Boy

BOY. Will you have any music, gentlemen?

COMPASS. Music amongst lawyers! here's nothing but discord. What, Ralph? Here's another of my young cuckoos I heard last April, before I heard the nightingale.[201] No music, good Ralph: here, boy; your father was a tailor, and methinks by your leering eye you should take after him; a good boy; make a leg handsomely; scrape yourself out of our company. [*Exit* BOY.] And what do you think of my suit, sir?

PETTIFOG. Why, look you, sir: the defendant was arrested first by Latitat in an action of trespass.

COMPASS. And a lawyer told me it should have been an action of the case: should it not, wife?

WIFE. I have no skill in law, sir: but you heard a lawyer say so.

PETTIFOG. Ay, but your action of the case is in that point too ticklish.

COMPASS. But what do you think? shall I overthrow my adversary?

PETTIFOG. Sans question. The child is none of yours: what of that? I marry a widow is possessed of a ward: shall not I have the tuition of that ward? Now, sir, you lie at a stronger ward; *tor partus sequitur ventrem*, says the civil law, and if you were within compass of the four seas, as the common law goes, the child shall be yours, certain.

COMPASS. There's some comfort in that, yet. O, your attorneys in Guildhall have a fine time on't!

LIONEL. You are in effect both judge and jury yourselves.

COMPASS. And how you will laugh at your clients, when you sit in a tavern, and call them coxcombs, and whip up a cause, as a barber trims his customers on a Christmas-eve, a snip, a wipe, and away!

PETTIFOG. That's ordinary, sir: you shall have the like at a *nisi prius*.

[*Enter* FIRST CLIENT.]

O, you are welcome, sir.

FIRST CLIENT. Sir, you'll be mindful of my suit?

PETTIFOG. As I am religious: I'll drink to you.

FIRST CLIENT. I thank you. By your favour, mistress. I have much business, and cannot stay; but there's money for a quart of wine.

COMPASS. By no means.

FIRST CLIENT. I have said, sir. [*Exit.*]

PETTIFOG. He's my client, sir, and he must pay. This is my tribute: custom is not more truly paid in the Sound of Denmark.

---

has been already recognized by Compass.

[201] He who happened to hear the cuckoo sing before the nightingale was supposed not to prosper in his love affairs.—Dyce.

[*Enter* SECOND CLIENT.]

SECOND CLIENT. Good sir, be careful of my business.

PETTIFOG. Your declaration's drawn, sir: I'll drink to you

SECOND CLIENT. I cannot drink this morning; but there's money for a pottle of wine.

PETTIFOG. O, good sir.

SECOND CLIENT. I have done, sir. Morrow, gentlemen. [*Exit.*]

COMPASS. We shall drink good cheap, Master Pettifog.

PETTIFOG. An' we sate here long, you'd say so. I have sate here in this tavern but one half hour, drunk but three pints of wine, and what with the offering of my clients in that short time, I have got nine shillings clear, and paid all the reckoning.

LIONEL. Almost a counsellor's fee.

PETTIFOG. And a great one, as the world goes in Guildhall; for now our young clerks share with 'em, to help 'em to clients.

COMPASS. I don't think but that the cucking-stool is an enemy to a number of brabbles that would else be determined by law.

PETTIFOG. 'Tis so, indeed, sir. My client that came in now sues his neighbour for kicking his dog, and using the defamatory speeches, *come out, cuckold's cur.*

LIONEL. And what shall you recover upon this speech?

PETTIFOG. In Guildhall, I assure you,[202]—the other that came in was an informer, a precious knave.

COMPASS. Will not the ballad of Flood[203] that was pressed make them leave their knavery?

PETTIFOG. I'll tell yon how he was serv'd; this informer comes into Turnbull street to a victualling-house,[204] and there falls in league with a wench;—

COMPASS. A Tweak, or Bronstrops: I learned that name in a play.[205]

PETTIFOG. —had, belike, some private dealings with her, and there got a goose.[206]

---

[202] Something is wanting here.

[203] Doubtless some ballad-history of the removal of an informer called Flood from the scene of his operations, by a Press Gang.

[204] Turnbull Street (more properly called *Turnmill* Street), a noted resort for courtesans and bad characters. Coffeehouses and other similar victualling-houses were then, as now, applied to evil purposes.

[205] In Middleton and Rowley's *Faire Quarrell*, the play to which, in all probability, our text alludes, *Tweak* is used for harlot, *Bronstrops* for bawd.—Dyce.

[206] "A sore in the groin, which, if it come by lechery, is called a *Winchester goose*, or a botch."—*Nomenclator*, 1585, p. 439 (Halliwell). The term "Winchester" was used, because the houses of ill fame along the river in Southward were under the control of the Bishop of Winchester.

COMPASS. I would he had got two: I cannot away with[207] an informer.

PETTIFOG. Now, sir, this fellow, in revenge of this, informs against the bawd that kept the house that she used cans[208] in her house: but the cunning jade comes me into th' court, and there deposes that she gave him true Winchester measure.

COMPASS. Marry, I thank her with all my heart for't.

[*Enter* DRAWER.]

DRAWER. Here's a gentleman, one Justice Woodroff, inquires for Master Franckford.

FRANCKFORD. O, my brother, and the other compromiser,[209] come to take up the business.

[*Enter* COUNSELLOR *and* WOODROFF.]

WOODROFF. We have conferr'd anil labour'd for your peace,
    Unless your stubbornness prohibit it;
    And be assur'd, as we can determine it,
    The law will end, for we have sought the cases.

COMPASS. If the child fall to my share, I am content to end upon any conditions; the law shall run on headlong else.

FRANCKFORD. Your purse must run by like a footman then.

COMPASS. My purse shall run open-mouthed at thee.

COUNSELLOR. My friend, be calm: you shall hear the reasons.
    I have stood up for you, pleaded your cause,
    But am overthrown; yet no further yielded
    Than your own pleasure: you may go on in law
    If you refuse our censure.[210]

COMPASS. I will yield to nothing but my child.

COUNSELLOR. [211]'Tis then as vain in us to seek your peace:
    Yet take the reasons with you. This gentleman
    First speaks, a justice, to me; and observe it,
    A child that's base and illegitimate born,
    The father found, who (if the need require it)
    Secures the charge and damage of the parish,
    But the father? who charg'd with education,
    But the father? then, by clear consequence,
    He ought, for what he pays for, to enjoy.

---

[207] Endure.

[208] i.e. I suppose, short measures.

[209] Arbitrator.

[210] Opinion, judgment.

[211] This speech, though originally printed as prose, was manifestly intended by the Author to be metrical.

Come to the strength of reason, upon which
The law is grounded: the earth brings forth,
This ground or that, her crop of wheat or rye;
Whether shall the seedsman enjoy the sheaf,
Or leave it to the earth that brought it forth?
The summer tree brings forth her natural fruit,
Spreads her large arms; who but the lord of it
Shall pluck [the] apples, or command the lops?
Or shall they sink into the root again?
'Tis still most clear upon the father's part.

COMPASS. All this law I deny, and will be mine own lawyer. Is not the earth our mother? and shall not the earth have all her children again? I would see that law durst keep any of us back; she'll have lawyers and all first, though they be none of her best children. My wife is the mother; and so much for the civil law. Now I come again, and y'are gone at the common law. Suppose this is my ground: I keep a sow upon it, as it might be my wife; you keep a boar, as it might be my adversary here; your boar comes foaming into my ground, jumbles with my sow, and wallows in her mire; my sow cries *week*, as if she had pigs in her belly—who shall keep these pigs? he the boar, or she the sow?

WOODROFF. Past other alteration, I am changed;
The law is on the mother's part.

COUNSELLOR. For me, I am strong in your opinion.
I never knew my judgment err so far;
I was confirm'd upon the other part,
And now am flat against it.

WOODROFF. Sir, you must yield;
Believe it, there's no law can relieve you.

FRANCKFORD. I found it in myself. Well, sir,
The child's your wife's, I'll strive no further in it;
And being so near unto agreement,
Let us go quite through to't: forgive my fault,
And I forgive my charges, nor will I
Take back the inheritance I made unto it.

COMPASS. Nay, there you shall find me kind too; I have a pottle of claret and a capon to supper for you; but no more mutton for you, not a bit.

RAYMOND. Yes, a shoulder, and we'll be there too; or a leg opened with venison sauce.

COMPASS. No legs open'd, by your leave, nor no such sauce.

WOODROFF. Well, brother and neighbour, I am glad you are friends.

OMNES. All, all joy at it.

[*Exeunt* WOODROFF, FRANCKFORD, *and* LAWYERS.]

COMPASS. Urse, come kiss, Urse; all friends.

RAYMOND. Stay, sir, one thing I would advise you;
    'Tis counsel worth a fee, though I be
    No lawyer;
    'Tis physic indeed, and cures cuckoldry, to keep
    That spiteful brand out of your forehead,
    That it shall not dare
    To meet or look out at any window to you;
    'Tis better than an onion to a green wound
    I' th' left hand made by fire.
    It takes out scar and all.

COMPASS. This were a rare receipt; I'll content you for your skill.

RAYMOND. Make here a flat divorce between yourselves, Be you no husband, nor let her be no wife; Within two hours you may salute again, Woo and wed afresh; and then the cuckold's blotted; This medicine is approv'd?

COMPASS. Excellent, and I thank you. Urse, I renounce thee, and I renounce myself from thee; thou art a widow, Urse. I will go hang myself two hours, and so long thou shalt drown thyself; then will we meet again in the pease-field by Bishops-Hall, and, as the swads and the cods shall instruct us, we'll talk of a new matter.

WIFE. I will be ruled: fare you well, sir.

COMPASS. Farewell, widow, remember time and place: change your clothes too, do ye hear, widow?

[Exit Wife.]

Sir, I am beholding to your good counsel.

RAYMOND. But you will not follow your own so far, I hope; you said you'd hang yourself.

COMPASS. No, I have devised a better way, I will go drink myself dead for an hour, then when I awake again, I am a fresh new man, and so I go a wooing.

RAYMOND. That's handsome, and I'll lend thee a dagger.

COMPASS. For the long weapon let me alone then.

[Exeunt.]

SCENE II.

[*Enter* LESSINGHAM *and* CLARE.]

CLARE. O, sir, are you return'd? I do expect
  To hear strange news now.
LESSINGHAM. I have none to tell you;
  I am only to relate I have done ill
  At a woman's bidding; that's, I hope, no news.
  Yet wherefore do I call that ill, begets
  My absolute happiness? You now are mine;
  I must enjoy you solely.
CLARE. By what warrant?
LESSINGHAM. By your own condition. I have been at Calais,
  Perform'd your will, drawn my revengeful sword,
  And slain my nearest and best friend i' th' world
  I had for your sake.
CLARE. Slain your friend for my sake?
LESSINGHAM. A most sad truth.
CLARE. And your best friend?
LESSINGHAM. My chiefest.
CLARE. Then of all men you are most miserable.
  Nor have you aught further'd your suit in this,
  Though I enjoin'd you to't, for I had thought
  That I had been the best esteemed friend
  You had i' th' world.
LESSINGHAM. Ye did not wish, I hope,
  That I should have murder'd you.
CLARE. You shall perceive more
  Of that hereafter; but, I pray, sir, tell me,—
  For I do freeze with expectation of it,
  It chills my heart with horror till I know,—
  What friend's blood you have sacrific'd to your fury,
  And to my fatal sport, this bloody riddle:
  Who is it you have slain?
LESSINGHAM. Bonvile, the bridegroom.
CLARE. Say? O, yuu have struck him dead thorough my heart!
  In being true to me you have prov'd in this
  The falsest traitor. O, I am lost for ever!
  Yet, wherefore am I lost? rather recover'd
  From a deadly witchcraft, and upon his grave
  I will not gather rue but violets

To bless my wedding strewings.[212] Good sir, tell me
Are you certain he is dead?

LESSINGHAM. Never, never to be recover'd.

CLARE. Why now, sir, I do love you
With an entire heart. I could dance methinks:
Never did wine or music stir woman
A sweeter touch of mirth. I will marry you,
Instantly marry you.

LESSINGHAM. This woman has strange changes. You are ta'en
Strangely with his death.

CLARE. I'll give the reason
I have to be thus ecstasied with joy:
Know, sir, that you have slain my dearest friend,
And fatalest enemy.

LESSINGHAM. Most strange.

CLARE. 'Tis true.
You have ta'en a mass of lead from off my heart
For ever would have sunk it in despair.
When you beheld me yesterday, I stood
As if a merchant walking on the downs,
Should see some goodly vessel of his own
Sunk 'fore his face i' th' harbour, and my heart,
Retain'd no more heat than a man that toils
And vainly labours to put out the flames
That burn his house to th' bottom. I will tell you
A strange concealment, sir, and till this minute
Never reveal'd, and I will tell it now
Smiling, and not blushing: I did love that Bonvile,
Not as I ought, but as a woman might
That's beyond reason. I did doat upon him
Though he ne'er knew oft, and beholding him
Before my face wedded unto another,
And all my interest in him forfeited,
I fell into despair; and at that instant
You urging your suit to me, and I thinking
That I had been your only friend i' th' world,
I heartily did wish you would have kill'd
That friend yourself, to have ended all my sorrow,
And had prepar'd it, that unwittingly
You should have don't by poison.

LESSINGHAM. Strange amazement.

CLARE. The effects of a strange love.

LESSINGHAM. 'Tis a dream sure.

---

[212] The flowers scattered before the bride in the wedding procession.

CLARE. No, 'tis real, sir, believe it.

LESSINGHAM. Would it were not!

CLARE. What, sir! you have done bravely: 'tis your mistress
    That tells you you have done so.

LESSINGHAM. But my conscience
    Is of counsel 'gainst you, and pleads otherwise.
    Virtue in her past actions glories still,
    But vice throws loathed looks on former ill.
    But did you love this Bonvile?

CLARE. Strangely, sir;
    Almost to a degree of madness.

LESSINGHAM. Trust a woman!
    Never! henceforward, I will rather trust
    The winds which Lapland witches sell to men.
    All that they have is feign'd, their teeth, their hair,
    Their blushes, nay, their conscience too is feign'd;
    Let 'em paint, load themselves with cloth of tissue,
    They cannot yet hide woman; that will appear
    And disgrace all. The necessity of my fate!
    Certain this woman has bewitch'd me here
    For I cannot choose but love her. O how fatal
    This might have prov'd! I would it had for me!
    It would not grieve me though my sword had split
    His heart in sunder, I had then destroy'd
    One that may prove my rival. O, but then
    What had my horror been, my guilt of conscience!
    I know some do ill at women's bidding
    I' th' dog-days, and repent all the winter after:
    No, I account it treble happiness
    That Bonvile lives; but 'tis my chiefest glory
    That our friendship is divided.

CLARE. Noble friend, why do you talk to yourself?

LESSINGHAM. Should you do so,
    You'd talk to an ill woman: fare you well,
    For ever fare you well. I will do somewhat
    To make as fatal breach and difference
    In Bonvile's love as mine: I am fix'd in 't:
    My melancholy and the devil shall fashion't.

CLARE. You will not leave me thus?

LESSINGHAM. Leave you for ever!
    And may my friend's blood, whom you lov'd so dearly,
    For ever lie imposthum'd in your breast,
    And i' th' end choke you! Woman's cruelty
    This black and fatal thread hath ever spun;
    It must undo, or else it is undone. [*Exit.*]

CLARE. I am every way lost, and no means to raise me
    But blest repentance. What two unvalued jewels
    Am I at once depriv'd of! Now I suffer.
    Deservedly. There's no prosperity settled:
    Fortune plays ever with our good or ill,
    Like cross and pile,[213] and turns up which she will.

[*Enter* BONVILE.]

BONVILLE. Friend.
CLARE. O, you are the welcoraest under heaven!
    Lessingham did but fright me: yet I fear
    That you are hurt to danger.
BONVILLE. Not a scratch.
CLARE. Indeed you look exceeding well, methinks.
BONVILLE. I have been sea-sick lately, and we count
    That excellent physic. How does my Annabel?
CLARE. As well, sir, as the fear of such a loss
    As your esteemed self will suffer her.
BONVILLE. Have you seen Lessingham since he return'd?
CLARE. He departed hence but now, and left with me
    A report had almost kill'd me.
BONVILLE. What was that?
CLARE. That he had kill'd you.
BONVILLE. So he has.
CLARE. You mock me.
BONVILLE. He has kill'd me for a friend, for ever silenc'd
    All amity between us. You may now
    Go and embrace him, for he has fulfill'd
    The purpose of that letter.

[*Gives her a letter.*]

CLARE. O, I know't. And had you known this, which I meant to have
    sent you

[*She gives him another.*]

    An hour 'fore you were married to your wife,
    The riddle had been constru'd.
BONVILLE. Strange! this expresses
    That you did love me.
CLARE. With a violent affection.

---

[213] The game now called *Heads or tails.*

BONVILLE. Violent indeed; for it seems it was your purpose
    To have ended it in violence on your friend.
    The unfortunate Lessingham unwittingly
    Should have been the executioner.
CLARE. 'Tis true.
BONVILLE. And do you love me still?
CLARE. I may easily
    Confess it, since my extremity is such
    That I must needs speak or die.
BONVILLE. And you would enjoy me
    Though I am married?
CLARE. No, indeed, not I, sir:
    You are to sleep with a sweet bed-fellow
    Would knit the brow at that.
BONVILLE. Come, come a woman's telling truth makes amends
    For her playing false: you would enjoy me?
CLARE. If you were a bachelor or widower,
    Afore all the great ones living.
BONVILLE. But 'tis impossible
    To give you present satisfaction, for my wife,
    My wife is young and healthful, and I like
    The summer and the harvest of our love,
    Which yet I have not tasted of, so well
    That, and you'll credit me, for me her days
    Shall ne'er be shorten'd. Let your reason, therefore,
    Turn you another way, and call to mind,
    With best observance, the accomplish'd graces
    Of that brave gentleman, whom late you sent
    To his destruction; a man so every way
    Deserving, no one action of his
    In all his life-time e'er degraded him
    From the honour he was born to. Think how observant
    He'll prove to you in nobler request that so
    Obey'd you in a bad one; and remember
    That afore you engag'd him to an act
    Of horror, to the killing of his friend,
    He bore his steerage true in every part,
    Led by the compass of a noble heart.
CLARE. Why do you praise him thus? You said but now
    He was utterly lost to you; now't appears
    You are friends, else you'd not deliver of him
    Such a worthy commendation.
BONVILLE. You mistake,
    Utterly mistake that I am friends with him
    In speaking this good of him. To what purpose

Do I praise him? only to this fatal end,
That you might fall in love and league with him:
And what worse office can I do i' th' world
Unto my enemy than to endeavour
By all means possible to marry him
Unto a whore? and there, I think, she stands.

CLARE. Is whore a name to be belov'd? if not,
What reason have I ever to love that man
Puts it upon me falsely? You have wrought
A strange alteration in me: were I a man,
I would drive you with my sword into the field,
And there put my wrong to silence. Go, y'are not worthy
To be a woman's friend in the least part
That concerns honourable reputation;
For you are a liar.

BONVILLE. I will love you now
With a noble observance, if you will continue
This hate unto me; gather all those graces
From whence you have fallen yonder, where you have left 'em
In Lessingham, he that must be your husband.
And though henceforth I cease to be his friend,
I will appear his noblest enemy, and work
Reconcilement 'tween you.

CLARE. No, you shall not,
You shall not marry him to a strumpet: for that word
I shall ever hate you.

BONVILLE. And for that one deed
I shall ever love you. Come, convert your thoughts
To him that best deserves 'em, Lessingham.
It's most certain you have done him wrong,
But your repentance and compassion now
May make amends; disperse this melancholy,
And on that turn of fortune's wheel depend,
When all calamities will mend or end.

[*Exeunt.*]

SCENE III.

[*Enter* COMPASS, RAYMOND, EUSTACE, LIONEL, GROVER.]

COMPASS. Gentlemen, as you have been witness to our divorce, you shall now be evidence to our next meeting, which I look for every minute, if you please, gentlemen.

RAYMOND. We came for the same purpose, man.

COMPASS. I do think you'll see me come off with as smooth a forehead, make my wife as honest a woman once more as a man sometimes would desire, I mean of her rank, and a teeming woman as she has been. Nay, surely I do think to make the child as lawful a child too as a couple of unmarried people can beget, and let it be begotten when the father is beyond sea, as this was: do but note.

EUSTACE. 'Tis that we wait for.

COMPASS. You have waited the good hour. See, she comes.

[*Enter* WIFE.]

A little room, I beseech you, silence and observation.

RAYMOND. All your own, sir.

COMPASS. Good morrow, fair maid.

WIFE. Mistaken in both, sir, neither fair nor maid.

COMPASS. No! a married woman?

WIFE. That's it I was, sir; a poor widow now.

COMPASS. A widow! Nay, then I must make a little bold with you; 'tis akin to mine own case; I am a wifeless husband too. How long have you been a widow, pray? nay, do not weep.

WIFE. I cannot choose, to think the loss I had.

COMPASS. He was an honest man to thee, it seems.

WIFE. Honest, quoth a', O!

COMPASS. By my feck,[214] and those are great losses. An honest man is not to be found in every hole, nor every street: if I took
    A whole parish in sometimes I might say true,
For stinking mackarel may be cried for new.

RAYMOND. Somewhat sententious.

EUSTACE. O, silence was an article enjoined.

COMPASS. And how long is it since you lost your honest husband?

WIFE. O, the memory is too fresh, and your sight makes my sorrow double.

COMPASS. My sight! why, was he like me?

WIFE. Your left hand to your right is not more like.

COMPASS. Nay, then I cannot blame thee to weep. An honest man, I warrant him, and thou hadst a great loss of him; such a proportion, so limbed, so coloured, so fed.

RAYMOND. Yes, faith, and so taught too.

EUSTACE. Nay, will you break the law.[215]

WIFE. Twins were never liker.

COMPASS. Well, I love him the better, whatsoever is become of him: and how many children did he leave thee at his departure?

---

[214] By my faith.

[215] i.e. of silence, just recalled to Eustace.

WIFE. Only one, sir.

COMPASS. A boy or a girl?

WIFE. A boy, sir.

COMPASS. Just mine own case still: my wife, rest her soul? left me a boy too, a chopping boy, I warrant.

WIFE. Yes, if you call him so.

COMPASS. Ay, mine is a chopping boy: I mean to make either a cook or a butcher of him, for those are your chopping boys. And what profession was your husband of?

WIFE. He went to sea, sir, and there got his living.

COMPASS. Mine own faculty too. And you can like a man of that profession well?

WIFE. For his sweet sake whom I so dearly lov'd, More dearly lost, I must think well of it.

COMPASS. Must you? I do think then thou must venture to sea once again, if thou'lt be ruled by me.

WIFE. [216]O, sir, but there's one thing more burdensome To us, than most of others' wives, which moves me A little to distaste it: long time we endure The absence of our husbands, sometimes many years, And then if any slip in woman be, As long vacations may make lawyers hungry, And tradesmen cheaper pennyworths afford Than otherwise they would for ready coin, Scandals fly out, and we poor souls [are] branded With wanton living and incontinency; "When, alas! consider, can we do withal?[217]

COMPASS. They are fools, and not sailors, that do not consider that: I am sure your husband was not of that mind, if he were like me.

WIFE. No, indeed, he would bear kind and honestly.

COMPASS. He was the wiser. Alack, your land and freshwater men never understand what wonders are done at sea: yet they may observe ashore that a hen, having tasted the cock, kill him, and she shall lay eggs afterwards.

WIFE. That's very true indeed.

COMPASS. And so may women, why not? may not a man get two or three children at once? one must be born before another, you know.

WIFE. Even this discretion my sweet husband had: You more and more resemble him.

COMPASS. Then, if they knew what things are done at sea, where the winds themselves do copulate and bring forth issue, as thus: in the old world there were but four in all, as nor', east, sou,' and west: these dwelt far from one another, yet by meeting they have

---

[216] I have followed Mr. Dyce in giving this speech, originally printed as prose, a metrical arrangement.

[217] Can we abstain.

engendered nor'-east, sou'-east, sou'-west, nor'-west,—then they were eight; of them were begotten nor'-nor' east, nor'-nor'-west, sou'-sou'-east, sou'-sou'-west, and those two sou's were sou'-east', and sou'-west', daughters; and indeed, there is a family now of thirty-two of 'em, that they have filled every corner of the world; and yet for all this, you see these bawdy bellows-menders, when they come ashore, will be offering to take up women's coats in the street.

WIFE. Still my husband's discretion.

COMPASS. So I say, if our landmen did understand that we send winds from sea, to do our commendations to our wives, they would not blame you as they do.

WIFE. "We cannot help it.

COMPASS. But you shall help it. Can you love me, widow?

WIFE. If I durst confess what I do think, sir, I know what I would say.

COMPASS. Durst confess! Why, whom do you fear? here's none but honest gentlemen, my friends: let them hear, and never blush for't.

WIFE. I shall be thought too weak, to yield at first.

RAYMOND. 'Tush, that's niceness: come, we heard all the rest: The first true stroke of love sinks the deepest; If you love him, say so.

COMPASS. I have a boy of mine own; I tell you that aforehand: you shall not need to fear me that way.

WIFE. Then I do love him.

COMPASS. So, here will be man and wife to-morrow, then: what, though we meet strangers, we may love one another ne'er the worse for that. Gentlemen, I invite you all to my wedding.

OMNES. We'll all attend it.

COMPASS. Did not I tell you, I would fetch it off fair? Let any man lay a cuckold to my charge, if he dares, now.

RAYMOND. 'Tis slander, whoever does it.

COMPASS. Nay, it will come to petty-lassery[218] at least, and without compass of the general pardon, too, or I'll bring him to a foul sheet, if he has ne'er a clean one: or let me hear him that will say I am not father to the child I begot.

EUSTACE. None will adventure any of those.

COMPASS. Or that my wife that shall be, is not as honest a woman as some other men's wives are.

RAYMOND. No question of that.

COMPASS. How fine and sleek my brows are, now!

EUSTACE. *Ay*, when you are married they'll come to themselves again.

COMPASS. You may call me bridegroom if you please now, for the guests are bidden.

OMNES. Good master bridegroom!

---

[218] i.e. petty larceny.

COMPASS. Come, widow, then: ere the next ebb and tide, If I be
  bridegroom, thou shalt be the bride.

[*Exeunt.*]

ACT V.

SCENE I.

[*Enter* ROCHFIELD *and* ANNABEL.]

ROCHFIELD. Believe me, I was never more ambitious,
    Or covetous, if I may call it so,
    Of any fortune greater than this one,
    But to behold his face.
ANNABEL. And now's the time;
    For from a much-fear'd danger, as I heard,
    He's late come over.
ROCHFIELD. And not seen you yet!
    'Tis some unkindness.
ANNABEL. You may think it so,
    But for my part, sir, I account it none.
    What know I but some business of import
    And weighty consequence, more near to him
    Than any formal compliment to me,
    May for a time detain him? I presume
    No jealousy can be aspersed on him
    For which he cannot well apology.
ROCHFIELD. You are a creature every way complete,
    As good a wife as woman, for whose sake,
    As I in duty am endear'd to you,
    So shall I owe him service.

[*Enter* LESSINGHAM.]

LESSINGHAM. [*aside.*] The ways to love and crowns lie both through
    blood,
    For in 'em both all lets must be remov'd:
    It could be styl'd no true ambition else.
    I am grown big with project—project, said I?
    Rather with sudden mischief, which without
    A speedy birth fills me with painful throes,
    And I am now in labour. Thanks, occasion,
    That giv'st me a fit ground to work upon!
    It should be Rochfield, one since our departure,

It seems, engrafted in this family:
Indeed, the house's minion, since from the lord
To the lowest groom, all with unite consent
Speak him so largely; nor, as it appears,
By this their private conference is he grown
Least in the bride's opinion; a foundation
On which I will erect a brave revenge.

ANNABEL. Sir, what kind offices lie in your way
To do for him, I shall be thankful for,
And reckon them mine own.

ROCHFIELD. In acknowledgment,
I kiss your hand: so with a gratitude
Never to be forgot, I take my leave.

ANNABEL. I mine of you, with hourly expectation
Of a long-look'd for husband. [*Exit.*]

ROCHFIELD. May it thrive
According to your wishes!

LESSINGHAM. Now's my turn.
Without offence, sir, may I beg your name?

ROCHFIELD. 'Tis that I never yet denied to any,
Nor will to you, that seem a gentleman;
'Tis Rochfield.

LESSINGHAM. Rochfield! You are then the man,
Whose nobleness, virtue, valour, and good parts
Have voic'd you loud: Dover, and Sandwich, Margate,
And all the coast is full of you.
But more, as an eyewitness of all these,
And with most truth, the master of this house
Hath given them large expressions.

ROCHFIELD. Therein his love
Exceeded much my merit.

LESSINGHAM. That's your modesty.
Now I, as one that goodness love in all men,
And honouring that which is but found in few,
Desire to know you better.

ROCHFIELD. Pray, your name?

LESSINGHAM. Lessingham.

ROCHFIELD. A friend to Master Bon vile?

LESSINGHAM. In the number
Of those which he esteems most dear to him
He reckons me not last.

ROCHFIELD. So I have heard.

LESSINGHAM. Sir, you have cause to bless the lucky planet
Beneath which you were born; 'twas a bright star,
And then shin'd clear upon you: for as you

Are every way well-parted,[219] so I hold you
In all designs mark'd to be fortunate.

ROCHFIELD. Pray, do not stretch your love to flattery,
'T may call it then in question: grow, I pray you,
To some particulars.

LESSINGHAM. I have observ'd
But late your parting with the virgin bride,
And therein some affection.

ROCHFIELD. How!

LESSINGHAM. With pardon,
In this I still applaud your happiness,
And praise the blessed influence of your stars.
For how can it be possible that she,
Unkindly left upon the bridal day,
And disappointed of those nuptial sweets,
That night expected, but should take the occasion
So fairly offer'd? nay, and stand excus'd,
As well in detestation of a scorn
Scarce in a husband heard of, as selecting
A gentleman in all things so complete
To do her those neglected offices
Her youth and beauty justly challengeth?

ROCHFIELD. [220]Some plot to wrong the bride, and I now
Will marry craft with cunning: if he'll bite,
I'll give him line to play on—Wer't your case,
You being young as I am, would you intermit
So fair and sweet occasion?
Yet, misconceive me not, I do entreat you,
To think I can be of that easy wit,
Or of that malice to defame a lady
Were she so kind so to expose herself;
Nor is she such a creature.

LESSINGHAM. [221]On this foundation
I can build higher still.—Sir, I believ't.
I hear you two call cousins: comes your kindred
By the Woodroffs or the Bonviles?

ROCHFIELD. From neither; 'tis a word of courtesy
Late interchang'd betwixt us; otherwise
We are foreign as two strangers.

LESSINGHAM. Better still.

ROCHFIELD. I would not have you grow too inward[222] with me

---

[219] Endowed.
[220] [*aside.*]
[221] [*aside.*]
[222] *Inward*, i.e. intimate.

Upon so small a knowledge: yet, to satisfy you,
And in some kind, too, to delight myself,
Those bracelets and the carcanet she wears
She gave me once.
LESSINGHAM. They were the first and special tokens past
Betwixt her and her husband.
ROCHFIELD. 'Tis confest; What I have said, I have said.
Sir, you have power,
Perhaps, to wrong me, or to injure her:
This you may do, but as you are a gentleman,
I hope you will do neither.
LESSINGHAM. Trust upon't.

[*Exit* BOCHFIELD.]

If I drown, I'll sink some along with me,
For of all miseries I hold that chief,
Wretched to be when none coparts[223] our grief.
Here's another anvil to work on: I must now
Make this my masterpiece, for your old foxes
Are seldom ta'en in springes.

[*Enter* WOODROFF.]

WOODROFF. What, my friend!
You are happily return'd, and yet I want
Somewhat to make it perfect. Where's your friend,
My son-in-law?
LESSINGHAM. O, sir!
WOODROFF. I pray, sir, resolve me;
For I do suffer strangely till I know
If he be in safety.
LESSINGHAM. Fare you well: 'tis not fit
I should relate his danger.
WOODROFF. I must know't.
I have a quarrel to you already
For enticing my son-in-law to go over:
Tell me quickly, or I shall make it greater.
LESSINGHAM. Then truth is, he's dangerously wounded.
WOODROFF. But he's not dead, I hope.
LESSINGHAM. No, sir, not dead:
Yet sure your daughter may take liberty
To choose another.

---

[223] Shares.

WOODROFF. Why, that gives him dead.

LESSINGHAM. Upon my life, sir, no: your son's in health, As well as I
    am.

WOODROFF. Strange! you deliver riddles.

LESSINGHAM. I told you he was wounded, and 'tis true;
    He is wounded in his reputation.
    I told you likewise, which I am loth to repeat,
    That your fair daughter might take liberty
    To embrace another. That's the consequence
    That makes my best friend wounded in his fame.
    This is all I can deliver.

WOODROFF. I must have more oft;
    For I do sweat already, and I'll sweat more:
    'Tis good, they say, to cure aches, and o' th' sudden
    I am sore from head to foot. Let me taste the worst.

LESSINGHAM. Know, sir, if ever there were truth in falsehood,
    Then 'tis most true your daughter plays most false
    With Bonvile, and hath chose for her favourite
    The man that now pass'd by me, Rochfield.

WOODROFF. Say?
    I would thou had'st spoke this on Calais' sands,
    And I within my sword and poniard's length
    Of that false throat of thine! I pray, sir, tell me
    Of what kin or alliance do you take me
    To the gentlewoman you late mention'd?

LESSINGHAM. You are her father.

WOODROFF. Why, then, of all men living do you address
    This report to me, that ought of all men breathing
    To have been the last o' th' roll, except the husband,
    That should have heard oft?

LESSINGHAM. For her honour, sir, and yours;
That your good counsel may reclaim her.

WOODROFF. I thank you.

LESSINGHAM. She has departed, sir, upon my knowledge,
    With jewels, and with bracelets, the first pledges
    And confirmation of th' unhappy contract
    Between herself and husband.

WOODROFF. To whom?

LESSINGHAM. To Eochfield.

WOODROFF. Be not abus'd; but now,
    Even now, I saw her wear 'em.

LESSINGHAM. Very likely:
    'Tis fit, hearing her husband is return'd,
    That he should re-deliver 'em.

WOODROFF. But pray, sir, tell me,

How is it likely she could part with 'em,
When they are lock'd about her neck and wrists,
And the key with her husband?

LESSINGHAM. O, sir, that's but practice:
She has got a trick to use another key
Besides her husband's.

WOODROFF. Sirrah, you do lie;
And were I to pay down a hundred pounds
For every lie given, as men pay twelvepence,
And worthily, for swearing, I would give thee
The lie, nay, though it were in the court of honour,
So oft, till of the thousands I am worth,
I had not left a hundred. For is't likely
So brave a gentleman as Rochfield is,
That did so much at sea to save my life,
Should now on land shorten my wretched days
In ruining my daughter? A rank lie!
Have you spread this to any but myself?

LESSINGHAM. I am no intelligencer.

WOODROFF. Why then 'tis yet a secret:
And that it may rest so, draw! I'll take order
You shall prate of it no further.

LESSINGHAM. O, my sword
Is enchanted, sir, and will not out o' th' scabbard.
I will leave you, sir; yet say not I give ground,
For 'tis your own you stand on.

[*Enter* BONVILE *and* CLARE.]

Clare here with Bonvile! excellent, on this
I have more to work: this goes to Annabel,
And it may increase the whirlwind. [*Exit.*]

BONVILLE. How now, sir!
Come, I know this choler bred in you,
For the voyage which I took at his entreaty;
But I must reconcile you.

WOODROFF. On my credit
There's no such matter. I will tell you, sir,
And I will tell it in laughter, the cause of it
Is so poor, so ridiculous, so impossible
To be believ'd: ha! ha! he came even now
And told me that one Rochfield, now a guest
(And most worthy, sir, to be so) in my house,
Is grown exceedingly familiar with
My daughter.

BONVILLE. Ha!

WOODROFF. Your wife; and that he has had favours from her.

BONVILLE. Favours!

WOODROFF. Love-tokens I did call 'em in my youth;
    Lures to which gallants spread their wings, and stoop
    In ladies' bosoms. Nay, he was so false
    To truth and all good manners, that those jewels
    You lock'd about her neck, he did protest
    She had given to Koehfield. Ha! methinks o' th' sudden
    You do change colour. Sir, I would not have you
    Believe this in least part: my daughter's honest,
    And my guess[224] is a noble fellow; and for this
    Slander deliver'd me by Lessingham,
    I would have cut his throat.

BONVILLE. As I your daughter's,
    If I find not the jewels 'bout her.

CLARE. Are you return'd
    With the Italian plague upon you, jealousy?

WOODROFF. Suppose that Lessingham should love my daughter,
    And thereupon fashion your going over,
    As now your jealousy, the stronger way
    So to divide you, there were a fine crotchet!
    Do you stagger still? If you continue thus,
    I vow you are not worth a welcome home
    Neither from her nor me. See, here she comes.

[*Enter* ROCHFIELD *and* ANNABEL.]

CLARE. I have brought you home a jewel.

ANNABEL. Wear it yourself:
    For these I wear are fetters, not favours.

CLARE. I look'd for better welcome.

ROCHFIELD. Noble sir,
    I must woo your better knowledge.

BONVILLE. O, dear sir,
    My wife will bespeak it for you.

ROCHFIELD. Ha, your wife!

WOODROFF. Bear with him, sir, he's strangely off o' th' hinges.

BONVILLE. The jewels are i' th' right place: but the jewel
    Of her heart sticks yonder. You are angry with me
    For my going over.

ANNABEL. Happily[225] more angry for your coming over.

---

[224] *Guess*, a corruption of *guest*, not unfrequently used by old writers.—Dyce.
[225] Haply, perhaps.

BONVILLE. I sent you my will from Dover.
ANNABEL. Yes, sir.
BONVILLE. Fetch it.
ANNABEL. I shall, sir, but leave your self-will with you. [*Exit.*]
WOODROFF. This is fine; the woman will be mad too.
BONVILLE. Sir, I would speak with you.
ROCHFIELD. And I with you of all men living.
BONVILLE. I must have satisfaction from you.
ROCHFIELD. Sir, it grows upon the time of payment.
WOODROFF. What's that? what's that? I'll have no whispering.

[*Enter* ANNABEL, *with a will.*]

ANNABEL. Look you, there's the patent
Of your deadly affection to me.
BONVILLE. 'Tis welcome.
When I gave myself for dead, I then made over
My land unto you: now I find your love
Dead to me, I will alter't.
ANNABEL. Use your pleasure.
    A man may make a garment for the moon,
    Rather than fit your constancy.
WOODROFF. How's this? Alter your will!
BONVILLE. "Tis in mine own disposing:
    Certainly, I will alter't.
WOODROFF. Will you so, my friend?
    Why then I will alter mine too.
    I had estated thee, thou peevish fellow,
    In forty thousand pounds after my death:
    I can find another executor.
BONVILLE. Pray, sir, do.
    Mine I'll alter without question.
WOODROFF. Dost hear me?
    And if I change not mine within this two hours,
    May my executors cozen all my kindred
    To whom I bequeath legacies.
BONVILLE. I am for a lawyer, sir. [*Exit.*]
WOODROFF. And I will be with one as soon as thyself,
    Though thou rid'st post to th' devil.
ROCHFIELD. Stay, let me follow and cool him.
WOODROFF. O, by no means!
    You'll put a quarrel upon him for the wrong
    H' has done my daughter.
ROCHFIELD. No, believe it, sir, he's my wish'd friend.
WOODROFF. O, come, I know the way oft:

Carry it like a French quarrel, privately whisper,
Appoint to meet, and cut each other's throats
With cringes and embraces. I protest,
I will not suffer you exchange a word
Without I overhear't.
ROCHFIELD. Use your pleasure.

[*Exeunt* WOODROFF *and* ROCHFIELD.]

CLARE. You are like to make fine work now.
ANNABEL. Kay, you are like to make a finer business oft.
CLARE. Come, come, I must solder you together.
ANNABEL. You! why I heard
    A bird sing lately, you are the only cause
    Works the division.
CLARE. Who, as thou ever loved'st me?
    For I long, though I am a maid, for't.
ANNABEL. Lessingham.
CLARE. Why then I do protest myself first cause
    Of the wrong which he has put upon you both,
    Which, please you to walk in, I shall make good
    In a short relation. Come, I'll be the clue
    To lead you forth this labyrinth, this toil
    Of a suppos'd and causeless jealousy.
    Cankers touch choicest fruit with their infection,
    And fevers seize those of the best complexion.

[*Exeunt.*]

SCENE II.

[*Enter* WOODROFF *and* ROCHFIELD.]

WOODROFF. Sir, have I not said I love you? if I have,
    You may believ't before an oracle,
    For there's no trick in't, but the honest sense.
ROCHFIELD. Believe it, that I do, sir.
WOODROFF. Your love must then
    Be as plain with mine, that they may suit together.
    I say, you must not fight with my son Bonvile.
ROCHFIELD. Not fight with him, sir?
WOODROFF. No, not fight with him, sir.
    I grant you may be wrong'd, and I dare swear
    So is my child; but he is the husband, you know,
    The woman's lord, and must not always be told

Of his faults neither: I say, you must not fight.
ROCHFIELD. I'll swear it, if you please, sir.
WOODROFF. And forswear, I know't,
    Ere you lay ope the secrets of your valour,
    'Tis enough for me I saw you whisper,
    And I know what belongs to't.
ROCHFIELD. To no such end, assure you.
WOODROFF. I say, you cannot fight with him,
    If you be my friend, for I must use you:
    Yonder's my foe, and you must be my second.

[*Enter* LESSINGHAM.]

Prepare thee, slanderer, and get another
Better than thyself, too: for here's my second,
One that will fetch him up, and firk him too.
Get your tools: I know the way to Calais sands,
If that be your fence-school. He'll show you tricks, faith;
He'll let blood your calumny: your best guard
Will come to a *peecavi*, I believe.
LESSINGHAM. Sir, if that be your quarrel,
    He's a party in it, and must maintain
    The side with me: from him I collected
    All those circumstances concern your daughter,
    His own tongue's confession.
WOODROFF. Who? from him?
    He will belie to do thee a pleasure then,
    If he speak any ill upon himself:
    I know he ne'er could do an injury.
ROCHFIELD. So please you, I'll relate it, sir.

[*Enter* BONVILE, ANNABEL, *and* CLARE.]

WOODROFF. Before her husband then,—and here he is,
    In friendly posture with my daughter too:
    I like that well.—Son bridegroom and lady bride,
    If you will hear a man defame himself,
    For so he must if he say any ill,
    Then listen.
BONVILLE. Sir, I have heard this story,
    And meet with your opinion in his goodness:
    The repetition will be needless.
ROCHFIELD. Your father has not, sir: I'll be brief
    In the delivery.
WOODROFF. Do, do, then: I long to hear it.

ROCHFIELD. The first acquaintance I had with your daughter,
 Was on the wedding-eve.
WOODROFF. So, 'tis not ended yet, methinks.
ROCHFIELD. I would have robbed her.
WOODROFF. Ah, thief!
ROCHFIELD. That chain and bracelet which she wears upon her,
 She ransom'd with the full esteem in gold,
 Which was with you my venture.
WOODROFF. Ah, thief again!
ROCHFIELD. For any attempt against her honour, I vow I had no thought
on.
WOODROFF. An honest thief, faith, yet.
ROCHFIELD. Which she as nobly recompens'd, brought me home,
 And in her own discretion thought it meet,
 For cover of my shame, to call me cousin.
WOODROFF. Call a thief cousin! why and so she might,
 For the gold she gave thee, she stole from her husband;
 'Twas all his now: yet 'twas a good girl too.
ROCHFIELD. The rest yon know, sir.
WOODROFF. Which was worth all the rest,
 Thy valour, lad; but I'll have that in print,
 Because I can no better utter it.
ROCHFIELD. Thus jade unto my wants,
 And spurr'd by my necessities, I was going,
 But by that lady's counsel I was stay'd,
 (For that discourse was our familiarity:)
 And this you may take for my recantation;
 I am no more a thief.
WOODROFF. A blessing on thy heart!
 And this was the first time I warrant thee, too.
ROCHFIELD. Your charitable censure is not wrong'd in that.
WOODROFF. No; I knew't could be but the first time at most;
 But for thee, brave valour, I have in store
 That thou shalt need to be a thief no more. [*Soft music.*
 Ha! what's this music?
BONVILLE. It chimes an Io peean to your wedding, Sir, if this be your
 bride.
LESSINGHAM. Can you forgive me? some wild distractions
 Had overturn'd my own condition,
 And spilt the goodness you once knew in me;
 But I have carefully recover'd it,
 And overthrown the fury on't.
CLARE. It was my cause
 That you were so possess'd; and all these troubles
 Have from my peevish will original:

I do repent though you forgive me not.

LESSINGHAM. You have no need for your repentance, then,
Which is due to it; all's now as at first It was wish'd to be.

WOODROFF. Why, that's well said of all sides.
But soft, this music has some other meaning:
Another wedding towards! good speed, good speed.

[*Enter* COMPASS *and the* FOUR GALLANTS, BRIDE *between*
FRANCKFORD *and another*, LUCE, NURSE, *and* CHILD.]

COMPASS. We thank you, sir.

WOODROFF. Stay, stay, our neighbour Compass, is't not?

COMPASS. That was and may be again to-morrow; this day, Master
Bridegroom.

WOODROFF. O, give you joy! but, sir, if I be not mistaken, you were
married before now: how long is't since your wife died?

COMPASS. Ever since yesterday, sir.

WOODROFF. Why, she's scarce buried yet, then.

COMPASS. No, indeed: I mean to dig her grave soon; I had no leisure
yet.

WOODROFF. And was not your fair bride married before?

WIFE. Yes, indeed, sir.

WOODROFF. And how long since your husband departed?

WIFE. Just when my husband's wife died.

WOODROFF. Bless us, Hymen! are not these both the same parties?

BONVILLE. Most certain, sir.

WOODROFF. What marriage call you this?

COMPASS. This is called *Shedding of Horns*, sir.

WOODROFF. How?

LESSINGHAM. Like enough, but they may grow again, next year.

WOODROFF. This is a new trick.

COMPASS. Yes, sir, because we did not like the old trick.

WOODROFF. Brother, you are a helper in this design, too?

FRANCKFORD. The father to give the bride, sir.

COMPASS. And I am his son, sir, and all the sons he has; and this is his
grandchild, and my elder brother: you'll think this strange now.

WOODROFF. Then it seems he begat this before you.

COMPASS. Before me! not so, sir; I was far enough off when 'twas
done: yet let me see him dares say, this is not my child and this my
father.

BONVILLE. You cannot see him here, I think, sir.

WOODROFF. Twice married! can it hold?

COMPASS. Hold! it should hold the better a wise man would think,
when 'tis tied of two knots.

WOODROFF. Methinks it should rather unloose the first,

And between 'em both make up one negative.

EUSTACE. No, sir, for though it hold on the contrary,
Yet two affirmatives make no negative.

WOODROFF. Cry you mercy, sir.

COMPASS. Make what you will, this little negative was my wife's
laying, and I affirm it to be mine own.

WOODROFF. This proves the marriage before substantial, Having this
issue.

COMPASS. 'Tis mended now, sir; for being double married
I may now have two children at a birth, if I can get 'em.
D'ye think I'll be five years about one as I was before?

EUSTACE. The like has been done for the loss of the wedding-ring,
And to settle a new peace before disjointed.

LIONEL. But this, indeed, sir, was especially done,
To avoid the word of scandal, that foul word
Which the fatal monologist cannot alter.

WOODROFF. Cuckoo!

COMPASS. What's that? the nightingale?

WOODROFF. A night-hird; much good may't do you, sir.

COMPASS. I'll thank you when I'm at supper. Come, father, child, and
bride: and for your part, father, whatsoever he, or he, or t'other
says, you shall be as welcome as in my t'other wife's days.

FRANCKFORD. I thank you, sir.

WOODROFF. Nay, take us with you, gentlemen:
One wedding we have yet to solemnize;
The first is still imperfect, such troubles
Have drown'd our music; but now, I hope, all's friends;
Get you to bed, and there the wedding ends.

COMPASS. And so good night. My bride and I'll to bed:
He that has horns, thus let him learn to shed.

[*Exeunt omnes.*][226]

THE END

---

[226] The enterprising publisher appends here an advertisement:—"If any gentlemen
please to repair to my house aforesaid, they may be furnished with all manner of English
or French histories, romances, or poetry; which are to be sold or read for reasonable
consideration."